'A' Level
ICT

P.M.Heathcote B.Sc.(Hons), M.Sc.

Published by

Payne-Gallway Publishers Ltd

76-78 Christchurch Street

Ipswich IP4 2DE

Tel 01473 251097

Fax 01473 232758

E-mail info@payne-gallway.co.uk

2000

Acknowledgements

I would like to thank the many colleagues and friends who have contributed to this book, and I am grateful to the following Examination Boards for permission to use questions from past examination papers:

The Associated Examining Board (AEB), Edexcel Foundation, Northern Examinations and Assessment Board (NEAB), Northern Ireland Council for the Curriculum, Examinations and Assessment (NICCEA), Scottish Qualifications Authority.

The answers in the text and in the teacher's supplement are the sole responsibility of the author and have neither been provided nor approved by the examination boards.

I would also like to thank the following organisations for permission to reproduce copyright material in the form of articles, photographs and artwork:

Armstrong Heathcare (Figure 4.1)

Bradford & Bingley Building Society (Fig 43.3)

British Telecom (Figures 5.2, 6.4)

British Software Alliance (Figs 10.3,47.1,47.3)

Cambs & Hunts Health Authority (Figure 8.2)

Canon (Figure 28.2)

Herts & Essex Hospital (Figure 8.3)

Formic Limited

Hewlett Packard Company (Figure 28.3)

Machinery

Network Associates (Figures 8.1, 48.1)

Polartechnics Limited

Sagesoft Limited (Figure 54.1)

Scanner Technologies Limited (Figure 15.5)

The Economist, London

The Guardian

Times Newspapers Limited

Graphics editor and designer: Flora Heathcote

Cover picture © "The North Unfolds" reproduced with the kind permission of Neil Canning

Cover photography © Mike Kwasniak, 160 Sidegate Lane, Ipswich

Cover design by Edward Morgan

First edition 1998. Reprinted 1999

Second edition 2000

A catalogue entry for this book is available from the British Library.

ISBN 0 95324908 5

Copyright © P.M.Heathcote 2000

Printed in Great Britain by

W M Print Ltd, Walsall, West Midlands

Preface

The aim of this book is to provide a comprehensive yet concise textbook covering all the topics studied for an Advanced Level course in Information Technology.

The book is divided into 5 sections covering all the material for each paper in a modular scheme such as that offered by the Assessment and Qualifications Alliance (AQA). Within a section, each chapter covers material that can comfortably be taught in one or two lessons, and the chapters are sequenced in such a way that practical sessions can be based around the theory covered in the classroom.

Section 3 contains topics that need to be covered in order for the student to tackle project work. Sections 1 to 3 cover all the requirements of the AQA AS specification, with the remaining sections being studied in the second year.

Sample examination questions and answers are included at the end of Sections 1 and 2 to show students the type of answers that are likely to score well in the examinations.

Throughout the book, case studies are used to illustrate the points made. Each chapter contains exercises and questions from past examination papers, so that the student can gain plenty of experience in 'exam technique'. Answers to all the questions are available, to teachers only, in a separate Teacher's Supplement which can be downloaded from our web site www.payne-gallway.co.uk

Contents

Table of Contents

SECTION 1

SECTION 3

SECTION 4

Section 1

Information: Nature, Role and Context

Chapter 1 – The Role of ICT

Computing – a look backwards

Within half a century, computers and information technology have changed the world and affected millions of lives in ways that no one could have foreseen. Here are some of the things that people have said about computers:

"I think there's a world market for maybe five computers." *(Thomas Watson, the chairman of IBM, in 1940)*

"I have travelled the length and breadth of this country and talked with the best people, and I can assure you that data processing is a fad that won't last out the year." *(The editor in charge of business books for Prentice Hall, in 1957)*

"There is no reason why anyone would want to have a computer in their home." *(President of Digital Equipment Corporation, in 1977)*

Contrary to these predictions, computers are transforming the ways in which we learn, communicate, do business, enjoy our leisure and live our everyday lives. Whatever career you pursue in the future, a knowledge of computer skills and concepts is likely to be beneficial or even essential. This course aims to make you competent and confident in the use of computers and to give you an understanding of the uses and impact of computers in society today.

In this chapter we'll look at some of the ways that information technology has changed patterns of work. We'll also examine how dependent we have become on computer systems, and what the consequences might be when these systems fail.

Computers and employment

Ever since the industrial revolution, people have feared that machinery will displace workers, and information technology is no exception.

In spite of dire predictions, however, there is no evidence that the introduction of computers has led to mass unemployment – in fact, overall more jobs have been created by computers than have been displaced by them. Nevertheless, in some areas computers have substantially replaced the workforce. In the 1980s, thousands of factory workers were made redundant by the introduction of robots on the factory floor making everything from biscuits to cars. In the 1990s, thousands of clerical and white-collar workers saw their jobs disappear with the introduction of company databases, desktop publishing, computerised accounting systems and increased automation in banks, building societies and organisations of all kinds, large and small.

The changing nature of employment

Today, most people no longer work in farms or factories but are found instead in sales, education, health care, banks, insurance firms and law firms. They provide services such as catering, writing computer software, or advertising and delivering goods. These jobs primarily involve working with, creating or distributing new knowledge or information. Knowledge and information work account for about 70% of the labour force in Britain and the US

Computers have taken over many of the tedious tasks that humans once performed. Consider that only a generation or so ago:

- Taking cash out from your bank account involved queuing at the bank's counter, having the cashier give you the money and manually note the transaction in a book;
- Putting a newspaper together involved picking up individual letters made out of lead and placing them manually in position, with correct spacing achieved by placing a strip of lead ('leading') between lines;
- All long distance calls had to go through an operator who manually made the connection.

The introduction of computers has in many instances led to a change in the types of job available. Many publishing firms feared that desktop publishing would result in fewer jobs in the publishing and printing industries. In fact thousands of new publishing and printing companies have been created in the last decade – a quick flip through the yellow pages under 'Printing' will verify this!

In many cases, workers displaced by computers are retrained to perform computer-related jobs that may be more satisfying than their original jobs.

- A secretary may find it more satisfying to use a word processor to produce high quality output which can be saved and amended, rather than having to retype whole pages because a minor error was made;
- An engineer or draughtsman may find it more satisfying to create designs using a computer-aided design system with complete accuracy, than drawing by hand;
- An accounts clerk may prefer to use an Accounts software package rather than to do the accounts manually.

> **Discussion: Computerisation often leads to a change in the tasks that a worker has to perform. In some cases the new tasks may be more satisfying, and in other cases, less satisfying. Think of some examples where computerisation has one of these two outcomes.**

Teleworking

Teleworking involves carrying out work away from the office and communicating with the employer through the use of computer and telecommunications equipment. Often teleworkers are based at home, but they can also work from telecentres, satellite offices or even on the move. Although a study done in 1995 at Newcastle University found that less than 1 worker in 100 was a teleworker (spending at least half of their working week at home using a computer), organisations are becoming increasingly interested in various forms of teleworking, which has benefits both for the employer and the employee. According to research done by Henley Business School in 1997, there are already 4 million teleworkers in the UK

Benefits of teleworking

- It may be easier to concentrate on work in a quiet environment at home than in a noisy office;
- Workers save on commuting time and costs, with the associated environmental benefits of keeping cars off the roads;
- Workers enjoy greater flexibility, and can arrange their working hours around other commitments such as picking children up from school;
- Employers save on the costs of office space and overheads such as heat and light;
- People in different locations can work in a team;
- People can be recruited from a much wider geographical area;

- People who are not able to take employment in standard office hours can be recruited.

The problems of teleworking

- Management may fear difficulties in controlling a workforce that is not in the office;
- There is a problem in ensuring that remote staff understand corporate goals and retain a sense of loyalty to the organisation;
- Employees may feel isolated and miss the social environment of an office full of colleagues;
- Employees may find it difficult to work in teams, or to get help when they need it;
- Some teleworkers may find it difficult to separate home from work, and find work encroaching on their leisure or family time. Conversely, it may be difficult to concentrate on work with children making demands on a parent's time.

Case study: Socket to 'em now

A survey of 200 companies published last summer by consultant Small World Connections suggests as many as three-quarters of employers have some form of teleworking, and 85% say they expect to be using teleworkers at some point in the future.

The advantages to employees of being able to work from home are obvious, but there is a business case for their employers, too. Employers can reduce their office costs, enabling them to replace permanent workstations with a smaller number of 'hot' desks.

It means they can increase their employees' productivity – one hour less commuting means one hour more work, theoretically. Supporters of teleworking say companies who use homeworkers also find it easier to recruit and retain staff, and it opens the door for companies to attract other sources of labour such as the disabled or women returners.

BT has more than 1,500 staff who telework on a full-time basis and another 15,000 who work from home occasionally. Teleworking has also been embraced by companies in sectors such as retailing, banking and the legal profession. Davis & Co, a firm of City solicitors, allows 30 of its lawyers to enjoy the benefits of teleworking. The firm offers clients 24-hour, seven-day-a-week access to home-working solicitors who use a combination of e-mail, audio-conferencing, faxes and voice mail to keep in touch.

On the down side, teleworking could deal a body blow to the unions, which find it easier to recruit and organise members who are clustered together, not scattered throughout the country. Without effective union representation, teleworkers could be open to exploitation. Research is needed on how well workers are able to cope with long periods of isolation from the office and how this impacts on their motivation, job satisfaction or promotion prospects.

Source: Ian Wylie, The Guardian 1 November 1997

Changing locations of work

Not only are the type of jobs we do changing, the location of work is changing too. When Britain changed in the 19th century from an agricultural to an industrial society, more and more workers were forced to move from farm work into towns and large industrial centres. The advent of communications technology is now starting to reverse this trend. There is no need for much of the work of an organisation to be done at a Head Office in a city; it is often more economical for it to be done in a more remote area where office rates and housing are cheaper, and employees can be paid less. Results of data processing can be transferred to wherever they are needed via a telecommunications line.

In fact, many large companies such as some airlines and the London Underground have their daily data processing carried out in countries like India where labour is cheap and plentiful.

Case study: Remote working

Injured Americans who wind up in emergency rooms at hospitals in Dallas, Denver and Seattle may owe their lives to a group of clerical workers on a farm in Northern Ireland. Emergency room doctors dictate diagnoses and other relevant information for clerks to type into the hospital computer's system. But clerical cover is limited at night, so the voice recording is digitised and transferred by ISDN line to the KITE (Kinawley Integrated Teleworking Enterprise) centre in the village of Kinawley, Co Fermanagh. Here it is typed and instantly transmitted back to the hospital, so that within minutes the patient's records are up-to-date.

KITE also works for Silicon Valley recruitment firms, taking CVs by e-mail and editing them into standard format. Kinawley's working day corresponds to California's night shift, so the finished CVs can be on the consultants' PCs by the time they come into work. "They can double their working day at minimal cost," says Sheila McCaffrey, KITE's director.

Because of its rural location, KITE can undercut the cost of American firms by up to a third. "Office space in the heart of Silicon Valley is £100 a square foot, compared with £3 or £4 per square foot here", says McCaffrey.

Kite is one of about 150 teleworking centres or 'telecottages' around Britain, many of them in disadvantaged rural areas.

Source: Paul Bray, The Sunday Times 27 April 1997

Personal qualities for ICT professionals

To rise to the top as an ICT professional, you will need more than technical knowledge and the right qualifications. A browse through a single day's advertisements for jobs in ICT will soon throw up commonly required characteristics in prospective employees. Look at the extracts shown in Figure 1.1 below and see what you can pick out.

- **Communication skills.** Many jobs such as those of a technical support engineer or systems analyst involve working with non-technical end-users. The ability to listen carefully and understand a user's problem or requirements is one of the most important skills required for a systems analyst. You have to act as a liaison between non-technical users and managers on one hand, and technical people on the other. You must be sensitive to the concerns of managers, programmers, end-users and employees. You must also be able to communicate the information and proposals in clear English in written reports, and give oral presentations when required.

- **Ability to take the initiative**. This is one of the most highly-rated skills for ICT professionals, according to a recent survey.

- **Management skills**. Project leaders, systems analysts, network administrators or database administrators, among others, need to be able to manage schedules, resources and people. They also need to be able to motivate the people working for them and may need to manage change within an organisation.

- **Design skills.** A systems analyst, for example, requires creative and critical thinking as well as the technical knowledge to design new systems.

- **Problem-solving abilities**. Anyone involved with user support, after-sales service or programming will need well-developed problem-solving abilities.

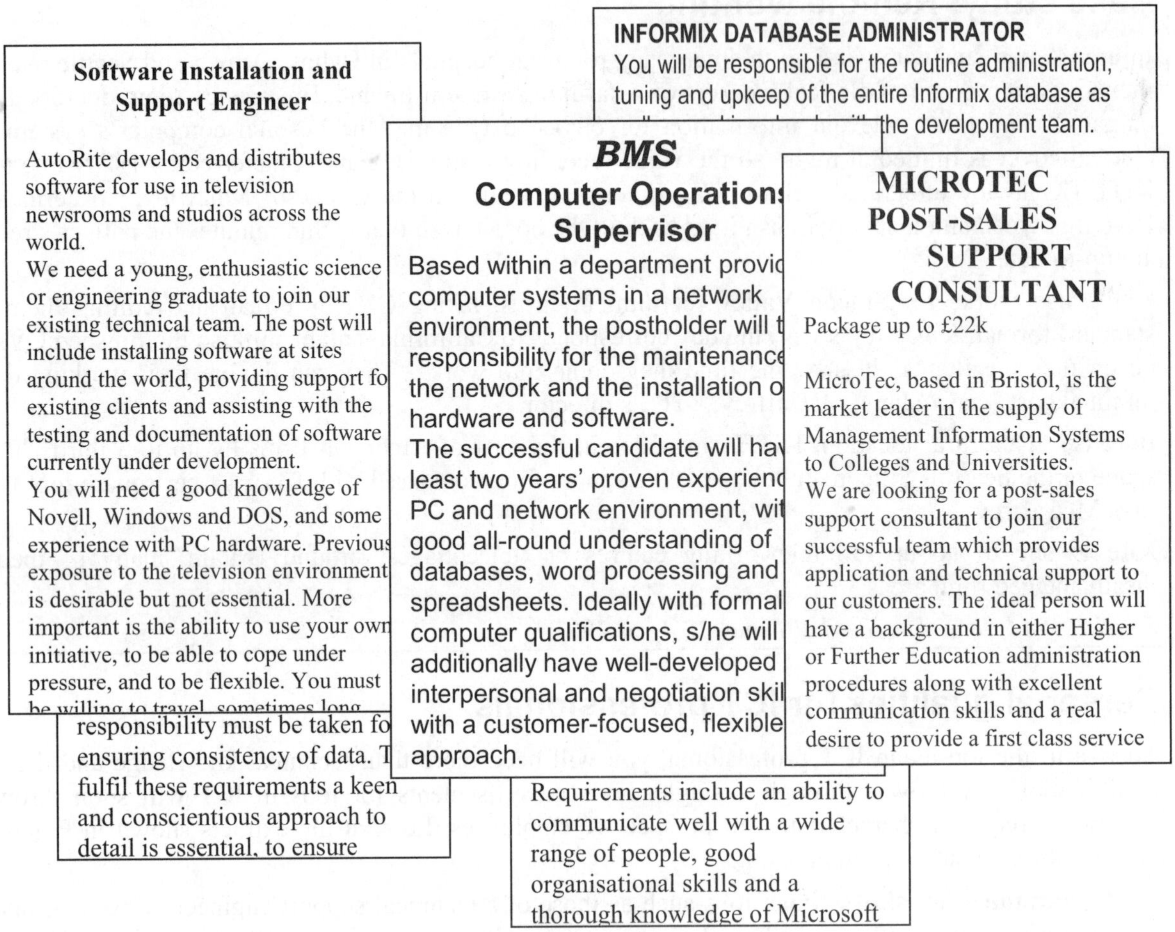

Software Installation and Support Engineer

AutoRite develops and distributes software for use in television newsrooms and studios across the world.

We need a young, enthusiastic science or engineering graduate to join our existing technical team. The post will include installing software at sites around the world, providing support for existing clients and assisting with the testing and documentation of software currently under development.

You will need a good knowledge of Novell, Windows and DOS, and some experience with PC hardware. Previous exposure to the television environment is desirable but not essential. More important is the ability to use your own initiative, to be able to cope under pressure, and to be flexible. You must be willing to travel, sometimes long

responsibility must be taken for ensuring consistency of data. T fulfil these requirements a keen and conscientious approach to detail is essential, to ensure

INFORMIX DATABASE ADMINISTRATOR

You will be responsible for the routine administration, tuning and upkeep of the entire Informix database as the development team.

BMS
Computer Operation: Supervisor

Based within a department provic computer systems in a network environment, the postholder will t responsibility for the maintenance the network and the installation of hardware and software.

The successful candidate will hav least two years' proven experienc PC and network environment, wit good all-round understanding of databases, word processing and spreadsheets. Ideally with formal computer qualifications, s/he will additionally have well-developed interpersonal and negotiation skil with a customer-focused, flexible approach.

Requirements include an ability to communicate well with a wide range of people, good organisational skills and a thorough knowledge of Microsoft

MICROTEC POST-SALES SUPPORT CONSULTANT

Package up to £22k

MicroTec, based in Bristol, is the market leader in the supply of Management Information Systems to Colleges and Universities.

We are looking for a post-sales support consultant to join our successful team which provides application and technical support to our customers. The ideal person will have a background in either Higher or Further Education administration procedures along with excellent communication skills and a real desire to provide a first class service

Figure 1.1: Careers in ICT

Exercises

1. Individuals and organisations have become so dependent upon I.T. systems that the consequences of their failure could be catastrophic to the individual or the organisation.

    Give **two** different examples of types of I.T. system for which failure would be catastrophic. In each case explain why the failure could prove to be catastrophic. (4)
    NEAB IT01 Qu 1 1997

2. Briefly describe **two** social impacts and **two** organisational impacts commonly identified as a result of introducing computerised information systems into business organisations. (8)
    NAEB IT0 1 Qu 2 1998

3. Through the 1990s an increasing number of people have become teleworkers. These are people who work from home using a personal computer linked to a Wide Area Network via a modem and the telephone system. Discuss, with the aid of specific examples, the advantages and disadvantages to individuals, organisations and society of this type of employment. (13)
    New question

4. Professional progression within the ICT industry requires more than just technical skills. Give **three** other necessary qualities and explain why they are important. (6)
    NEAB IT01 Qu 6 1997

Chapter 2 – ICT in Business and Commerce

New products and services

No matter what career you decide to take up, you will almost inevitably need to be able to understand and use information technology. Information technologies are used to create and keep track of documents in offices, seek out and exploit new ways of marketing, control factory production, design and create new products and enable service industries to function on a global scale.

Information technologies have changed the way that business is done. The explosion of knowledge and information has resulted in a mind-boggling range of products and services that were undreamt of two decades ago. Automated teller machines (ATMs), fax machines, mobile telephones, CD players, video recorders and computer games are some of the new products. New services include a range of telephone services such as caller ID and ring back, shopping and banking via the Internet, e-mail, barcode scanning at supermarket checkouts and libraries.

> ➢ **Discussion: Describe some other new products and services that have appeared in the last decade.**

Changing shape of organisations

Without information technology, businesses large or small cannot remain competitive. As the range of goods and services continues to increase, and markets expand world-wide, some trends can be noted:

- More and more people are going into business for themselves, or working for small businesses.
- Large organisations are becoming 'flatter' and less hierarchical. People work together in groups rather than individually. Information workers need far less supervision than factory workers because they have knowledge – they know what to do and when and how to do it. They need information, not supervision.
- More and more workers are recruited because of their knowledge and skills in problem-solving, communications, their ability to use their initiative and make appropriate use of new technology.

Case study: Britain's fastest growing companies

Fast Track 100 is a league table that ranks the fastest-growing unquoted companies between 1993 and 1996. It shows these firms are creating jobs and pioneering technological innovation. Half of the firms in the top 100 are technology-related industries.

But the record of the Fast Track 100 companies cannot disguise the fact that Britain needs to develop many more growth firms. When compared with the huge loss of jobs that big businesses in manufacturing and banking suffered during the early 1990s, the employment creation is small: the 12,500 jobs created in the sector could be offset by just one redundancy programme at a big group.

Six different types of company were identified in the top ranking small companies:

- Those with a star product such as Eyretel. In 1990, Roger Keenan decided to develop and market his own digital voice recorder. His first big order, worth £80,000 came from an emergency-service base in Virginia, USA, and from then on sales quickly began to grow in America, Britain and Asia.

- Those that identified customer service as the key to growth, such as Simply Computers and Software Warehouse.

- Companies that excel in marketing their goods, such as Vivid Imaginations and Roldec.

- Management leaders such as Wolfe, a building contractor.

- 'People champions' such as Lexis Public Relations.

- Acquirers, who take over other companies to achieve growth.

The successful entrepreneurs cited the key factor in their success as customer service, ahead of marketing and the product itself.

(Source: The Sunday Times 7 December 1997)

➢ **Discussion: In what ways do you think information technology helps these companies to be successful? Consider the three areas of customer service, marketing and the manufacture of the product.**

BUSINESS SECTOR PROFILE

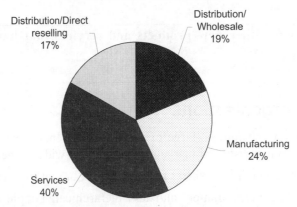

Figure 2.1: Types of company in the Top 100 small companies (Source: Fast Track 100)

Using ICT to set up a small business

Information technology can play a crucial part in the success or failure of a new enterprise. For example:

- A **spreadsheet** can be used to draw up a business plan and to calculate expected income and expenses. It can also be used to perform 'What-if' calculations to test out the effects of raising the price but lowering sales, using less expensive components, subcontracting the distribution of goods, and so on.

- A **graphics package** can be used to design the company logo, headed stationery and business cards.

- A **word processing package** can be used to design invoice stationery and send mailshots.

- A **desktop-publishing package** can be used to design advertising or promotional material.

- A **database package** can be used to keep a mailing list of customers.

- An **accounts package** can be used to set up the company accounts.

- A **PC** with associated peripherals such as a laser printer is needed to run the software.

- A **fax machine** can be used to communicate with potential suppliers, wholesalers, distributors, printers etc.
- The **Internet** can be used to sell products to new and existing customers, and as a valuable research tool.
- **E-mail** can be used to correspond with customers or suppliers.
- **Online banking** can enable you to keep tabs on your cash flow.
- The **telephone** and **answering machine** are essential to every small business.

ICT in banking

The banking industry makes extensive use of ICT in all its operations.

- Using telephone banking, a customer can ring in to check a balance or pay a bill, 24 hours a day, 365 days a year. One major bank has 750 phone banking staff taking up to 50,000 calls a day from 600,000 customers. As soon as the call is answered, the operator asks what service the customer requires, and selects one of 40 items on screen. The customer is then asked for their name and postcode, which enables their details to be retrieved in less than 2 seconds from the mainframe computer in Andover, Hants. As well as handling account queries and transactions, operators can access the bank's central credit-scoring system, empowering them to agree loans and overdrafts on the spot in many cases. If further discussion is needed, the system can arrange for the customer to visit their branch, by automatically booking a slot in the branch's electronic diary.
- Using ATMs, cash can be withdrawn at thousands of cashpoint machines all over the country.
- Using a debit card, purchases can be made at petrol stations, supermarkets, department stores, etc and the customer's account balance checked. If sufficient funds are available, the amount of the purchase is automatically debited to the account.
- Credit cards can be used to make purchases over the phone or via the Internet.
- Millions of cheques are processed each day using MICR (Magnetic Ink Character Recognition).
- Salaries and bills can be paid automatically by Direct Debit.
- Electronic smartcards such as Mondex store money on a microchip which can be topped up just like cash. Goods can be paid for by inserting the card into a reader and typing in the amount to be deducted. Such a card could eventually replace cash.

Shopping on the Internet

Online shopping is just beginning to attract the attention of all kinds of retailers. In the early days of the Net, small specialist traders found it a useful way of reaching a new, wider market, but today the big retailers are beginning to explore the potential of the 'virtual store'. A Web site can be used as a 'shop-front' and customers can browse 24 hours a day from anywhere in the world. It can be used to build up a database of customers by asking customers to 'register' when they first visit the Web site, giving their name and address and sometimes other information about products they are most interested in. (See Chapter 7.)

Thousands of companies do business on the Internet, including:

- Online Waterstone's, where a 'Bookseeker' mechanism can be used to search for titles by publisher, keyword and title (www.waterstones.co.uk);
- AutoHunter, the car site, has more than half a million private and trade advertisements, uploaded daily from 700 newspapers. These can be searched by location, make, model, year, price and even colour – to the relief of one young man who crashed his mother's estate car one Saturday night and was able to find an exact replica by the following Tuesday (www.adhunter.co.uk);

- Dell, the computer manufacturer, sells £3 million worth of computers a day at its sites (www.dell.com).
- Supermarkets such as Tesco have online shopping facilities in many areas of the country (see Chapter 7).

The drawbacks

What are the drawbacks in this scramble to jump on the technology bandwagon in which the microchip is a key component to practically everything we do? This new information revolution is comparable to the industrial revolution, only far more wide-ranging in its effects. Information replaces raw materials as the driving force of successful world economics. In future, individuals and countries will only be as good as the marketable skills and knowledge they have accumulated. You are what you know.

But at the other end of the scale, a new underclass is being created in Britain. A survey published in November 1996 reported that 40% of the population did not regularly use any of the weapons of the information revolution such as computers or mobile phones. 80% did not know how to get connected to the Internet, and of those online, only 9% used it regularly.

Worse still is the social profile: only 9% of working people (the C2/E/Ds of the socio-economic grading) have ever used the Internet, compared with 25% of the middle and upper classes. This paints a depressing picture of a new two-nation Britain even more polarised in terms of access to the advantages of the information age than the monetary gulf between the rich and the poor that so shamed the eighties. The dream of a new age of equal opportunities for all once again appears to be foundering.

Just as in mediaeval times when many of the great cathedrals were built, the Freemasons represented an elite body of people with specialist skills in stonemasonry which they jealously guarded, so today those with ICT skills are the indispensable builders of the information age.

The dangers

A reliance on technology brings with it unavoidable dangers. Faulty hospital equipment that delivers the wrong dose of radiation, 'fly-by-wire' aircraft that develop hardware or software faults and fall out of the sky, software bugs that corrupt data held in massive databases, are just some of the catastrophes that can result from our dependence on technological wonders.

Case study: Charity database corrupted

George is a computer consultant who recently travelled to London to arrange some consultancy work with a large national charity, with annual donations of £2.5 million, and a donor database of nearly half a million people worldwide. George was asked to investigate methods of speeding up data entry but, when he examined the application, he discovered that the software had been written some 7 years previously and added to by well-meaning volunteers at different times to cope with each new need. They were using Version 1 of the database software, since superseded by versions 2.0, 2.1 and 3.1...6. He took the details of what was required, and went home to prepare a quote. One problem was that this version of the software was no longer available and he only had a much more up-to-date version. This meant the work would have to be done on-site, which would mean traveling up to London every day instead of making the changes on his home PC and going up once to install them. Also, knowing that the early software had suffered from many bugs, he asked whether they had ever experienced problems with data corruption. The boss was not sure.

A week later he received a panic call from the charity. They had just sent out a major mailshot, and now discovered that thousands of people on the database had somehow been given identical 'unique reference numbers'. Their backup copies all showed the same problem. It would now be impossible to update the correct donor's record when a donation was received.

> ➢ **Discussion: Could this problem have been foreseen or averted? What course of action will George recommend now?**

Exercises

1. 'The development of Information Technology has had significant effects on society, individuals and organisations.'
    With the aid of specific examples discuss this statement. Include in your discussion:
    -   the effects of Information Technology on society at large;
    -   the effects of Information Technology on employment and work methods;
    -   the effect of Information Technology on individuals. (20)
    NEAB IT01 Qu 8 1996

2. Discuss in an essay the concept of a cashless society and the assertion that we will become one. You should refer to steps taken by banks and other financial institutions to move us towards a cashless society and explain why some people feel that it may never be possible to achieve such a goal. (15)
    London Computing Paper 1 Qu 11 1996

3. List **four** different software packages that a small business would find useful, explaining in each case why they would be useful. (8)
    New question

4. Replacing a manual system by a computerised system can have certain unwelcome consequences. Suggest **three** different examples of these unwelcome consequences at least **one** of which should be social and at least **one** economic. (3)
    AEB Computing Paper 1 Qu 3 1997

Chapter 3 – ICT in Manufacturing

Introduction

In the face of ever-increasing competition from international markets, many labour-intensive manufacturing companies face a stark choice: *automate*, or *evaporate*. Here are some of the many ways in which computers are used in the manufacturing world.

- Order entry and processing systems accept and process customer orders. A fully integrated system will also calculate the quantity and cost of materials needed to make the items ordered, produce reports on any shortages of materials in stock that need to be ordered and raise the purchase order. It will then track the progress of the order through the manufacturing process so that customer queries can be answered.

- Project management software provides management with the information necessary to keep projects within budget and on time. Reports can be produced showing actual costs versus projected costs, and the number of days ahead or behind schedule.

- Expert systems can be used in a multitude of ways from calculating the cost of a new multi-storey office block to detecting when a batch of beer is ready for the next stage of the brewing process.

- Computer-aided design systems are used in thousands of different applications from designing a new jumbo jet to the design of the most aerodynamic material for a ski racer's suit.

- Computer-aided manufacture enables components to be manufactured with the utmost precision.

- Robots are used in every kind of industry from car manufacture to sorting items on an assembly line.

Case study: The sweet smell of success

Bass the brewers has built a machine that can perform the daunting task of smelling beer and deciding if it's up to snuff. The technology that makes this possible is neural computing, the revolutionary process that mimics the way the human brain works. The artificial nose makes a complex series of judgements based on the electrochemical stimuli received by its gas sensors, and could save the brewers a fortune.

"By detecting an over-active yeast or a weak crop of hops at an early stage in the fermentation process, the nose could save us having to throw away a whole batch – 345,600 pints of beer", explained Ian Morris of Bass.

It is not just brewers who are interested in the artificial nose. Manufacturers of instant coffee, perfume and other aromatic products are spending huge sums, in co-operation with researchers at several universities, to build a better-than-human olfactory sensor.

Source: Garth Alexander, The Sunday Times 19 September 1993

Computer-aided design (CAD)

CAD systems allow designers and engineers to create designs on screen for thousands of products ranging from the tiniest computer chip to bridges, buildings and aeroplanes. The software allows users to create 3-dimensional 'solid' models with physical characteristics like volume, weight and centre of gravity. The models can be rotated and viewed from any angle, edited and stored. The computer can perform calculations to evaluate its performance under different stresses, or crash-test a new design of car before it is even manufactured.

Animation software can be used to enable a viewer to 'walk through' a 3-D model of say, a building, that exists only in the computer's memory.

CAD systems ('vector-based' graphics packages) store data in a different way from Paint ('bitmapped') packages. Paint packages store a picture as a two dimensional array, with each element of the array representing one pixel (dot) on the screen. A CAD package stores drawings as a collection of objects such as lines and circles, each represented by specifying coordinates, thickness and so on. This has many advantages, including the following:

- Drawings can be scaled or resized without distortion;

- Drawings are device independent; a drawing created using one type of VDU can be transferred to a screen of a different resolution without distortion;

- The files created tend to be smaller than for equivalent bitmapped images;

- Drawings can be made with a very high degree of accuracy by specifying coordinates.

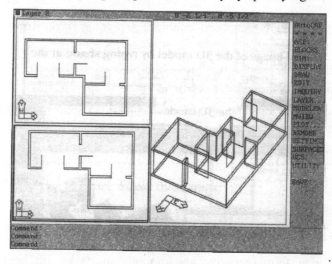

Figure 3.1: A simple drawing being made in AutoCAD

Computer-aided Manufacturing (CAM)

Computer-aided design is often linked to *computer-aided manufacturing* (CAM). CAD/CAM systems are used in the design and manufacture of thousands of applications from aeroplane and car parts to office furnishings and sports equipment. When the design of the product is completed, the specifications are input directly into a program that controls the manufacturing of parts.

A great advantage of these systems is their flexibility: individual items can be manufactured to a customer's exact specifications.

Case study: Subcontracting sector uses ICT

Precimax was founded in 1988 and has grown to a 30-employee company with an anticipated turnover in 1997 of £1.4 million. It offers a full manufacturing service from initial design through to supply of fully-finished components and assemblies. Production is predominantly on CNC (computer numeric control) turning and machining centres, and programs can be created from customer drawings or directly from CAD via modem or disk. Batches range from one-off up to 5000, but are more typically in the 50 to 500 bracket. In size, turned components measure up to 250mm diameter.

Precimax is a major supplier of components for train braking and door systems and is currently producing parts for use in the platform edge doors for London Underground's new Jubilee Line extension. It also has a contract with a postal equipment manufacturer for monthly deliveries of rollers and other parts for letter-sorting machines.

Precimax uses Datatrack for Windows for keeping track of its annual 3000 orders. The system includes estimating and quoting, sales order processing, purchasing, job costing and delivery. The commercial director commented "A system to handle this level of business is absolutely essential. Without it, we would be lost. It enables us to control cost and better understand our trading and manufacture. It gives us accurate information, so we can communicate with our customers on costs and deliveries quickly and with confidence."

Source: Machinery 5/19 December 1997

➢ **Discussion: In what major ways are computers being used at Precimax?**

Robots

The word 'robot' comes from the Czech word 'robotnik', meaning slave. Robots come in many different forms and shapes, but they all have the same basic components:

- Sensors, which capture information from the environment;
- A microprocessor to process the information;
- Actuators to produce movement or alter the environment in some way, for example by turning an electronic switch on or off.

Robots may be used for spray painting, spot welding and car assembly. They are also used as security devices inside homes and office buildings, as vehicles in space exploration, as intelligent wheelchairs for disabled people, and as underwater maintenance workers for oil rigs. Hundreds of applications use robots in one form or another.

Why use robots?

- Robots can tirelessly perform repetitive and monotonous tasks, lift heavy loads and reach long distances. They are used, for example, by the US Navy to scrape and repaint ships.
- Labour costs can be substantially reduced. Robots are widely used in car manufacturing as well as in many other industries including printing and publishing. Robots can carry tons of paper coming off presses, bind and trim books and apply book covers. It has been estimated that each industrial robot will replace an average of six workers.
- Quality of work is consistent. A robot is never tired or bored or having an off day.
- Robots can work 24 hours a day, do not need breaks and do not go on strike.
- They can work in total darkness, at low temperatures, thus saving on electricity bills.
- They can be used in hazardous areas, such as fume-filled rooms or radioactive environments. Tests are currently being carried out to set robots to work on clearing mine fields.

➢ **Discussion: Robots are immensely expensive to buy and install, and need to be used for a high proportion of each day in order to recoup the cost. What happens when demand for a product slumps? Would a manufacturer be better advised to stick with manual workers, who can be laid off and rehired when times improve?**

Exercises

1. Computers and information technology are widely used in manufacturing industries. Give **three** different examples of their use in manufacturing, and in each case discuss
   (a) The benefits to the company, the customers and the employees
   (b) The possible drawbacks to the company, the customers and the employees. (12)
   New question

2. Research an application of computers and ICT in manufacturing. Describe briefly the end product, the reasons for using ICT and the software and hardware used. (8)
   What group of people benefits most from the use of ICT in the application you have described? Is any other group of people disadvantaged? Briefly explain your answers. (4)
   New question

3. Describe briefly **one** application for robots in industry. (2)
   Explain **two** advantages of using robots in the application you describe. (2)
   New question

4. Some manufacturers are deciding to re-employ people on the shop floor and retire their robots. Give **one** argument to support this action and **one** argument against it. (2)
   AEB Computing Paper 1 Qu 3 1996

5. The use of computer-controlled machinery in manufacturing and product assembly has become widespread. Give **two** benefits for the manufacturer, other than financial, and **two** implications for the employees of such automation. (4)
   NEAB AS Computing Qu 3 1995

Chapter 4 – ICT in a Caring Society

Introduction

In this chapter we'll take a look at some of the ways in which information technology is used in medicine, and the benefits that it has brought to people with disabilities.

Computers in medicine

Computers have had a very significant impact on the quality of medical services. For example:

- Medical records stored in hospital information systems improve the quality of patient care. They are more accurate, they can keep track of prescriptions and tests administered, hospital admissions, dietary requirements and so on. Records are less likely to go astray than manual records and they can be made available to authorised people at any location.

- Databases of organ donors and patients needing transplants mean that when an organ becomes available, a match can quickly be found.

- Computerised devices such as pacemakers, artificial organs and prostheses (artificial limbs) have enabled tens of thousands of people to live longer and have a fuller life.

- Computerised monitoring devices can keep a 24-hour watch on critically ill patients and sound the alarm if vital signs change for the worse.

- Expert medical systems can help to diagnose diseases often at remote locations far from the care of a specialist. Vast amounts of data on symptoms and illnesses are stored in a 'knowledge base' which can help a doctor to arrive at a preliminary diagnosis.

- Surgeons can perform operations at remote locations using a remotely controlled robot arm. (See case study below.)

- Computers can model new drugs and test their effects, significantly reducing the time taken for new drugs to come onto the market.

Case study: Robot surgeon operates

A British robot will next week carry out a biopsy on a live patient in what is believed to be the world's first international robotic operation. A £100,000 robotic arm designed and manufactured by Armstrong Healthcare in High Wycombe, Bucks, will perform the operation on a patient in Lisbon, but the surgeon controlling it will be in Italy.

The robotic arm, called Pathfinder, is similar in shape and function to a human arm. It will seek out a vital organ in the patient, probably the liver, and then extract a piece of tissue. The surgeon in Italy will be guided by ultrasound images taken simultaneously by the arm. He will be able to see live video and ultrasound pictures from the robot, sent down a special high-speed telephone line. To control the robot, the surgeon will hold a 3D computer mouse that can operate both the arm and the needle.

Once the needle is in place over the patient, the surgeon can use the mouse to insert it and remove a biopsy sample for examination. According to Patrick Finlay, the managing director of Armstrong Healthcare, the Pathfinder is actually more accurate than a surgeon's hand, with no risk of shaking or wavering.

Source: Roger Dobson, The Guardian 7 December 1997.

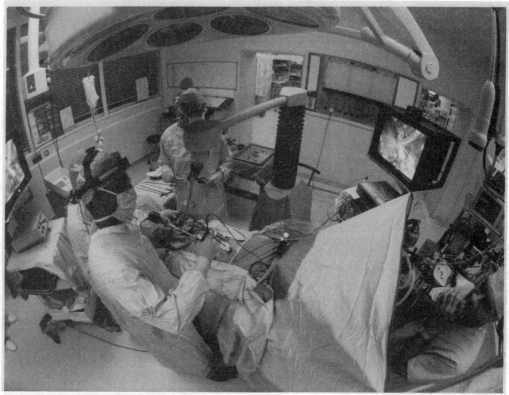

Figure 4.1:The robot surgeon operates (Photograph by permission of Armstrong Healthcare Ltd)

Case study: Deeper Blue checks cancer drugs

The supercomputer technology giving world champion Gary Kasparov a run for his money is to help halve the time it takes to bring new drugs to market.

According to IBM, which developed the Deeper Blue chess-playing computer, the ability to compute millions of calculations a second will be used within two years to enable scientists to model new drugs and test their effects. They claim this could reduce the average 12-year development period for a drug to about 6 years.

A supercomputer the company is building will be able to model within a day the effect of 1m atoms on each other during a split second. Instead of using valuable laboratory time and space, scientists can model a variety of chemicals on the computer and mimic the condition they are designed to combat. The supercomputer can then calculate the reaction of the drug, showing scientists whether they are on the right track within a day, rather than months.

Source: Sean Hargrave, The Sunday Times, 11 May 1997.

Expert systems used in medical diagnosis

Expert systems are computer programs that attempt to replicate the performance of a human expert on some specialised reasoning task. Also called **knowledge-based systems**, they are able to store and manipulate knowledge so that they can help a user to solve a problem or make a decision.

An expert system of this type is being developed in Australia to assist doctors in the diagnosis of melanoma, one of the most common types of cancer which manifests itself as dark patches similar to moles on the skin. In order to build the expert system, 45 different cancerous melanomas and 176 similar but benign non-melanomas were photographed and the images processed to remove hair, oil bubbles, etc. to extract the essential features. From these pictures and the known correct diagnoses, a set of 'rules' can be programmed into the expert system so that when presented with a photograph of a new skin lesion, the computer can make a diagnosis with a high degree of accuracy. The next step is to develop a real-time device.

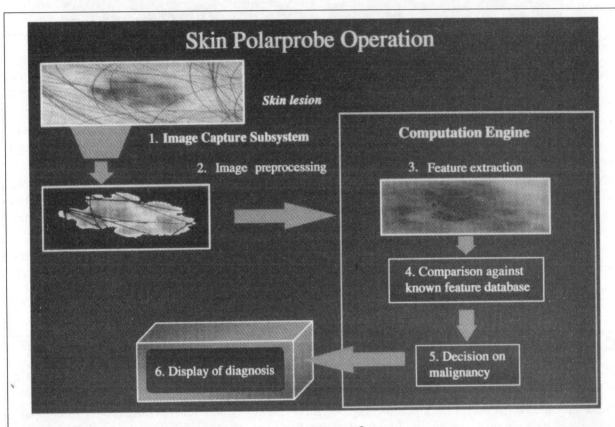

1. An image of the lesion is captured by the Polarprobe® camera system and downloaded onto the Polarprobe® computer system.

2. Calibration is performed. Image preprocessing follows to mask out hairs and oil bubbles and to identify the boundaries of the lesion.

3. The image is analysed by the Skin Polarprobe® software algorithms to extract diagnostic features of the lesion that facilitate the identification of melanoma using multiple discriminants such as colour segmentation, lesion patterns and geometry.

4. The computer algorithms, developed in collaboration with CSIRO, compare the values with stored values inside the computer database. The stored values are based on a large amount of empirical data which has been collected in a data library by Polartechnics and the Sydney Melanoma Unit, Royal Prince Alfred Hospital.

5. The Skin Polarprobe® computes the data using the detection algorithms and a decision is made as to whether the lesion is a melanoma or not.

6. The physician is informed of the computer's diagnosis immediately.

(Reproduced with permission from Polartechnics Ltd, Sydney, Australia)

> ➢ **Discussion: What are the benefits and drawbacks of using such a system for the diagnosis of melanomas?**

Computers and the disabled

About ten percent of people in Britain have some kind of disability. For many of them, new computer technology can dramatically improve their quality of life, their ability to communicate and their opportunities for independence and employment.

Case study: Eyes in the sky

A satellite navigation system for the blind is expected to transform the way visually handicapped people get around towns and cities, and will make travelling to unfamiliar places overseas less of an ordeal and more of a pleasure. It is to be tested by several visually handicapped people in Birmingham.

The system hinges on the Global Positioning System (GPS) of satellites encircling the earth. Receivers picking up the signals from the satellites can calculate precisely where they are on earth. People from yachtsmen to motorists using in-car navigation devices now use the system.

The blind person's version is essentially a portable computer plus a satellite receiver. The computer, fitted with a speech synthesiser so that it can 'talk' to the user, contains electronic Ordnance Survey maps of an area or city. A blind person trained on a keyboard taps into the system his or her location and where they want to go, and it automatically plots the route.

Once this has been done, the user is ready to go and steps out of the house. The computer will then say things like "Walk 100 yards, turn left and then right". It will also inform you of landmarks on the way, such as a fire station, and mention the numbers of houses or buildings on a street.

Source: Nick Nuttall, The Sunday Times, 27 March 1996.

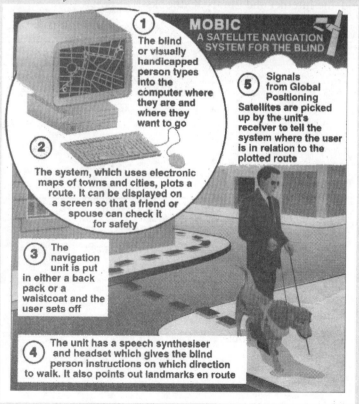

Today there are systems based on personal computers that can talk, listen, teach, communicate and translate. People with control over just an eyelid or a toe, for example, can communicate by means of the proper equipment attached to a PC

For example:

- Scanners can convert printed text to verbal output for the visually impaired;

- Voice recognition equipment converts speech to printed or displayed output for the hearing impaired;

- People with physical disabilities can use special pointing devices, pens or touch screens instead of keying devices for interacting with a computer;

- Vision systems have sensors built into special glasses;

- Implanted computerised devices can help physically impaired people to become more mobile.

Exercises

1. Computers and microprocessors are being used to help the physically disabled in many different ways. For each of **two** different types of handicap, briefly describe a way in which patients can be helped by this new technology. (4)
    AEB Computing Paper 1 Qu 1 1995

2. Briefly describe **two** examples of how computers could aid surgeons performing operations. You must show clearly the role of the computer in your answer. (4)
    AEB Computing Paper 1 Qu 6 1997

3. Research an application of information technology in one of the following areas: medicine, the home, education, helping people to overcome disabilities, environmental work. Prepare and deliver a short presentation. Your sources could include magazines and newspapers, TV programs such as Tomorrow's World, the Internet and library textbooks. (10)
    New question

Chapter 5 – ICT in Education

Computers in schools

In the 1980s money was found to put at least one microcomputer in every school in Britain. Since then, microcomputers have had a mediocre track record in the classroom, with many computers being left unused in a corner. Many of these computers are old, not sufficiently powerful to run modern software, and incompatible with more modern machines. Schools which made a one-time investment in computer technology may not have sufficient funds to train teachers how to use them effectively, to buy the latest software and to upgrade hardware as needed.

Yet in spite of these problems, there is general agreement that computer technology is a crucial resource in education today. Computers and ICT can bring benefits such as:

- The use of productivity tools like word processors, desktop publishing and spreadsheet software for use in projects and other school activities;

- The use of interactive teaching packages available on CD for many different subjects;

- Access to the Internet and thousands of online databases;

- Distance learning facilities for those who are unable to attend school or college, or for minority subjects (such as Russian or Japanese) which do not justify a full-time teacher in a single school;

- Links with other schools or colleges, or with industrial or business organisations;

- Special facilities available for students with disabilities – for example partially-sighted students may be able to change text size and background colour, blind people can use text-to-speech conversion packages, people with arthritis or cerebral palsy may control the computer by speaking to it instead of using the keyboard or mouse.

Case study: John Cabot City Technology College

If the network goes down at John Cabot City Technology College in Bristol, it is the pupils who complain the loudest. "The network has become an essential crutch for them", says Keith McCorkindale, the school's principal. "It's not so much an add-on as a way of life."

The school has several overlapping networks, including one for its 600 students. They can store their work online, e-mail each other and publish minutes of student council meetings. They automatically receive copies of school announcements and they can e-mail their teachers, even at the weekend if they have a computer at home.

And there is always the Internet. Learning to use the Net effectively can be an education in itself. "Meandering from hot link to hot link is a superb way of wasting time" says McCorkindale. "Pupils – and teachers – need training on how to use it effectively, just as they would with a big library. And it becomes frustratingly slow after 11am when all the Americans go online."

So the staff at John Cabot prefer to download Web pages onto the schools own Intranet. Then access times can be guaranteed, as can the quality of information and its freedom from pornography and other unsuitable material.

Students are encouraged to establish two-way links. When a group of year 10 students were doing a project on under-carriage control systems for their GCSE in Design and Technology, they probed engineers at British Aerospace for advice.

Source: Paul Bray, The Sunday Times 27 April 1997

Will computers replace teachers?

The fear is sometimes expressed that technology will make teachers redundant, and that pupils will lose the skills of social interaction as they become more and more isolated in their own little 'cyber-world'. Computer-aided learning packages have many advantages:

- Students can work at their own pace, repeating sections they don't understand;
- Computers are endlessly patient;
- The material is presented in a consistent way – you are not dependent on the skills of a particular teacher;
- Once the package is paid for, it can be cost-effective as fewer teachers are required.

At the same time, there are disadvantages in this method of learning. It can be very boring sitting in front of a computer screen, and a computer may not motivate students in the same way as a good teacher.

> ➤ **Discussion: Do you think that computers could replace teachers for at least part of the timetable? Would this be desirable from the point of view of the school administration, the teachers, and the pupils?**

Multimedia in schools

Multimedia is the combination of several elements such as text, graphics, animation, video and sound using a computer. To create or run multimedia software, a fairly powerful computer with a large memory, hard disk and a CD ROM drive is desirable. There are hundreds of CD ROMs available for every level of the National Curriculum, on virtually any topic from 'talking stories' for 6-year-olds, to The Complete Physics from BTC, which shows quality animations of solar eclipses and 'Algorithms and Data Structures' from Payne-Gallway Publishers for A Level Computing students. (Figure 5.1.)

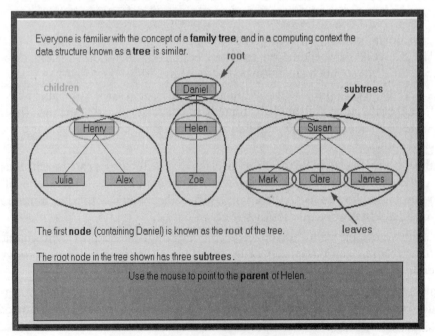

Figure 5.1: Interactive multimedia tutorial

Authoring software

To allow authors from school children to professionals to create multimedia software, *authoring software* is needed which allows text to be entered, graphics to be added and animated, photographs, video and sound files to be imported.

Internet-based services

The Internet provides many sites specifically for education, as well as being a source of more general information. Below is an advertisement for a BT home-learning service.

Figure 5.2: BT HomeCampus service

Exercises

1. The *Internet*, initially set up by the US Defence Department, now has many millions of users around the world. In the UK many schools and colleges have access to this web of computer networks.

    Describe **one** advantage and **one** disadvantage of allowing young people unrestricted access to the Internet. (2)

    AEB AS Computing Paper 1 Qu 8 1997

2. Describe briefly **five** ways in which information technology can aid pupils studying subjects **other** than computing or information technology. (5)

    New question

3. Give **three** advantages and **three** disadvantages of computer-aided learning packages compared with conventional classroom teaching. (6)

    New question

Chapter 6 – Role of Communication Systems

Introduction

The late 20th century has become known as the 'information age'. It would be impossible to conduct modern day businesses without the use of communication technologies such as the telephone, fax machine and computer communications networks. Communications and computer technology have become inextricably linked, resulting in *telecommunications*, the transmission of data of all kinds (text, graphics, sound and video) over a variety of different communication channels such as public telephone lines, private cables, microwave and satellite. In this chapter we'll look at some of the important developments in communications.

The Internet

The Internet is the largest wide area network in the world. In fact it is not a single network, but a collection of thousands of computer networks throughout the world. These linked networks are of two types:

- LAN (Local Area Network), covering an office block or University campus, for example;
- WAN (Wide Area Network) connecting computers over a wide geographical area, even over several countries.

All LANs and some WANs are owned by individual organisations. Some WANs act as **service providers**, and members of the public or businesses can join these networks for a monthly charge.

There is no central authority or governing body running the Internet; it started with an initial 4 computers in 1969 and grew over the next ten years to connect 200 computers in military and research establishments in the US Today there are more than 4 million host computers, any of which could be holding the information you are looking for, and as many as 50 million people connected, any of whom could be future customers, friends or problem-solvers.

Figure 6.1: The opening screen of CompuServe, an Internet service provider

The World Wide Web

The Web is a collection of pages stored on computers throughout the world, and joined by *hypertext* links. A hypertext link enables you to click on a word or graphic, and be taken automatically to the related Web page. It is the fastest-growing part of the Internet, owing much of its popularity to Web-browsing software such as Netscape, which enables you to quickly find references to any particular topic.

Online information services

Hundreds of companies such as CompuServe and BT now provide online information services, enabling subscribers to gain access to the latest news, share prices, weather and sport as well as providing services such as home banking or shopping, education and entertainment and access to thousands of online databases all over the world.

Case study: Those little white lies

You know you're the best person for that dream job you've seen advertised, but your CV doesn't quite convey this. Surely it wouldn't hurt to shove in an extra language GCSE and exaggerate your knowledge of Excel?

Checking job applicants' CVs for little white lies is about to get much easier. Credit reference company Experian announced last week that it had struck a deal with the UK's universities to compile a database of all degree results after 1995, available to sceptical employers for a fee. Interviewers will simply need to call Experian to check candidates' grades (it plans an Internet service soon). By collating the information centrally and accessibly, the company has allowed firms to become merciless in their attempts to distinguish the fraudulent from the faithful.

Source: Kate Halpern, The Guardian 24 January 2000

Electronic bulletin boards

Electronic bulletin boards are Internet sites for groups of people with similar interests to exchange information and discuss issues. Bulletin boards are used by thousands of different user groups from University 'Open Learning' providers and software manufacturers user groups to less savoury groups interested in terrorist activities or paedophilia.

Intranets

An Intranet is a company-wide network run along the lines of the World Wide Web, making it possible to share documents, databases and applications. Intranets have the potential to revolutionise the way that organisations share information internally, just as the Internet will revolutionise the way that businesses communicate with external suppliers, customers and consultants.

The software to implement Intranets is already available. The latest Microsoft Office suite will let you surf Word and Excel documents, reading them in a local Web site just as if they had been produced by a Web page designer.

Electronic mail (E-mail)

E-mail systems allow you to send memos, letters and files containing data of all types from your computer to any other computer with an e-mail address and a modem, simply by typing the recipient's name and pressing the 'Send' button.

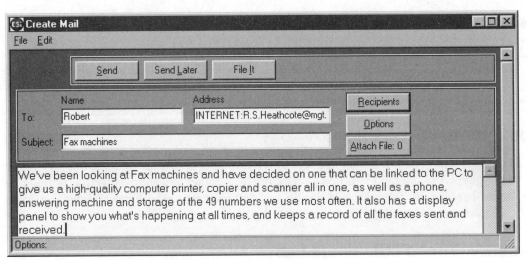

Figure 6.2: Creating an e-mail letter

E-mail has many advantages over both ordinary mail and the telephone. For example:

- A message can be sent anywhere in the world at the price of a local call, without having to leave your desk;

- The same message can be sent simultaneously to a group of people;

- The message will arrive in at most a few hours, and can be picked up the next time the recipient looks at their e-mail;

- It is very easy to send a reply to an e-mail as soon as it is received, using a 'Reply' button;

- Long files including video, sound and graphics can be sent automatically when the cheap rate starts after 6pm;

- Graphics and text can be electronically transmitted and placed in a document by the recipient. The BSA advertisement in Chapter 10, for example, was transmitted by the advertising agency via e-mail and imported straight into this manuscript using MS Word.

Case study: Monitoring employee e-mail

Monitoring employees e-mail is considered by many to be unethical and an invasion of privacy, but is considered legitimate by many companies who claim they need to know that their facilities are being used to further business goals. Some also argue that they need to be able to search electronic mail messages for evidence of illegal activities, racial discrimination or sexual harassment. Others argue that the company needs access to business information stored in e-mails, just as if it were stored in filing cabinets.

➢ **Discussion: Many companies have stated policies regarding e-mail. Do you think employees should be granted privacy, or should companies have the right to monitor e-mail?**

Hardware required to access the Internet

The basic hardware needed to set up online communications is a computer, a modem and a telephone line. The overall speed of online communication is governed by the speed of the modem and the speed of the communications link. An ordinary telephone line is the cheapest but not the fastest link. An ISDN line has a greater bandwidth and will send data much faster.

A **modem** (**Mo**dulator/**DEM**odulator) converts the data from your computer from digital form (0s and 1s) into analogue or wave form so that it can be sent over the telephone line, which was originally designed for speech. Modems typically transmit data at rates of between 28,800 bps (bits per second) and 56,600bps. A second modem at the receiving end translates the analogue signal back into digital form.

Figure 6.3: Modem

Many computers come equipped with an internal **modem card** in one of the free expansion slots inside the computer. (Most PCs have four to eight expansion slots into which you can plug a variety of peripheral devices.)

In the near future you will be able to access the Internet, send e-mails and order your shopping online using a mobile phone, as described below.

Software and services required to access the Internet

To connect to the Internet you need to sign up with an **Internet Service Provider (ISP)** who will supply you with a user account on a host computer and a complete software package that includes:

- A browser which enables you to download and view pages from the World Wide Web (see Chapter 22);

- Communications software which allows your computer to transmit and receive data using the Internet TCP/IP communications protocol (see Chapter 22);

- An e-mail package to enable you to send and receive e-mails;

- A newsreader which you use to read and post messages to the Usenet groups;

- An FTP client which you can use to download and upload files and software.

A good ISP should provide you with all of these at no charge. There are over 200 ISPs in the UK including Virgin and BT who charge a monthly rate for unlimited access, and Freeserve from the High Street retailer Dixons, which is free. (Further details on http://www.freeserve.net).

- Some users may want to install filtering software which blocks access to certain sites and let you set times during which the net can or cannot be used.

Telephones

It seems incredible that only a decade or so ago, mobile phones were almost unknown. In little more than a decade, the mobile phone has changed from a yuppie toy to a vital piece of kit for 40% of Britons.

Case Study: The Internet revolution

"We're at the beginning of the Internet revolution", says Brian Greasley, general manager of BT Cellnet's internet service provider, Genie Internet. He means that mobile phones, rather than the computers we've been using so far, are going to deliver that revolution.

"If you look at the Internet today, it's based on a PC platform of 350 million PCs worldwide. If you roll that figure forward to 2003, there will be around 400-500 million PCs. But there will be one billion mobile phones, and every one of them will have an Internet browser built in.."

Greasley is referring, at least in part, to new "internet phones". They send information using a new standard called Wireless Application Protocol (WAP).

The new mobile phones will be used not just for talking – we'll use them to send messages, find out the latest news and football scores, access information and use services on the Internet.

And, here's the crunch, the amount of "bandwidth" these phones have – the amount of information they can receive or send in a second – will eclipse today's conventional phones. This summer, you could have the equivalent of an expensive ISDN line to your mobile phone. In the near future, you will quite easily have the kind of power that will make receiving high quality sound and video on the move quite straightforward and rewarding, reshaping the way we get information and entertainment.

Source: Neil McIntosh, The Guardian 27 January 2000

Facsimile transmission (Fax)

The popularity of fax machines has exploded over the past decade. They are now regarded as indispensable by even the smallest business and have played a large part in speeding up business transactions. A fax machine scans and digitises images (text or graphics) on a page and transmits them in analogue form over a telephone line to another fax machine, which then reproduces a copy of the image on a piece of paper.

Photo courtesy of BT (BT Products and Services Catalogue Summer 1997)

Figure 6.4: Fax machine from BT

Voice mail

Voice mail is a more sophisticated version of the telephone answering machine. A voice mail system can act as an automated switchboard so that when you dial a company number, you may hear a message along the lines of 'Hello – this is the Customer Service Department of XYZ. If you would like information on new services, press 1. If you have a query about your bill, press 2. For other information, press 3.'

A voice mail system also allows you to leave a recorded message for someone who is absent from the office. The recipient can then save it, delete it or forward it to someone else on another extension.

Teleconferencing

Teleconferencing allows people in different physical locations to exchange ideas and information interactively using either the telephone or e-mail. A more advanced form of teleconferencing is videoconferencing, which allows participants to see and hear one another. A videoconferencing system includes video cameras, special microphones, large television monitors and a computer with a special device called a *codec* that can convert analogue video images and sound waves into digital signals and compress them for transfer over digital telephone lines. (An ISDN – Integrated Services Digital Network

– line with a high bandwidth is required to transmit video.) At the other end, another computer reconverts the digital signals to analogue for displaying on the receiving monitor. Such systems are familiar from television programmes in which people on the other side of the Atlantic are interviewed from a studio in London, for example.

Microcomputer-based desktop videoconferencing systems are also available, where users can see each other and simultaneously work on the same document.

Exercises

1. A multi-national company is considering the use of 'teleconferencing'.
    (a) What is meant by the term 'teleconferencing'. (3)
    (b) List the minimum facilities required to enable 'teleconferencing' to take place. (4)
    (c) Discuss **two** advantages and **two** disadvantages to the firm of using 'teleconferencing' as compared to traditional methods. (4)
    NEAB IT01 Qu 5 1997

2. A large company has introduced a communication system which includes electronic mail. This system will be used for both internal use within the company and for external links to other organisations.
    (a) Describe **two** features of an electronic mail system which may encourage its use for internal communication between colleagues. (2)
    (b) Contrast the use of an electronic mail system with each of fax and the telephone. (6)
    (c) Describe **two** functions the communication system might have, other than the creation and reception of messages. (4)
    NEAB IT01 Qu 7 1996

3. A company specialises in organising international conferences for doctors. The company has decided to make use of the Internet for advertising and organising the conferences.
    (a) State, with reasons, the hardware that the company would need, in addition to their PC and printer, in order to connect to the Internet. (4)
    (b) State the purpose of the following software when used for the Internet:
        (i)   Browser
        (ii)   Editor
        (iii) E-mail software (3)
    (c) Explain **three** potential advantages for this company of using the Internet as opposed to conventional mail/telephone systems. (6)
    NEAB IT01 Qu 7 1999

4. Facsimile and computer based electronic mailing systems are different forms of message systems.
    (a) For each of these systems, describe **two** of the facilities offered. (4)
    (b) Discuss the relative strengths and weaknesses of each of these systems. (10)
    NEAB IT01 Qu 7 1998

Chapter 7 – The Internet in Business

Doing business on the Web

Almost no business can afford to ignore the Internet. It is fast becoming an essential business tool for everyday correspondence, marketing, customer feedback and customer support. For businesses from a small country hotel to the world's largest airline, the Web can act as a shop front where customers can browse 24 hours a day, 365 days a year.

The Internet Music and Video shop is one example of a company that does all its business over the Internet. Log on by typing in the address http://www.yalplay.com and you will see the following screen:

Figure 7.1: The Internet Music and Video Shop opening screen

You can then click on **Secure Checkout** followed by **First Time Visitor's Guide** to register and leave your credit card details, or if you are a regular customer, browse through new releases or search for a particular title. Once you have made your selection and proceeded to the checkout, your order details will be displayed on the screen. You'll receive an e-mail confirming your order the next day, and your CD should arrive within a few days.

Couldn't be simpler!

Advantages to business

For a business such as Yalplay, this way of doing business has numerous advantages.

- There is a huge saving on overheads: no costly warehouse space, rent, heating or employee facilities;
- The 'virtual shop' can stock every one of the 16,000 or so CDs produced in the last year whereas a conventional store would stock only between 5-10,000;
- The Internet shop has arrangements for 'Just In Time' delivery from its suppliers, so does not get left with CDs which it cannot sell;
- It is a valuable market research tool – a list of customers' names and addresses, purchases, likes, dislikes and suggestions can be built up at absolutely no cost and used to improve the service provided.

Advantages to the customers

There are advantages to the customers, too. They can:

- Visit the music shop without having to leave home, at any hour of the day;
- Hear snatches of the song before deciding to buy;
- Shop without being jostled by crowds, having to listen to music that is not to their taste.

Yalplay estimate that 6% of visitors to their site make a purchase, as opposed to only 1% who respond to a direct mail shot. 40% of their customers return to make further purchases.

Doing the weekly shopping online

It is no longer necessary to fight the crowds in Tesco on a Saturday morning. Customers can register and then do their grocery shopping from the comfort of their own home, to have it delivered for a modest £5.00 charge. To make the weekly order, the customer logs on, types in their user number and password, and has the latest up-to-date list of products and prices downloaded. The customer's shopping list is saved and can be recalled to help compile next week's list, a 'recipe for the week' can be downloaded and ingredients automatically put in the shopping trolley, quantities can be edited and notes added to any product ordered, such as 'Green bananas please'.

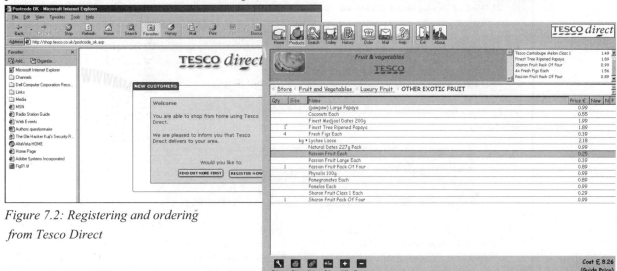

Figure 7.2: Registering and ordering
from Tesco Direct

> ➤ **What kind of people do you think are most likely to use the Internet for their grocery shopping? What do you think are the advantages and disadvantages?**

The drawbacks of online commerce

Inevitably, there are drawbacks to buying goods online. For one thing, there are worries about the security of giving a credit card number over the Internet. It is possible that hackers could retrieve thousands of credit card numbers and use them to order goods. Secondly, when companies post up information about new products and services, it is not only their customers who will visit the site – competitors will also be regular visitors, indulging in a little industrial espionage to make sure they don't get left behind.

Thirdly, because Internet sites can be accessed from all over the world, companies have to be aware of the laws regarding data protection in every country. Different countries have different laws regarding the holding and passing on of personal information about individuals.

Several companies have experienced problems with people who have set up web sites using their own company's trademark. They then demand large sums of money for the Web address.

Case study: British Petroleum

British Petroleum is taking legal action over a bogus Web site created by a motorist, John Bunt, who claims his vehicle was destroyed in a car wash at a BP service station in Exeter. The site (www.britishpetroleum.co.uk), with a home page identical to that on BP's own site (www.bp.com), offers links to a range of information detailing the vehicle damage and the action since taken, or not, by BP and the service station manager. While the manager says "Talk to BP" and BP says the matter is in the hands of its insurer, Commercial Union, Bunt has put the bogus site's domain name up for sale at £7,000 – and turned a drama into a crisis at one stroke. An expert on the registration of domain names is really put out by Bunt's action, and urges BP to sort out the renegade. "The site causes confusion and could be libellous." It might also win Bunt some attention for his claim.

Source: The Guardian 28 January 1998

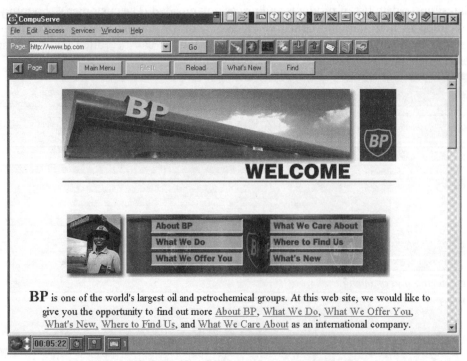

Figure 7.3: BP's Home Page – genuine or an impostor?

Business-to-Business

One of the major growth areas on the Internet is trading between businesses – for example distribution and delivery of manufactured goods. International carriers can make huge savings by taking orders over the Internet, and customers can not only make savings but also get online information about exactly where their goods are, and when they are delivered.

Finding new suppliers

The Internet is increasingly being used by businesses to find new suppliers of goods and services. Japan Airlines, for example, has used the Internet to post orders for in-flight materials such as plastic cups. On its Web site it advertises drawings and specifications (such as JAL's logo, which the cups must carry) in order to solicit business from any firm that comes across its site, rather than the usual Japanese suppliers.

Setting up a Web site

It doesn't take much to set up a Web site – a PC and a modem, and a subscription to a Service Provider of about £10 per month will typically include space of between 5-10Mb to use for your own personal site. Huge, complex sites on the other hand can cost up to £500 per month – but savings can be impressive. BA estimates that if they can sell just 1% of tickets over the Internet, it will save them around £6m a year.

> ➤ **Discussion: Imagine you have been asked to set up a Web site for a small publisher specialising in 'A' Level textbooks. What features would you include on the Web site? Who would benefit from the Web site, and what would the benefits be?**

Exercises

1. 'Networked computer systems (e.g. Internet) will revolutionise the way we shop.' With the aid of specific examples, discuss this statement. Include in your discussion:

   - The types of organisation likely to advertise on such systems.
   - The capabilities and limitations of such systems for this activity.
   - The potential security risks for the customers in using such systems.
   - The organisational impact of such systems.
   - The social impact of such systems.

   (20)
   NEAB IT01 Qu 9 1997

2. Over the past few years, many companies have tried to sell their products over the Internet, but have failed. Give **three** possible reasons.

   (3)
   New question

3. A major bookshop uses the Internet for an online bookshop. Give **three** advantages to customers of using the Internet to shop for books, and **three** advantages to the bookshop.

   (6)
   New question

Chapter 8 – Knowledge, Information and Data

Input-process-output

The main purpose of using computers is to process data as quickly and efficiently as possible to produce useful information.

Computers read incoming data called **input**, process or operate on it and display or print information called **output**.

Examples of **input data** include:

- The mark achieved by candidate 1342 in A-level Information Technology Paper 1;
- The time at which Jane Rowe clocked in for work at McDonald's on Monday morning;
- The sale of a can of baked beans in a supermarket.

Examples of **information** that might be obtained from processing many items of similar data include:

- The percentage of candidates gaining 'A' grades in Information Technology in a particular year;
- The total number of hours worked last week by Jane Rowe;
- The total weekly cost of paying all employees;
- The total weekly value of goods sold in a supermarket;
- A list of items that need to be reordered.

Data and information

Data can be defined as the stream of raw facts representing events occurring in organisations before they have been organised and arranged into a form that people can understand and use.

Information is data that has been processed into a form that is useful. Information is needed in organisations for the day-to-day running of a business ("How many cans of baked beans do we need to order today?") and to support decision-making and control. Information systems may also help managers to analyse problems, create new products, and find the best solutions to questions such as whether or in which direction to expand.

Knowledge

Data and information are generally concerned with facts and figures. We all carry round a huge number of facts that enable us to function in our daily lives, but we also have a different kind of knowledge in the form of **rules**, or the likely effects of certain courses of action. For example:

- Students are likely to get a good grade in this course IF they attend regularly and IF they do all the homework set;

Chapter 8 – Knowledge, Information and Data

- A new restaurant is likely to succeed IF the food is good, the location is good and the price is reasonable;

- Double-clicking an icon in Windows will open an application.

'Knowledge workers' are generally people in professions such as engineering, medicine, management or teaching. Their specialised knowledge makes them experts in their field, able to create new products, provide services and make decisions, based on formal and informal facts and rules that they have learned through training or experience.

Many of these rules are based on probabilities, not certainties. Computers can be programmed with a 'knowledge' on particular subjects, consisting of facts, rules and probabilities, and then deliver advice to someone. These so-called 'expert systems' or 'knowledge-based systems', which store the knowledge of a human expert, are used in many areas such as medical diagnosis, oil exploration, the stock market and fault diagnosis of all kinds.

> ➤ **Discussion: A doctor could order various tests for a patient such as blood tests, X-rays and so on. From the results of the tests she would have *information* about the condition of the patient. What *knowledge* would she need to be able to make a diagnosis?**

Access to knowledge

An example of a 'knowledge base' is the McAfee HelpDesk Suite. This software uses an expert system with a knowledge base containing instant answers to over 25,000 questions commonly asked by users having trouble with their hardware or software. The user simply loads the software and uses the 'Knowledge Wizard' to type in the problem. The software may then ask a series of questions before coming up with a diagnosis of the problem. (Figure 8.1.)

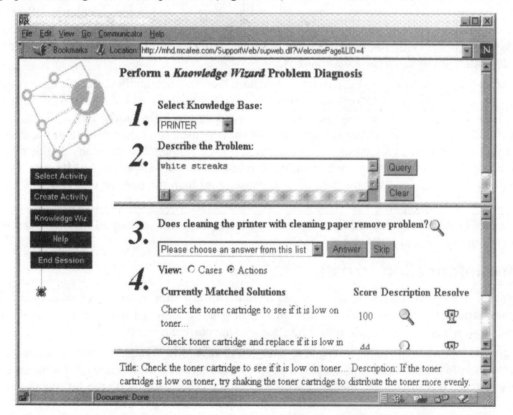

Figure 8.1: McAfee HelpDesk Suite 'Knowledge Wizard'

Case study: Collecting information

Will Havercroft spends his days touring Britain looking for attractive towns for new Waterstones bookshops.

In an age of sprawling out-of-town shopping centres and vast indoor malls, finding new retail space is not a problem but Waterstones does not want anonymous sites in Arndale Centres. Mr Haverstock scours the country looking for unusual locations, such as an old church in Reading and a former cinema in Swansea.

In the last six months he has visited 70 towns from Dunfermline to Torquay. "I have been to many lovely towns I had not been to before, like Kings Lynn, Rugby and Bury St Edmunds. I think about whether it is an attractive place to shop which people who live nearby will travel to. I look at what sort of food is on sale and whether there are nice markets and restaurants. I look out for nice jewellery shops, as they are often a good indicator of the type of town it is, and I size up the competition.

I'm looking, wherever possible, for architecturally interesting buildings, but they must be adaptable for retail use."

Source: The Guardian 2 January 1998

➤ **Discussion: Mr Haverstock is visiting towns and gathering data to help aid management decisions. What other ways could he get data? What *knowledge* does he have which makes his visits a worthwhile exercise? Could this knowledge be coded and entered into a computer? If no decision is made for a year, is the information he collected still useful?**

Sources of data

Data can be collected from many sources, either directly or indirectly. Data which is collected for a specific purpose is said to be collected **directly**. For example, the times at which an employee clocks in and out may be collected by punching a time card, and this data is used in the calculation of the weekly pay packet. Similarly, when a library book is borrowed, data about the book and the borrower is collected by scanning the bar codes of the book and the borrower's library card. This data is used directly to produce information on where a particular book is.

On the other hand, information can be derived from data which was originally collected for a completely different purpose – in other words, collected **indirectly**. For example a credit card company collects data about each transaction or purchase made so that the customer can be billed at the end of the month. This is the **direct** collection of data. At a later date, the data may be used to build a profile of the customer – perhaps they often use their credit cards for holiday travel, for example. The company could sell a list of all such customers to a travel company who would use it in a direct mail advertising campaign. This is the **indirect** collection of data – use of the data for a purpose other than the one for which it was originally collected.

➤ **Discussion: Think of several examples of data which is originally collected for one purpose, and then used for additional purposes.**

Encoding information as data

Another way of looking at the difference between data and information is to regard data as an encoded form of information. *Information* about hours worked or grades achieved may be input as a string of numbers, i.e. *data* which is meaningful only when put into the correct context.

Precision may be lost when attempts are made to encode information as data. Although it seems desirable in some ways to hold as much information about people or things as possible there are problems in doing so, not only because it is difficult to maintain accuracy but for other reasons, as the following case study illustrates.

Case study: 'Nightmare' scheme to track every pupil

Government proposals are afoot for a national computer record of the educational attainment of every child. Ministers plan to provide every child with a 13-digit identity number which would be used to track progress from the start of primary school through to University.

The Department for Education and Employment would control a central database with information on every pupil's social, economic and ethnic background as well as academic results and special educational needs.

A child's records would start with the score achieved in the proposed 'baseline' test at age 5, measuring elementary verbal and social skills. It would take in results of national assessment tests at 7, 11 and 14, GCSEs, A levels and vocational qualifications.

The file would also include more personal information such as a behaviour record, eligibility for free school meals and whether English was the child's native language.

But the Office of the Data Protection Registrar said the creation of a central databank about individual pupils raised 'nightmare' possibilities of abuse if it was not accompanied by adequate controls on access.

"There would have to be clear rules on access because this would set up a source of information that would be very attractive to somebody who might wish to find a particular child – for example a parent denied access because of violence."

The database on the other hand could reduce form-filling in schools by stopping repeated collection of the same data, and would provide the basis for much useful analysis.

Source: The Guardian 1 January 1998

➢ **Discussion: How could data about a pupil's behaviour be recorded? Who would decide what to encode? Would it be on a scale of 1 to 10?**

➢ **Are there any difficulties in recording a pupil's eligibility for free school meals?**

➢ **What are the benefits and dangers of this proposal to (a) the individual (b) society as a whole?**

Quality of data

To be useful, data must be:

- Accurate;
- Up-to-date;
- Complete.

This is often hard to achieve. Encoding the information from a doctor's notes, for example, could lead to the coarsening of the precision and context of the data, just as the encoding of a pupil's behaviour in the case study above is not likely to give a complete or accurate picture in all cases.

There may be huge costs involved in keeping data up-to-date. Here are a couple of examples:

- An insurance agent may compile a list of which particular insurance company is most competitive for each of hundreds of different types of policy. But insurance companies change their rates all the time; in a few weeks, the research may have to be repeated.

- A company which markets the names and addresses of particular types of organisation, such as educational establishments or firms making agricultural equipment, may spend months gathering the information. But how can they be sure it is up-to-date? Colleges change their names, firms move or go bust and new ones start up. It is useful to **'date stamp'** each item of information, by recording the date that the information was last updated. Then at least someone can check each entry over a certain age.

Exercises

1. Travelling sales representatives working in the UK can make extensive use of company credit cards to pay for goods and services. A company credit card is one that is issued by a company to its representative. All charges and information relating to each transaction are sent directly to the company.

    (a) List **four** items of data which are captured each time the card is used. (4)

    (b) Other than payment information, suggest **one** other potential use for information which can be derived from this data. (2)

    NEAB IT01 Qu 2 1997

2. (a) Describe briefly what is meant by *data*, *information* and *knowledge*, giving examples of each. (6)

    (b) Describe briefly **three** ways in which data can be or become of 'poor quality'. (3)

    New question

3. What is meant by *direct* and *indirect* sources of data? Give an example of each, and describe the purposes for which the data is used in each case. (4)

    New question

4. Look at Figures 8.2 and 8.3 below. The first is an advertisement for a 'Chief Knowledge Officer' and the second is for an 'Information Analyst'.

    (a) Describe the differences between these two jobs. (4)

    (b) What are the similarities and differences in the desired qualities and abilities of prospective candidates? (4)

    New question

Figure 8.2: Knowledge in demand

Information Management and Technology

Information Analyst

A&C Grade 5/6
£13,580 - £19,328 plus £194 Fringe London Weighting Allowance p.a.
37 hours per week

The Princess Alexandra Hospital is a progressive NHS Trust. The hospital is situated centrally in Harlow Town. The town offers a wealth of leisure facilities and is surrounded by beautiful Essex countryside. Cambridge, London and Stansted Airport are easily accessed via the M11.

We are currently seeking an Information Analyst to join our friendly team.

Duties will include:

♦ provide information for monitoring, planning and management

♦ support Theatre and A&E Systems and develop systems for monitoring the data contained.

♦ carry out statistical analyses and provide statistical support to managers and clinicians.

♦ work with managers to determine their information needs.

The successful candidate will:

♦ be a graduate in a numerate discipline.

♦ have knowledge of Microsoft applications.

♦ have a high level of numeracy, analytical and problem solving skills.

♦ have good interpersonal and organisational skills.

♦ have an interest in measuring effectiveness of healthcare.

For an application form and job description, please contact Recruitment Services, York House, Herts & Essex Hospital, Haymeads Lane, Bishop's Stortford, Herts CM23 5JH.

Please quote ref: AC-40-203.

Closing date for receipt of completed applications: 4 February 1998.

Interviews will take place 17 February 1998.

Working Towards Equal Opportunities

We operate a No smoking policy.

Figure 8.3:Advertisement for an information analyst

Chapter 9 – Information as a Commodity

The importance of information

Almost overnight, it seems, success in almost any field has become impossible without information technology. In manufacturing, health care, education, policing, retailing, banking, farming and thousands of other fields, information is as valuable a resource as capital or people. Information is gathered about market trends, buying preferences, customer profiles; computers analyse, summarise and present this data to managers who use it as the basis for decision-making.

Accessible, accurate and up-to-date information can help to ensure that decisions of all kinds are likely to be correct, from how many thousands of a particular toy to manufacture in time for Christmas, to whether or not to open a new factory.

Case study

A million Teletubby toys were manufactured for Christmas in 1997. The manufacturers got it wrong; a million would have been enough if only children wanted them, but adults (including large numbers of students, and people buying them as collectors' items) bought them as well, and three million toys were needed to satisfy demand.

In 1996 shortages of Buzz Lightyear cost Disney and Mattell £300 million in lost sales.

➢ **Describe some items of information that would help a manufacturer to accurately predict sales of a particular toy at Christmas time.**

Collecting and analysing data

Data can be collected for a specific purpose, or it may be collected for one purpose and then used for some other purpose. If it is personal data, then care would have to be taken not to contravene the Data Protection Act ('Data must not be used for any reason incompatible with its original purpose').

Tesco's, for example, collects huge amounts of data on customer buying patterns through its Loyalty card. This massive amount of data can be analysed in thousands of different ways to help predict likely sales, or to suggest new marketing ploys. For example, a probably apocryphal tale is told of how a computer analysis of sales data showed that large numbers of disposable nappies were bought by men in their 20s and 30s on Friday evenings. This led the astute manager to position cans of beer in the same area of the store as nappies, on the basis that most men would pop a few cans in their shopping trolley as they were passing. Sales of beer rocketed!

➢ **Discussion: In the example discussed above, sales data is collected directly for the purposes of printing an itemised bill and keeping track of sales and stock levels. The data is used indirectly to target particular customers.**

Think of other examples where data is collected for one purpose initially and then used for a different purpose.

Information as a commodity

Have you ever wondered why YOU in particular, or your family, are targetted for particular mail advertisements? Every time you make a credit card purchase, enter a competition or order goods by phone or mail, information about who you are and the products you bought goes onto a database. This information can then be used to direct advertising to the people who are most likely to be interested in particular products.

Usefulness of data

Data is of poor 'quality' if it is out-of-date, inaccurate or incomplete. Companies who sell their products through direct mail, for example, need up-to-date lists of names and addresses of people who are likely to be interested in their product, and such lists are enormously valuable to them. But unless the list is kept up-to-date, it soon ceases to be of much value. People move away, grow old, die, or change their interests or purchasing habits.

Charities, for example, may sell their mailing lists to other charities, thus raising extra funds for themselves. Without knowing who on the list are regular donors and who is simply a 'one-off' donor of several years ago, the list is probably not very useful. The information can be 'date-stamped' by including for each person not only their address but the date of their last donation.

Coding value judgements

What is a value judgement? The answer is, any description such as 'tall', 'dark', 'handsome', 'green-eyed', 'old'. If you have ever filled in a questionnaire on which you were asked to tick a box rating something from 'Poor' to 'Excellent' you will know how difficult this is.

> **Fill in the following questionnaire:**
>
> *(2)   The library facilities at school/college are:*
>
> Excellent ☐   Good ☐   Fair ☐   Poor ☐
>
> *(3)   The computing facilities are:*
>
> Excellent ☐   Good ☐   Fair ☐   Poor ☐
>
> *(4) The amount of homework set on this course is:*
>
> Far too much ☐   A bit too much ☐   About right ☐   Too little ☐
>
> *(5)   The course is:*
>
> Very interesting ☐   Quite interesting ☐   Quite dull ☐   Very dull ☐

> **Discussion: Summarise the responses gathered from the class. Analyse the data and present a summary report.**
>
> Notice how difficult it is to code such value judgements. To get a more accurate and complete picture, comments, exceptions or reasons need to be included, but these are very difficult to encode and analyse.

The benefits of ICT

Information technology systems have become indispensable in many businesses today. The benefits include:

- **Speed of processing.** Modern banking systems, for example, could not function without information technology. An MICR reader can sort and process over 2,400 cheques per minute.

- **Vast storage capacity.** Hundreds of thousands of transactions can be stored on disk for processing and analysing in organisations such as banks, building societies, government departments, hospitals and retail stores.

- **Ability to search and combine data in many different ways.** Retail stores can analyse purchases to identify trends and preferences. The police computers can analyse thousands of different pieces of information to help catch criminals.

- **Instant response.** Real-time systems such as airline reservation systems can give an instant response to a query about seat availability, and update their information as soon as a booking is made. When a customer pays for their groceries or other goods using a credit or debit card, the information on the card can be captured and the status of the account checked almost instantly. If sufficient funds are available, the transaction will be accepted.

- **Accurate results.** A computer can calculate the company payroll or the electricity bills for thousands of people with 100% accuracy every time.

- **Communication.** Electronic mail can be used to keep people in different branches of an organisation in touch. Data and information can be sent from one branch to another.

- **Improved company image.** A company can use word processors, desktop publishing and presentation graphics to enhance its image.

Case study: Ford and Microsoft invest in joint venture

By March 2000 Ford's customers will be able to order new vehicles from web sites including Microsoft's www.carpoint.com and Ford's www.ford.com. The jointly-developed *Carpoint* software system will provide access to real-time information such as vehicle availability and delivery schedules, and will be integrated with manufacturer and dealer systems.

The new system will enable customers to customize a car to their own requirements, and manufacturers and dealers hope that the system will give them greater insight into customer buying patterns and preferences. The software will include an online management system to enable dealers to respond to Internet-based queries, and vehicles will continue to be delivered through dealers.

➢ **Discussion: What benefits will the new system bring to dealers, manufacturers and customers? Can you foresee any problems arising from the new system?**

Limitations in the use of information technology systems

New systems nearly always have some drawbacks. These could include:

- Job losses among employees;
- Faults in the software may mean the new system does not work as planned, which may lead to chaos, loss of customers and low employee morale;
- Inadequate hardware may lead to bottlenecks in the flow of data around an organisation;

- Managers may be simply overloaded with information. It is not uncommon for an individual in an organisation to receive several hundred e-mails in the space of a week. If he or she goes away for a week's holiday, it can be almost impossible to catch up with the backlog.

- It may be difficult to extract data from a system in the form required by a user. If the requirements of a new system has not been correctly specified it may not be possible to produce the information that management subsequently finds they need.

- The information can only be as good as the data that is input – garbage in, garbage out, as the saying goes. If employees are not aware of how important it is to enter data accurately, or there are insufficient checks built in to the system to ensure accurate data entry, the information produced may be useless. The difficulty of coding value judgements and the problems of aging data are described above. Poorly designed data entry forms can also contribute to problems of inaccurate data entry.

Exercises

1. With the aid of an example, describe **one** problem which may arise when coding a value judgement.

    (2)

    NEAB IT01 Qu 2 1996

2. A college maintains an extensive database of its full-time students. The database contains personal data, the courses students attend, and higher education or employment applications.

    (a) Describe how the college might keep the personal data of the students up to date. (3)

    (b) The college wishes to sell the personal data to a local sports retailer. An agreement is to be written between the college and the retailer. Describe **three** issues, relating to the data, that should be included in the agreement.

    (3)

    NEAB IT01 Qu 4 1997

3. A telephone company collects the telephone numbers of people who receive calls through a 'Friends and Family' scheme. Under this scheme, subscribers receive discounts on phone calls to numbers they dial most frequently. The customer has to inform the telephone company which numbers are to be included on their 'Friends and Family' list.

    (a) Describe briefly **one** way in which the telephone company could use this data to their advantage. (2)

    (b) How can the telephone company keep their data up-to-date and accurate? (2)

    New question

4. Low quality information can be misleading, distorted or incomprehensible. This type of information is of little value to the decision maker. The output of good quality information is costly and dependent upon many factors.

    (a) Identify **three** factors which affect the quality of information. (3)

    (b) State **two** factors which affect the cost of providing good quality information. (2)

    NEAB IT01 Qu 4 1998

Chapter 10 – Computer Crime and the Law

Computer crime and abuse

New technologies generally create new opportunities for crime; as soon as one avenue is blocked to the criminal, another one is discovered. As information technology has spread, so too have computer crime and abuse. The Internet, for example, is used not only by innocent members of the public but also by fraudulent traders, paedophiles, software pirates, hackers and terrorists. Their activities include planting computer viruses, software bootlegging, storing pornographic images and perpetrating all sorts of criminal activities from credit card fraud to the most complex multinational money laundering schemes. **Computer abuse** refers to acts that are legal but unethical.

Hacking

Hacking is defined as unauthorised access to data held on a computer system. The extent of hacking is extremely difficult to establish as it is usually only discovered by accident, with only about two percent of security breaches discovered as a result of positive action on the part of security staff. (*Digital Crime* by Neil Barrett, page 40.)

Hacking is often perpetrated by employees of a company who have acquired inside knowledge of particular user Ids and passwords. The ability of such hackers to carry out illegal actions without being detected is often hampered by the audit and monitor software that all computer operating systems supply.

The motive behind hacking can often be mischievous rather than anything more sinister: computing students who are learning about operating systems may take delight in penetrating a University's security system to prove that it can be done, or to gain access to exam questions and answers.

In November 1997 Mathew Bevan, a 23 year-old computer technician obsessed with the X-Files and the search for alien spacecraft, and Pryce, a teenager working independently, walked free after a 3 year-long case against them collapsed. They had quite separately penetrated US Air Force computers, Mathew partly motivated by a belief that a captured alien spacecraft was being held secretly at a remote Nevada airbase, and Pryce by an interest in Artificial Intelligence. They were traced not by infowar techniques but by traditional police methods, when Pryce boasted to an undercover informant of his activities on an Internet chat line and gave him his London phone number. They were charged with three offences under the Computer Misuse Act 1990, but eventually it was decided that they in fact presented no threat to national security and they were acquitted after the prosecution offered 'No Evidence'.

Mathew Bevan is now forging a career in Information Security and has a web site www.bogus.net/kuji full of interesting information which you might like to look at.

Theft of money

Not all hackers are motivated purely by fascination with technology. In a recent case, police in San Diego claimed to have cracked an informal ring of about 1,000 hackers that had obtained credit information from computers at one of the nation's three major credit bureaus, and made fraudulent credit card purchases that may have totalled millions of dollars. Other methods of using credit cards fraudulently include stealing them (either from the owner, or in the post before they reach the owner) or getting details from a credit card receipt and using these details to order goods over the phone or Internet.

Theft of data

Data can be stolen by illegally accessing it, or by stealing the computer on which the data is stored. In December 1990 Wing Commander Farquhar's notebook computer was stolen from his car when he left it unattended for a few minutes. It contained the preliminary Allied invasion plan for the impending Gulf war, and could have had potentially disastrous consequences.

Fraud on the Internet

The most common form of fraud on the Internet takes place between traders that appear to be legitimate and innocent purchasers of goods that are offered for sale. A trader could for example represent himself as a particular organisation (say, Selfridges) but in fact be entirely unconnected. They could then take orders and payment for goods and not deliver them.

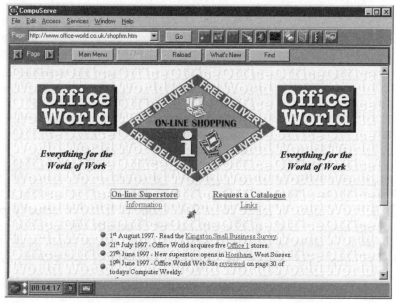

Figure 10.1: Legitimate online merchandising

Another type of trade involves the purchase of software, which the buyer provides payment for and then expects to be able to download. The fraudulent trader can take the money and then develop a persistent 'fault' which means that the software arrives scrambled or is not transmitted at all.

Viruses

Viruses are generally developed with a definite intention to cause damage to computer files or, at the very least, cause inconvenience and annoyance to computer users. The first virus appeared at the University of Delaware in 1987, and since then the number of viruses has escalated to over 9000 different variations in 1997. The virus usually occupies the first few instructions of a particular program on an 'infected' disk and relies on a user choosing to execute that program. When an infected program is executed, the virus is the first series of instructions to be performed. In most cases the virus's first action is to copy itself from the diskette onto the PC and 'hide' within obscure files, the operating system code or within unused disk blocks which are then marked as being 'bad' and unavailable for reuse. The virus can then proceed to perform any of a number tasks ranging from the irritating to the catastrophic such as reformatting the hard disk.

Some viruses lie dormant, waiting to be triggered by a particular event or date – the 'Friday 13th' virus being a well-known one. The virus then infects other diskettes, perhaps by modifying operating system programs responsible for copying programs. From there, the next PC to use the diskette will be infected.

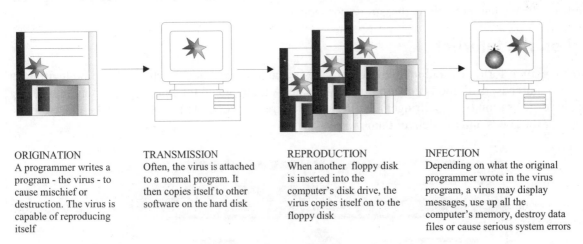

ORIGINATION
A programmer writes a program - the virus - to cause mischief or destruction. The virus is capable of reproducing itself

TRANSMISSION
Often, the virus is attached to a normal program. It then copies itself to other software on the hard disk

REPRODUCTION
When another floppy disk is inserted into the computer's disk drive, the virus copies itself on to the floppy disk

INFECTION
Depending on what the original programmer wrote in the virus program, a virus may display messages, use up all the computer's memory, destroy data files or cause serious system errors

Figure 10.2: How a virus works

'Logic bombs'

A 'logic bomb' is similar to a virus and is sometimes delivered by means of a virus. The 'bomb' can be written to destroy or, worse, subtly change the contents of an organisation's computer systems. However, it does not begin this activity until signalled to do so by the hacker or extortionist, or it may be activated if a cancelling signal fails to arrive. In many cases the bomb itself is not actually planted; a warning message alerting the organisation to the placing of a bomb is usually sufficient to persuade vulnerable institutions to hand over huge sums of money. Estimates suggest that at much as £500 million has been handed to extortionists threatening attacks on computer installations between January 1993 and June 1996.

Digital crime and the law

The rapid progress of computer technology has led to the need for new laws to be introduced so that all perpetrators of computer crime can be prosecuted. Laws in the US impact on computer users in this country, since the majority of systems and Internet content is American. A general approach to a common standard for Internet-related laws throughout the European Union formed part of a proposed European Commission directive discussed by member states in October 1996.

The Computer Misuse Act of 1990

In the early 1980s in the UK, hacking was not illegal. Some universities stipulated that hacking, especially where damage was done to data files, was a disciplinary offence, but there was no legislative framework within which a criminal prosecution could be brought. This situation was rectified by the Computer Misuse Act of 1990 which defined three specific criminal offences to deal with the problems of hacking, viruses and other nuisances. The offences are:

- unauthorised access to computer programs or data;
- unauthorised access with a further criminal intent;
- unauthorised modification of computer material (i.e. programs or data).

To date there have been relatively few prosecutions under this law – probably because most organisations are reluctant to admit that their system security procedures have been breached, which might lead to a loss of confidence on the part of their clients.

Case study 1

A Sunday Times investigation in 1996 established that British and American agencies were investigating more than 40 'attacks' on financial institutions in New York, London and other European banking centres since 1993. Victims have paid up to £13m a time after the blackmailers demonstrated their ability to bring trading to a halt using advanced 'information warfare' techniques learnt from the military.

Criminals have penetrated computer systems using 'logic bombs', electromagnetic pulses and 'high emission radio frequency guns' which blow a devastating electronic 'wind' through a computer system. They have also left encrypted threats at the highest security levels, reading: "Now do you believe we can destroy your computers?"

In most cases victim banks have given in to blackmail rather than risk a collapse of confidence in their security systems.

➤ **Under which clause of which act could a hacker leaving a threatening message as described above, be prosecuted?**

Software copyright laws

Computer software is now covered by the Copyright Designs and Patents Act of 1988, which covers a wide range of intellectual property such as music, literature and software. Provisions of the Act make it illegal to:

* copy software;
* run pirated software;
* transmit software over a telecommunications line, thereby creating a copy.

Software can easily be copied and bootlegged (sold illegally). In addition, the programming *ideas* and *methods* can be stolen by a competitor. Microsoft was sued (unsuccessfully) many years ago by Apple Computers for copying the 'look and feel' of their graphical user interface. It is possible for an expert programmer to 'reverse engineer' machine code to establish the specific algorithms used, so that they can be copied. Some software manufacturers put 'fingerprints' into the code – little oddities which do not affect the way the program runs – so that if the same code is found in a competitor's program, they can prove that it was illegally copied.

The Business Software Alliance in 1998 targeted some 20,000 small- and medium-sized companies to ensure that all software being used is correctly licensed. Offences include using 'pirate' copies of software and using software on more machines than is permitted under the terms of the licence.

Figure 10.3: BSA Advertisement 1997

Case study 2

Bill Gates's empire is being jeopardised by Russian software pirates. Microsoft Office '97 is being sold for £3 on the Russian black market, a minute fraction of the normal retail price of £315. In 1996, 91% of software programs being used in Russia were pirate copies.

Gates recently travelled to Moscow in an attempt to persuade those trading in pirated copies of software programs to refrain from doing so. The overall cost of this illegal activity to the software industry is around £300 million each year. However, it is unlikely that this personal appeal will succeed while fines for being caught in possession of pirated materials are insignificant in comparison with the revenue generated from the pirate industry itself, set at over £500,000 per month. As one stallholder reportedly said: "Mr Gates has gone home and we are trading happily – he makes about £18 million a month, so we do not feel too bad about selling these copies to people who cannot afford to buy it."

(Computer Consultant October 1997)

➢ **Who are the stakeholders (the people affected) in this story? Who are the victims? Is the stallholder acting ethically?**

Using computers to combat crime

Although computers are often involved in criminal activities, there is a more positive aspect to computers in crime; they can prove invaluable in the detection and prevention of crime. Detection is very often about collecting and collating huge amounts of information until a key piece of evidence emerges. In the search for Peter Sutcliffe, the 'Yorkshire Ripper', literally millions of hand- or type-written cards were stored in a mass of filing cabinets and desktop rotating card-holders while investigators pored over them and tried to pull together threads from the often conflicting evidence. Sutcliffe himself was interviewed several times but overlooked before the key evidence against him emerged from the mass of data. This case acted as the impetus for the implementation of the 'HOLMES' system (Home Office Large Major Enquiry System).

Databases of fingerprints, stolen vehicles and criminal records are all essential tools in today's fight against crime. Data matching exercises which match, for example, a 'modus operandi' ('style' of crime) with possible suspects can narrow the search field. Analysis of tax returns against the average profits for a particular type of business in a particular area can highlight possible tax fraud.

Exercises

1. The Computer Misuse Act defines three types of offence. With the aid of examples, describe each of these **three** types of offence. (9)

   NEAB IT01 Qu 7 1997

2. The illegal use of computer systems is sometimes known as computer-related crime.
   (a) Give **three** distinct examples of computer-related crime. (3)
   (b) Give **three** steps that can be taken to help prevent computer-related crime. (3)

   NEAB Sample Paper IT01 Qu 4

3. Describe **three** ways in which a person could gain unauthorised access to information stored on a computer. (6)

   New question

Chapter 11 – Protecting ICT Systems

Internal and external threats to ICT systems

Data and programs within an information technology system are vulnerable to deliberate and accidental destruction or loss, both from within an organisation and from outside it. At one end of the scale it may be a floppy disk which after months of loading your project without complaint, comes up with a message 'Disk unreadable'. At the other end of the scale criminal syndicates hacking into major organisation's computer systems can steal millions of pounds, for example by transferring money to phoney accounts or making fraudulent credit card purchases. What can be done to protect systems against loss?

Internal threats to ICT systems include:

- Hardware failure. A disk head crash, for example, can make the contents of a hard disk unreadable.

- Faulty procedures. A poorly trained employee who does not fully understand how to make entries into an Accounts system can wreak havoc over quite a short period of time.

- Natural disasters. Fire, flood, hurricanes and earthquakes can destroy a building, taking every last customer record with it.

- Employees using laptop computers outside the office may neglect to take backups and lose data through loss of or damage to hardware;

- Dishonest employees. Computer systems are vulnerable to fraud and theft of data both from inside and outside the organisation.

External threats to ICT systems include:

- Hackers gaining entry to company databases and stealing or corrupting data or using the information gained to carry out fraudulent transactions;

- Viruses being downloaded from the Internet;

Unless systems are perceived to be secure, companies may suffer from a lack of confidence in a particular company. Banks, for example, are generally reluctant to disclose how much money they have lost through insecure systems. Many people are unwilling to give credit card numbers when making purchases over the Internet.

Case study: Safety and Privacy of NHS records

Computer records, coded with each patient's unique NHS number and accessible via a UK-wide network, NHSNet, will be linked to patients' names by a new tracking system, the NHS Strategic Tracing Service. Ross Anderson, a computer security expert at Cambridge University says that plans to protect privacy will not work. The proposed use of Smart cards to access the system and firewalls between NHSNet and the Internet will be inadequate because of the large number of health staff involved. The stakes are high, because it is vital for public health that individuals are confident their privacy will be respected.

The NHS executive says security for the tracking system will follow two basic principles: access will occur only where there is a clear need, and all transactions will be strictly monitored.

Why would anyone want to steal NHS data? here are some possible reasons:

1. Insurance companies may want to know how big a risk you are.

2. Extremist anti-abortionists may want to know who has terminated a pregnancy.

3. Blackmailers could access health records of public figures.

4. Information could be used to make obscene phone calls, or even identify subjects for stalking or attacks.

5. Lawyers may want to contact certain kinds of patients to suggest litigation.

6. Companies selling drugs and medical appliances could try to market directly to relevant people.

7. Funeral parlours may try to find out who is seriously ill.

(Adapted for an article in The Guardian, January 29 1999)

Measures to protect ICT systems from illegal access

Measures that can be taken include:

- Physical restrictions to the building and/or computer departments. Most medium and large-size organisations require all employees to wear an ID badge and all visitors to sign in and wear a temporary ID while on the premises. The Computer department is commonly protected from access by a locked door which can only be opened by authorised personnel.

- When using a computer terminal, employees are normally required to sign on with a user-id and password. Company policy commonly states that passwords must not be written down, must not be composed of common names, words or dates and must be changed frequently.

- Access to various data files on the computer can be restricted to those people who need it, identified by their user ID. Any piece of data in a database can have restrictions placed on who can look at it and who can change it, by setting appropriate access rights. Restrictions can also be placed on the location and time at which terminals can be used to access certain data, so that for example a user in the Sales Department will not be able to access any data after 6pm, and will not at any time be able to access Personnel records.

- Special software can be installed on a computer system which will maintain an 'audit trail' of who has logged on, from which terminal and for how long. This will enable any unusual activity to be spotted and investigations made.

- Data can be encrypted before being transmitted. Data is 'scrambled' using an encryption technique so that even if it is intercepted it cannot be read without decoding it first. It is then decrypted at the receiving end. Cryptography researchers are constantly coming up with better techniques for encrypting data. Strong encryption means that the code is virtually impossible to crack, whereas weak encryption means that it would be difficult for most individuals or companies to decrypt, but it could be done by an organisation with sufficient resources and motivation.

Case study: Numbers up as encryption code cracked

The code used by the majority of major financial institutions and e-commerce Web sites has been broken. Researchers led by the Dutch National Research Institute for Mathematics and Computer Science have determined the two prime numbers used to generate a single 512-bit RSA key.

The breakthrough was announced by RSA, the authors of the system used by many companies, websites and banks to encrypt financial data. It's the code that secures your credit cards when you buy online.

It wasn't easy. It took scientists at eleven sites in six countries seven months and 292 different computers, working for 35 years of computing time, to find the two 155 digit-long prime numbers needed.

RSA continually challenges its researchers to break its codes, which depend on the multiplication of two prime numbers. By proving it is possible to factor the RSA key, the researchers have reinforced the view that current codes are not strong enough. Criminals with access to enough computing power could, it appears, interfere with banking and e-commerce transactions.

Source: Ben Hammersley, The Times 'Inter//face' 1 September 1999

> ➤ **Discussion: In some countries *strong encryption* is illegal because governments want to be able to decode messages from terrorists, drug traffickers or other criminals. However, *weak encryption* is not sufficient to prevent determined criminals from stealing confidential data such as credit card numbers used over the Internet.**
> **Do you think strong encryption should be legal in this country?**

Types of backup

Online backup

Backup of all data on a company database is crucial. Many companies cannot afford to lose even a few minutes worth of online transactions, let alone a day's worth. One method of ensuring that data is not lost if for example a disk head crashes, or a bomb is exploded in the vicinity, is to write each transaction to three separate disks more or less simultaneously. Two of the disks will be at the main computer centre, so that in the event of one disk drive failing, the data is safe on the other drive until the problem is fixed. The third disk drive will be situated at a remote, secure location so that if the whole computer centre is destroyed the data is still safe.

Periodic backups

For many companies it is sufficient to make daily backups of all data files. Data is transferred, maybe overnight, to a backup tape or disk and the backup copy is then stored in a fireproof safe. It is necessary to have the previous day's backup copy stored securely, preferably offsite to guard against data loss in the case of fire.

A relatively recent development is the technique of backing up files onto the Internet, so that your files are safely tucked away overnight in San Diego or somewhere truly remote. America's biggest backup provider, @Backup (www.backup.com) enables a user to download a compact little application and then backup important files in off-peak hours. One reason that this method has been slow to catch on, apart from the cost of the phone calls, is the worry about security. @Backup claims that its encryption is so tight that even its own staff cannot tell what is in the files backed up on its hardware.

Backing up laptop data

Having a laptop computer stolen while travelling on business can be disastrous. The NetStore Group provides a backup service called PCRefresh, which for a monthly fee backs up any changed files on a laptop automatically every day. Using this service a laptop user anywhere in the world can be supplied with a new machine with the original data already installed.

Other security measures

Other measures to guard against accidental or deliberate destruction of data include:

- Installing virus checkers on all networks. Viruses are small programs written by sad people who wish to cause others disaster or at least inconvenience and annoyance. New viruses are constantly being written and software companies such as Network Associates issue regular updates of their anti-virus software which can be downloaded from the Internet. Many companies forbid employees to download games and other free software from the Internet as it is prone to virus attack.

- Careful vetting of staff before hiring can help to ensure that potential hackers or fraudsters are not employed. When an employee is fired for any reason it is common in some organisations for them to be escorted immediately from their desk out of the building so that they are not given the chance to destroy data in a 'revenge attack'. Their user-id is removed from the system at the same time.

- Staff training to ensure that all employees who use the computer know the correct procedures and understand the importance of following them can prevent data from being corrupted by faulty data entry, for example.

- Careful siting of the mainframe computer in a large organisation to minimise danger of flooding, with smoke alarms and automatic fire-quenching systems installed. Frequently mainframes are sited in anonymous, unmarked buildings to minimise the threat of extremist attacks.

Issues surrounding access to the Internet

With so much material on the Internet, there are other considerations beyond merely making the transfer of data secure.

- Parents and schools do not want children accessing, for example, pornographic material. They also want to protect children who post material on the Internet for a school project being contacted by undesirable strangers.

- Companies want some control over e-mails and jokes being sent over the Internet from their offices.

Many organisations including businesses, schools and colleges set up their own company-wide **intranet**. This is effectively the same as providing all the facilities commonly used on the Internet, such as browsing software and e-mail facilities for internal use. A proxy server to control access to the Internet and to control access from outside, together with other hardware and special software can be used to maintain security. This is known as a **firewall**. Using an Intranet, a school for example can control what is accessible to pupils which will prevent unsuitable material being downloaded.

> ## Case study: Caught on the Net
>
> In December 1999 twenty-three office staff at the New York Times were fired after company managers discovered they had been e-mailing smutty jokes, jokes about bosses and pornographic pictures while tapping away on screen.
>
> The New York Times has a policy specifying that "communications must be consistent with conventional standards of ethical and proper conduct, behaviour and manners". Staff are banned from using their computers to "create, forward or display any offensive or disruptive messages".
>
> In 1997 Norwich Union paid £450,000 in an out-of-court settlement and had to make a public apology when an e-mail on the intranet disparaging a competitor got out. Workers in the city have been sacked for downloading and distributing pornography. Working with a sexually explicit screensaver could constitute harassment if it offended other staff.
>
> Employers are advised to spell out what is and is not acceptable. Abuse of e-mail, for example, may be treated as a disciplinary offence if employees breach them.
>
> *Source: Helen Hague, The Guardian 3 December 1999*

Exercises

1. (a) State the three levels of offence under the Computer Misuse Act of 1990. Illustrate each answer with a relevant example. (6)

   (b) Describe four separate measures that can be taken to prevent accidental or deliberate misuse of data on a stand-alone computer system. (8)

   NEAB IT01 Qu 5 1999

2. Some companies have policies governing the acceptable use of the Internet. Describe briefly **three** examples of activity that might be covered in such a policy statement. (6)

   New question

Chapter 12 – Data Protection Legislation

Personal privacy

The **right to privacy** is a fundamental human right and one that we take for granted. Most of us, for instance, would not want our medical records freely circulated, and many people are sensitive about revealing their age, religious beliefs, family circumstances or academic qualifications. In the UK even the use of name and address files for mail shots is often felt to be an invasion of privacy.

With the advent of large computerised databases it became quite feasible for sensitive personal information to be stored without the individual's knowledge and accessed by, say, a prospective employer, credit card company or insurance company to assess somebody's suitability for employment, credit or insurance.

Case study: James Wiggins – a true story

In the US, James Russell Wiggins applied for and got a $70,000 post with a company in Washington. A routine pre-employment background check, however, revealed that he had been convicted of possessing cocaine, and he was fired the next day, not only because he had a criminal record but because he had concealed this fact when applying for the job. Wiggins was shocked – he had never had a criminal record, and it turned out that the credit bureau hired to make the investigation had retrieved the record for a James Ray Wiggins by mistake, even though they had different birthdates, addresses, middle names and social security numbers. Even after this was discovered, however, Wiggins didn't get his job back.

If the pre-employment check had been made *before* Wiggins was offered the job, he would not have been offered it and no reason would have been given. The information would have remained on his file, virtually ensuring that he would never get a decent job – without ever knowing the reason why.

The Data Protection Act

The Data Protection Act 1984 grew out of public concern about personal privacy in the face of rapidly developing computer technology. It provides rights for individuals and demands good information handling practice.

The Act covers 'personal data' which are 'automatically processed'. It works in two ways, giving individuals certain rights whilst requiring those who record and use personal information on computer to be open about that use and to follow proper practices.

The Data Protection Act 1998 was passed in order to implement a European Data Protection Directive. This Directive sets a standard for data protection throughout all the countries in the European Union, and the new Act was brought into force in March 2000. Some manual records fall within the scope of the Act and there will also be extended rights for data subjects.

The Data Protection Principles

The Data Protection Act became law on 12th July 1984 and was updated in 1998.

Once registered, data users must comply with the eight Data Protection principles of good information handling practice contained in the Act. Broadly these state that personal data must be:

1. obtained and processed fairly and lawfully;

2. held for the lawful purposes described in the data user's register entry;

3. used for those purposes, and disclosed only to those people, described in the register entry;

4. adequate, relevant and not excessive in relation to the purposes for which they are held;

5. accurate and, where necessary, kept up-to-date;

6. held no longer than is necessary for the registered purposes;

7. accessible to the individual concerned who, where appropriate, has the right to have information about themselves corrected or erased;

8. surrounded by proper security.

Useful definitions from the 1984 Act

'PERSONAL DATA'

information about living, identifiable individuals. Personal data do not have to be particularly sensitive information, and can be as little as a name and address.

'AUTOMATICALLY PROCESSED'

processed by computer or other technology such as document image processing systems. The Act doesn't currently cover information which is held on manual records, e.g. in ordinary paper files.

'DATA USERS'

those who control the contents and use of a collection of personal data. They can be any type of company or organisation, large or small, within the public or private sector. A data user can also be a sole trader, partnership, or an individual. A data user need not necessarily own a computer.

'DATA SUBJECTS'

the individuals to whom the personal data relate.

(The Schedules of the Act may be downloaded from the web site www.hmso.gov.uk and following links for Legislation, United Kingdom, Acts of the UK Parliament. This site contains a lot of information on this topic.)

Data Subjects

We are all 'data subjects'. All types of companies and organisations ('data users') have details about us on their computers. This growth of computerised information has many benefits but also potential dangers. If the information is entered wrongly, is out of date or is confused with someone else's, it can cause problems. You could be unfairly refused jobs, housing, benefits, credit or a place at college. You could be overcharged for goods or services. You could even find yourself arrested in error, just because there is a mistake in the computerised information.

The Data Protection Registrar

The Act established the office of **Registrar**, whose duties include:

- Maintaining a register of data users and computer bureaux and making it publicly available.
- Disseminating information on the Act and how it works.
- Promoting compliance with the Data Protection Principles.
- Encouraging the development of Codes of Practice to help data users to comply with the Principles.
- Considering complaints about breaches of the Principles or the Act.
- Prosecuting offenders, or serving notices on those who are contravening the Principles.

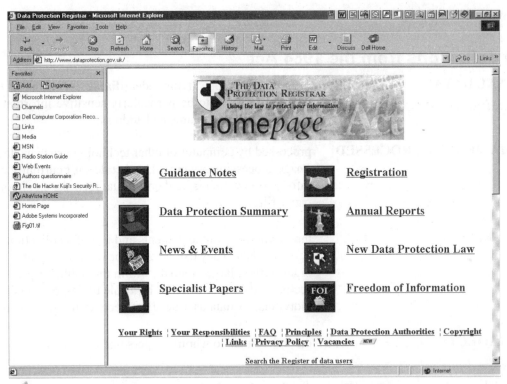

Figure 12.1: The Data Protection Registrar's Home Page

A data user's Register entry

With few exceptions, all data users have to register, giving their name and address together with broad descriptions of:

- Those about whom personal data are held;
- The items of data held;
- The purposes for which the data are used;
- The sources from which the information may be obtained;
- The types of organisations to whom the information may be disclosed i.e. shown or passed on to;
- Any overseas countries or territories to which the data may be transferred.

Exemptions from the Act

- The Act does not apply to payroll, pensions and accounts data, nor to names and addresses held for distribution purposes;
- Registration may not be necessary when the data are for personal, family, household or recreational use;
- Subjects do not have a right to access data if the sole aim of collecting it is for statistical or research purposes, or where it is simply for backup;
- Data can be disclosed to the data subject's agent (e.g. lawyer or accountant), to persons working for the data user, and in response to urgent need to prevent injury or damage to health.

Additionally, there are exemptions for special categories, including data held:

- in connection with national security;
- for prevention of crime;
- for the collection of tax or duty.

The rights of data subjects

The Data Protection Act allows individuals to have access to information held about themselves on computer and where appropriate to have it corrected or deleted.

As an individual you are entitled, on making a written request to a data user, to be supplied with a copy of any personal data held about yourself. The data user may charge a fee of up to £10 for each register entry for supplying this information but in some cases it is supplied free.

Usually the request must be responded to within 40 days. If not, you are entitled to complain to the Registrar or apply to the courts for correction or deletion of the data.

Apart from the right to complain to the Registrar, data subjects also have a range of rights which they may exercise in the civil courts. These are:

- Right to compensation for unauthorised disclosure of data;
- Right to compensation for inaccurate data;
- Right of access to data and to apply for rectification or erasure where data are inaccurate;
- Right to compensation for unauthorised access, loss or destruction of data.

Case Study: Employers to face tighter control of employee data usage

At her Annual Report media conference today the Data Protection Registrar, Elizabeth France announced that a draft Code of Practice governing the uses of personal data by employers is to be circulated for consultation with representatives of employers and employees.

The Code of Practice will be published under the Data Protection Act 1998 once it has been brought into force and will serve as guidance as to good practice for employers. The draft is to be developed following a study on the use of personal data in employment undertaken by Robin Chater of the Personal Policy Research Unit, which was completed at the end of February 1999 and has just been published by the Registrar on her website.

The Code of Practice will introduce tighter control over the use of employee records in three key areas:

1. Employee surveillance involving collection of data to monitor performance or detect problems e.g. interception of e-mail and use of CCTV.

2. Automated processing e.g. CV scanning, aptitude and psychometric testing and the extent to which employment decisions might be taken by automatic means.

3. Collection of new and sensitive information e.g. genetic tests or results of alcohol or drug testing.

Once it is in place, failure to comply could lead to enforcement action by the Registrar, or a claim for compensation by any individual who has suffered as a result. Mrs France said:

"The development of new technology is threatening personal privacy in the workplace. Employers want to know more and more about their staff who are often not in a position to resist. This Code will set out clear ground rules to ensure employers' information practices are fair to employees."

Source: Internet web site www.dataprotection.gov.uk 1999

Discussion: How do the requirements of Data Protection Legislation impact upon data collection and use within the workplace?

Exercises

1. A company is storing details of its customers on a database. Describe **three** obligations the company has under the Data Protection Act. (6)

   NEAB Computing Paper 1 Qu 7 1997

2. A particular college uses a computer network for storing details of its staff and students and for managing its finances. Network stations are provided for the principal, vice-principal, finance officer, clerical staff and teaching staff. Only certain designated staff have authority to change data or to authorise payments.

   (a) What are the legal implications of storing personal data on the computer system? (4)

   (b) Outline **two** methods of controlling access to the stored data. (4)

   (c) What precautions should be taken to guard against loss of the data? (3)

   New Question

3. State what is meant by the term 'data subject' and outline **two** common criticisms of the Data Protection Act from the data subject's point of view. (5)

   NISEAC Computing Paper 2 Qu 4 1996

Chapter 13 – Health and Safety

Computers and health

Computers can be held responsible for a whole raft of health problems, from eyestrain to wrist injuries, back problems to foetal abnormalities, stomach ulcers to mental collapse. Articles appear regularly in the newspapers relating stories of employees who are suing their employers for computer-related illnesses.

Not so long ago it was thought that the widespread use of these fantastic machines, that could perform calculations and process data with lightning speed and complete accuracy, would free up humans to work maybe only two or three hours a day, while the computer did the lion's share. In fact, people seem to be working harder than ever, trying to keep up with the output of their computers. Human beings are the weak link in the chain, needing food, rest, a social life; prone to headaches, stress, tired limbs and mistakes.

Figure 13.1: Stress at work

Stress

Stress is often a major factor in work-related illness. Simply thinking about computers is enough to cause stress in some people. It is stressful to be asked to perform tasks which are new to you and which you are not sure you can cope with. It is stressful to know that you have more work to do than you can finish in the time available. It is stressful, even, to have too little to do and to be bored all day.

The introduction of computers into the workplace can have detrimental effects on the well-being of information workers at many different levels in an organisation. For example:

- Some companies may use computers to monitor their workers' productivity, which often increases their stress levels. Symptoms include headaches, stomach ulcers and sleeplessness.

- Many people are afraid of computers and fear that they will not be able to learn the new skills required, or that their position of seniority will be undermined by younger 'whizz kids' with a high level of competence in ICT

- It can be almost impossible for some people to get away from work. Pagers, mobile phones, laptop computers and modems mean that even after leaving the office, there is no need to stop work – indeed, should you even *think* of stopping work? As a busy executive, can you afford to waste 45 minutes on the train to Ipswich reading the newspaper or just gazing out of the window, when you could be tap-tap-tapping on your laptop, or infuriating your fellow passengers by holding long and boring conversations on your mobile phone?

- 'Information overload' means that managers are often bombarded with far more information than they can assimilate, producing 'information anxiety'. Try typing the words 'Information Overload' into one of the World Wide Web's search engines and within seconds, it will have searched millions of information sources all over the world and come up with thousands of references all presorted so that those most likely to be of interest are at the top.

- A survey of 500 heads of ICT departments revealed that over three quarters of respondents had suffered from failing personal relationships, loss of appetite, addiction to work and potential alcohol abuse. The continuing developments within ICT ensure that it is always in the minds of business executives and also that it is blamed for most corporate problems. The very speed of development, for which ICT is now famous, and the need to keep pace with this is also a major contributing factor to ICT stress-related illness.

Case study: Information overload

Val Kerridge is an ICT manager in an Engineering company:

"I have to monitor everything to do with computers that might affect the firm, from fax-modems to new operating systems or network capabilities. I'm always being asked what I think of new hardware or software products, so I feel obliged to read everything – computer magazines, e-mails, user group communications on the Internet, mailshots from suppliers – there was so much it made me ill. I couldn't sleep properly, I had constant headaches and neck pains from staring at a screen, and I never had time to eat properly in a 12 to 14 hour day at the office."

Peter Harris is a management consultant:

"I was away for four days and when I came back, there was a huge pile of mail and faxes and dozens of e-mail messages. I couldn't tell from the titles whether they were important or not, and I spent 10 hours or more in front of a screen dealing with it all. I didn't know what information overload was until I came across the research and then I thought, 'Yes, that's me.'

When I go into organisations I find it very common in all departments. There's too much information and not enough communicating.

I now have a survival strategy. I am very strict with the amount of information I use. I scan it and throw it away or file it. I've learned to say 'No, I don't need that information'".

> **Discussion: Do you suffer from computer-related stress? How can it be alleviated?**

Repetitive strain injury (RSI)

RSI is the collective name for a variety of disorders affecting the neck, shoulders and upper limbs. It can result in numbness or tingling in the arms and hands, aching and stiffness in the arms, neck and shoulders, and an inability to lift or grip objects. Some sufferers cannot pour a cup of tea or type a single sentence without excruciating pain.

The Health and Safety Executive say that more than 100,000 workers suffer from RSI. It is not a new disease; Bernard Ramazzini, an Italian physician, noted of scribes and notaries in 1717:

> "The diseases of persons incident to this craft arise from three causes … constant sitting … the perpetual motion of the hand in the same manner, and the attention and application of the mind … constant writing also considerably fatigues the hand and the whole arm on account of the continual tension of the muscles and tendons."

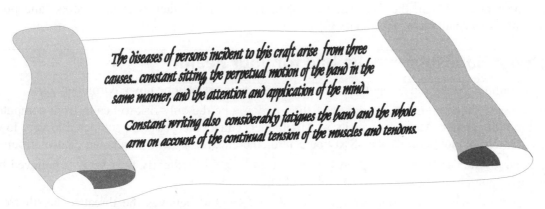

Figure 13.2: Recognition of RSI is not new!

Now, as then, the constant pain "can be removed by no medicines".

Case study: Bank staff 'driven to injury'

Keyboard operators at the Midland Bank's factory-style processing centre at Frimley, Surrey developed severe cases of repetitive strain injury after their work rate was sharply increased, a court was told yesterday.

Five former part-time workers who put cheque details into computers are claiming compensation for upper limb disorders including aches, stiffness and shooting pains in their arms, fingers, wrists, shoulders and necks.

The five former Midland workers, all women, were required to key in transaction records at an intensive stroke rate, on inadequately designed equipment, with a poor working posture and negligible training.

There was a lack of breaks or variation of tasks and there was strong pressure on staff to maintain and increase speed. The fastest operators – who keyed four strokes a second with their right hand, while holding cheques in their left – were awarded gold badges and their names were publicised by the bank.

In 1989, the Midland Bank had to pay £45,000 compensation to an RSI sufferer.

Source: Seumas Milne, The Guardian November 25 1997

➢ **What factors were cited as contributing to the onset of RSI among the employees?**

Eyestrain

Computer users are prone to eyestrain from spending long hours in front of a screen. Many computer users prefer a dim light to achieve better screen contrast, but this makes it difficult to read documents on the desk. A small spotlight focussed on the desktop can be helpful. There is no evidence that computer use causes permanent damage to the eyes, but glare, improper lighting, improperly corrected vision (through not wearing the correct prescription glasses), poor work practices and poorly designed workstations all contribute to temporary eyestrain.

Extremely low frequency (ELF) radiation

In normal daily life we are constantly exposed to ELF radiation not only from electricity mains and computer monitors but also naturally occurring sources such as sunshine, fire and the earth's own magnetic field. Research into the effects of ELF radiation is increasing and seems to indicate that it may be connected to some health problems. Several studies have tried to establish whether there is a link between monitor use and problems in pregnancy such as early miscarriages. The results are not clear-cut, because although some studies seem to show a correlation between an increased rate of miscarriages and long hours spent at a VDU in the first trimester of pregnancy, other factors such as stress and poor ergonomic conditions could have played a part.

Case study: Handsets may be bad for your health

The safety of mobile phones and computer monitors is again being questioned by environmentalists.

Research in France suggests that microwave radiation may not be the only risk to health from computer screens and mobile phones. At the University of Montpelier, chick embryos were subjected to very low-frequency radiation for eight hours a day. Sixty percent died compared with 17 percent in control groups.

And a large survey funded by the European Union, due to be published early next year, is believed by activists to have found a strong link between mobile phone use and cancer.

Green Party activist and bioelectromagnetics expert Roger Coghill believes the threat to health from heavy mobile phone use is so great that handsets should have a warning sticker on them.

Coghill Research Laboratory Web site: www.cogreslab.demon.co.uk

Source:Chris Partridge, The Sunday Times 10 December 1997

Computers, health and the law

Occupational health and safety legislation in Britain is researched, guided and structured by the Health and Safety Executive (HSE), a government body. An EEC Directive on work with display screen equipment was completed in the early 1990s, with member states required to adapt it to become part of their own legislation. As a consequence, the Health and Safety at Work Act of 1974 incorporated legislation pertaining to the use of VDUs, and the relevant section is now referred to as The Health and Safety (Display Screen Equipment) Regulations 1992.

This legislation is intended to protect the health of employees within the working environment, and employers, employees and manufacturers all have some responsibility in conforming to the law.

Employers are required to

- Perform an analysis of workstations in order to evaluate the safety and health conditions to which they give rise;
- Provide training to employees in the use of workstation components;
- Ensure employees take regular breaks or changes in activity;
- Provide regular eye tests for workstation users and pay for glasses.

Employees have a responsibility to

- Use workstations and equipment correctly, in accordance with training provided by employers;
- Bring problems to the attention of their employer immediately and co-operate in the correction of these problems.

Manufacturers are required to ensure that their products comply with the Directive. For example, screens must tilt and swivel, keyboards must be separate and moveable. Notebook PCs are not suitable for entering large amounts of data.

Screen must **tilt**..

.. and **swivel**

Figure 13.3: Workstations must be ergonomically designed

Classrooom menace: ignore it and you may end up in court

Schools should not only teach children good posture and ensure they take regular screen breaks, but also scrutinise the equipment they provide. Chairs and screens should be adjustable for each child and foot- and back-rests may be needed.

"Some schools may be buying laptops because they are relatively cheap and easy to store but they are terrible for kids and long-term use. The screens are too low and the little workstations sold for them put kids into horrid positions," says Ms Martin, a specialist remedial therapist with extensive experience teaching RSI victims.

Tom Jones, of Thompsons solicitors, the UK's largest personal injury law firm, says schools ignoring RSI may find themselves in court.

"Schools have a duty of care over computer use in the same way they have at a school rugby match."

Source: Caroline Palmer, The Guardian 2 December 1997

The ergonomic environment

Ergonomics refers to the design and functionality of the environment, and encompasses the entire range of environmental factors. Employers must give consideration to

- **Lighting**. The office should be well lit. Computers should neither face windows nor back onto a window so that the users have to sit with the sun in their eyes. Adjustable blinds should be provided.

- **Furniture**. Chairs should be of adjustable height, with a backrest which tilts to support the user at work and at rest, and should swivel on a five-point base. It should be at the correct height relative to a keyboard on the desk.

- **Work space**. The combination of chair, desk, computer, accessories (such as document holders, mouse and mouse mats, paper trays and so on), lighting, heating and ventilation all contribute to the worker's overall well-being.

- **Noise**. Noisy printers, for example, should be given covers to reduce the noise or positioned in a different room.

- **Hardware**. The screen must tilt and swivel and be flicker-free, the keyboard must be separately attached.

- **Software**. Software is often overlooked in the quest for ergonomic perfection. The EEC Directive made a clear statement about the characteristics of acceptable software, requiring employers to analyse the tasks which their employers performed and to provide software which makes the tasks easier. It is also expected to be easy to use and adaptable to the user's experience.

Software can be hazardous to your health

Bad software can be extremely stressful to use. Software that slows you down by crashing frequently, giving incomprehensible error messages, using non-standard function keys and displaying badly structured menus, for example, can leave a user longing to throw the computer from the nearest window. Repeated failure with a new software package very quickly becomes frustrating, boring and depressing. Feelings of inadequacy and alienation mean that people may begin to dread their daily encounters with the computer and productivity suffers.

Human-computer interaction is a growing field of study within computing and seeks to understand, among other things, what makes software difficult or unpleasant to use, and how it can be improved. The principles of good, usable software design are based on extensive research.

Exercises

1. (i) Describe briefly **four** computer-related illnesses from which a VDU operator may suffer. (8)

   (ii) Describe **four** ways in which an employer can help to ensure that VDU operators will not suffer from computer-related illnesses. (8)

   New question

2. Describe **three** health hazards associated with computer use. (6)

   NEAB IT01 Sample Paper

3. The introduction of computer terminals and personal computers has been associated with a number of physical health hazards.

   (a) State **three** health hazards which have been associated with prolonged use of computers. (3)

   (b) Describe **five** preventative actions which may be taken to avoid computer related health hazards, explaining clearly how each action will assist in preventing one or more of the hazards you have described in part (a). (10)

   NEAB IT01 Qu 6 1998

IT01 – Sample Questions and Answers

1. (a) Information processing is concerned with:

    Input
    Processing
    Output
    Feedback

    Briefly describe these four elements of information processing, using a diagram to illustrate your answer. (6)

    (b) Explain the difference between 'knowledge' and 'information'.

    NEAB IT01 Qu 1 1998

Notes:

In Chapter 8 you will find a block diagram which shows the stages of Input, Processing and Output. *Feedback* is an easy concept to understand and as it has not been explicitly covered in the text, you will have to use common sense to add it to the diagram. Feedback always goes back from the output to the input phase and the purpose of it is to have some effect on the input. Think of occasions on which you have been asked for feedback, perhaps on the quality of a product or the 'A' Level course you are studying. In your written explanation, try and give enough detail to score the marks – it is all too easy to write a superficial answer which will not satisfy the mark scheme. For example if you write 'Feedback is the response from the user to the output he/she receives' this will probably get you one mark, but not the two marks allocated.

In part (b), remember that knowledge consists of the facts and rules that you know about a particular topic.

Suggested answer:

(a) **Input** is the capturing of the raw data or facts representing events occurring in organisations. (1)

Processing is the conversion of these raw facts into a form that is useful for some purpose, for example by summarizing, finding subsets of data satisfying some given criteria (e.g. all items which need reordering). (1)

Output is the production of reports (on-screen or hard copy) from the processed information which goes to the end-user. (1)

Feedback is the response to the output that a user receives, which is returned to appropriate members of the organisation to help them refine or correct the input phase. (2)

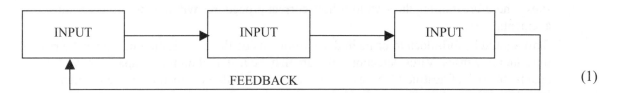

(1)

(b) Information is data which has been processed into a meaningful and useful form whilst knowledge is a set of concepts, rules and procedures used by people to create, collect, store and share information. (2)

2. A multi-national organisation maintains an information technology system which holds a large amount of vital and sensitive data.

    (a) Describe **three** steps which should be taken to protect the data against deliberate theft or corruption. (6)

    (b) Describe **three** steps which should be taken to protect the data against accidental loss. (6)

NEAB IT01 Qu 4 1996

Notes:

It always helps when answering questions to try and relate them to your own personal experience and use any knowledge gleaned from the course combined with a large dose of common sense – don't leave home without it. Have you ever visited a large organisation? What happens as you enter the front door? Would it be possible to get into their Computer Department? If you had a few week's work experience with such an organisation, what would prevent you from looking at or corrupting sensitive data?

For Part (b), be aware that you will not get full marks with one-word answers or short phrases without some explanation or expansion of your answer. Often one mark goes for the phrase such as 'Take regular backups' or 'Staff training' and the second mark for further explanation. Think what else you can say about backups. For example how often will they be done, what will they be stored on, where will they be kept? Get used to allowing your mind to float around a subject, exploring it from different angles.

Suggested answer:

    (a) Physical restrictions can be placed on the building so that anyone entering has to sign in or show an ID badge. This will prevent unauthorised people from gaining access to computer terminals inside the building. Physical access to sensitive areas can be restricted to badge-holders or more sophisticated techniques such as iris recognition technology.

        Each employee can be given a user-id and password which has to be frequently changed and not written down anywhere. Access rights to data can be made dependent on the user-id of the person signing on.

        Staff should be carefully vetted before they are hired to ensure as far as possible that they are honest and reliable and not likely to indulge in hacking or theft of data. They can be asked to sign a document laying down the company's regulations and code of practice. If staff are fired for any reason they should be escorted from the building immediately and their user-id removed from the system so that they have no chance for 'revenge attacks'.

        (You could also gain points for describing data encryption, call-back system for logging on, keeping an audit trail etc if you are familiar with these techniques.)

    (b) Periodic backups of the data could be made. For example a backup of all files that have changed could be made every evening onto a backup tape which is stored in a secure, fireproof safe. Once a week an extra backup copy could be stored off-site.

        Accidental loss may be caused by not following correct procedures for example when updating files. Therefore training the staff to follow correct procedures will help to protect against accidental loss.

        Staff should be forbidden to bring in disks from outside the organisation to reduce the risk of introducing viruses. Virus detection software may be installed on the company network to guard against the risk of destructive viruses being accidentally downloaded from the Internet or introduced from a floppy disk.

3. Give two advantages and one disadvantage of a firm using electronic mail as a method of keeping in touch with its large number of travelling salespersons. (3)

NEAB Specimen Paper IT01 Qu 2

Notes:

Before you put pen to paper consider what you are comparing electronic mail with. Contact by letter? By mobile phone? By a note in the internal mail to be picked up on return to the office? By fax? Be careful to avoid answers such as 'quicker', 'cheaper', 'more reliable' which will not score any marks. Can you think of any facilities that e-mail has which are not available with other means of communication? What scenario are you imagining for these salesmen? Do they return to the office every day, or are they away for several days at a time? Try to put yourself in the position of the salesperson (or the boss) before you start to answer the question.

Suggested answer:

Advantages: Using e-mail the same message can be sent to a group of salespersons in a single operation, thus saving the time that would be spent writing or telephoning each individual.

The salesperson can look at his/her e-mail messages at a convenient time, and so would not be interrupted by a telephone call in the middle of a meeting with a client.

(Could also say: Compared with sending a letter, the advantages are that e-mail will arrive far quicker, and the sender will know that the message has been received at the salesperson's computer – if it is not, a message such as 'e-mail returned' is sent back to the sender.)

Disadvantage: The salesperson may not look at his/her e-mail regularly – it is reliant on following good practice and checking e-mail, maybe on a laptop, at least once a day.

---

4. Recent changes in communications technology have resulted in a blurring of the distinction between telecommunications and computing. Information services are starting to be provided on what is becoming known as the Information Super Highway (ISH).

(a) State the minimum facilities needed to gain access to these services. (3)

(b) Identify and briefly describe three types of information service you would expect to find when linked to the ISH. (6)

NEAB IT01 1998

Notes:

'Facilities' refers to the hardware and software needed to access the Internet. (*Information Super Highway* is not a phrase that has stood the test of time.) This should be straightforward to answer – you need to mention 3 different things to get 3 marks. Part (b) will be easier if you have spent time using the Internet. You will get one mark for naming an information service and two marks for a brief description making two good points.

Suggested answer:

(a) Hardware needed: A PC with a modem, and a telephone line or ISDN connection.

   Software: Browser such as Internet Explorer.

(b) Home shopping: Can browse through a catalogue, select goods and transfer them to a 'shopping basket', then proceed to 'checkout' and give credit card details and delivery address. Goods will be delivered to address.

   Entertainment: Videos, music and games software can be downloaded and saved.

   News service: the BBC and national newspapers have online news so that you can check weather, football or cricket scores, current affairs as the news breaks.

   (Could also describe online banking, stock market dealing, software help, university places, job vacancies etc.)

5. Briefly describe **two** social impacts and **two** organisational impacts commonly identified as a result of introducing computerised information systems into business organisations. (8)

NEAB IT01 Qu 2 1998

Notes:

The Mark Scheme specifies that "There must be a clear statement of the issues. Whilst lengthy discussion is not required, short phrases of 4 or 5 words are unacceptable at A Level." You will get no marks for writing, for example, "The business will become more efficient and it will be easier and quicker to find out information."

The key to getting good marks on questions like this, which look superficially easy, is to first consider very carefully what the question means. Is it asking for the social impact on the employees or the general public? When you have decided, imagine a particular business, and consider how computerisation affects that business. What are you envisioning when you consider the social impact of introducing a computerised information system? A person in the stock room at a garage, who has to know whether a particular part is in stock? A car salesman who has a customer wanting a silver Puma with blue interior and who wants to know the delivery time? These examples may help with the organisational impact. They may not have much of a social impact so now think of another situation. What about a Travel company who has information available over the Internet on holidays available at short notice? What about telephone banking? What about e-mail? Use your own personal experience wherever possible.

Suggested answer:

Social impacts: Computerised information systems may have the effect of shifting the locations of work. For example many high street banks may close, and employees lose their jobs unless they are willing to relocate to say the Scottish highlands where the new telephone banking centre is set up. Some employees in other organisations may be able to work from home using a PC and modem, linked to the company network, so they will not need to travel to work. This may be convenient but may result in a feeling of isolation.

(Could also discuss issues of stress from speed of change or information overload when a manager is required to deal with 50-100 e-mails every day.)

Organisational impacts: The type of work done by employees often changes, and this may mean that training programmes have to be introduced. The organisation may become 'flatter' as all levels of worker in the company use the computerised information system and there is less need for middle managers.

The skill level of the workforce may rise and it may be harder to recruit people with the right skills than for the unskilled workforce previously required.

---

6. List **six** factors which could give rise to health or safety problems associated with the use of information technology equipment. (6)

NEAB IT01 Qu 3 1996

Notes:

The question says 'list' so you don't need a long explanation of each point you make. Generally it is not considered very hazardous to health to sit down at a computer for the duration of an ICT lesson or for long enough to type up your homework, so you probably need to be thinking of people whose job it is to enter data at a computer all day long.

Suggested answer:

Incorrect positioning of computer facing window can lead to eyestrain from screen glare.

Incorrect seating position can lead to backache.

Constant typing with inadequate breaks can lead to RSI (repetitive strain injury).

Printer noise can contribute to stress.

Badly designed software can cause stress and a desire to throw the computer out of the nearest 6th floor window.

Trailing electric cables can be a safety hazard.

---

7. A software house is advertising for an analyst programmer to join one of their development teams. State four personal qualities that the company should be looking for in the applicants. (4)

    NEAB IT01 Qu 2 1999

Notes:

 The word 'team' should give you at least one clue. Also, what does an analyst programmer do? Analyses systems, of course … and how is this carried out? Think of the people in your class you would most like to have in your team for a joint assignment and you've probably got the answer.

Suggested answer:

Ability to work as part of a team, *(but this on its own won't score you the mark!)* i.e. exchange views, share information, listen to the other team members' ideas.

Good oral communication skills, able to interact easily and confidently with users, ask the right questions and understand the user's requirements.

Good written communication skills for documenting results of interviews, writing technical documentation for programmers.

Good problem-solving abilities since systems analysis is a high-level skill requiring insight as well as technical knowledge.

(Could also mention: ability to work under pressure and meet deadlines; organisational management skills, i.e. ability to take orders and give them, be responsible for own work and delegate where necessary.)

---

8. Many market research firms use questionnaires as a means of gathering raw data for companies about the popularity of their products.

    (a) Explain why Information Technology is widely used in Market Research. (4)

    (b) Once the data has been collected, it can be used to give the client information about their products. Explain the difference between information and data in this context. (4)

    NEAB IT01 Qu 4 1999

Notes:

In part (a), try to think how Market Research would be done without using computers. The data would be collected on forms, then presumably answers would be totted up manually (how long would that take??), calculations laboriously worked out … with quite a few mistakes probably creeping in and a few made-up results along the way. Now think of reasons why computers are used for this task.

In part (b) be careful to avoid answers such as "data is raw data, and information is data which has been processed" for which you will get no marks. Many great minds have struggled to explain the difference between data and information and not all of them agree but you will have to try and add something of note to the debate!

Suggested answer:

(a) Data can be input directly from the documents on which it is collected, thus avoiding transcription errors and allowing more accuracy.

The data will be processed very much more quickly which is important to companies which require feedback quickly so that they can respond to consumer demands.

(could also mention that the data can be manipulated more easily using statistical packages, graphs can be produced, etc. to present the information in a variety of ways for different audiences e.g. management, the general public. Or, that a far greater volume of results can be handled than would be possible manually so more accurate results will be achieved.)

(b)   The data is the raw facts or figures which are fed into the computer, and which have no meaning until a context is given to them. Information is data which has been processed to give it meaning. For example the numbers representing answers to the questions on the questionnaire (data) are input and processed, and information is produced such as '83% of the population do not think that the shape of a toothbrush is an important factor in deciding whether to purchase.'

---

9.   The term 'data protection' covers the maintenance of the integrity, quality and ownership of data handled by information technology systems. There are many ways to protect data, and there is also legislation to ensure that data is kept private and secure.

Discuss the Data Protection Act 1984, including reference to:

- objections to the Act;

- the information that should be recorded when registering with the Office of the Data Protection Registrar;

- the likely future of the Act and the consequences for data owners/users as a result of the EU Directive on Data Protection. (15)

Quality of language will be assessed in this question

NEAB IT01Qu 8 1998

Notes:

In this question 4 marks are allocated to 'quality of language'. The criteria for gaining full marks are as follows:

The candidate has expressed complex ideas clearly and fluently. Sentences and paragraphs follow on from one another smoothly and logically. Arguments will be consistently relevant and well structured. There will be few, if any, errors of grammar, punctuation and spelling.

This is an essay question and you should pay attention to how your answer is constructed. Start by making rough notes of any points that you think are relevant, and number them in the order you think they should be written so that they follow a logical progression. (The points mentioned in the question itself are not in a particularly logical order.) Then start your essay, trying to address the specified points without waffling. It is quality, not quantity, which counts.

Suggested answer:

The Data Protection Act of 1984 was brought into force as a result of growing public concern over the amount of personal data kept on computers. Basically the Act requires that, with very few exceptions, all data users who hold personal data on a computer must register with the Office of the Data Protection Registrar. The information that they must give includes their name and address and broad information on:

- those about whom personal data are held;
- the items of data held;
- the purposes for which the data are used;
- the sources from which the information may be obtained;
- the types of organisations to whom the information may be disclosed i.e. shown or passed on to;
- Any overseas countries or territories to which the data may be transferred.

(This covers the second bullet point in the question – there is a maximum of 4 marks for each bullet point in the Mark Scheme.)

Some objections have been made to the Act, or omissions from it. For example, manual records are not covered by the Act and it is therefore quite legal to hold personal records in a manual filing system without registering with the Data Protection Registrar. Also, the Act does not cover the types of data that may be collected about employees in the workplace, and how the data is collected. For example, e-mails could be monitored, or the results of aptitude tests recorded. Employees may not be aware that this type of data is stored about them. Some people may object to the number of exceptions to a data subject's right to view data, for example data held for purposes of tax collection or in connection with national security. Who decides whether it would be a breach of national security for a data subject to view his or her personal data?

(That's enough on the second point. The third point is tricky as you, like me, probably have no idea what the European Data Protection Directive said. However, the Act was updated in the year this question was asked and you will just have to make intelligent guesses.)

The Act was amended in 1998 as a result of a European Data Protection Directive. The same legislation will apply to both manual and computerized records. All EU countries will have to incorporate the Act into their domestic legislation. Data users may have to implement quality control systems or redesign their own internal systems to ensure that they comply with the Act. There may be some provision to cover e-mail usage.

There may also be some strengthening of individual rights so that data users are obliged to get the consent of data subjects before storing data about them.

Section 2

Information: Management and Manipulation

Chapter 14 – Introduction to Computer Systems

The components of a computer

All computers, whatever their size or function, have certain basic components. They have input devices for reading data into main memory, a central processing unit (CPU) for processing the data, output devices for printing, displaying or outputting information, and storage devices for permanent storage of programs and data.

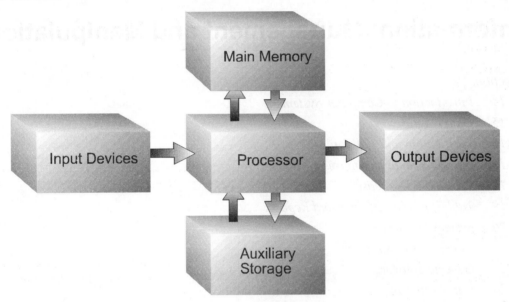

Figure 14.1: Block diagram of a computer system

Input and output devices

Input devices include the keyboard, mouse, barcode readers or scanners and many other devices. We will be looking at some of these and their uses in more detail in the next chapter. Output devices include various types of printer and plotter as well as the VDU (screen).

> ➤ **Discussion: Can you think of some other input devices? In what circumstances or environment is the device you have named appropriate?**

The processor

The processing power of a computer is measured in terms of its speed of operation, the amount of memory it has, and the number of input/output devices it can handle. All computer operations are under the control of the CPU, which has the following functions:

- It controls the transmission of data from input devices to memory;
- It processes the data held in main memory;

- It controls the transmission of information from main memory to output devices.

Most computers use integrated circuits, or chips, for their CPUs and main memory. A chip is about ½" square and can hold millions of electronic components such as transistors and resistors. The CPU of a microcomputer is called a **microprocessor**. The CPU and main memory of a PC are commonly held on a single board called a main circuit board.

Main memory

Instructions and data are held in main memory, which is divided into millions of individually addressable storage units called **bytes**. One byte can hold one character, or it can be used to hold a code representing, for example, a tiny part of a picture, a sound, or part of a computer program instruction. The total number of bytes in main memory is referred to as the computer's memory size. Computer memory sizes are measured as follows:

1 Kilobyte (Kb)	=	1,000 bytes (or to be exact, 1024 bytes)
1 Megabyte (Mb)	=	1,000,000 (1 million) bytes
1 Gigabyte (Gb)	=	1,000,000,000 (1 billion) bytes
1 Terabyte (Tb)	=	1,000,000,000,000 (1 trillion) bytes

As with processing power, the amount of memory that comes with a standard PC has increased exponentially over the past 20 years. In about 1980, BBC microcomputers with 32K of memory were bought in their thousands for home and school use. In 1981, Bill Gates of Microsoft made his famous remark "640K ought to be enough for anybody". In 2000, a PC with 64Mb of memory is standard, costing around £1,000 including bundled software.

RAM and ROM

There are basically two kinds of memory; Random Access Memory (RAM) which is the ordinary kind of memory referred to above, used for storing programs which are currently running and data which is being processed. This type of memory is **volatile** which means that it loses all its contents as soon as the machine is switched off.

Read Only Memory (ROM) is the other type of memory, and this is non-volatile, with its contents permanently etched into the memory chip at the manufacturing stage. It is used for example to hold the **bootstrap loader**, the program which runs as soon as the computer is switched on and instructs it to load the operating system from disk into memory. To assist software development, some types of ROM are programmable (PROM) and may also be erasable (EPROM).

Auxiliary storage

All standalone PCs come equipped with an in-built hard disk, the capacity of which is also measured in bytes. A typical storage capacity for a Pentium PC is between 1 and 10 gigabytes.

- The hard disk is used for storing software including the operating system, other systems software, application programs and data.
- Floppy disks consist of a thin sheet of mylar plastic encased in a hard 3½" casing. The standard High Density disk has a capacity of 1.44Mb.
- CDs have a capacity of approximately 650Mb.
- Many PCs also have a drive for Zip disks, which have a capacity of 100Mb.

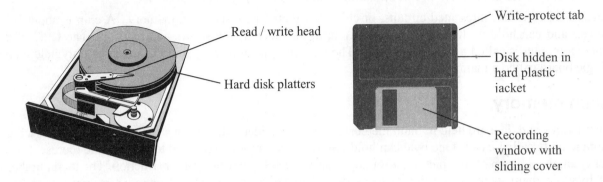

Read / write head

Hard disk platters

Write-protect tab

Disk hidden in hard plastic jacket

Recording window with sliding cover

Figure 14.2: Hard disk and floppy disk

Internal storage of data

One of the things that many people find most amazing about computers is their seeming ability to understand and interpret all kinds of information fed in via a keyboard, mouse, scanner, microphone or sensor of some kind.

All digital computers use the **binary** system for representing data of all types – numbers, characters, sound, pictures and so on. A binary system uses just 2 symbols to represent all information. The symbols could be anything like a dot and dash (as in Morse code), + and -, or 0 and 1. The great advantage of the binary system is that the digits 1 and 0 can be represented by electrical circuits that can exist in one of two states – current is either flowing or not flowing, and a circuit is either closed or open, on or off.

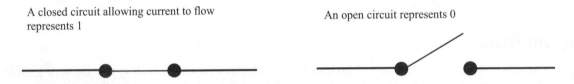

A closed circuit allowing current to flow represents 1

An open circuit represents 0

Figure 14.3: Electrical circuits can represent 1 or 0

The ASCII code

A binary digit (1 or 0) is known as a '**bit**', short for **BI**nary digi**T**. In most computers today, bits are grouped together in 8-bit **bytes**. A byte can hold 2^8 different combinations of 0s and 1s, which means that, for example, 256 different characters can be represented.

Over the years, different computer designers have used different sets of codes for representing characters, which has led to great difficulty in transferring information from one computer to another. Most personal computers (PCs) nowadays use the ASCII code (American Standard Code for Information Interchange), but many mainframe computers use a code called EBCDIC (Extended Binary Coded Decimal Interchange Code — pronounced EB-SUH-DICK or EB-SEE-DICK according to taste).

ASCII originally used a 7-bit code, but a later version that is now more common uses 8 bits. The 128 different combinations that can be represented in 7 bits is plenty to allow for all the letters, numbers and special symbols, and the extra 128 combinations are used for symbols such as Ç, è, ü, ©, ®, Œ, etc.

> ➢ **Discussion: About how many different combinations of 0s and 1s are required to represent all the keys on a keyboard? (Remember to include uppercase and lowercase letters.)**

The ASCII codes are shown below.

Character	ASCII	Char	ASCII	Char	ASCII	Char	ASCII
space	0100000	8	0111000	P	1010000	h	1101000
!	0100001	9	0111001	Q	1010001	i	1101001
"	0100010	:	0111010	R	1010010	j	1101010
£	0100011	;	0111011	S	1010011	k	1101011
$	0100100	<	0111100	T	1010100	l	1101100
%	0100101	=	0111101	U	1010101	m	1101101
&	0100110	>	0111110	V	1010110	n	1101110
'	0100111	?	0111111	W	1010111	o	1101111
(	0101000	@	1000000	X	1011000	p	1110000
)	0101001	A	1000001	Y	1011001	q	1110001
*	0101010	B	1000010	Z	1011010	r	1110010
+	0101011	C	1000011	[	1011011	s	1110011
,	0101100	D	1000100	\	1011100	t	1110100
-	0101101	E	1000101	]	1011101	u	1110101
.	0101110	F	1000110	^	1011110	v	1110110
/	0101111	G	1000111	_	1011111	w	1110111
0	0110000	H	1001000	`	1100000	x	1111000
1	0110001	I	1001001	a	1100001	y	1111001
2	0110010	J	1001010	b	1100010	z	1111010
3	0110011	K	1001011	c	1100011	{	1111011
4	0110100	L	1001100	d	1100100			1111100
5	0110101	M	1001101	e	1100101	}	1111101
6	0110110	N	1001110	f	1100110	~	1111110
7	0110111	O	1001111	g	1100111	del	1111111

Figure 14.4: ASCII codes

> ➤ **Discussion: The name JACK can be held in 4 bytes of a computer's memory. What will be the binary code representing this name? (You can assume that the leftmost bit in each byte is 0.)**

Note that a particular binary pattern in 4 consecutive bytes could represent 4 characters, a number, a sound, a tiny portion of an image or an instruction to the computer. Its interpretation depends entirely on the context in which it is read.

Exercises

1. Find some advertisements for PCs and write down the specifications and prices. Are prices still falling and computers still becoming more powerful? (6)

    New question

2. A given combination of binary digits in a byte may be interpreted in many different ways. Name **four** different things that it could represent. (2)

    New question

3. Name **four** different types of auxiliary storage found in a typical PC. Give **one** use for each of these types of storage. (4)

    New question

Chapter 15 – Data Capture

Keyboard data entry

The keyboard is the most common input device, suitable for a wide range of applications from entering programs to typing all kinds of documents using a word processor, or entering personal details of customers or patients at a hospital, etc. Data entered at a keyboard is commonly copied from a source document, and as such has disadvantages:

- It is easy to make **transcription** errors – that is, copy the data wrongly from the document.

- It is time-consuming.

- Data entry operators who enter data all day every day are prone to **repetitive strain injury** (RSI), a condition which renders them unable to do any further data entry or even perform everyday tasks such as pouring a cup of tea.

Voice data entry

The user speaks the text into a microphone and special software such as IBM's VoicePad or Dragon's Naturally Speaking interprets the text and displays it on a screen, where it may be edited using the keyboard and exported to a word processing package such as Word. The accuracy of the voice recognition system is improved by 'training' it to a particular user's voice – an embarrassing process of speaking a given set of a few hundred short sentences to your computer, repeating any that are not accurately interpreted.

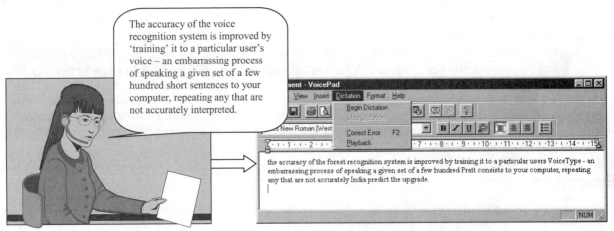

Figure 15.1: Voice recognition: not always 100% accurate!

Scanners and OCR

An optical scanner can be used to scan graphical images and photographs, and software can then be used to edit or touch up the images. Scanners can also be used to read typed or even hand-written documents and OCR (Optical Character Recognition) software can then be used to interpret the text and export it to a word processor or data file. Scanners are also used to input large volumes of data on preprinted forms such as credit card payments, where the customer's account number and amount paid are printed at the bottom of the payment slip.

Case study: Automating college enrolment

Enrolling thousands of college students on hundreds of different courses is a year-long administrative headache for colleges. Unravelling the mysteries of what students and staff have written on the enrolment forms and then entering all this information onto computer, checking it and resolving it can take weeks. One college has slashed this time and eliminated many of the errors by investing in a scanning solution from Formic.

Formic has a proven track record in scanning survey questionnaires using graphical imaging and intelligent character recognition technologies which produce clean, validated data with minimal human intervention. Its new ACE product (Automated College Enrolment) links a scanner with a digital camera and identity card printer to offer immediate and complete enrolment in the presence of the student.

Students select their courses with the help of teaching staff, who then attach official peel-off stickers to the form. Stickers are preprinted with course names and barcodes for reliable scanning. This simple procedure has eliminated much administrative frustration of trying to identify which course a student really meant to enrol for, and made it impossible for students to enrol on courses that do not exist.

Students present themselves at the enrolment desk for their form to be scanned by computer. Handwriting is converted to letters and numbers, answers are checked and validated against a postcode database. This way, all omissions and inconsistencies are picked up and resolved while the student is still there. Finally, a plastic identity card is produced bearing the student's name, enrolment number and smiling face in full colour etched securely into its tough surface. The same digital picture is stored for use later. The whole process typically takes two to three minutes from start to finish.

Source: Tim Macer, Formic magazine

➢ **Discussion: What are the benefits of the scanning system? What output could be obtained from the information gathered at enrolment time? What other use could be made of the digital photographs?**

Key-to-disk systems

In organisations where large amounts of data are collected on forms which then have to be keyed in for later processing (a **batch processing** system) an entire computer system consisting of a processor, dozens of terminals and central disk storage may be dedicated entirely to data entry. One terminal is nominated as the supervisor's terminal, from whose screen the supervisor can see exactly what every data entry operator is working on and how many keystrokes per hour and how many errors everyone is making. Completed batches of data are stored on disk from where they are either downloaded to the main computer over a communications link, or transferred to magnetic tape which is physically removed and taken to the main computer room.

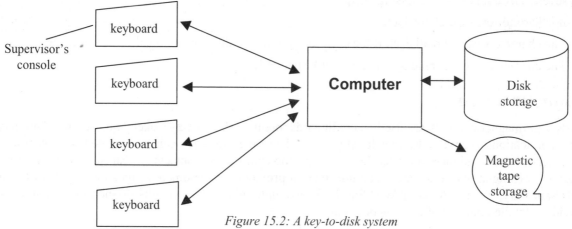

Figure 15.2: A key-to-disk system

Using a key-to-disk system, each data entry operator calls up the data entry program for her particular batch of data (e.g. payroll data entry, Council Tax payments, student grant applications) and keys in the data, which is automatically validated by the computer program.

When the batch of data has been entered and stored on disk, the source documents are passed to a second data entry operator who switches her machine to **verify** mode and keys in the data a second time. The keystrokes are compared with the data already stored on disk and any discrepancy causes the machine to beep so that the error can be corrected.

Banks, for example, no longer process routine transactions (such as paying in cheques) in branches. Instead, the work is sent to giant processing centres where the staff do nothing but key in data.

"It's like a factory", said one Barclay's worker. "There's just crates and crates of work everywhere. They call them customer service centres, but you never see a customer".

The trend is raising health and safety concerns among the banking unions. Four employees at one Midland Bank processing centre took their employer to court in 1998 claiming they developed repetitive strain injury (RSI) after being required to key in 2000 cheque details per hour.

In order to ensure the accuracy of the data entered, it is commonly **batched** and **verified** – that is, entered twice by different operators with the second version being automatically compared with the first version and any discrepancies brought to the operator's attention. (See **batch processing** in Chapter 24.)

Mouse, joystick, light pen, touch screen

The mouse and its variants such as a trackball is well known to all users of PCs. A light pen is a device which incorporates a light sensor so that when it is held close to the screen over a character or part of a graphic, the object is detected and can be moved to create or modify graphics.

A touch screen allows the user to touch an area of the screen rather than having to type the data on a keyboard. They are widely used in tourist centres, where tourists can look up various local facilities and entertainments, in fast food stores such as McDonald's for entering customer orders, in manufacturing and many other environments.

Magnetic Ink Character Recognition (MICR)

All banks use MICR for processing cheques. Along the bottom of a cheque the bank's sort code, customer account number and cheque number are encoded in special characters in magnetic ink. The amount of the cheque is encoded in magnetic ink when it is handed in at a bank. The cheques can then be processed extremely fast by high-speed MICR devices that read, sort and store the data on disk. MICR has several advantages for processing cheques:

- It is hard to forge the characters;
- The characters can be read even if the cheque is crumpled, dirty or smudged;
- The characters are readable by humans, unlike bar codes.

Magnetic stripe

Cards with magnetic stripes are used as credit cards, debit cards, railway tickets, phone cards and many other applications such as customer loyalty cards. The magnetic strip can be encoded with up to 220 characters of data, and there are over 2.4 billion plastic card transactions every year in Britain, with 83% of adults owning at least one card. The information provided when someone signs up for a loyalty card with Sainsbury, Tesco, Boots or W.H.Smith, for example, plus a few months of shopping records, can provide a detailed portrait of customers' habits.

The day is not far off when you will be able to wake up on Saturday morning (or whichever is your regular shopping day) to an e-mail from Sainsbury suggesting what you need to buy this week.

Nevertheless, three factors threaten to destroy the lucrative business that high street banks have made out of plastic: crime, the cost of cash and competition. In 1996 card fraud cost the banks £97.1 million, with £13.3 million of it from fake magnetic stripe cards. The 220 characters are simply too easy to copy, which is why the stripes will eventually disappear and be replaced by a chip, which is almost impossible to fake.

Smart cards

Smart cards look similar to plastic cards with a magnetic stripe, but instead of (or as well as) the magnetic stripe, they contain a 1-millimetre square microprocessor embedded in the middle, behind a small gold electrical contact. Instead of swiping the card, you plug it into a reader.

Chip cards cost only about £1 to produce, and can hold millions of characters of data. Banks plan to introduce a 'supercard' which in addition to debit and credit facilities, can be loaded with digital cash so that smaller items such as bread, milk and newspapers can be bought without the need to carry cash. BT will adapt local payphones in a trial area to load the cards, and NCP car parks will accept the cards. When your card runs out of digital cash, you reload it from a cashpoint machine.

The Mondex card was introduced in Swindon in 1994 for a trial period, and incorporates the 'electronic purse' idea but no debit or credit facilities. However even this card has proved not to be entirely tamper-proof, which leaves open the possibility that dishonest users could simply load their cards with as much money as they like.

Figure 15.3: the Mondex smart card

> ➤ **Discussion: It has been suggested that other information such as kidney donor record and driving licence could be held on the same chip card that allows you to withdraw cash and pay for goods.**
>
> ➤ **What would be the benefits of doing this?**
>
> ➤ **What other information would it be useful to hold on a card of this sort?**

Optical Mark Recognition (OMR)

An optical mark reader can detect marks made in preset positions on a form. It is widely used for marking multiple-choice exams and market research questionnaires.

Bar code reader or scanner

Bar codes appear on almost everything we buy. The pattern of thick and thin bars represents the 13-digit number underneath the bar code. There are four main pieces of information on a bar code;

The first two (or sometimes three) digits indicate in which country the product has been registered. The code for the UK and Ireland is 50.

The next five digits represent the manufacturer's code – Cadbury's for example is 00183.

The second group of five digits represents the product and package size, but not the price.

The last digit is a check digit, which is calculated from the other digits in the code and ensures that the barcode is keyed in or read correctly.

Figure 15.4: A product bar code

Benefits of using bar codes

The major benefit of using bar codes at point of sale is that management is provided with very detailed up to date information on key aspects of the business, enabling decisions to be made quicker and with more confidence. For example:

- Fast-selling items can be identified quickly and automatically reordered to meet demand.

- Slow-selling items can be identified, preventing a build-up of unwanted stock.

- The effects of repositioning a given product within a store can be monitored, allowing fast-moving more profitable items to occupy the best space.

- Historical data can be used to predict seasonal fluctuations very accurately.

Bar code scanners are relatively low cost and extremely accurate: only about one in 100,000 entries will be wrong.

Photograph courtesy of Scanner Technologies

Figure 15.5: A bar code scanner

> ➤ **Discussion: A supermarket has a file of all stock items, which is on-line to the point-of-sale terminals at each checkout. What data is held on the stock file? What processing takes place when an item is scanned by the barcode reader? What is the output from the process?**

Other uses of bar codes

Bar codes can be used in a wide range of applications that require fast and accurate data entry. These include:

- Warehousing. Bar coded containers of raw materials are stored in racks of bins which are also bar coded. When goods are put into the warehouse, the computer system instructs an automatic crane to retrieve the nearest available empty bin. The filled bin is then returned to an empty location. The crane relies entirely on bar codes to move goods in and out.

- Transport and distribution. All major road freight carriers now use bar codes. Individual packages are bar coded as are depot consignments. The exact location of any package is known at any one time together with details of the type of service used. Individual customers can be billed quickly and missing parcels traced more easily.

- Manufacturing. Very accurate data relating to work in progress can be obtained using bar codes as the data entry method. Management can obtain up to date data on the progress of unfinished goods, enabling bottlenecks and over-production to be reduced and production efficiency to improve.

- Marketing. Many polling companies now use bar coded multiple choice questionnaires to enter data quickly and accurately. Survey times can be dramatically reduced.

- Medical. Bar codes are commonly used to identify blood and other samples. Hospital patients' and outpatients' records are increasingly bar coded for fast retrieval and better accuracy.

- Libraries. Bar codes are used to record loans and provide more information on stock.

- Banking, insurance and local government. Bar codes are used extensively for accurate document control and retrieval. Many cheque book covers, insurance claim files and council tax forms are bar coded.

Hand-held input devices

Portable keying devices are commonly used in such applications as reading gas or electricity meters, where the meter reader displays the next customer name, address and location of meter on a small screen, then reads the meter and keys in the reading. At the end of the day all the readings can be downloaded via a communications link to the main computer for processing.

Exercises

1. Speech recognition systems for Personal Computers are now becoming more affordable and useable.

   (a) State **two** advantages to a PC user of a speech recognition system.   (2)

   (b) Give **two** different tasks for which a PC user could take advantage of speech recognition.   (2)

   (c) Speech recognition systems sometimes fail to be 100% effective in practice. Give **three** reasons why this is so.   (3)

   NEAB IT02 Qu 6 1999

2. Most banks now dispense cash via Automated Teller Machines (ATMs). After inserting a plastic card which is read by the ATM, the customer types requests and responses on a special keypad.

   (a) Describe fully the procedure that the customer follows when making a cash withdrawal. (2)

   (b) The information on the card is encoded onto a magnetic strip. Name **three** customer attributes that are stored on the strip. (3)

   AEB AS Paper 1 Qu 2 1996

3. The use of Point of Sale (POS) terminals in supermarkets is now commonplace. What is meant by *Point of Sale*?

   Suggest **two** advantages to the customer of POS terminals connected to the central computer. (3)

   AEB AS Paper 1 Qu 3 1994

4. Describe briefly an appropriate application for each of the following methods of input:

   (i) MICR

   (ii) Key-to-disk

   (iii) Video camera

   (iv) Touch screen

   (v) Smart card (10)

   New question

5. (a) Why is MICR used in preference to OCR in cheque processing systems? (1)

   (b) Why is OCR used in preference to MICR in invoicing systems? (1)

   (c) (i) What is Optical Mark Reading (OMR)?

   (ii) Give **one** situation where OMR might be used. (2)

   NEAB Computing Paper 2 Qu 3 1997

Chapter 16 – Verification and Validation

Data capture

In the last chapter we looked at different input devices and situations in which they would be appropriate. The particular method used to capture data will be chosen because it offers advantages in terms of speed, accuracy, and/or cost.

Methods of 'direct data capture' which cut out the need to key in data from input documents are likely to have all these advantages, and so are becoming more and more common. However, we are a long way off from escaping the chore of filling in forms of one sort or another, a large number of which will then have to be keyed into a computer system.

> ➢ **Discussion: Name (a) some applications which use direct data entry, eliminating the need for keying in data and (b) applications which require data to be keyed in.**

Types of error

Figure 16.1 shows an example of an order form filled in by customers of a mail order company.

ORDERED BY						
MR/MRS/MISS/MS			CUSTOMER NO			
SURNAME			POST TO:			
ADDRESS			MANSION HOUSE, MAIN STREET			
			BANSTEAD			
			LAKE DISTRICT			
POSTCODE			LA31 8TR			
DAYTIME TEL NO						

PAGE NO	CODE	COLOUR	SIZE	QTY	DESCRIPTION	PRICE
					GOODS TOTAL	
					P & P	£2.50

CARD NO.	VALID FROM	EXPIRY DATE	TOTAL PAYABLE

Figure 16.1: A Mail Order form

The information from this form will be keyed in to the computer and then processed to produce a set of documents including a delivery note and invoice for the customer, as well as updating stock and sales records. There are several possible sources of error before the data are processed:

- The customer could make a mistake, entering the wrong product codes, adding up the total cost wrongly, forgetting to enter their address or card expiry date, etc.;

- The person keying in the data could make a **transcription** error, keying in the wrong product code or quantity, misreading the customer's name, adding an extra couple of 0's to the total price by keeping a finger down too long, and so on;

- A form could be blown into the bin by a sudden draught as a fan starts up or someone flounces out, slamming the door – or the operator might decide the writing was so bad it simply wasn't worth the effort of struggling with, and bin it;

- A bored keypunch operator, chatting to a colleague, could enter the same form twice without realising it;

- A faulty connection between hardware components such as the processor and the disk drive could mean that some characters are wrongly transmitted.

Now clearly a mail order company would not stay in business very long if this was how the operation worked! So what can be done to minimise the possibility of error?

Batch processing

In a batch processing system, documents such as the sales orders described above are collected into batches of typically 50 documents. A **data control clerk** has the responsibility of:

- counting the documents;

- checking each one visually to see that the customer has entered essential details such as their name and address, card details if that is the payment method, and total payable;

- calculating a control total of some crucial field such as Total Payable, for the entire batch of 50 documents;

- calculating **hash totals** of other fields such as size or quantity (see below);

- filling in a batch header document which will show, for example:

  ❑ batch number

  ❑ number of documents in batch

  ❑ date received

  ❑ control total

  ❑ hash total

- logging the batch in a book kept for this purpose.

A hash total is a sum of values calculated purely for validation purposes. For example, if the sizes of all garments ordered on a batch of forms (12, 10, 12, 34, 36, etc.) are added together and the total entered on the batch header and keyed in, the computer will be able to perform the same calculation and if the figures don't match, then the batch must have an error in it somewhere.

Control totals and hash totals have a similar purpose: the data from the batch header is keyed in as well as the contents of all the documents in the batch, and the computer performs the same summing calculations that the data entry clerk made manually. If there is any discrepancy, an error is reported and the batch is rechecked. The difference between the two types of total is only that a hash total has no meaning, whereas a control total (e.g. number of documents in the batch) does.

The stages in batch processing are discussed in Chapter 24.

Validation checks

As the data is being keyed in, a computer program controlling the input can perform various validation checks on the data. For example:

1. **Presence check.** Certain fields such as customer number, item code, quantity etc must be present. The data control clerk may have visually checked this but the program can perform a second check. Also, if this is a new customer, a number could be automatically assigned.

2. **Format check** (also called **picture check**). For example the code perhaps has a pattern of 2 letters followed by 4 numbers. The quantity and price must be numeric.

3. **Range check.** The expiry date of a card must have a month number between 1 and 12, and the date must be later than today's date.

4. **File lookup check.** If the customer has filled in their customer number, the computer can look this up on the customer file and display the name and address. The data entry operator can check that it tallies.

5. **Check digit check.** (see below).

6. **Batch header checks.** The total number of records in the batch should be calculated by the computer and compared with the figure on the batch header. The control totals and hash totals are also calculated and compared.

Check digits

Code numbers such as a customer number, employee number or product number are often lengthy and prone to error when being keyed in. One way of preventing these errors occurring is to add an extra digit to the end of a code number which has been calculated from the digits of the code number. In this way the code number with its extra check digit is self-checking.

The best-known method of calculating check digits is the modulus-11 system, which traps over 99% of all errors. The calculation of a check digit is shown below.

1. Each digit of the code number is assigned a 'weight'. The right hand (least significant) digit is given a weight of 2, the next digit to the left 3 and so on.

2. Each digit is multiplied by its weight and the products added together.

3. The sum of the products is divided by 11 and the remainder obtained.

4. The remainder is subtracted from 11 to give the check digit. The two exceptions are:

   • If the remainder is 0, the check digit is 0, not 11.

   • If the remainder is 1, the check digit is X, not 10.

Example:

To calculate the check digit for the number 1587:

Original code number	1	5	8	7
Weights	5	4	3	2
Multiply digit by its weight	5	20	24	14
Add products together	5 + 20 + 24 + 14 = 63			
Divide by 11	5 remainder 8			
Subtract remainder from 11	11 - 8 = 3			

Check digit = 3. The complete code number is 15873.

To check that a code number is valid, it is not necessary to recalculate the check digit completely. If the check digit itself is assigned a weight of 1, and the products of the digits (including the check digit) and their respective weights are calculated, their sum will be divisible by 11 if the check digit is correct.

All books have an ISBN number which has a modulus-11 check digit. Try checking whether the ISBN number 1858051703 is valid.

Verification

Verification is the process of entering data twice, with the second entry being compared with the first to ensure that it is accurate. It is common in batch processing for a second data entry operator to key in a batch of data to verify it. You have probably come across another example of verification when setting a password; you are asked to key the password in a second time to ensure that you didn't make a keying error the first time, as it is not echoed on the screen.

Detecting transmission errors

In order to guard against the possibility of data being wrongly transmitted between the various hardware components of a computer, a **parity bit** is added to each character. In an even parity machine, the total number of 'On' bits in every byte (including the parity bit) must be an even number. When data is moved from one location to another, the parity bits are checked at both the sending and receiving end and if they are different or the wrong number of bits are 'On', an error message is displayed.

Thus a character code of 1101010 will have a parity bit of 0 appended to it, and a character code of 1101110 will have a parity bit of 1 appended.

Data is transmitted over a transmission line between computers in **blocks** of say 256 bytes. A **checksum** may be calculated by adding together the numeric value of all the bytes in a block, and this sum is transmitted with the data, to be checked again at the receiving end.

Accuracy and validity

When primary data is collected for surveying prospective customers or following the launch of a new product, for example, the research organisation has to be careful that the sample of the population chosen to be asked questions accurately reflects the whole population. If for example the researcher collects data from random members of the public in a town between 10am and 12 noon each morning for a week, they are probably going to interview mainly pensioners or people not currently employed.

Figure 16.2: A Market Research Society card

> ➤ **Discussion: Look back at the order form shown in Figure 16.1. Is it possible that some of the data entered on the form could be *valid* but *inaccurate*?**

Exercises

1. *(see case study below)*

Case study: Market research survey

The National Readership Survey is a survey about the newspapers and magazines people read (and the ones they don't), how much television they watch, and how much they listen to the radio. The research is used by publishers and editors to help them identify, for instance, what people of different ages are interested in, so they can produce newspapers and magazines to suit their readers.

The people to be interviewed (35,000 annually) are a cross-section of the population, and in order to make sure that a representative sample is chosen, interviewees are asked questions about their age, occupation, income and other descriptive details. They are also asked for their name and telephone number. Each interviewer is equipped with a battery-powered laptop computer with a single floppy disk drive and a modem. The program for each particular survey is posted to them in advance together with a list of addresses to visit and a list of questions to ask. The interviewer types the respondent's answers straight into the computer from where the data is saved onto the floppy disk. Each evening the data is transferred by telephone link to the company's mainframe computer. The data is analysed and distributed within two weeks of collection.

> ➤ **Questions:**
>   a. How can a householder be sure that the interviewer is genuinely employed by a Market Research Organisation? (1)
>   b. Name **two** advantages of entering data straight into the computer rather than onto hand-written forms. (2)
>   c. Describe briefly **two** advantages and **two** disadvantages of using laptop computers that have only a single floppy drive and no hard disk. In each case say whether the advantage or disadvantage is to the market research company or to the interviewer. (4)
>   d. The interviewees' names, addresses and telephone numbers are stored on the mainframe computer system, but held separately from the answers given in the interview and not linked to them in any way. Why are interviewees asked to supply this information? Explain why names and addresses are held separately from the rest of the data. (3)
>   e. The survey includes questions on which sections (home news, foreign news, sport, computers, finance etc) people read in newspapers and also questions on major purchases made by members of the household over the past year or two. How would this information be useful to the organisations which use the data? (2)

2. A well designed information system should be able to check that input data is valid, but it can never ensure that information is accurate.
   (a) Explain the distinction between accuracy of information and validity of data. Illustrate this distinction with a suitable example. (4)
   (b) Describe **two** ways in which data capture errors may arise, together with techniques for preventing or reducing these errors. (4)

NEAB IT02 Qu 6 1997

3. Most banks and building societies now offer cash withdrawal facilities through the use of Automatic Teller Machines (ATMs). The data that needs to be entered before a transaction can take place will include the customer's account number and Personal Identification Number (PIN).

    (a)   (i)   State **three** validation checks that should be made on the customer's account number.   (3)

          (ii) State **one** validation check that should be made on the PIN.   (1)

    (b)   These transactions will normally involve transmission of data from and to an ATM via a communications link. State **one** security precaution that should always be taken, giving a reason why it is needed.   (2)

    NEAB IT02 Qu 8 1999

4. Name and describe two validation checks that could be used when a product code number is input.
    (4)
    AEB AS Computing Qu 2 1997

5. A school uses an information system to store details of students' examination entries and results. As part of this system a program is used to check the validity of data such as candidate number, candidate names and the subjects entered.

    (a)   Suggest **three** possible validation tests which might be carried out on this data.   (3)

    (b)   Explain, with an example, why data which is found to be valid by this program may still need to be verified.   (2)
    NEAB IT02 Qu 5 1996

6. With the aid of an example, distinguish clearly between a batch/control total and a hash total.   (4)
    NISEAC Computing Paper 2 Qu 3 1996

7. Briefly explain what is meant by verification during data entry in batch processing systems.   (2)
    NEAB Computing Paper 2 Qu 2 1997

Chapter 17 – Introduction to Databases

What is a database?

A database is a collection of data. It may be something as simple as a list of names and addresses or details of the CDs in your personal collection, or it may contain details of all the customers, products, orders and payments in a large organisation. The word database often now refers to data held on a computer but non-computerised databases also exist. Some smaller schools, for example, may hold a card index file with details about all the pupils in the school. A school library may hold a card-index file with details about each book.

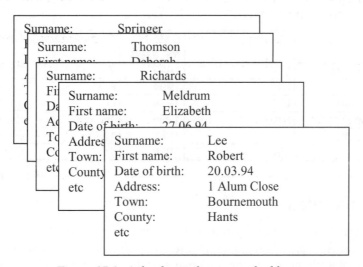

Figure 17.1: A database of names and addresses

Retrieving information from a database

The main difference between computerized and non-computerised databases is the speed with which data can be accessed. Information that would previously have taken weeks or even years to gather and collate can now be gathered in a few seconds. A doctor's surgery, for example, may hold details on each patient. To find the names and addresses of all patients over 65 in a manual system would involve a painstaking search through every record. The answer could be retrieved from a computerized database in a second or two.

A computerized database also makes it possible to analyse data in ways that were previously unthinkable. Retail stores such as Tesco and Sainsbury's collect data on customer purchases every time a loyalty card is used. This data can be held in a database and used to build up a profile of what each customer is likely to purchase. Health Authorities can carry out complex analyses linking various illnesses to other factors such as diet or environment. Police databases are used to build up profiles of crimes and criminals and come up with possible suspects.

Databases vs. Database Management Systems

The software that is used to access, update and manipulate the data in a computerised database is known as a Database Management System. There are many different ways in which data can be organised in a database, but by far the most common is the **relational database model**. Microsoft Access is an example of a Relational Database Management System (RDBMS).

Flat files

A flat file is a database held in a single file. This allows only very simple structuring of the data, and the software that accesses and updates the data is commonly called a File Management System.

File management systems (such as the one which forms part of the integrated package MS Works) have been around for a number of years and differ from true Database Management Systems in that the data stored in one file cannot easily be linked to data stored in another file. These so-called 'flat-files' are useful for storing data such as a list of contact names and addresses, a list of student grades or details of a video collection. A spreadsheet can be used as a flat-file database, with a column representing a field and a row representing a record.

Video number	Title	Country	Date released	Classification	Star
1	A Few Good Men	US	1992	15	Tom Cruise
2	The Mask	US	1994	PG	Jim Carrey
3	The Flintstones	US	1994	U	John Goodman
4	Trainspotting	UK	1996	18	Ewan McGregor
5	Crocodile Dundee	AUS	1986	15	Paul Hogan
6	*Elizabeth*	UK	1998	15	Cate Blanchett
etc					

Problems with flat files

There are several drawbacks to holding anything except very simple data in a single file. As an example, consider a file that contains details about customer orders for an electrical goods store. If all the data is to be held in a single file, the file needs to contain details of the customer (such as name and address), the items ordered, the employee who sold the item and probably the supplier of the item as well. We could end up with a file of data similar to that shown below:

ORDERTABLE

OrderNo	OrderDate	ItemNo	Description	Price	Supplier	Customer	Employee Firstname	Employee Surname	Date Employed
1	10/01/00	54112	Oven	475.00	Atag	Harris	James	Noakes	09/10/99
2	10/01/00	87123	Dihswasher	260.00	Phillips	Jenner	Rebecca	Maynard	01/02/98
3	11/01/00	44433	CD Player	500.00	Toshiba	Bemrose	James	Nokes	09/10/99
4	11/01/00	81723	Dishwasher	260.00	Philipps	Akbar	Rebecca	Maynard	01/02/98
5	11/01/00	54112	Oven	475.00	Atag	Payne	James	Noaks	01/01/99
6	11/01/00	18293	Hairdryer	24.50	Phillips	Campbell	Paul	Smith	05/06/97

We would also need to hold details of the customer such as their title and initials, address and phone number, and additional details both on the item sold and the employee. Even with the small number of fields shown it is obvious that the file has serious shortcomings. These are described in the following paragraphs.

Redundant data

The table contains a vast amount of repeated data. Names, prices and dates are all stored several times, wasting disk space and slowing down any queries that we might make to retrieve information from the table. Data entry will be time-consuming since every time an order is entered, the employees name, date of employment and other details will have to be typed in as well. The description and price of the item will also have to be typed in along with the supplier details. If we sell 500 dishwashers, the price, description and supplier details will have to be recorded 500 times.

Errors on input

Typographical errors are bound to occur if all these details have to be entered every time a sale is made. In the table above, employee *Noakes* has had his name spelt wrongly twice. A query to find out the total value of sales made by Noakes will not find them all – he will not be pleased when his bonus for selling goods worth over £2000 per day is wrongly calculated as a result!

Problems with updating data

Suppose Rebecca Maynard, one of the employees who has made thousands of sales since she was employed, gets married and changes her name. Instead of having to make this change only once, every record that contains her name would have to be updated. Similarly, if details such as address and telephone number of each employee were stored (which they certainly would be), these details would have to be changed in every record if the employee moved or changed their phone number.

Problems with modifying data

With a single table, problems arise if records need to be added or deleted. When a new employee joins the sales force, there is no way of adding their details to the database until they make their first sale. Similarly, if a record is to be deleted, information will be lost. For example if record number 3 is deleted the information about the price and supplier of the CD Player will be lost.

Summary

In summary, the problems that arise with flat file databases are:

- Redundant data, which makes the file large, wasting space on disk, and also makes it slow to retrieve information;
- Errors which arise from typing the same data many times in different records;
- Difficulties in updating and modifying data.

These problems can be solved in the most efficient way possible by using multiple tables to store the data.

Using multiple tables

We can move the data about employees into a separate table. At the same time, we will give each employee a unique ID number since it is quite possible that the store could hire two people with identical names and with the current information stored there would be no way of distinguishing between them.

The two tables shown below hold the same data as before.

EMPLOYEETABLE

EmployeeID	Employee Firstname	Employee Surname	Date Employed
1	James	Noakes	09/10/99
2	Rebecca	Maynard	01/02/98
3	Paul	Smith	05/06/97

ORDERTABLE

OrderNo	OrderDate	ItemNo	Description	Price	Supplier	Customer	EmployeeID
1	10/01/00	54112	Oven	475.00	Atag	Harris	1
2	10/01/00	87123	Dishwasher	260.00	Phillips	Jenner	2
3	11/01/00	44433	CD Player	500.00	Toshiba	Bemrose	1
4	11/01/00	81723	Dishwasher	260.00	Philipps	Akbar	2
5	11/01/00	54112	Oven	475.00	Atag	Payne	1
6	11/01/00	18293	Hairdryer	24.50	Phillips	Campbell	3

What we have done is leave the employee ID in the ORDERTABLE to act as a pointer to which employee sold the item. All the information about a particular employee can then be looked up in the EMPLOYEETABLE.

Using the same principle, we could set up a separate table for Item to hold the description, price and supplier, and a fourth table to hold details of customers. We would need to assign each customer a unique ID number just as we did for employees, and leave the ItemNo and CustomerID as pointers in ORDERTABLE.

> ➤ **Discussion: What would each of the four tables EMPLOYEETABLE, CUSTOMERTABLE, ITEMTABLE and ORDERTABLE look like, holding the same information as the single table that we started with? Show the contents of each table.**
>
> **Notice that this structure does not allow for an order consisting of more than one item! You would need yet another table to cater for this, or there will still be redundant data on the tables. Try using another table called ORDER-LINE, or ignore this complication for now.**

It is quite likely that details on each supplier would be held as well. A further table could be set up to hold these details.

This principle of giving each *entity*, (or *object* or *thing*) its own table and linking the tables by means of a pointer like EmployeeID or CustomerID is the principle behind **relational databases**. Relational database management systems (RDMSs) such as MS Access make the process of referring to several different tables to look up data completely transparent to the user.

Solving the problems of single table databases

One of the problems with holding the data in a single table was the amount of redundant data that needs to be stored. Using a separate table for each entity means that the information only needs to be entered once. This also avoids the problems of typographical errors arising from typing the same data in many different records.

The difficulties which arise in modifying and updating data in a single table also disappear when multiple tables are used. We can, for example, add a new employee as soon as they are hired, before they have made a sale.

In the next chapter we will look in more detail at how to design the best database structure for a particular application.

Flat file information storage and retrieval systems

Before database management systems became popular, it was common practice for each department in a large company to keep their own data on separate files. Thus for example the Payroll department would keep data on employees and their salaries, tax information and so on. The Personnel Department might have a very similar file holding much of the same information, but with some non-overlapping fields. The Sales Department might have a file holding sales figures from which employee bonuses were calculated, which would have to be passed to the Payroll Department.

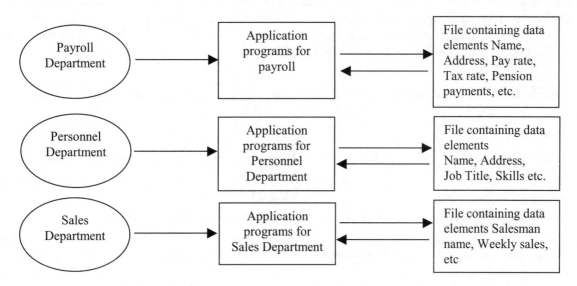

Figure 17.2: Data files in a traditional flat file system

This type of system (the 'traditional file approach') is also loosely known as a 'flat file information storage and retrieval system'. In addition to the problem of redundant data being stored in several different files, problems arose when it became necessary to add new fields to a file, because all the programs using the file had to be updated to reflect the change even if they did not use the new fields.

The advantages of a database system over such a system may be summarised as:

- data independence
  i.e. the structure of the database does not affect the programs which access the database;

- quality of management information
  information is more useful as it is based on a single, comprehensive set of data;

- control over redundancy
  the data is not stored several times in separate files

- consistency of data
  because the data is only stored once, there is no possibility of holding different data on different files (e.g. different addresses for the same employee);

- more information available to users
  because the data is held in a single, company-wide database, all users have access to it;

- greater security of data
  a database management system enables different levels of access to be specified so that users can only view or update the parts of the database that they are authorised to access or change;

- less time spent inputting data
  because it is held only once, there is no duplication of effort inputting the same data into different files.

Exercises

1. Explain by means of an example:
   (i) what is meant by *data redundancy* in a flat file information and retrieval system; (2)
   (ii) how data in such a system might become *inconsistent*. (2)

   New question

2. A publishing company keeps records of all the books they publish, and the authors of each book in a flat file system, for the purposes of calculating royalty payments to each author. Each author is paid a royalty based on an agreed percentage of gross sales over the previous 6 months. An advance on royalties is paid when a manuscript is delivered and this is deducted from the first royalty payment. (Only one column is shown for address to save space in the example but there will in practice be several columns).

   The file called BOOK contains fields as shown below. Some sample contents are also shown.

BOOK

Book No	Title	Author	Address1	Date Published	Royalty%	Advance
156	Basic Spreadsheets	Donaldson,G	3 Elgar Close	01/03/99	7.5%	£0
157	Programming in Visual Basic	Noakes,K	White House	01/04/99	10%	£500
160	Intermediate Spreadsheets	Donaldson,G	3 Elgar Close	01/02/00	8%	£250
163	Basic Windows 2000	Woods,R	6 Bullen Ave	01/03/00	10%	£0

   (i) Explain, with reference to the above table, what is meant by **redundant data**. (2)

   (ii) Describe briefly two problems which arise from holding the data in a single table. (2)

   (iii) Show how the data could be rearranged in two tables to solve these problems. (4)

   New question

Chapter 18 – Relational Databases

Relational databases

Within a relational database, data is stored in **tables**. A very simple database such as one that contains a list of names and addresses may have all the data stored in a single table, whereas a more complex database such as the one discussed in the previous chapter holding details of customers, orders, employees, items for sale and suppliers will require several tables.

Putting data into the correct tables

When you set out to design a database for a particular application, how do you know how many tables to use, and what data to put in which table? The answer lies in the fact that the database will be storing information about real-world objects or entities such as students, subjects and teachers, or doctors and patients at a GP's surgery. Relationships exist between these entities – for example a student can study many subjects, and a subject may be studied by several students. A doctor will be responsible for many patients but a patient will only see one doctor.

Databases have to store information about these different objects and the relationships that exist between them. Generally the commonsense rule to follow is: *create a table for each separate entity in the database*.

Example 1: A library database

Let's see how this works in practice. Suppose you are going to build a database to keep track of books in a library, and who has books out on loan. We will assume that a borrower may have several books out on loan at any one time. The two obvious entities in this system are BORROWER and BOOK, so we will create a table for each of these entities. Next you have to decide what fields to put in each table. One rule is that each record in the table must have a unique identifier by which it can be distinguished from every other record in the table. It is usually a good idea to use a simple numeric identifier.

The BORROWER table could have the following fields:

> BorrowerID (This is the unique identifier, also known as the *primary key*)
> Surname
> Firstname
> Title
> AddressLine1
> AddressLine2
> Town
> County
> Postcode
> DateofBirth

The BOOK table could have the following fields:

> BookID (This is the unique identifier or *primary key* – it could be the accession number of the book)
> DeweyCode
> Title
> Author
> DatePublished
> Publisher

Using **standard database notation**, these tables can be described as follows:

BORROWER (<u>BorrowerID</u>, Surname, Firstname, Title, AddressLine1, AddressLine2, Town,
County, Postcode, DateofBirth)

BOOK (<u>BookID</u>, DeweyCode, Title, Author, DatePublished, Publisher)

(Note that the table name is shown in uppercase and the primary key is underlined.)

You may be able to think of several other fields that we could have on each table.

The next problem is that these tables do not tell us anything about who has which books on loan. To solve this, we can look at 3 different possibilities:

Option 1.   On the BORROWER table, add fields showing which books the individual has out on loan and when they are due back;   *or*

Option 2.   On the BOOK table, include fields to show whether the book is out on loan, who has borrowed it and when it is due back;   *or*

Option 3.   Create a brand new table holding details about books on loan.

Option 1 is a bad one because we don't know how many fields to set aside for books that have been borrowed. The majority of borrowers may have no books on loan at any particular time, many borrowers may have just one or two, and a few borrowers may have the maximum, say 6 books, out on loan. It will be a waste of space to allow 6 fields for books borrowed, (not to mention 6 more for date due back) on every customer record. It will also be very difficult to query the database to find who has a particular book out, since we won't know which of 6 fields to look in.

Option 2 is better, and will involve adding 2 extra fields to the BOOK table – BorrowerID and DateDue. BorrowerID acts as a pointer or link to the BORROWER table and all the details about the borrower can be looked up as required. It will be easy to query the BOOK table to find out who has the book out on loan.

The only drawback to this solution is that most libraries have tens of thousands of books on the shelves and relatively few out on loan at any one time. Therefore, queries to find out who has overdue books, or when a particular book is due back, may take a very long time because so many records have to be searched. Let's look at Option 3.

Option 3 involves creating a new table which we will call LOAN. This needs only 3 fields:

BookID   (This is also a *foreign key* because it is a primary key of the BOOK table, not this one)

BorrowerID (This is known as a *foreign key* because it is a primary key of another table, not this one)

DateDue

This is the best solution to the problem. The LOAN table will be relatively small, queries will be performed very quickly, and there is very little redundant data. (this solution does use one more field in total and the tables will take up a little more space than the two tables for Option 2 but the benefits far outweigh the disadvantages.) The table will be structured as follows:

LOAN (<u>BookID</u>, BorrowerID, DateDue)

Note that BookID is a unique primary key only if the loan records are deleted as soon as the book is returned. If the loan record remains on the table, no one else will be able to borrow the book because the database will not allow two records which have the same primary key to be added to the table!

Example 2: A vet keeps a database to hold information about the treatments that each animal has had. Owners are notified when, for example, a cat is due to be vaccinated against cat flu. What tables are required for this application, and what fields should be specified on each table?

When designing a database it is important to have a clear idea of what information you hope to get out of it. There is no point collecting and keeping data unless it is required on a report or as part of an answer to a query.

Step 1:   Identify the entities. Obvious entities include PET, OWNER, VISIT and possibly TREATMENT. There may be other entities such as DRUG.

Step 2.   Decide what fields need to be held on each table. Identify a primary key for each table.

Step 3.   Make sure the relationships between the tables are correctly represented by means of foreign keys linking the tables together.

As a first try, the tables might have fields defined as follows:

PET

>   PetID   *(Primary key)*
>   Type of animal (Dog, Cat, etc)
>   Breed
>   Date of Birth

OWNER

>   OwnerID   *(Primary key)*
>   Surname
>   Initials
>   Title
>   Address (probably split into 4 or 5 fields)

VISIT

>   PetID   *(Part of Primary key)*
>   Date   *(Part of Primary key)*
>   Flu Vaccine (Y/N)
>   Other treatments (Notes)

Notice that in the VISIT table, the PetID on its own is not sufficient to uniquely identify the record, since a pet may have several visits. Assuming that an animal only ever has one visit on a particular date, the two fields PetID and Date together form a unique identifier and can be used as the primary key.

Looking at Step 3, we must make sure that the relationships are correctly represented.

> ➢ **Discussion: What additional field(s) need to be added to which table(s) to represent the relationship 'One owner may have several pets'?**

Creating a database table in MS Access

We have seen that before you can begin to store data in a database table, you have to specify the format of a record in the table. Each record in the table will have the same format or structure, specified by defining the characteristics of each field in a record. You must specify:

1. The **order** in which the fields are stored in the record.

2. The **name** of each field.

3. The **field type**. The database software will offer a number of field types including

   - Text (also referred to as Character or Alphanumeric)

   - Numeric (integer, or real with a specified number of decimal points)

   - Date (in a number of different formats)

   - Yes/No (or True/False)

   - Memo (for writing notes about a client, for example).

4. For some types of field such as a text field, the field length. This should be large enough to hold the maximum expected length of data – for example, 20 characters could be allowed for a surname.

Once the structure of the database table has been specified, the empty table can be given a name and saved.

The significance of field types

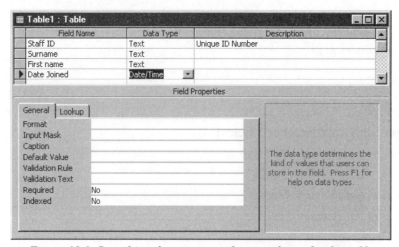

Figure 18.1: Specifying the structure of a record in a database file

Does it really matter whether you specify a date or numeric field as a text type, or a field such as a telephone number as numeric? The answer is YES – for several reasons.

- Certain field types are automatically validated when the user enters data. Thus, if you specify a field named Date of Birth as a date field, the software will not allow a user to enter 31/2/76 because this is not a valid date. If you have specified the field as a text field, no automatic validation is possible.

- Similarly, if a field is defined as currency or numeric, the user will not be able to enter a non-numeric character in the field by mistake.

- On the other hand, it is unwise to define a telephone number as numeric because a user may want to leave a space or hyphen between the area code and the rest of the number, and a numeric field will allow only numbers and a decimal point to be entered

- Numeric fields are held differently inside the computer from text fields, and if the field will be involved in any type of calculation, it MUST be defined as numeric (or date, or currency) or an error will be reported when the computer tries to perform the calculation.

- The length specified for a text field should also be chosen carefully and documented for future reference. If a student ID, for example, is defined as 6 characters in one file and 10 characters in another file, errors will occur when the two files are linked through this common ID number.

Primary key

Each individual row or record in a database file needs to be given a unique identifier, and this is termed the **primary key**. It needs to be carefully chosen so that there is no possibility of two people or items being confused; Surname, for example, is no use as an identifier. The primary key sometimes consists of more than one field: for example several stores in a national chain may each have a store number, and each store may have Departments 1,2,3 etc. To identify a particular department in a particular store, the primary key would be composed of both Store number and Department number.

> ➤ **Discussion: What would be a suitable primary key for: a book in a bookshop?**
> **a book in a library?**
> **a hospital patient?**
> **a car owned by a car-hire firm?**

Exercises

1. Express in standard database notation the tables for PET, OWNER and VISIT described in this chapter. (3)

   New question

2. The data requirements for a booking system are defined as follows.

   An agency arranges booking of live bands for a number of clubs. Each band is registered with the agency and has its name (unique) recorded, together with the number of musicians, the type of music played and hiring fee. Each band is managed by a manager. A manager may manage several bands. Each manager is assigned an identification number and managers have their name, address and telephone number recorded. Each club is assigned an identification number and clubs have their name, address and telephone number recorded.

   The agency records details of each booking made between a band and a club for a given date. A band will never have more than one booking on any particular date.

   (a) Four entities for the booking system are Manager, Club, Band and Booking.

   Suggest an identifier, with justification, for **each** of the entities Manager, Club and Band. (3)

   (b) A relational database is to be used. Describe tables (i.e. suggest field names) for the following entities underlining the primary key in each case:

   (i) Manager; (2)

   (ii) Club (2)

   (iii) Band; (4)

   (iv) Booking. (5)

   New question

Chapter 19 – Tables, Forms, Queries and Reports

The basic components of a database

The four basic components of a database are:

- tables
- forms
- queries
- reports

In order to demonstrate how each of these components is used, we will build a simple database of library borrowers, books and loans as described in Chapter 18.

The tables for the Library application

Three tables are needed for this application which we will call **tblBorrower**, **tblBook** and **tblLoan**. The structure of each table is shown below.

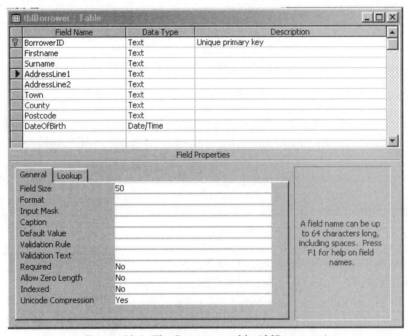

Figure 19.1: The Borrower table (tblBorrower)

Data can be entered into this table in one of two ways: straight into the table in what Access calls Datasheet view, or using a form specially designed for the purpose. In Figure 19.2 two records have been added in Datasheet view.

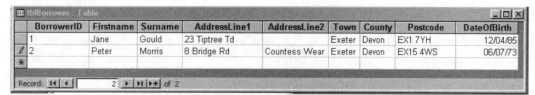

*Figure 19.2: Data entered into **tblBorrower** in Datasheet view*

Next we will create the structures for tblBook and tblLoan.

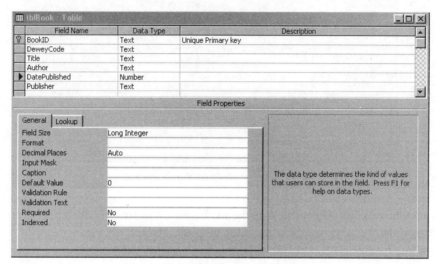

Figure 19.3: The Book table (tblBook)

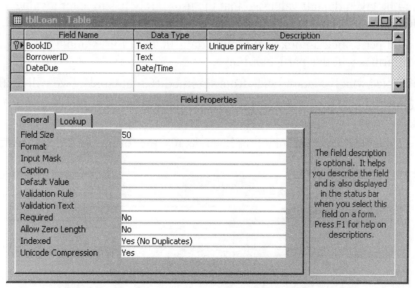

Figure 19.4: The Loan table (tblLoan)

Note that the primary key of the loan table is BookID. This is sufficient to uniquely identify the record provided that a Loan record is deleted from the table as soon as the book is returned by the borrower. Both BorrowerID and BookID are *foreign keys* because they are primary keys in tblBorrower and tblBook respectively.

Forms

We can create a data entry form for entering data into each of the tables. The data entry form for the Borrower table might look like the one shown below:

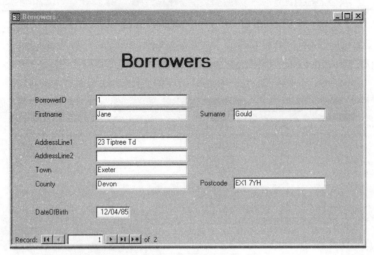

Figure 19.5: Data entry form for Borrowers

A form like this can be very quickly created using an Access 'wizard'. Forms have several advantages as a means of entering data:

- they present a much more attractive appearance to the user;

- the fields can be placed on the form in a convenient order for data entry;

- some fields can be given default values so that the user rarely has to enter a value – for example, the town could default to 'Exeter' if this was a library in Exeter;

- validation can be performed automatically on certain fields – for example the program could check that the date of birth is within a particular range;

- forms can be created which contain fields from several different tables – we will do this below.

- several data entry forms can be created for different purposes, each showing just the relevant fields from the table(s).

If we use a wizard to create a form for inputting Loan details, the following form is created:

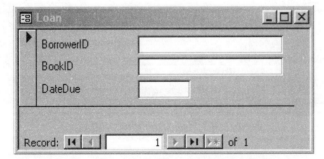

Figure 19.6: First attempt at form for entering Loans

This is not a good form because it gives the user no opportunity to check the name of the borrower or the title of the book. These details are not held on the Loans table – they are on tblBorrower and tblBook. We need to combine the data from the three tables before creating the form, and to do this, we use a **query**.

Queries

Queries are very powerful tools in a database. They are most commonly used to find subsets of the data, such as for example all loans for books which are overdue, or all borrowers over 16 years old. Reports or mail-merge letters can then be created from these subsets of the data.

In a multi-table database queries can pull together all the information needed from different tables, creating a new **answer** table from which forms and reports can be created. When data in the original tables (called the **base** tables) changes, the changes will automatically be reflected in the answer tables. Queries can also be used to summarise data, delete or update all records satisfying particular criteria, append data to one table from another, or make a brand new table.

We'll look at how a query can combine data from tblBorrower, tblBook and tblLoan. First of all the relationships between the three entities needs to be defined.:

<blockquote>
One borrower may have many books on loan;   (a one-to-many relationship)

Each book may appear on one loan record.   (a one-to-one relationship)
</blockquote>

The relationship between Borrower and Book can be specified in Access (using Edit, Relationships) and is depicted as shown below:

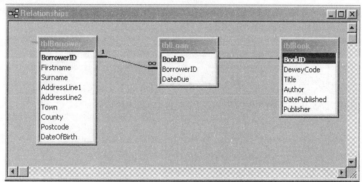

Figure 19.7: Setting up relationships between entities

The query is now created as shown below, using fields from all three tables. The query has been saved with the name **qryLoanForm** and this will also be used by Access as the name of the Answer table from which our new form will be created.

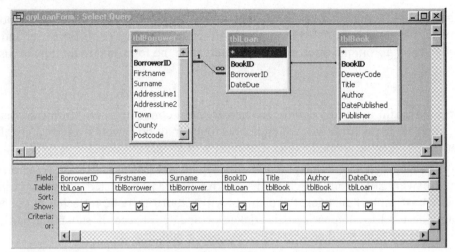

Figure 19.8: Creating a query to combine fields from 3 tables

Note: When a book is returned, the Loan record for that book must immediately be removed from the Loan table, or it will not be possible to add a new Loan record for the book. if, say, the same Borrower wants to take it out again the next day.

Creating the Loan form from the new query

Now the new form can be created using the new query as the source. A possible layout is shown below. As soon as the user enters the BorrowerID, the borrower's name is automatically shown, and similarly, the book title and author are shown when the BookID is entered.

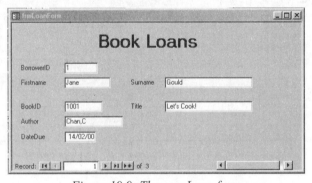

Figure 19.9: The new Loan form

Reports

Queries are commonly used to pick out records satisfying particular criteria and to sort or summarise them ready to be printed on a report. For example, suppose we wanted a list, sorted by borrower name, of all books overdue by more than one week. These borrowers could then be mailed a postcard reminding them to return their books.

The first step is to perform a query to pick out the fields that are needed on the report and to set the criteria, expressed in the DateDue column as *<Date()-7* (Note that *Date()* gives today's date.) The report will be sorted in the order in which the fields appear on the query unless we specify otherwise. In the example below we have specified that the records are to be sorted in ascending order of Surname and Firstname.

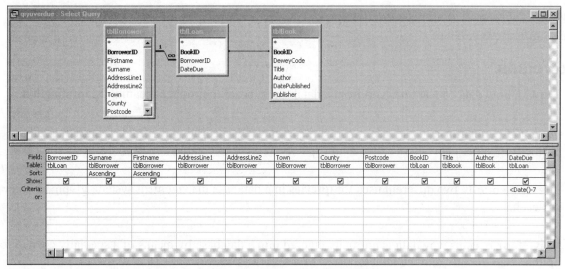

Figure 19.10: Query to find overdue books

Now a report can be created based on the records in the Answer table.

Overdue books   *22 February 2000*

ID	Surname	Firstname	Address		BookID	Title	Author	DateDue
6	Arnot	Mark	7 Exe Vale Road		1009	Wild Swans	Chang	10/02/00
			Exeter					
			Devon	EX8 7HG				
4	Baker	Neil	7 School Lane		1011	Business Information	Cleary,T	09/02/00
			Countess Wear					
			Exeter					
			Devon	EX11 9KP				
4	Baker	Neil	7 School Lane		1010	The Road Ahead	Gates,Bill	09/02/00
			Countess Wear					
			Exeter					
			Devon	EX11 9KP				

Figure 19.11: A report on overdue books

Selecting a suitable output format

Reports can contain any data from any table or combination of tables, sorted and summarised as required. The report can be suitably **formatted** by selecting appropriate headings, fonts, spacing and sequence of fields across the page. In the example above the address fields have been arranged in just two columns so that the fields fit across the page.

You can download all the instructions to build this database in Access 2000 from the web site www.payne-gallway.co.uk

Exercises

1. Explain how data can be retrieved from a database in order to produce meaningful information.   (4)
    New question

2. A **report generator** allows a user to generate a report by specifying the fields required on the report. Name **four** other parameters a user might specify in order to create a report in the desired format.   (4)
    New question

3. Describe briefly two different uses for **queries** in a database management system, giving an example of each.   (4)
    New question

4. Give **four** reasons why data is normally entered into a database by means of a specially created form rather than directly into the tables.   (4)
    New question

Chapter 20 – Systems Software

What is an operating system?

Computers require two types of software: **applications software** such as word processing, spreadsheet or graphics packages, and **operating systems software** to control and monitor the running of application programs, and to allow users to communicate with the computer.

The operating system consists of a number of programs which are typically 'bundled' with the hardware; in other words, when you buy a new PC, for example, you will also be supplied with a CD containing the latest version of the Windows operating system. This then has to be installed by running a special installation program supplied on the CD, which will copy the operating system to your hard disk and customise it to your particular hardware configuration.

The part of the operating system that manages the computer's resources (the CPU, memory, storage devices and peripherals) is called the **kernel** (or **supervisor** or **control program**). Each time you switch on your PC, the kernel will be copied from the hard disk into memory, which takes a couple of minutes.

Functions of an operating system

Obviously, the operating system (OS) for a standalone microcomputer system will be very much simpler than that of a supercomputer which is controlling hundreds of terminals and running many different kinds of job simultaneously. Nevertheless, all operating systems perform certain basic functions, including:

- **Memory management**. Most computers nowadays are capable of holding several programs in memory simultaneously, so that a user can switch from one application to another. The operating system has to allocate memory to each application – as well as to itself!

  If the OS detects that there is insufficient memory to load an application that the user has asked for, it may swap another application (or part of it) out to disk temporarily, and reload it when required, swapping something else out to disk. This takes time, which is why increasing memory may have the effect of speeding up the computer's performance.

  The technique of swapping part of the contents of memory out to disk is known as **virtual memory**, because it makes the computer appear to have more memory than it actually does.

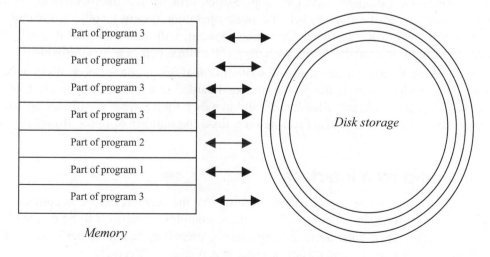

Figure 20.1: Virtual memory

- **Resource allocation and scheduling**. In larger computer systems which are capable of running several programs at once (**multiprogramming**), the OS is responsible for allocating processing time, memory and input-output resources to each one.

- **Backing store management**. The OS controls the transfer of data from secondary storage (e.g. disk) to memory and back again. It also has to maintain a directory of the disk so that files and free space can be quickly located.

- **Interrupt handling**. The OS detects many different kinds of interrupt such as for example a user pressing the Enter key on the keyboard, a printer sending a message that it is out of paper, the real-time clock interrupting to indicate that the processor should be allocated to the next user in a multi-user system, a hardware or software malfunction.

- **Allowing a user to communicate with the computer**. The user gives instructions to the computer to start a program, copy a file, send a message to another user, and so on by typing in commands recognised by the operating system or by using a mouse to point and click in a graphical user interface such as Windows 95.

Utility programs

As well as the basic operating system, the systems software available to users includes numerous **utility programs**, such as:

- **Virus checkers** which check disks and memory for viruses and delete them if detected;

- **Security and accounting** software which checks user IDs and passwords, counts and reports the number of attempts made to log on under each user ID, the amount of processor time used at each session, total login time and so on;

- **File management utilities** which attempt to repair corrupted files, reorganise files on disk so that free space is 'defragmented' (which can improve performance), 'zip' (compress) files so that they occupy less space if for example you want to make a backup copy of a large file onto a floppy disk.

The DOS operating system

Two operating systems currently dominate the microcomputer world; Windows and the Apple Macintosh (MacOS) operating system.

In 1981, IBM purchased from a tiny company called Microsoft Corporation an operating system which it called PC-DOS (Personal Computer Disk Operating System) for its new microcomputer. Bill Gates, the head of Microsoft, retained the right to sell the same operating system to other computer companies, under the name MS-DOS (Microsoft Disk Operating System), with the result that it rapidly became the most popular operating system in the world, with over 150 million copies sold worldwide.

DOS tells the computer how to format, read and write information on either floppy disks or hard disks. It manages peripheral devices such as the printer and keyboard, and controls the execution of application software. It also specifies how many files can be held in a disk folder, what constitutes an acceptable file or folder name, the number of bytes that can be on a disk, the number of bytes of memory usable by a program.

The command-driven interface

DOS is essentially a command-driven interface, meaning that the user has to type in commands in exactly the correct syntax to perform any operation. This allows complex commands to be entered to customise the operating system for a particular user, and experienced users may be able to perform operations faster using DOS than by using a mouse and menus or icons in a Windows interface.

A DOS prompt appearing on a blank screen shows which drive and folder are current, e.g.
C\WINDOWS>

To change drive, the user types the characters shown in bold
C\WINDOWS>**A:** and the prompt changes to
A:>

To display a folder of files held on A, the user types the word **DIR**
A:>**DIR**   and a folder is shown (Figure 20.2)

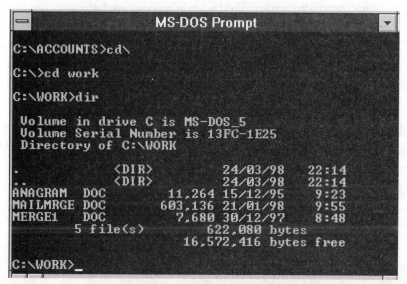

Figure 20.2: MS DOS Command line interface

The Apple Macintosh graphical user interface (GUI)

While Microsoft were developing their DOS operating system, the Apple Computer Corporation were working on a completely different way of communicating with a microcomputer. In 1984, Apple brought out their most powerful PC, the Macintosh, complete with the WIMP interface that has now become universal. WIMP stands for Windows, Icons, Mouse and Pull-down menus or alternatively, Windows, Icons, Menus, Pointer – and the term 'user-friendly' was more or less invented to describe this approach.

The Macintosh could do things that the IBM PC could not, such as having more than one application open at once, each in its own 'window', and transferring data between applications.

Unfortunately for Apple, from being the most popular PC in the late 1970s, they rapidly fell behind IBM even after the success of their graphical user interface. What went wrong? The major problem lay in the lack of software packages written especially for the Mac. Apple, unlike IBM, owned both the hardware and the operating system, and refused to license the operating system to any other company, so that while sales of PC 'clones' mushroomed, Apple retained a much smaller niche market. Software developers concentrated on developing software for PCs running MS-DOS because this was a much larger market, even though the operating system was inferior to Apple's.

DOS with Windows

It was not long before Microsoft, headed by Bill Gates, began to develop its own Windows interface. The early versions of Windows, including Windows 3.1 and 3.11, were not full operating systems. They provided an operating environment or *graphical user interface* (GUI) that operated under the control of DOS, acting as a kind of bridge between the user and DOS. Because Windows 3.11 is not an actual operating system, DOS has to be loaded into memory first when the machine is switched on.

One primary objective of Windows 3.1 was to allow **multi-tasking**, allowing a user to have several applications running simultaneously and to switch between them. With multi-tasking, there is no need to close one application before starting another. The concept is analogous to working at a desk; you might start to write a report, then decide to check your diary and make a phone call, and use your calculator to work out a couple of figures to include in the report.

Several desktop 'accessory' programs are supplied with Windows, including

1. Calculator.
2. Calendar, for displaying a calendar in month or day format and setting alarms to 'beep' at specific times.
3. Notepad, for writing brief notes.
4. Card file, for keeping a card index, say of names and addresses.
5. Clock for displaying the current time.
6. Paintbrush, a simple drawing package.
7. Write, a simple word processing package.
8. Clipboard, for temporarily saving anything such as text, a graphic, spreadsheet or screenshot, temporarily in memory so that it can be pasted into another application.
9. Terminal, for communicating with another computer.

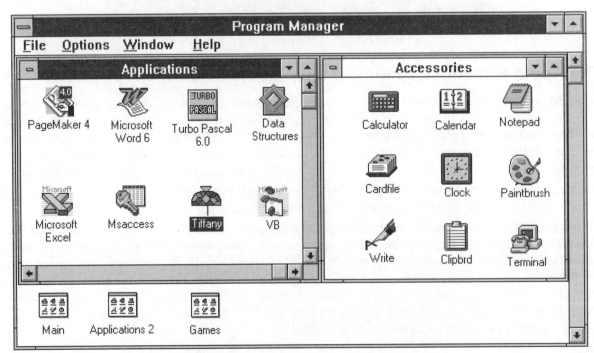

Figure 20.3: The Windows 3.11 Graphical User Interface

Windows 95, 98, 2000 – a full operating system

Windows 95, unlike previous versions of Windows, was in itself a full operating system offering true multi-tasking, and taking full advantage of the 32-bit architecture of newer PCs. This means, effectively, that applications will run faster under Windows 95 (and its successors) than under Windows 3.11. Other improvements include a completely redesigned interface, and the ability to use long file names rather than being restricted to 8 characters.

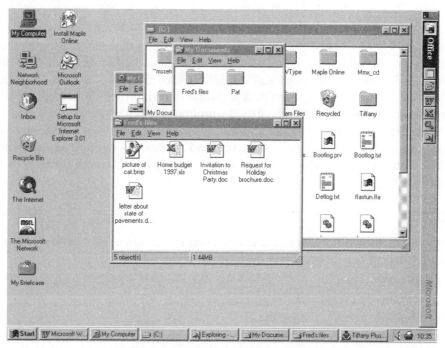

Figure 20.4: Windows 95 Interface

Windows 95 and subsequent versions also provide 'Plug and Play' support designed to make it easier to install peripherals such as a new printer. The device merely needs to be plugged in and the user can then select 'Add New Hardware' from Control Panel in the Settings menu to be taken through a few easy steps for the device to be automatically configured with the appropriate driver. That is the theory anyway but many users view such tasks with a degree of trepidation and scepticism and refer to the procedure as 'Plug and Pray'.

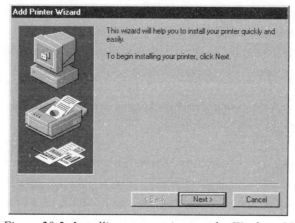

Figure 20.5: Installing a new printer under Windows 95

UNIX

UNIX is a general-purpose, multi-user, multi-tasking operating system written in C, which has been around since the early 1970s. Unlike other operating systems, UNIX is available on a wide variety of platforms, which is to say that it can be used on computers from many different manufacturers. This means that users can select hardware from different manufacturers and use the same software on different types of hardware, which is not the case with other operating systems traditionally supplied with the hardware.

Linux

Linux is an operating system created by Linus Torvalds, an altruistic Finnish programmer. It has been developed by thousands of volunteers, many of whom are regarded as some of the best programmers in the world. It is available entirely free and can be downloaded from the Internet, and for many young programmers, the beauty of it is that you can pick it up and start improving it immediately. It is said to be far more bug-free than Windows 2000, which at 35 million lines of code, is the biggest program ever written. In the year 2000, there are not many applications that will run under Linux, and Microsoft has a virtual monopoly with Outlook, Explorer, Word, Excel and Access. Soon, however, Microsoft's old rivals such as Corel and Borland will be offering Linux versions of their software and just possibly, Microsoft Windows' dominance may one day be buried.

Exercises

1. At present there are many different computer operating systems in existence. If operating systems were standardised, give one different benefit for each of the following:

    (a) the user of computers;

    (a) the manufacturer of computers;

    (a) developers of software for computers.

    Give **one** technical reason why this is not likely to happen. (4)
    AEB Computing Paper 1 Qu 8 1993

2. Describe three housekeeping utilities normally provided with the operating system for a single-user personal computer. Your description should include a typical task for which each utility is used. (6)
    NEAB Computing AS Paper 1 Qu 9 1996

3. When using any applications software package on a network, the user is often unaware that an operating system is working 'behind the scenes', managing system resources. Give **three** of these resources and in each case briefly explain the role of the operating system in its management. (6)
    NEAB IT02 Qu 4 1997

4. In recent years there has been a move from command driven interfaces to WIMP driven interfaces.

    (a) Compare and contrast command and WIMP driven interfaces. (3)

    (b) Discuss factors which have led to the development and increased use of WIMP driven interfaces. (2)
    SEB Computing Studies Paper 1 Qu 9 1995

5. Disk directories record information about the files that are stored on disk. State **three** items of information that, typically, would be recorded. (3)
    AEB Computing Paper 2 Qu 4 1997

6. From the experienced user's viewpoint, give **three** functions of an operating system. (3)
    NEAB IT02 Specimen Paper Qu 5

7. Give **two** reasons why additional memory might be useful to the user of a PC. (2)
    New question

Chapter 21 – Categories of Software

Categorising software

Software is the general term used to describe all the programs which run on a computer. There are three general categories of software: systems software, applications software and general-purpose software. This categorisation is not rigid, however, and some people would say that general-purpose software and applications software can be lumped together. You will soon discover that very little in computing is black and white; whatever you read, someone will soon come up with an apparently contradictory statement on most topics, leaving you to choose your own truth!

Systems software

In the last chapter we looked at the functions of an operating system, which must be installed on every computer and is independent of any applications that a user may wish to run. The operating system comes under the general heading of **systems software**, as do the utility programs mentioned in the last chapter. Here is a list of some of the different types of systems software.

1. **Operating system.** Already discussed.

2. **Utility programs.** These are programs designed to make life easier for computer users. Utility programs perform common tasks that thousands of computer users need to do at one time or another, such as search for lost files, sort files of data into a particular sequence, copy disk files to magnetic tape for backup purposes and so on.

3. **Programming language compilers/interpreters**. Compilers and interpreters are different types of program used to translate the statements in a programming language such as Pascal, Visual Basic or C into a form that the computer can understand.

4. **Performance monitoring software**. This is used to monitor, analyse and report on the performance of a computer and its components. It can provide information such as the overall utilisation of the processor and number of disk accesses over a given period of time. In a mainframe environment, this can assist management in monitoring the current and future hardware requirements.

5. **Communications software**. In a mainframe environment, communications software is executed on a separate, dedicated processor ('front-end processor') and controls the flow of data to and from remote locations.

Applications software

Applications software is written to perform specific tasks such as order entry, payroll, stock control or hospital appointments. The software may be designed specifically for one particular company, ('bespoke software') and written especially for them using a programming language or software such as a database management system. Alternatively, the software may be purchased 'off the shelf'.

General purpose software

All common application packages such as word processing, desktop publishing, spreadsheet, database, computer-aided design (CAD) and presentation graphics packages fall into this category. Most general purpose software is sold as a package, including a CD containing the software and manuals to help you get started and to be used as a reference.

Figure 21.1: General purpose software

Integrated packages and software suites

The main productivity tools used by organisations include word processing, spreadsheets, databases, presentation graphics and communications software to enable users to communicate with each other either locally or across the world in an international company.

Integrated packages which combined features from all five of these products were once very popular, because they offered capabilities from all these packages in a single product at a relatively low price, and data could be transferred between applications. However, a single integrated package (e.g. Microsoft Works) has fewer and less sophisticated features than are found in separately-purchased packages.

Today, complete **software suites** such as Microsoft Office or Lotus SmartSuite offer four or more software products packaged together at a much lower price than buying the packages separately.

Microsoft Office, for example, includes Word, Excel, Access and a multimedia presentation graphics package called PowerPoint.

Terminology in the computer world soon becomes fuzzy and MS Office is sometimes referred to as an integrated suite. The advantage of buying such a suite of programs is that the individual applications are completely compatible so that there is no difficulty importing or exporting data from one package to another, if for example you wish to put a spreadsheet in a word processed report. Also, the packages all have the same look and feel, with the same shortcut keys used for various operations (such as Ctrl-S for Save) and this makes learning new software an easier task.

Generic and specific software

Note that software such as word processing, spreadsheet and database software is sometimes referred to as **generic** software. This simply implies that any of the dozens of spreadsheet packages, for example, can be made to do many different tasks, and is not designed specifically for one type of application. The other type of application software such as a payroll or stock control system mentioned above, or a software package such as a program to help fill in an income tax return, is in contrast **specific** because it is designed to do one particular task.

Exercises

1. Describe the difference between applications software and systems software, giving an example of each. (4)

   NEAB IT02 Qu 2 1996

2. When purchasing software, it is often possible to buy either an 'integrated package' or separate application packages that run under a common operating system environment.

   (a) What is meant by the term 'integrated package'? (2)

   (b) What applications would you normally expect an 'integrated package' to offer? (4)

   (c) What are the relative advantages and disadvantages of an 'integrated package' over a collection of separate applications packages running under a common operating system environment? (4)

   NEAB IT02 Sample Paper Qu 2

3. Give **three** points a user should consider before deciding to purchase a software package. (3)

   NEAB AS Computing Paper 1 Qu 1 1996

4. Describe **three** housekeeping utilities normally provided with the operating system for a single-user personal computer. Your description should include a typical task for which each utility is used. (6)

   NEAB AS Computing Paper 1 Qu 8 1996

Chapter 22 – Generic Software

Generic software

This is a general term sometimes used to describe the application packages that are used to perform operations that are an integral part of day-to-day business operations. The most common ones are word processors, spreadsheets, database management systems and electronic mail. These four applications form the basis of both integrated packages and software suites from many different software manufacturers, and all have many features in common.

Word processing

A word processing package is a program or set of programs used to enter, edit, format, store and print documents. A document may be anything from a simple memo to a complete book. In addition to data entry and editing facilities, word processors have several important features:

- **Spelling and grammar checker**. Each word in a document can be checked against words held in the package's dictionary, and in some packages misspelt words and grammatically incorrect sentences are underlined. If the original word is correctly spelt but was highlighted by the spell checker, it can be added to the dictionary.

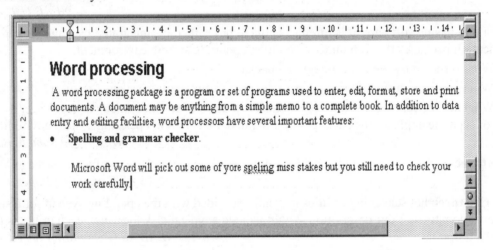

Figure 22.1: a spelling checker underlines misspelt words

- **Automatic creation of index and table of contents**. Any word in the text can be marked for inclusion in an index. Headings and subheadings in a given style can be included automatically in a table of contents, which can be updated at any time.
- **Import files**. Tables, photographs, graphics and even video and sound files can be imported from other sources and inserted in a document.

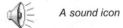   *A sound icon*

To play the sound, double-click its icon. (This could be used to insert a verbal message or some music in a document, for example.)

- **Mail Merge**. A document and a list of names and addresses can be merged to produce personalised letters. (see Figure 22.2)

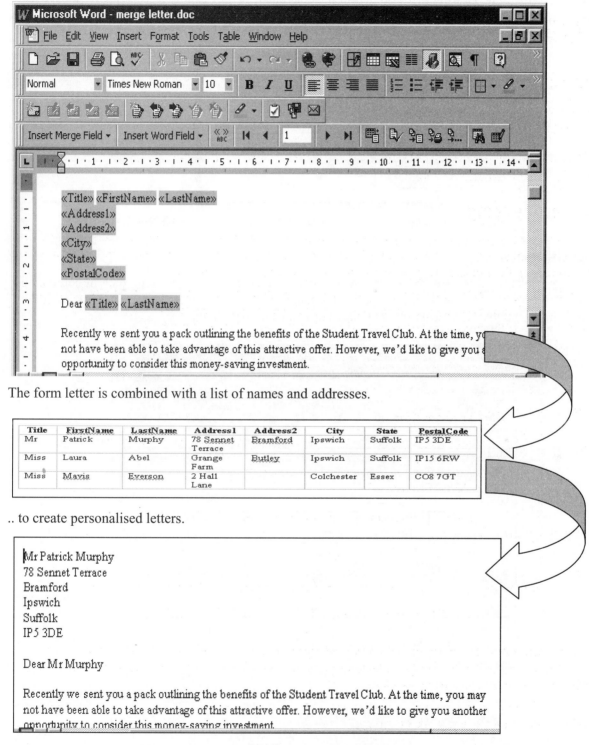

The form letter is combined with a list of names and addresses.

Title	FirstName	LastName	Address1	Address2	City	State	PostalCode
Mr	Patrick	Murphy	78 Sennet Terrace	Bramford	Ipswich	Suffolk	IP5 3DE
Miss	Laura	Abel	Grange Farm	Butley	Ipswich	Suffolk	IP15 6RW
Miss	Mavis	Everson	2 Hall Lane		Colchester	Essex	CO8 7GT

.. to create personalised letters.

Mr Patrick Murphy
78 Sennet Terrace
Bramford
Ipswich
Suffolk
IP5 3DE

Dear Mr Murphy

Recently we sent you a pack outlining the benefits of the Student Travel Club. At the time, you may not have been able to take advantage of this attractive offer. However, we'd like to give you another opportunity to consider this money-saving investment.

Figure 22.2: Mail merge

- **Creation of templates** with preset text styles, margins, formatting, letterheading, etc.
- **WYSIWYG** capability. This acronym stands for 'What You See Is What You Get', and refers to the ability to display on screen exactly what you will get when the text is printed. Many word processors

have more than one viewing mode so that in page layout view, for example, you can see a page as it will be printed, and in 'normal' view can see and edit text but not see imported pictures or text laid out in columns.

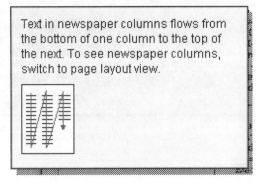

Figure 22.3: Columns can be viewed in 'Page Layout' view in MS Word

Spreadsheets

Spreadsheet packages allow a user to create worksheets (spreadsheets) representing data in column and row form. Spreadsheets are used for any application that uses numerical data, such as budgets, cash flow forecasts, profit and loss statements, student marks or results of experiments.

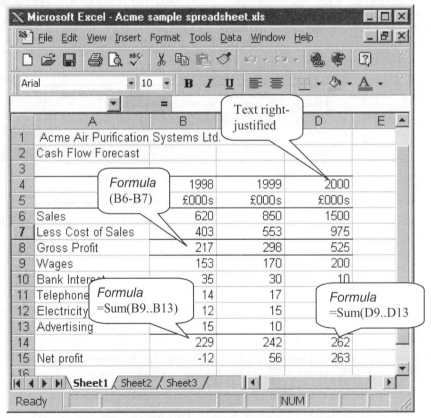

Figure 22.4: Spreadsheet containing numbers, text and formulae

Spreadsheet features

Spreadsheets offer the following facilities:

- Format cells, rows and columns, specifying for example, the alignment of text, number of decimal points, height and width of cell;

- Copy cell contents to other locations, with automatic adjustment of formulae from say B9 to C9, D9 etc.;

- Determine the effect of several different hypothetical changes of data; this facility is termed 'what-if' calculation;

- Insert, move or delete rows and columns;

- Use functions such as SUM, AVERAGE, MAX, MIN in formulae;

- Create a simple database and sort or query the data to produce a report of, say, all females earning over £20,000 for a list of employees;

- Write macros to automate common procedures;

- Create templates – spreadsheets with formats and formulae already entered, into which new figures may be inserted;

- Create 'multi-dimensional' spreadsheets using several sheets, and copy data from one sheet to another;

- Create many different types of charts and graphs (see Figure 22.5).

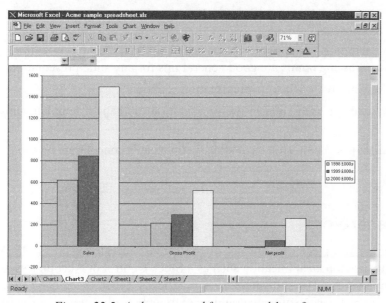

Figure 22.5: A chart created from spreadsheet figures

Databases and Electronic Mail

These two applications are each discussed elsewhere (see chapters 17-19, 6) and are not covered here.

> ➢ **Discussion: Many integrated suites share common features such as menus, toolbars and shortcut key combinations to perform common tasks. Do you know some of these shortcuts? Do you know how to display toolbars that are not currently on the screen? Do you make use of the 'Help' menu when you are stuck?**

Presentation Graphics

Presentation graphics software such as PowerPoint is useful for putting together a presentation which can be delivered using a computer attached to a projection device, using transparencies and an ordinary overhead projector or as a self-running presentation in, say, a shopping mall or cinema. The software allows the user to quickly create 'slides' combining text, graphics and pictures and to create animation or sound effects and 'transition' effects between slides.

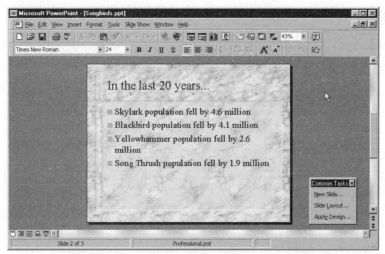

Figure 22.6: Creating a PowerPoint presentation

When creating a presentation it is important to consider how the presentation will be given, and to what type of audience. The following points are good general tips for any slide presentation:

- Start with a title screen saying what the presentation is about.

- Use a consistent style for each slide in the presentation, perhaps a template showing the company logo.

- Don't put more than 4 or 5 points on each slide. People can't concentrate on too much information at once.

- Be sure the font size is large enough to be read from all parts of the room.

Application generators

An application generator is a piece of software, often database-oriented such as MS Access or Paradox, which allows a user to develop an application such as a Stock Control or Accounts system without having to do very much programming. The software will automatically generate the code from tables, forms and reports specified by the user. Such software could be extremely useful in, say, a Recruitment department of a large company that wants to keep track of applicants, where they come from, what qualifications they have, and so on in order to plan future recruitment campaigns.

Report generators

A report generator is a piece of software that allows a business user who may have little knowledge of programming to specify the format and content of a printed report to be composed using values from a database or calculations performed by a computer. Visual Basic, for example, uses a report generator called Crystal Reports which can generate reports automatically. In the programming language RPG (Report Program Generator), the user designs reports using statements similar to programming language statements. In Access, 'wizards' are used to generate reports without having to write any code.

Web browsers

Software called a **Web Browser** is used to view information stored on the World Wide Web. The browser interprets the information, displays it on the screen and enables you to move between linked items. Examples of Web browsers include Microsoft Internet Explorer and Netscape.

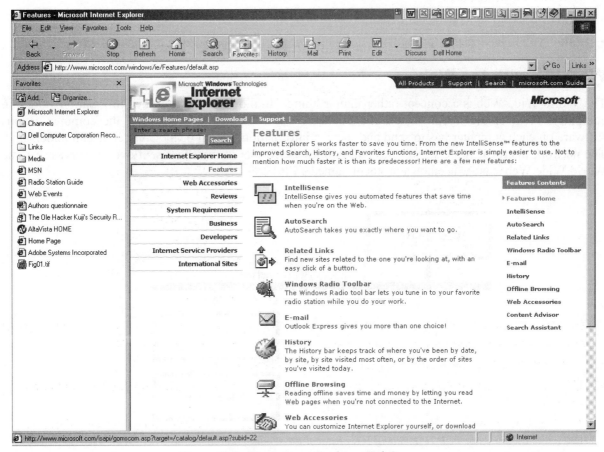

Figure 22.7: The Internet Explorer Web Browser

Facilities offered by a browser

A web browser is a program that enables a computer to download and view pages from the world-wide web. Browsers can also perform tasks that previously needed special software. A browser will:

- Show a web page for which you have either entered the address or URL (Uniform Resource Locator) or clicked on a 'hot' link;

- Browse back and forward through the most recently viewed pages;

- Allow you to customise the basic options such as the opening page, content censorship, security levels and whether to download the page as text only to speed up transmission;

- 'Bookmark' pages for quick reference later;

- Keep a 'History' list of pages visited within a specified period;

- Save the most recently visited pages for viewing off-line;

- Show animation sequences programmed in Java script;

- Play back sound, video clips and multimedia if the appropriate 'plug-in' software (usually a Visual Basic ActiveX control) is installed, e.g. Shockwave;
- Download files to a local hard disk;
- Allow you to fill in an on-line form and submit it by e-mail;
- Give links to search engines;
- Allow access to some personal e-mail;
- Allow you to have pages 'pushed' at you (Netcasting) rather than having to request them.

Working with the Web

The World Wide Web is a concept rather than a 'thing'. It allows people to view information stored on computers all over the world. When you connect your computer to a network, the communications software on each computer has to send and receive information that all of the computers can understand. The network **protocol** is the set of rules that defines the format of messages sent over the network. The World Wide Web standardised on a protocol named TCP/IP.

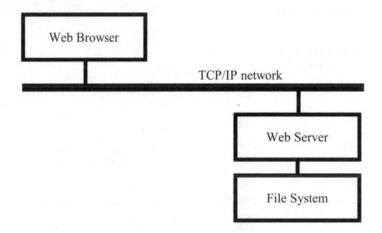

Figure 22.8: TCP/IP Protocol is a protocol for sending data over the World Wide Web

What your computer sends within the packaging parameters of a protocol depends on the applications sending and receiving the information – the *application* protocol. When you copy a file to a local server using Windows Explorer, Explorer packages up your file information in a format that the receiving file system understands. Windows than wraps these packages in a *transport* protocol (TCP/IP) for sending over the network.

When you work on the World Wide Web, the browser uses standard application protocols to send and receive information. Two of the most common Web protocols are *Hypertext Transport Protocol* (HTTP) for transmitting things like Web pages and pictures, and *File Transfer Protocol* (FTP) for uploading and downloading files.

Exercises

1. A particular word processing package is described as having a WYSIWYG (what you see is what you get) output capability. Give the advantages of using such a package rather than one which does not possess this capability.   (3)
    NEAB IT02 Qu 1 1996

2. A mail-order book club holds its customer data on a computer file. The club wishes to contact its customers who have not ordered a book for one year or more. Briefly describe the stages involved in the necessary mail merge.   (3)
    NEAB Computing AS Qu 2 1995

3. A cell in a typical electronic spreadsheet can contain a data value or a formula. Describe briefly **two** other types of cell contents.   (6)
    NISEAC Computing Paper 1 Qu 5 1996

4. One common business application package is the spreadsheet. Give **two** different reasons why a spreadsheet package is particularly useful as a decision-making tool.   (2)
    AEB Computing Paper 1 1996

5. An office worker has created a macro which imports data from one spreadsheet file to another and then performs some calculations. However, the macro fails to work as expected when it is used.
    (a) Explain the term "macro" as used in the above description.   (2)
    (b) What could the office worker have done to reduce the chance of the macro failing when it was used?   (3)
    NEAB IT02 Qu 3 1999

6. (a) The following is an example of an advertisement appearing in a computing magazine:
        "For sale: 386 16MHz microprocessor with 4Mb RAM, 180Mb hard disk, mouse and installed operating system and user software (including DTP, Clip Art and integrated software). Best offer secures."
        (i)   Describe the main features you would expect to find in each of the DTP, Clip Art and integrated software offered with this microcomputer.   (9)
        (ii) What operational difficulties might arise with the software already installed on this microcomputer if the original disks are not available? How might these difficulties be prevented?   (6)
    NISEAC Paper 1 Qu 15(a) 1995

7. The head of a sales team has developed a presentation. It is planned for members of the sales team to deliver this presentation as part of a sales talk to large audiences at various locations throughout the country.
    (a) State **three** advantages to be gained using presentation software as opposed to the use of traditional methods, e.g. OHP.   (3)
    (b) State **three** design considerations that should be taken into account when the head of the sales team is developing the presentation.   (3)
    NEAB IT02 Qu 4 1999

Chapter 23 – Capabilities of Software

Object Linking and Embedding (OLE)

Using OLE, it is possible to share information between programs. For example, if a report is being written in Word which requires the use of a spreadsheet or chart created in Excel, the spreadsheet can be either linked to, or embedded in, the document.

In the Word menu, selecting Insert, Object and then 'Create from file' in the next window brings up the following screen:

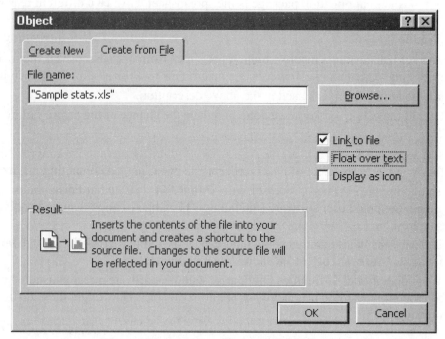

Figure 23.1: Linking a file to another document

The spreadsheet 'Sample Stats.xls' is then linked into the report.

Mortimer College A Level Statistics 1997-98							
Cumulative Percentage of Candidates at each grade							
	A	B	C	D	E	N	U
1997	8.35	18.22	37.00	58.63	74.19	88.99	100.00
1998	9.11	24.55	53.07	73.66	92.28	98.81	100.00

Figure 23.2: This spreadsheet is linked to the original in Excel

About linked and embedded objects

The main differences between linked objects and embedded objects are where the data is stored and how it is updated after you place it in the destination file.

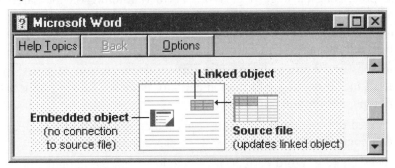

Figure 23.3: The difference between linked and embedded objects

Use **linked** objects if:

- you want the information to reflect any changes to the original data, or

- file size is a consideration.

With a **linked object**, the original information remains stored in the source file. The destination file displays a representation of the linked information but stores only the location of the original data. The linked information is updated automatically if you change the original data in the source file. For example, if you select a range of cells in a Microsoft Excel workbook and then paste the cells as a linked object in a Word document, the information is updated in Word if you change the information in your workbook.

In contrast, an **embedded object** becomes part of the destination file. Because an embedded object has no links to the source file, the object is not updated if you change the original data. You can still edit a spreadsheet or other object embedded in Word, though, by double-clicking it to open and edit it using Excel.

The need for portability of data

Portability is the ability to run the same program on different types of computer. It can also refer to the ability to transfer a file from one computer to another.

For all sorts of reasons, it's important to be able to transfer data between applications and between computers of the same or different types, perhaps using different operating systems. For example:

- You're writing a report in Word and you want to be able to insert an Excel spreadsheet in the report.

- You're using a desktop publishing system and you want to be able to import some graphics from a drawing package.

- You're doing a research assignment and want to download articles from the Internet on 'Computers and Dolphins'.

- You want to e-mail your friend on a Unix machine in Hull from your PC in Southampton, and send her a scanned photograph she requested.

Files (binary, text or graphical) can be downloaded from the Internet using **ftp** (File Transfer Protocol) – software that can copy files between different types of computer.

Problems with portability

There are several reasons why files may not be portable.

- A document created using one word processing package (e.g. Word) commonly cannot be read by a different word processing package (e.g. Word Perfect) running on the same computer. Different formatting codes are used by different packages; for example, the information that a word or paragraph is in bold text must be stored along with the actual text, but exactly how this information is coded varies between packages.

  For this reason, most word processing packages allow documents to be stored in 'Text only' format. This strips out all the formatting information and any graphics, leaving only the text, which can be read into a different package and reformatted.

- A document created on one computer using a particular word processor appears differently on the screen of another computer running the same word processing package.

  Some word processors (e.g. Word Perfect) lay out a document based on the printer that is being used. If the document is transferred to another computer, and a different printer specified, the document may appear with a completely different layout, with line breaks and page breaks appearing in different places.

Another reason why a document may appear differently on a different computer is that it may not have the same fonts (typefaces) installed. An alternative font will be substituted, which usually changes the layout.

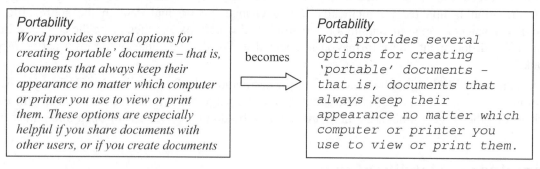

Figure 23.4: Transferring a document to another computer can change its appearance

Upgradability

Software manufacturers commonly bring out upgrades about every two years, to the intense annoyance of many customers who soon find themselves either using out-of-date software or having to pay for the upgrade. Software upgrades frequently cause some or all of the following problems:

- Documents or applications produced by the upgraded software are not 'downwardly compatible'. In other words, a document written in Version 6 can usually be read in Version 7, but not vice versa. Usually, the newer version allows the user to save the file as a 'Version 6 file' so that it can be read by the earlier version.

- The new version is likely to contain new features non-existent in earlier versions, so that data or formatting may be lost if it is converted to the earlier version for another user.

- The upgraded software frequently needs more memory, more disk space and a faster processor to work efficiently, meaning that hardware has to be upgraded.

On the other hand, of course, the march of progress brings its advantages and a new version often brings impressive improvements in ease of use, functionality and speed.

> ➢ **Discussion: A College has several independent local area networks in different open-access rooms, each with its own file server. Periodically the oldest computers are replaced with the most up-to-date hardware available. Why does the College continue to run older versions of software on the new computers?**

Criteria for selecting a software package

The most important factor in evaluating software is how well the software meets your needs, but there are many other factors to consider as well.

1. Compatibility with existing hardware. Will the software run on existing equipment?

2. Compatibility with existing software. Can files from other packages be imported or exported to and from the new package to other packages?

3. Quality of documentation.

4. Ease of learning. How good is the on-line help? Are tutorials available?

5. Ease of use. Is the package easy to use? Are there shortcuts for advanced users?

6. Technical support. Is this available, and at what cost?

7. Upgrade policy. Will future upgrades be available at a discount? Can files created in older versions be used without change?

8. Speed. How long does it take to perform complex but frequently performed operations such as database queries. Some database packages, for example, are very fast with small amounts of data but grind to a halt when presented with several thousand records.

9. Cost. This may involve simply the cost of an individual package. If the package is to be used throughout an organisation, the cost of a licensing agreement that specifies how many copies of the software may legally be made, or how many users can use it on a network, has to be investigated.

Evaluating software

Before selecting a particular software package you could:

- Read reviews of it in a computer magazine. Magazines commonly compare similar software packages on dozens of different criteria;

- Consult other users who have experience of the type of software you are thinking of purchasing;

- Perform benchmark tests (performance tests) to see how fast various packages perform a number of different tasks. Computer magazines often publish the results of benchmark tests.

Software reliability

As software becomes increasingly complex, it becomes more and more difficult to test. Batch systems, where the data is entered together in a batch, processed and output produced, are relatively easy to test. Test files can be created and expected results of all processing calculated and compared with actual results. If something is wrong, the program can be fixed and the same set of tests run again.

With GUI interfaces and on-line systems, however, this type of testing is not possible. It may be impossible to recreate the conditions under which a program crashed. The difficulties arise because:

- There is no single, well-defined flow of events at the user interface;

- It is often impossible to restore a database to the condition it was in before a bug was detected. In a client-server environment, the data may be held on different servers and across networks;

- Rapid, iterative and continuous development techniques mean that software continues to develop and new, weekly versions of systems are released by programmers. Testing simply cannot keep pace with these rapid changes;

- Users often use new software in ways which were not anticipated by the software engineers who wrote the system. When the system finally crashes, ("I was just trying to add a new record and it crashed") it is impossible to retrace the sequence of events that caused the crash;

- Performance testing is difficult to set up. An on-line, multi-user system that works well when tested with 1,000 records and 2 users may fall over when a million records are added and hundreds of users are simultaneously accessing the database.

Exercises

1. Most word processors provide users with the facility to save a document as 'text only' as well as in the 'usual' format. Explain briefly the difference between the versions of a document stored in each of these two ways giving **one** reason why the 'text only' option is provided. (6)

    NISEAC Computing Paper 1 Qu 6 1995

2. Given an existing hardware platform, selecting the most appropriate software package for a specific application can be a difficult process.

    (a) Describe the criteria and methods you would use to select the most appropriate software package for a specific application. (16)

    (b) Users may encounter problems when software manufacturers upgrade a software package. With reference to specific examples describe **two** such problems. (4)

    NEAB IT02 Specimen Paper Qu 9

3. A freelance reporter who regularly contributes articles to various newspapers and magazines is considering which word processing package she should purchase. A friend has said that 'most modern applications packages enable users to produce files which are portable'.

    With the aid of specific examples discuss this statement. Include in your discussion:

    - An explanation of what portability means in this context;

    - Why portability is important;

    - How the Information Technology industry can encourage this portability. (16)

    NEAB IT02 Qu 10 1996

4. Explain briefly what is meant by the term *software portability*. (4)

    NISEAC Computing Paper 1 Qu 4 1994

Chapter 24 – Modes of Processing

Processing methods

There are several different ways in which data can be processed, the main distinction being made between **batch processing** and **pseudo real-time processing**. You will also see or hear the terms **on-line processing**, **interactive processing** and **transaction processing** – unfortunately in computing these terms tend to be used rather loosely and seem to mean different things to different people. All these types of processing involve processing transactions, so what exactly is a transaction?

Transactions

Transactions are events which need to be recorded in connection with the production, sale and distribution of goods and services.

Many organisations have to keep track of thousands or millions of transactions every day. Every time you withdraw cash from a cashpoint machine, for example, you are performing a transaction that has to be recorded and, at some point in time, used to update the balance in your account. Some banks do not update the balance until late at night when all customers' balances are updated. Other banks use a system which updates the bank balance straight away. That is the basic difference between a batch system and a pseudo real-time system.

Other examples of transactions include:

- Buying an item in a store;
- Paying a gas bill;
- Taking out a library book;
- Applying for a driving licence;
- Enrolling on a college course;
- Applying for a University place;
- Notifying a new employer of your full name, address and bank account details;
- Clocking in and out at work.

> ➢ **Discussion: Which of the above transactions need to be processed straight away, and which can wait for a few hours or even days? Think of some more examples of transactions.**

Master files and transaction files

A **master** file is a collection of records holding information about an entity such as a person or good. For example, an employee payroll master file will contain a record for each employee, with dozens of different fields holding an employee's surname, first name, several lines of address, department, date joined, pay rate, tax code, national insurance number and bank account number. These are all fields which will not change very often – maybe once or twice a year. In addition, there will be fields which change regularly – fields such as gross pay to date (since the start of the tax year), tax paid to date, N.I. contributions to date.

A **transaction** file holds information about events occurring in the organisation. Notice that in the case of an employee payroll file, there will be basically two different kinds of transactions. There will be the weekly or fortnightly transaction file containing information about hours worked which will be used to calculate each employee's wages or salary. Every so often there will be other transactions to process – additions, changes and deletions to the file.

- When a new employee is hired, a new record must be added;
- When an employee leaves, their record is (eventually) deleted;
- An employee may change address, bank account, etc.

> ➤ **What fields might be included on a record in a stock file in a supermarket? What different types of transaction will cause data on the master file to be changed?**

Batch processing

With batch processing, a group of similar transactions are collected together over a period of time and processed in one operation. The transactions may be input to the computer over a period of time (as with cashpoint machine withdrawals) or they may be collected together as pieces of paper (like orders sent by customers to a mail order firm). These documents are then batched as described in the last chapter before being entered into the computer. Either way, the actual processing of the transactions is delayed until a convenient time, which may be later the same day, at night, or once a week, for example.

> ➤ **Discussion: Look again at the examples of transactions given above. What processing needs to be carried out in each of these examples?**

Stages in batch processing

In a typical, large-scale batch system where data is collected on paper documents (such as applications for renewal of a TV or driver's licence) the following stages are gone through:

1. The paper documents are collected into batches of say 50, checked, control totals and hash totals calculated and written on a batch header document.

2. The data is keyed in off-line (i.e. to a separate computer system used solely for data entry, not the main computer) and validated by a computer program. It is stored on a transaction file.

3. The data is verified by being entered a second time by a different keypunch operator. Any discrepancies are followed up and corrected.

4. The transaction file is transferred to the main computer. This may be a matter of carrying a magnetic tape from one room to another, or it may be transferred electronically between computers.

5. Processing begins at a scheduled time – maybe overnight when the computer is not busy dealing with on-line users. All the processing steps (beginning with step 6) can take place without operator intervention.

6. The transaction file may be sorted into the same sequence as the master file (using a sort utility program) since this may speed up the processing of the data.

7. The master file is updated.

8. Any required reports are produced.

Interactive processing

In interactive processing, data is entered and processed straight away. Organisations such as insurance companies are often able to make changes to a customer's household insurance, for example, while the customer is on the phone. The insurance clerk simply calls up details of the customer's policy on the screen, and types in any required changes which immediately update the customer's record. A report of the change would be automatically generated and a copy sent to the customer.

Some interactive systems allow queries to be made, but cannot process transactions right away. Examples include:

- Cashpoint machines which allow you to query your balance and withdraw cash but do not update the balance until late at night;

- Point-of-sale terminals which can access a stock file to look up the description and price of an article when the bar-coded label is scanned, but do not alter the quantity in stock when a sale is made. (This is done later in batch mode.)

Real-time and pseudo real-time processing

Real-time processing occurs when a computer responds instantly to events occurring. The term is normally used in the context of, say, a computer controlling the flight of an aeroplane where on-board computers respond instantly to changes in wind speed, air pressure and so on. In data processing of a more mundane nature (selling tomatoes in Sainsbury's or borrowing a library book) a system where the computer records a transaction and more or less immediately updates the master file is termed 'pseudo real-time' because a delay of a few seconds is quite acceptable, unlike genuine real-time processing.

An example of a pseudo real-time processing system is the British Airways Booking System which is operated by a central computer at Heathrow linked to thousands of British Airways agents in the UK and overseas. A person wanting to book a seat can enquire at any airline office or travel agent about a flight on a particular day, and the booking clerk can call up details on a screen. A booking can be made if a free seat is available, or alternative choices offered. Such systems need to have methods of ensuring that the same seat is not booked simultaneously by two different agents at different terminals. (This would be a function of a *database management system.*)

Criteria for choice of processing mode

The choice of whether to use a batch processing system or a pseudo real-time system depends on such factors as:

- Whether the information obtained from the system needs to be completely up-to-date at all times.

- The scale of the operation. Batch systems are well suited to very high volumes of data, when it becomes economical to have an off-line key-to-disk system for data entry.

- Cost. A real-time system is generally more expensive because of the more complex backup and recovery procedures required to cope with power failures or breakdowns in hardware.

- Computer usage. The advantage of a batch system is that it can make use of spare computer capacity overnight or at times when the computer would otherwise be idle. Batch processing is often carried out on mainframe computers.

Many applications use a combination of batch and interactive processing.

Exercises

1.   A chain of estate agents has eighty branches. Daily transactions relating to house sales, purchases and enquiries are processed using a batch system based on a mainframe computer at head-office.

   (a)   Outline the flow of data through such a batch processing system.   (4)

   (b)   The company is considering changing from the batch system to an interactive system. Describe the advantages and disadvantages of moving to an interactive system.   (4)

   NEAB IT02 Qu 3 1996

2.   A proposal has been put forward by a school's management to introduce a computerised system for recording pupils' attendance. Two different systems are under consideration:

   -   The register books currently in use will be filled in manually as they are now, and these registers will be batch processed.

   -   Pupils will record their own presence directly into the computer system.

   (a)   Describe briefly what is meant by **batch processing** in this context.   (2)

   (b)   Suggest, with a reason, how often the batch processing should take place.   (2)

   (c)   Suggest and justify a method by which pupils could record their own presence into the system.

   (3)

   (d)   Describe **one** advantage and **one** disadvantage of the proposed batch system over the other proposal.   (2)

   New question

3.   The management of a company which sells goods to customers by mail order is considering computerising the sales accounts of its customers.

   The system would record details of new orders, issue invoices, and record payments received from customers. In particular the management is considering whether to implement a batch processing system or an on-line transaction processing system.

   (a)   State **two** advantages of batch processing and **two** advantages of on-line transaction processing.   (4)

   (b)   Describe **four** criteria which should be considered when choosing the processing method.   (4)

   (c)   State **three** validation checks which should be made to ensure that customers' accounts are correctly updated when payments are received.   (3)

   (d)   Describe **two** steps which should be taken to protect against the consequences of the system failing. Explain and justify how often these steps should be taken.   (4)

   London Computing Paper 1 Qu 9 1996

4.   A nation-wide chain of retail clothing stores processes its daily sales transactions using a batch system based on a mainframe computer at a central location.

   (a)   Outline the flow of data through such a batch processing system.   (6)

   (b)   The company is considering a change from the batch system to an interactive system. Describe the advantages and disadvantages of moving to an interactive system.   (4)

   NEAB IT02 Qu 9 1999

Chapter 25 – Processing Different Types of Data

Types of data

In this chapter we will look at how computers can process data in the form of numbers, pictures and sound. All these different types of data can be represented in a computer's memory using the binary code – different combinations of 0s and 1s.

Representing numbers

We have seen that each character has a corresponding code, so that if for example the 'A' key on the keyboard is pressed, the code '01000001' will be sent to the CPU. If the key '1' is pressed, the code '00110001' will be sent to the CPU. To print the number '123', the codes for 1, 2 and 3 would be sent to the printer. (Look back at Figure 14.4 for the table showing the ASCII code representing each character.)

This is fine for input and output, but useless for arithmetic. There is no easy way of adding two numbers held in this way, and furthermore they occupy a great deal of space. Numbers which are to be used in calculations are therefore held in a different format, as **binary numbers**.

Before we look at the binary system, it is helpful to examine how our ordinary decimal or **denary** number system works. Consider for example the number '134'. These three digits represent one hundred, three tens and four ones.

100	10	1	
1	3	4	$100 + 30 + 4 = 134$

As we move from right to left each digit is worth ten times as much as the previous one. We probably use a **base 10** number system because we have ten fingers, but essentially there is no reason why some other base such as 8 or 16 could not be used.

In the binary system, as we move from right to left each digit is worth twice as much as the previous one. Thus the binary number 10000110 can be set out under column headings as follows:

128	64	32	16	8	4	2	1	
1	0	0	0	0	1	1	0	This represents $128 + 4 + 2 = 134$

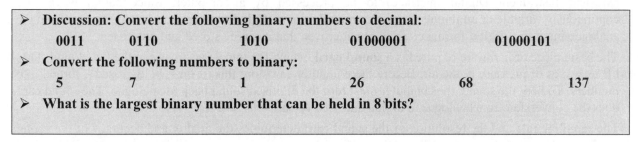

> ➢ **Discussion: Convert the following binary numbers to decimal:**
>   0011   0110   1010   01000001   01000101
> ➢ **Convert the following numbers to binary:**
>   5   7   1   26   68   137
> ➢ **What is the largest binary number that can be held in 8 bits?**

Obviously, using only one byte (8 bits) to hold a number places a severe restriction on the size of number the computer can hold. Therefore two or even four consecutive bytes are commonly used to store numbers.

Binary arithmetic

One advantage of this method of storing numbers is that arithmetic becomes easy. To see how the 'carry' system works, first count from 1 to 16 in binary. Copy and complete the table below:

Decimal	Binary	Decimal	Binary	Decimal	Binary
0	00000	6		12	
1	00001	7		13	
2	00010	8		14	
3		9		15	
4		10		16	
5		11			

We can now try some binary addition:

```
    00011001
+   01010110
=   01101111
```

> **Discussion: Convert the above sum to decimal to make sure it is correct.**
>
> **Add together the binary equivalents of 7 and 9.**

Real numbers

Numbers with a decimal point are known as **real numbers**. These numbers are represented differently inside the computer, enabling very large and very small numbers to be represented with a high degree o accuracy.

A discussion of how negative numbers and real numbers are held is beyond the scope of this course. The main thing is to have an appreciation of the fact that numbers which are going to be used in calculations have to be defined as such, and not held as 'text', or individual characters.

Digitised sound

Sound such as music or speech can be input via a microphone, CD or electronic keyboard with MIDI (Musical Instrument Digital Interface) to be processed by a computer. Since sound waves are continuously variable or **analogue** in nature, an **analogue to digital converter** is needed to transform the analogue input to a **digital** form, i.e. a binary pattern, so that it can be stored and processed.

The basic piece of hardware required is a **sound card**, which fits into a vacant slot in the PC. Sound starts off as waves of pressure in the air. Before the computer can store this, it must be digitised – turned into numbers. To hear the sound, the computer must turn the digitised sound back to analogue. The sound card does the conversion from analogue to digital and vice versa.

The sampling rate and the resolution of the sound card determines the quality and accuracy of the sound produced. The **sampling rate** tells you how often the sound card takes a digital snapshot of the sound wave – the higher the sampling rate, the greater the accuracy of the sample (see Figure 25.1). 'CD quality' sound requires a sampling rate of about 44,000 samples per second: a 44kHz frequency.

The **resolution** of the sound card determines how accurately the amplitude of the sound can be measured. An 8-bit sound board uses 8 bits of data to measure sound wave amplitude giving 256 (2^8) sound levels, whereas a 16-bit sound card using 16 bits can represent 65,536 (2^{16}) levels of amplitude.

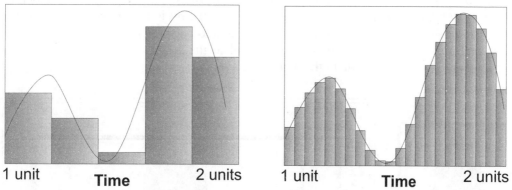

Figure 25.1: Increasing the number of samples in 1 time 'unit' (fraction of a second) means that the sound is more faithfully represented.

The sound card also has a built-in **synthesiser** for producing music and sound effects.

MIDI (Musical Instrument Digital Interface)

MIDI is an industry standard applied to electronic musical instruments as well as hardware, cables, connectors and data formats. Adding a MIDI interface to a computer allows it to communicate with, say, a MIDI keyboard, drum pad or guitar.

The MIDI data system stores all the information about each note to be played on the synthesiser, including the pitch, length, dynamics and type of sound. MIDI data in this format is very compact, taking only about 1/20th of the space on disk of even the lowest quality recorded sound samples. For example, a minute's worth of MIDI synthesised music occupies about 30Kb of disk space compared with 600Kb of low quality recorded sound.

Floppy disks and CDs containing MIDI music files can be loaded into a PC's memory and played through a sound card or synthesiser. Because the data is stored as 'instructions' rather than recorded sound, you can speed it up or slow it down, change the pitch, turn a keyboard solo into a voice or guitar solo, or alter the balance between several synthesised instruments.

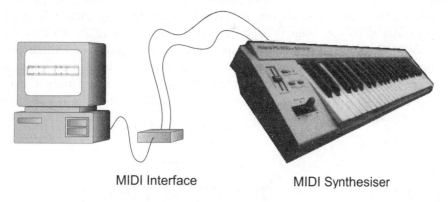

MIDI Interface   MIDI Synthesiser

Figure 25.2: A MIDI interface connects a keyboard to a computer

Bit-mapped graphics

In a bit-mapped system for displaying text and graphics on a VDU, the screen is divided up into a grid, and each square on the grid is called a **pixel** (picture element). A low resolution screen may have 320 by 240 pixels, and a high resolution screen may have 1024 by 1024 pixels or more. A monochrome screen will need just one bit in memory to represent each pixel; if the bit is 1, the pixel is on, and if it is 0, the pixel is off. On a colour screen, each pixel may correspond to one byte in memory, giving a possible 256 colours for each pixel. The memory used is additional to the RAM used for programs and data; it is supplied on a graphics 'card' specific to the type of screen.

If the screen was magnified you would be able to see the individual pixels. The more pixels to the square inch, the higher the resolution and the smoother the image.

Figure 25.3: An image on the screen is composed of thousands of pixels

Bitmapped versus vector-based graphics

There are two different kinds of graphics; **bitmapped** (also known as pixel-based) and **vector-based** (also known as object-oriented). Paint programs and scanners produce bitmapped images in the form of a collection of pixels, creating images by altering the colours or attributes of each individual pixel, and the amount of memory taken up by the image is dependent on the resolution of the display adapter where the image was first created. As a result, finished bitmap images are difficult to edit when you transfer them from one application to another. If you increase the size of a finished bitmap image, you see unsightly white spaces and jagged edges. If you greatly decrease the size of a finished bitmap image, parts of the image may 'smudge' because of the compression involved. Distortion can occur if you transfer bitmapped images to another computer that has a different display resolution.

(i)   (ii)   (iii)

Figure 25.4 - Bitmapped graphic image created in a PAINT package: (i) original size (ii) expanded (iii) shrunk

Object-oriented graphics, on the other hand, have none of these limitations. The information used to create and represent a drawing is real geometric data, rather than graphic data. For example, a line is defined by its endpoints, length, width, colour, and so on. A CAD program (and object oriented graphics software such as CorelDRAW!) then uses this information to create a representation of the line on the computer screen. Since this method of storing information has nothing to do with the resolution of a given display adapter, line-art is considered to be **device-independent**. No matter what computer you use to create an object-oriented graphic, you can stretch, scale and resize it flexibly without distortion. Object-oriented graphics also tend to create smaller files than bitmapped images because the computer does not have to store the attributes of each individual pixel.

(i)   (ii)   (iii)

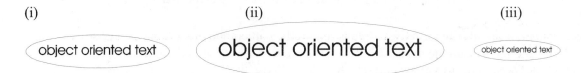

Figure 25.5 - an object oriented graphic created in CorelDRAW!: (i) original size, (ii) expanded, (iii) shrunk.

Another characteristic of CAD programs is the degree of accuracy that can be attained. Since a CAD program works with real geometric data, you can easily draw lines that meet exactly at a point, or move a line to a precise location, or draw an arc of an exact degree. When you zoom in on a portion of a line, no degradation occurs, and you can get an infinite degree of magnification. (The resolution of the laser printer may, as in this case, make the image appear less than perfectly smooth.) Using bitmapped graphics, by contrast, a line degrades when you zoom in and you see the individual pixels.

Exercises

1. Give 3 advantages of using vector-based graphics rather than bit-mapped graphics for a Computer-aided design package. (3)
   New question

2. Describe how music can be input and stored in a computer's memory. What additional hardware is required to do this? (5)
   New question

Chapter 26 – Storage Devices

Primary and secondary storage

A computer's main memory (RAM) is known as **primary storage**. In order to execute a program, the program instructions and the data on which it is to operate have to be loaded into main memory. Primary storage, however, is **volatile**; when the computer is switched off, all the contents of memory are lost. This is one good reason to perform frequent saves to disk when working on, for example, a word processed document.

A more permanent, **non-volatile** form of storage is required by all computer systems to save software and data files. Magnetic tape, magnetic disks, CD-ROM (Compact Disk Read Only Memory), and microfilm are all examples of what is known as **secondary storage**.

File processing concepts

Data stored on secondary storage is typically stored in **files**, with a file of data being defined as a collection of records. A payroll file, for example, will contain a record for each employee, and a stock file will contain a record for each stock item. The manner in which these files are **processed** depends on whether every record in the file is to be processed one after the other, or whether individual records will be processed in no particular sequence. These two methods of processing are known as sequential and random processing.

Sequential processing. Each record in the file is read. If only the 200th record on the file needs altering, the first 199 records must be read anyway, and left as they are. Sequential processing is very fast and efficient for an application such as payroll where every record needs to be processed because every person in the company will be paid.

Random processing. Each record on the file has its own address, which can either be calculated from its unique key, or held in a separate Index, so the record can be directly accessed. This type of processing is essential if for example you want to look up the price of an item of stock on a file of 20,000 items.

These two types of processing are similar to the different ways in which you would access a particular song on a cassette tape and on a CD. On a tape, you have to wind forward until you find the song you want, whereas on a CD, you just select the track and press the correct button. Note, however, that whereas you can 'process' a CD sequentially (listen to all the tracks from beginning to end) you cannot go directly to a particular song on a tape.

Similarly, some files need to be processed sequentially on some occasions, and randomly on others.

> **Discussion: Many files need to be processed sequentially on some occasions and randomly on others.**
>
> **When would the following files need to be processed (a) sequentially? (b) randomly?**
>
> **(i) Payroll file   (ii) Electricity billing file   (iii) Library book file**

Floppy disks and Zip disks

The standard 3½" floppy disk is a thin, flexible plastic disk coated in metal oxide, enclosed in a rigid plastic casing.

- A high density disk has a storage capacity of 1.44 Megabytes.

- It has a write-protect hole with a built-in tab which can be positioned to leave the notch open, which write-protects it so that it cannot be written to. Positioning the tab so that the hole is closed enables the disk for writing.

No hole in this corner indicates a double density disk, capacity 720Kb

Write-protect tab

Recording window with sliding cover

Figure 26.1: A floppy disk

- A Zip disk is slightly larger and thicker than a floppy disk, and has its own disk drive. These disks hold 100Mb or 250Mb of data and cost about £10.00 each in 2000.

How data is stored

A diskette consists of two surfaces, each of which contains typically 80 concentric circles called tracks. Each track is divided into sectors. Microcomputer disks are soft-sectored: the sectors are not present when you buy a new floppy disk, but are defined when you first format the disk. If you reformat a disk that already has data on it, all the data will be erased (although you can also do a 'quick format' which erases only the file folder).

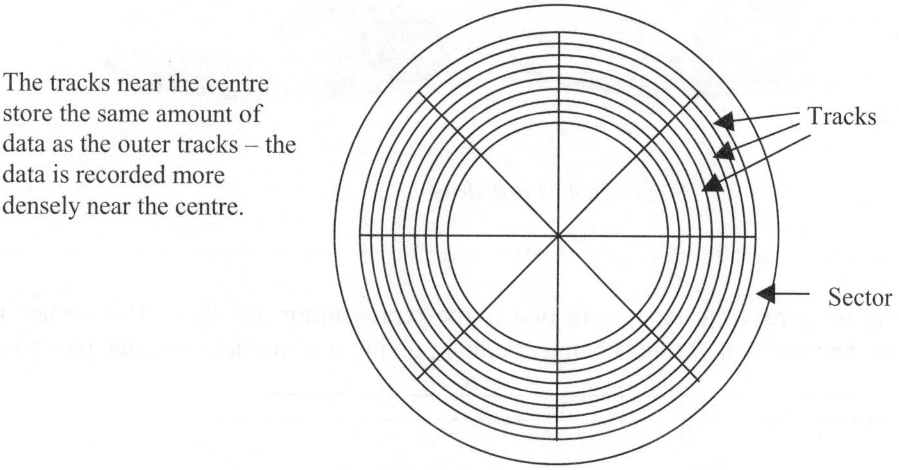

The tracks near the centre store the same amount of data as the outer tracks – the data is recorded more densely near the centre.

Tracks

Sector

Figure 26.2: Tracks and sectors on a magnetic disk

Hard disks for microcomputers

The hard disk used with PCs consist of one or more disk platters permanently sealed inside a casing. Hard disks typically have a capacity of between 500Mb and 5Gb. (1Gb = 1,000Mb.)

Each surface has its own read-write head. The heads are mounted on a single spindle so they all move in and out together.

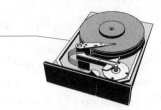

Figure 26.3: A microcomputer hard disk drive

External hard drives which can be plugged into a microcomputer are available as extra storage.

Hard disks for minis and mainframes

For large-scale applications storing huge amounts of data, several hard disk units will be required. The disks may be either fixed (sealed inside the unit) or removable. Fixed disks are faster, more reliable, and have a greater storage capacity.

As with other types of disk, data is stored on concentric tracks, with tracks being divided into sectors. All the tracks that are accessible from one position of the read-write heads form a **cylinder**; data is recorded cylinder by cylinder to minimise movement of the read-write heads, thereby minimising access time.

tracks
read-write heads move in and out together
cylinders (all the tracks accessible from one position of the read-write heads)
disks

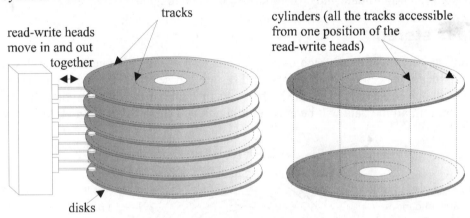

Figure 26.4: A disk drive

Magnetic tape

Data is recorded in 'frames' across the tape, with one frame representing one byte. The frames form tracks along the length of the tape, with 9 tracks being common, giving 8 data tracks and one parity track.

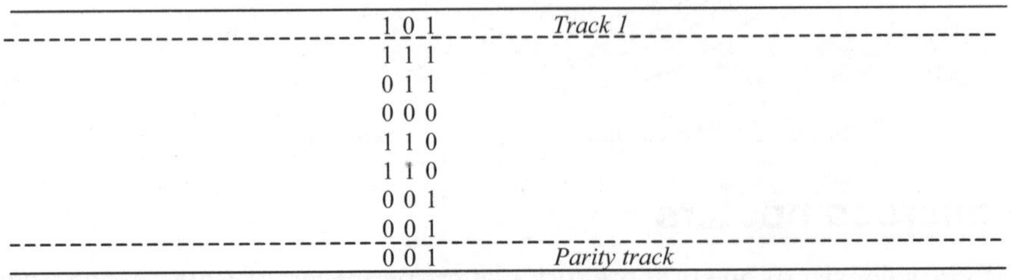

1 0 1
Track 1
1 1 1
0 1 1
0 0 0
1 1 0
1 1 0
0 0 1
0 0 1
0 0 1
Parity track

Figure 26.5: Tracks on a magnetic tape

Magnetic tape is a serial medium, meaning that an individual record can only be accessed by starting at the beginning of the tape and reading through every record until the required one is found. Likewise, it is impossible to read a record, amend it in memory, then backspace to the beginning of the block and overwrite the old record. Therefore, updating a magnetic tape file always involves copying the file to a new tape with the amendments made.

Uses of magnetic tape

Tape is a cheap and convenient medium for backup, and is also used for **archiving** past transactions or other data that may be needed again, such as for example, weather records collected over a number of years.

Cartridge tape drives are in common use for backing up the hard disk of personal computers, being much more convenient than using dozens of floppy disks. Cartridge tapes storing up to 7Gb can be bought for under £10, or about £50 for a 20Gb capacity tape.

> ➢ **Discussion: Discuss the relative advantages of hard disks, floppy disks and magnetic tape.**

CD-ROM

CD-ROMs can store around 680Mb of data, equivalent to hundreds of floppy disks. The data may be in text form, or may be in the form of graphics, photographic images, video clips or sound files. Although they do not transfer data as fast as a hard disk drive, their speed is increasing every year and is acceptable for most applications.

As the name suggests, the disks are read-only. When the master disk is created, a laser beam burns tiny holes in the surface of the disk, which (unlike a magnetic disk) has a single spiral track divided into sectors. To read data from the disk, a laser beam is reflected off the surface of the disk, detecting the presence or absence of pits which represent binary digits.

WORM disks

Write Once, Read Many optical laser disks look similar to CD-ROM disks, but they are often gold rather than silver in colour. An end-user company can use these disks to write their own material, typically for archiving or storing say, graphic or photographic images which will not be changed.

These disks are also widely used for pirated software; whereas silver CDs are pressed in factories, gold CDs are usually written one at a time on PCs in garages and back bedrooms. A £5 blank disk can hold £20,000 worth of software and sell for £50 to £80, and they are sometimes used by less reputable PC manufacturers who install the software on their PCs to make a more attractive deal for the unknowing customer. However, because there is a lot of competition among pirates, these CDs sometimes carry viruses which can cause havoc on a hard drive.

Magneto-optical disks

Magneto-optical disks integrate optical and laser technology to enable read and write storage. A 5½" disk can store up to 1,000Mb. These disks may in the future replace current magnetic disks, but at present the technology is still developing and the disks are too expensive, slow and unreliable to be in widespread use.

Microfiche

COM (Computer Output on Microfilm) devices are used to prepare microfiche, a 4" by 6" hard-copy film that is sometimes seen in libraries and bookshops being used for reference purposes. Each microfiche sheet is divided into as many as 270 frames each containing a page of information which can be read using a special viewer. COM is also extensively used for archiving material such as old cheques or income tax returns.

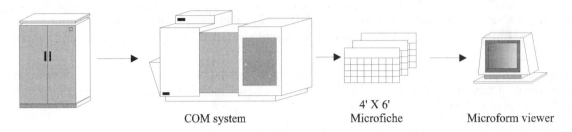

COM system   4' X 6'
                 Microfiche   Microform viewer

Figure 26.6: Computer Output to Microfilm

> ➢ **Discussion: What are some of the applications of CD-ROM? Why is CD-ROM particularly suitable for these applications?**

Exercises

1. Why do many software manufacturers now prefer to sell their software on CD-ROM rather than on floppy disk? (2)
   NEAB Computing Paper 1 Qu 1 1997

2. Give **one** appropriate use with clear justification for:
   (a) floppy disks;
   (b) hard disks;
   (c) CD-ROMs (6)
   AEB Computing Paper 1 Qu 9 1997

3. WORM (Write Once Read Many times) is an acronym sometimes used for certain types of data storage.
   Give **one** example of this type of storage and describe a typical use for your example.
   Give **one** feature of WORM type of storage which makes it appropriate for the example you have given. (3)
   AEB Computing Paper 1 Qu 5 1995

4. Although large disk storage devices are now readily available for computer systems, the use of magnetic tape is still widespread.
   Describe **two** distinct uses of magnetic tape and explain its suitability in each case. (4)
   London Computing Paper 1 Qu 8 1995

5. (i) Describe, with the aid of a diagram, the layout of data on one surface of a magnetic disk pack. (2)
   (ii) Why is data storage on a magnetic disk pack organised in cylinders? (2)
   (iii) Why is it necessary to format a magnetic disk before it can be used? (2)
   NEAB Computing AS Qu 7 1995

Chapter 27 – Security of Data

Issues of privacy

Everyone has a right to privacy – the right not to have details about our lives to be held or circulated without our knowledge. Data of a personal nature are regularly collected by numerous different organisations – for example:

- **Employers** hold personnel records that include data on address, age, qualifications, salary, sick leave, dependents and so on;

- **Stores** hold details on credit card payments, account history, items purchased;

- **Banks** hold details on salary, income and withdrawals, direct debits to various organisations;

- **Insurance companies** hold details of property, cars, accidents, claims and health.

The list is endless, and modern technology has made it possible not only to store vast quantities of data about individuals, but to view it from anywhere in the world, and to correlate data held in different databanks to produce a comprehensive profile of an individual.

Case study: TRW Information Service

TRW is a company that sells thirty-five million credit reports each year to 24,000 subscribers in the United States. Every month TRW receives data from thousands of companies containing the status of their customer accounts. They then process and organise this data to build up a comprehensive credit history of each person, so that when a customer wants to buy an item on credit from a store who subscribes to the TRW service, they can carry out an immediate credit check.

The downside is that TRW do not carry out any checks on the accuracy of their data. Each year some 350,000 people register formal complaints about errors in TRW reports and about 100,000 of these result in changes to the data held by TRW. But how many errors pass unnoticed, resulting in people being denied credit completely erroneously?

Threats to information systems

Computer-based information systems are vulnerable to crime and abuse, natural disaster and human error. In this chapter we'll look at some of the ways that an organisation can protect the **integrity** of data (by preventing inaccurate data entry, malicious or accidental alteration), and simple measures that can be taken to protect the **security** of data from theft or destruction.

Data integrity

This refers to the **correctness** of the data. The data held in a computer system may become incorrect, corrupted or of 'poor quality' in many different ways and at many stages during data processing.

1. **Errors on input**. Data that is keyed in may be wrongly transcribed. A batch of transaction data could go astray, or be keyed in twice by mistake.

2. **Errors in operating procedure**. An update program could for example be run twice in error and quantities on a master file would then be updated twice.

3. **Program errors could lead to corruption of files**. A new system may have errors in it that will not surface for some time, or errors may be introduced during program maintenance.

Standard clerical procedures

To protect against input and operating procedure errors, standard procedures may be documented and followed for both input and output.

Input

- Data entry must be limited to authorised personnel only;
- In large volume data entry, data may be verified (keyed in twice by different operators) to guard against keying errors;
- Data control totals must be used wherever possible to verify the completeness and accuracy of the data, and to guard against duplicate or illegal entry.

Output

- All output should be inspected for reasonableness and any inconsistencies investigated;
- Printed output containing sensitive information should be shredded after use.

> ➢ **Discussion: What are 'data control totals'? Give an example of a data control total that could be used by an Examining Board entering marks from students' 'A' Level scripts.**

Write-protecting disks

A simple measure such as write-protecting disks and tapes so that they cannot be accidentally overwritten can be effective in guarding against operator error. Both disks and tapes have write-protect mechanisms.

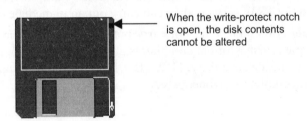

When the write-protect notch is open, the disk contents cannot be altered

Figure 27.1: Write-protecting a floppy disk

User IDs and passwords

Each user in an organisation who is permitted to access the company database is issued with a user ID and a password, which will normally give them a certain level of access rights set by the database manager. Common rules issued by companies regarding passwords include the following:

- Passwords must be at least 6 characters;
- Password display must be automatically suppressed on screen or printed output;
- Files containing passwords must be encrypted;
- All users must ensure that their password is kept confidential, not written down, not made up of easily guessed words and is changed regularly, at least every 3 months.

> ➢ **Discussion: Describe several ways by which a password may become known to an unauthorised person.**

Access rights

Even authorised users do not normally have the right to see all the data held on a company database. In a hospital, for example, receptionists may have the right to view and change some patient details such as name, address and appointments but may not access the patient's medical records. In a stock control system, salesmen may be permitted to view the price, description and quantity in stock of a particular item, but not to change any of the details held.

Access rights to a particular set of data could typically be set to Read-Only, Read/Write, or No Access. This ensures that users within a company can only gain access to data which they are permitted to see, and can only change data on the database if they are authorised to do so.

Likewise, the computer can also be programmed to allow access to particular data only from certain terminals, and only at certain times of day. The terminal in the database administrator's office may be the only terminal from which changes to the structure of a database may be made. An 'access directory' specifying each user's access rights is shown in Figure 27.2.

Access Profile: User ID 26885

Data	*Access right*	*Terminal number*	*Permitted time*	*Security level*
Customer Number	Read only	04,05	0830-1800	7
Credit Limit	Read Write	04	0830-1800	10
Payment	Read/Write	04,05	1830-1700	7
Credit Rating	No Access			12

Figure 27.2: A security access table as part of a database

Securing against fraudulent use or malicious damage

Organisations are often exposed to the possibility of fraud, deliberate corruption of data by disgruntled employees or theft of software or data which may fall into the hands of competitors. Measures to counteract these risks include the following:

- Careful vetting of prospective employees.

- Immediate removal of employees who have been sacked or who hand in their resignation, and cancellation of all passwords and authorisations.

- 'Separation of duties'; i.e. trying to ensure that it would take the collusion of two or more employees to be able to defraud the company. The functions of data preparation, computer operations and other jobs should be separate, with no overlap of responsibility.

- Prevention of unauthorised access by employees and others to secure areas such as computer operations rooms, by means of machine readable cards or badges or other types of locks.

- The use of passwords to gain access to the computer system from terminals.

- Educating staff to be aware of possible breaches of security, and to be alert in preventing them or reporting them. This can include politely challenging strangers with a "May I help you?" approach, not leaving output lying around, machines logged on, or doors unlocked.

- Appointing a security manager and using special software which can monitor all terminal activity. Such software can enable the security manager to see, either with or without users' knowledge, everything being typed on any screen in a network. It will also record statistics such as number of logins at each terminal, hours of login time, number of times particular programs or databases were accessed and so on. It will even log the security manager's activities!

Protection against viruses

Steps can be taken which minimise the risk of suffering damage from viruses. These include:

- Making sure that all purchased software comes in sealed, tamper-proof packaging;
- Not permitting floppy disks containing software or data to be removed from or brought into the office. (This is a sackable offence in some companies);
- Using anti-virus software to check all floppy disks before use. (This is sometimes known as a 'sheep-dip station'.)

Biometric security measures

Passwords are only effective if people use them properly: if obvious passwords are used, or people tell them to their friends or write them down on a piece of paper blue-tacked to the computer, they are useless. *Biometric* methods of identifying an authorised user include fingerprint recognition techniques, voice recognition and face recognition. One such system uses an infra-red scanner to capture the unique pattern of blood vessels under the skin, and can even differentiate between identical twins by comparing the scan with the one on disk stored for each person.

Case study: Iris recognition technology

The Nationwide Building Society started customer trials in March 1998 of 'iris recognition technology' – cash machines which are capable of recognising an individual's unique 'eye-print'. Special cameras are installed at the counter of the Swindon Head Office branch and at the cash machine. The camera captures a digital image of a person's iris, and from then on, every time a customer uses the cash machine, the system verifies their iris record within seconds.

However, retina verification can be unreliable, as checking the iris requires a person to look into a device at exactly the same angle each time.

Communications security

Telecommunications systems are vulnerable to hackers who discover a user ID and password and can gain entry to a database from their own computer. One way of preventing this is to use a callback procedure so that when a remote user logs in, the computer automatically calls them back at a prearranged telephone number to verify their access request before allowing them to log on.

Data encryption can also be used to 'scramble' highly sensitive or confidential data before transmission.

Disaster planning

The cost of lack of planning for computer failure can be ruinous. IBM estimates that 70% of organisations that experience a failure (caused by fire, flood, power failure, malice etc) cease operating within 18 months. The main consequence of a computer failure is loss of business, but other problems include loss of credibility, cashflow interruptions, poorer service to customers and loss of production.

Case study: Safe as Houses

One summer evening last year, the heart of Tony Pidgeley's computer system was stolen. "Someone walked into the office at 6pm and walked away with the network server. Incredible!" he says.

The consequences could have been catastrophic for Pidgeley's construction business. "We would have lost everything – all our accounts and land acquisition programmes," he says.

The firm was saved from disaster by a small cartridge no bigger than a couple of cigarette packets. Inside was a tape containing a backup copy, made the previous evening, of everything on the server's 1Gb hard disk. All that was lost was one day's data input, which was re-keyed in a couple of hours. The firm's PC dealer worked through the night to set up a replacement server, and insurance covered the hardware cost.

The firm's backup is run every evening. It takes most of the night, but this does not matter since it can run unattended. The next day, somebody takes the tape home, in case fire or flood should destroy the entire office. Once a month, a tape is checked to make sure the backup is working properly.

Source: Paul Bray, The Sunday Times 19 October 1997

➤ **Discussion: What are the main points of Tony's backup strategy?**

Many companies have comprehensive emergency plans, and even after suffering severe bomb or fire damage, can be up and running after a day or two. They generally subscribe to disaster recovery services offered by companies specialising in this field. Smaller companies may not need such elaborate backup and recovery procedures, but a backup system is still vital.

Periodic backups

The most common technique used to ensure that data is not lost is to make **periodic backups**, by copying files regularly and keeping them in a safe place. This scheme has several weaknesses:

- All updates to a file since the last backup may be lost;
- The system may need to be shut down during backup operations;
- Backups of large files can be extremely time-consuming;
- When a failure occurs, recovery from the backup can be even more time-consuming.

A **benefit** of periodic backups is that files which may have become fragmented by additions and deletions can be reorganised to occupy contiguous space, usually resulting in much faster access time.

An important feature of all backup systems is the safe storage of the backup copies: it is usually necessary to store one backup copy in a fire-proof safe in the building, and another copy off-site.

Backup strategies

The simplest backup strategy for a small business is to copy the contents of a computer's hard disk at the end of each day to a tape or removable disk.

However, it is not necessary to copy software programs except when they are changed, so a better solution is to keep data files in separate directories from the software and selectively back up only certain directories.

If this still results in backing up huge quantities of data, it can be reduced by backing up only those files which have changed since the last backup – an 'incremental backup'. Backup devices come with special software that helps you to select which files to copy, when and how.

Backup hardware

- For small quantities of data, removable disks are the simplest. Iomega's Zip drive costs around £100 and takes 100Mb disks similar to floppy disks costing £10 each.
- SuperDisk drives from manufacturers such as Panasonic take 120Mb disks and can also read ordinary 1.44Mb floppy disks.

- For larger backups, magnetic tape is the preferred medium. Low-cost tape drives such as Hewlett-Packard's Colorado range and Iomega's Ditto range costing around £100 use 2Gb tape cartridges costing around £20. An 8Gb drive costs around £250.

- A rewriteable optical disk drive costs around £280 and holds about 650Mb.

- RAID (Redundant Array of Inexpensive Disks) – see below.

Backing up on-line databases

When a database is on-line and being constantly updated, precautions have to be taken to ensure that data is not lost in the event of hardware failure such as a disk head crash. Methods used include:

- **Transaction logging.** Information about every updating transaction is recorded on a separate transaction file. A *before-image* and an *after-image* of any record being updated is saved so that if part of the database is destroyed by a disk failure, an up-to-date copy can be created from the backup copy together with the transaction log using a utility program.

- **Using RAID (Redundant Array of Inexpensive Disks).** These devices use a technology which enables data to be written simultaneously to several disks. Three copies of the database may be held, two in the same room and one at a remote location, and all three copies are kept completely up-to-date. Then if one disk fails, the data is still safe on the other two disks.

Factors in a backup strategy

When a company is planning its backup strategy, there are several factors to be taken into account. For example:

- **Frequency of backups.** Many organisations, such as a school or college, find it sufficient to back up data once or twice a day. On-line databases (for example in a hospital or airline booking system) need to be backed up constantly to prevent any loss of data.

- **Backup medium.** Magnetic tape is cheap, compact and can store large amounts of data, and is used by many organisations to back up data from hard disks every night. Smaller amounts of data may be backed up on removable disks using a Zip drive.

- **Location of backup storage.** The data needs to be held in a secure location in case of fire or burglary. Many organisations have a fireproof safe for the latest backups, with another set of backups being stored off-site.

- **Number of generations to be kept.** A typical strategy is to:
  - keep the daily backups for a week;
  - keep Friday's backup for a month;
  - keep one backup each month for a year;
  - give each tape or disk a serial number and keep a log book, to prevent mix-ups.

- **Responsibility for implementing the backup strategy.** Although the regular backup routine may be performed by a computer operator or an office worker, a senior manager should have overall responsibility for ensuring that all aspects of the backup strategy are properly implemented.

- **Testing of recovery procedures**. At regular intervals the effectiveness of the backup strategy needs to be tested to ensure that the organisation can recover quickly from loss of data. It would be rather tragic to discover that the magnetic tapes that were supposed to store the backup data were in fact blank!

Recovery procedures

A contingency plan needs to be developed to allow rapid recovery from major disruptions. In addition to file back-up procedures, it is necessary to:

- Identify alternative compatible equipment and security facilities, or implement a service agreement which provides replacement equipment when needed. This may also include putting up temporary office space;

- Have provision for alternative communication links.

Exercises

1. An on-line information retrieval system holds confidential personal data.
   (a) What precautions should be taken to
       (i) minimise unauthorised access
       (ii) detect unauthorised access? (4)
   (b) Why might different users be given different access privileges? (2)
   (c) Explain how the data should be protected from corruption. (4)
   NEAB IT01 Qu 6 Sample Paper

2. A company equips its sales staff with portable notebook computers. The I.T. department feels that a set of 'procedures' is required to ensure the integrity of the data and software held on the notebooks. Suggest **four** different items that the company might include in its set of procedures. (4)
   NEAB IT01 Qu 7 1997

3. A computer system, that is normally in use 24 hours a day, holds large volumes of different types of data on disk packs. The main types of data stored are:
   - Applications software that changes only occasionally during maintenance;
   - Data master files that are updated regularly every week;
   - Transaction files which are created daily;
   - Database files which are changing constantly.

   It is vital that these different types of files can be quickly recovered in the event of file corruption.

   Outline a suitable back up strategy for each of these types of file explaining what data is backed up and when, the procedures to be followed, and the media and hardware needed. (8)
   NEAB IT02 Sample Paper Qu 8

4. Describe briefly **three** different types of threat to data held in a computer system, and methods to combat each of these threats. (6)
   New question

5. A small company holds records of customer accounts, invoices and payments, stock records and mailing list on a hard disk on one of three networked PCs. Describe procedures that they should adopt to ensure that this data is not lost or corrupted. (10)
   New question

Chapter 28 – Output Devices

Printers

Printers come in all shapes and sizes, and the type of printer chosen will depend on several factors such as:

- **volume of output** – for high volumes, a fast, heavy-duty printer is required;

- **quality of print required** – business letters and reports to clients, for example, will require a high quality print, probably on special headed stationery;

- **location of the printer** – if the printer is going to be situated in a busy office, the noise that it makes is an important consideration;

- **requirement for multiple copies** – some printers cannot produce multiple copies;

- **requirements for colour** – does the output need to be in colour?

Dot matrix printer

A dot matrix printer is an **impact printer**, producing its image by striking the paper through a ribbon. Its print head consists of a number of small pins, varying between 9 and 24 depending on the manufacturer. A 24 pin print head will produce a better quality of print than a 9 pin print head because the dots are closer together.

As the print head moves across the page, one or more pins strike the ribbon and make a dot on the paper. The figure below shows how the letter F is produced.

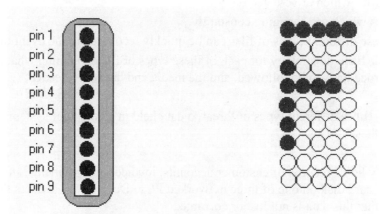

Figure 28.1 — Dot matrix print head

In order to produce 'near letter quality' (**NLQ**) print, a line is printed twice, with the print head being shifted along very slightly in the second printing so that the spaces between the dots are filled in. The disadvantage of this technique is that the document then takes approximately twice as long to print. Many dot matrix printers are 'bidirectional', meaning that they can print in either direction, thus eliminating the need to start printing each line from the left hand side of the page.

Dot matrix printers are extremely versatile, with most of them able to print in condensed, standard and enlarged mode, in 'bold' or normal print.

Many dot matrix printers have a graphics mode that enables them to print pictures and graphs by activating individual print head pins separately or in combination to produce any shape or line. With appropriate software any typeface can be produced, and using a special 4-colour ribbon (red, yellow, blue and black), colour output for, say, a graphical presentation can be produced. However the quality of colour is not as good as that produced by other types of colour printer.

One of the main drawbacks of a dot matrix printer is its noise; in an office environment it can be an irritating distraction. Covers can be obtained to cut down the noise, but it is still audible.

Ink jet printers

Ink jet printers are a popular type of non-impact printer, with prices ranging between £150 and £1500; a popular colour inkjet printer such as Hewlett Packard's DeskJet 690C costs around £150. They are compact and quiet, and offer resolution almost as good as a laser printer. However, they are slow in operation; on average 3 pages per minute are printed, but a complex combination of text and colour can take several minutes for a single sheet.

Inkjet printers such as the HP Deskjet fire a droplet of ink at the page by boiling it in a microscopic tube and letting steam eject the droplet. Heating the ink can damage the colour pigments and matching the ink chemistry to the broad range of papers used in the office is a technical challenge. Large areas of colour can get wet, buckle, and the ink may smear. Printing an ink jet colour page can cost as much as 75p if all colour inks are supplied in a single cartridge; more thrifty printers will use separate red, blue, yellow and black cartridges which can be individually replaced. Although ordinary photocopy paper can be used, special smooth-coated paper may produce a more satisfactory result.

Figure 28.2: A Canon Bubble Jet Printer BJC7000

Laser printers

Laser printers are becoming increasingly popular, with prices dropping rapidly to under £500 for a PostScript printer suitable for desktop publishing applications. Laser printers use a process similar to a photocopying machine, with toner (powdered ink) being transferred to the page and then fused onto it by heat and pressure. A laser printer produces output of very high quality at a typical speed in the region of ten pages per minute, and is virtually silent in operation. The main running expenses are the toner, which costs about £75 for a cartridge lasting for around 5,000 copies, and a maintenance contract which is typically up to £300pa.

A high quality colour laser printer may cost between £4,000 and £5,000.

Plotters

A plotter is an output device used to produce high quality line drawings such as building plans or electronic circuits. They are generally classified as pen (vector plotters) or penless (raster plotters). The former use pens to draw images using point-to-point data, moving the pen over the paper. Pen plotters are low in price and hold a large share of the plotter market.

Penless plotters include electrostatic plotters, thermal plotters and laser plotters. They are generally used where drawings of high densities are required, for example drawings of machines, printed circuit boards or maps. Colour electrostatic plotters are increasingly being used in, for example, assembly drawings of machines and building plans, making them easier to read and understand.

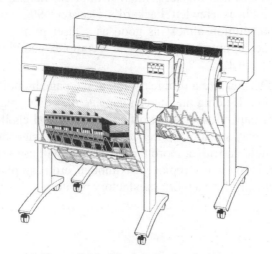

Photograph courtesy of Hewlett Packard Company

Figure 28.3: Hewlett-Packard plotters

Visual display unit (VDU)

A VDU has three basic attributes: size, colour and resolution. It has its own fixed amount of RAM associated with it to store the image being displayed on the screen, and the amount of RAM it has will determine the resolution and the maximum number of colours that can be displayed. Note that:

- The resolution is determined by the number of pixels (addressable picture elements) used to represent a full-screen image;

- the number of colours that can be displayed is determined by how many bits are used to represent each pixel. If only one bit is used to represent each pixel, then only two colours can be represented. To display 256 colours, 8 bits per pixel are required, and to display 65,536 (i.e. 2^{16}) colours, 16 bits (2 bytes) per pixel are needed. It is usually possible to adjust both the resolution and the number of colours - *if a high resolution is selected you won't be able to have as many colours because of the memory limitations of the VDU.*

For example, if a resolution of 800x600 pixels is selected together with 65,536 colours, the amount of video RAM required will be 800x600x2 bytes = 960,000 bytes, i.e. almost 1Mb. If 1Mb is all the video RAM supplied by the manufacturer, the resolution cannot be increased to say, 1000x800 unless the number of bytes used to represent each pixel is reduced, thus limiting the number of colours which can be displayed.

On a PC, the number of colours and the resolution of the screen can be adjusted on the Display option of the Control Panel.

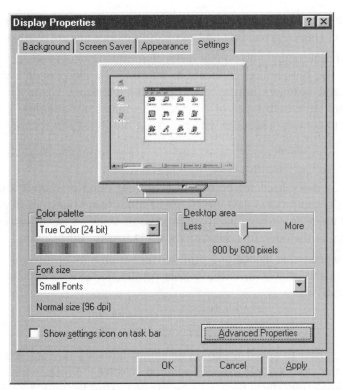

Figure 28.4: Adjusting the number of colours and resolution of a PC

Communicating with the CPU

Data, addresses and control signals are transferred between the various components of a computer by means of **buses**. The name originates from the analogy of carrying many people at once around town in a double-decker, but in this case it is simply a set of wires connecting components. There are two sorts of buses:

- **internal buses** which connect the various registers and internal components of the CPU
- **external buses** which connect the CPU to main memory and to the input-output units.

Input and output units vary enormously in their speed, mode of operation, code conversion requirements and so on, and so cannot be connected directly to the CPU by means of a simple bus. Instead, each device comes with its own **interface unit**, which in turn is connected to the bus.

Parallel and serial data transmission

Data may be transferred in either **parallel** or **serial** mode. A parallel bus with 8 lines can transfer one byte at a time, whereas a serial bus transfers one bit at a time. A commonly used serial interface is the 25-pin RS232C interface, used for example to connect an external modem to the CPU. A mouse commonly uses a 9-pin serial interface.

Figure 28.5: Different types of serial interface connectors

Although only one line is used for transmitting data, other lines are needed for control signals, timing signals, secondary data channels, grounding and so on. Some lines are not used at all.

Transferring data in parallel mode is obviously faster than transferring in serial mode because 8 bits are transferred simultaneously, but parallel connections can only be made over a short distance of two or three metres. Printers and scanners normally use parallel interfaces when the printer is close to the computer. Many printers have both types of connector so that if for example the parallel port on your computer is being used to connect a scanner, you could use the serial port for the printer.

Buffering

A buffer is an area of memory used for holding data during input or output transfers to and from I-O devices. Because the CPU can process data thousands of times faster than, say, a printer can print it, input and output are handled independently of the main processor. Once an I-O operation is initiated, a special I-O channel takes control of the operation, leaving the CPU free for other tasks.

Information that is to be printed is placed in a print buffer which may be several megabytes long, located either in the computer or the printer, or both. A laser printer, for example, comes with its own memory buffer of say 1 or 2 megabytes.

Spooling

Spooling is a technique used to speed up communication between devices which operate at differing speeds. Output to a printer, for example, may be spooled (written) to disk, which is a high-speed device. When the printer becomes free, the output will be printed. This technique enables several users on a network to share a single printer without their output getting muddled up. Each user's output is spooled to a different position on the disk, and printed using a queuing system.

Installing hardware devices such as a printer

When you add a new device such as a printer, scanner, mouse, soundcard or videodisk player to a computer system, you have to install a piece of software called a **device driver** to control the device. For example, when you attach a new printer to a computer, you have to do the following before you can print anything:

- Install the printer-driver file for the printer;
- Select the port you want to assign the printer to.

A printer-driver file is a piece of software that specifies information about the printer, including details about printer features, descriptions of fonts (sizes and styles) and control sequences that the printer uses to produce various formats. When you give an instruction to print, the driver translates the information about fonts, formatting, highlighting etc. into a form that the printer can understand.

Exercises

1. A printer fails to work or perform as the user expects when a document has been sent to be printed. The user has checked that the on-line light of the printer is illuminated and the printer paper is correctly inserted. Give **two** other possible reasons why the printing process failed. (2)

   AEB Computing Paper 1 Qu 1 1997

2. Explain the relationship between the resolution of a screen and the number of colours that it can display. (3)

   New question

3. (a) Describe the process of producing a printout when a print spooler is used.   (3)
    (b) Explain why a print spooler is desirable in
        (i)   a multi-user system,
        (ii) a single-user system.   (4)

NEAB Computing Paper 1 Qu 10 1996

4. When installing or configuring a particular word processing package, the documentation states that the correct printer driver must also be installed. What is a printer driver, and why is it necessary? (4)

NEAB IT02 Qu 2 1997

Chapter 29 – Network Environments

Communications networks

A Local Area Network (LAN) is a collection of computers and peripherals confined to one building or site, connected together by a common electrical connection. A LAN can be connected to other LANs, or to a Wide Area Network.

A WAN connects computers or networks over a wide geographical area; for example different sites, towns or continents.

Advantages and disadvantages of LANs

A network has several advantages over a collection of stand-alone microcomputers:

- It allows the sharing of resources such as disk storage, printers, image scanners, modems and central servers;

- It allows sharing of information held on disk drives accessible by all users;

- It is easier to store application programs on one computer and make them available to all users rather than having copies individually installed on each computer;

- It allows electronic mail to be sent between users;

- It is easier to set up new users and equipment;

- It allows the connection of different types of computer which can communicate with each other.

The main **disadvantages** of networks are:

- Users become dependent on them; if for example the network file server develops a fault, then many users will be unable to run application programs. (On many sites, a back-up file server can be switched into action if the main server fails).

- If the network stops operating then it may not be possible to access various hardware and software resources.

- The efficiency of a network is very dependent on the skill of the system manager. A badly managed network may operate less efficiently than stand-alone machines.

- It is difficult to make the system secure from hackers, novices or industrial espionage.

- As traffic increases on the network the performance degrades unless it is properly designed.

Server-based vs peer-to-peer networks

There are two types of local area network: a server-based network is generally used when there are more than 3 or 4 computers on the network. A peer-to-peer network is suitable for a small company with a few computers in different offices because data can easily be accessed from any computer, and documents can be printed on any of the printers connected to any computer, for example.

In *client-server architecture*, different devices on the network are treated as clients or servers. The client devices send requests for service, such as printing or retrieval of data, to specific server devices that perform the requested processing. For example, the client devices might consist of twenty workstations in a room, and the server devices might be a laser printer and a computer dedicated to managing the network (the file server).

Peer-to-peer architecture is an alternative to client-server for small computer networks. In peer-to-peer, each workstation can communicate directly with every other workstation on the network without going through a server. Peer-to-peer is most appropriate when the network users mostly do their own work but occasionally need to share data or communicate with each other. One disadvantage of this arrangement is that if the workstation from which a user wishes to retrieve data is switched off, the data cannot be retrieved!

Any sort of network requires maintenance – someone has to be responsible for ensuring that:

- Response time is adequate;
- Hardware is upgraded when necessary;
- The required software is loaded;
- Software is upgraded when necessary and users are kept informed of changes;
- A system of regular backups is adhered to;
- Network security is maintained.

The differences between the client-server and peer-to-peer networks are summarised in the table below:

Server-based networks	*Peer-to-peer networks*
Example: Novell's NetWare	***Example: Microsoft Windows for Workgroups***
A central backing store is available to all users.	Storage facilities are distributed throughout the network.
Software is centrally held and shared. The server distributes the programs and data to the other microcomputers in the network (the 'clients') as they request them. Some processing tasks are performed by the desktop computer; others are handled by the file server. This is **termed 'client-server'** architecture. The use of servers provides the network with more speed and power, but adds expense and complication.	Copies of software may be held on individual machines. Peer-to-peer networks provide basic network services such as software, file and print sharing, and are less expensive and less difficult to administer than those set up with servers. They are most appropriate for smaller businesses that do not need the power and speed of client-server architecture.
User IDs, passwords and access levels are controlled by the central computer.	Security is not centrally controlled.
Backup facilities are centralised; data and information held centrally are backed up regularly.	Backup is the responsibility of individual computer users.
All users are reliant on the service provided by the central facility. If the central computer goes down, all users are affected.	No reliance on a central computer.
All communication takes place through the central computer. Computers on the network may be of different types (from different manufacturers) and the central node computer controls the communications protocol.	The individual computers on the network must have software to control communication with other computers of the same or different types on the network.

Figure 29.1: Comparison of client-server and peer-to-peer networks

Wide area networks

When the devices in a network are close together, for example in the same building, they can be linked by means of cables, and this is what is meant by a Local Area Network. However, when devices are separated by more than a few hundred yards, data has to be sent over a communications link (e.g. telephone line) and extra equipment such as a modem is required.

A wide area network is a collection of computers spread over a wide geographical area, possibly spanning several continents. Communication may be via microwave, satellite link or telephone line, or a combination of these. The use of global networks (including the Internet) has increased enormously over the past few years, owing to:

- Changeover of telephone networks from old-style analogue to high-speed digital technology;
- Reduction in cost of connecting to and using networks;
- Improved compression techniques which allow faster transmission of text and graphics.

Communications links

In the UK, British Telecom, Mercury and other telecom operators provide services and data links. Telephone lines may be either:

- Public lines, on which the cost of sending data depends on the length of time taken;
- Private or leased lines, for which there is a fixed annual fee and the line can be used as often as needed for no extra cost.

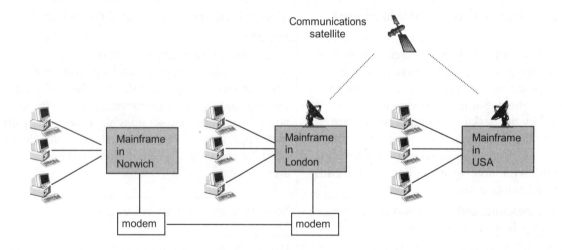

Figure 29.2: Satellite transmission

Communications media

Communication may take place over a combination of different media:

- Twisted pair (copper cable), used in much of the telephone network;
- Coaxial cable – high quality, well insulated cable that can transmit data at higher speeds;
- Fibre optic cable through which pulses of light, rather than electricity, are sent in digital form;
- Microwave – similar to radio waves. Microwave stations cannot be much more than 30 miles apart because of the earth's curvature as microwaves travel in straight lines. Mobile telephones use microwave radio links.

- Communications satellite, using one of the hundreds of satellites now in geosynchronous orbit about 22,000 miles above the earth. (Geosynchronous orbit means that they are rotating at the same speed as the earth, and are therefore stationary relative to earth.)

ISDN lines

The amount of data that can be sent over a line depends partly on the **bandwidth**, which is the range of frequencies that the line can carry. The greater the bandwidth, the greater the rate at which data can be sent, as several messages can be transmitted simultaneously.

A network that is capable of sending voice, video and computer data is called an **Integrated Services Digital Network (ISDN)**, and this requires a high bandwidth.

Bridges and gateways

A **bridge** is a connection between two local area networks. Wide area networks may be connected through a system of **gateways**, a gateway being a computer which acts as a point of connection between different networks.

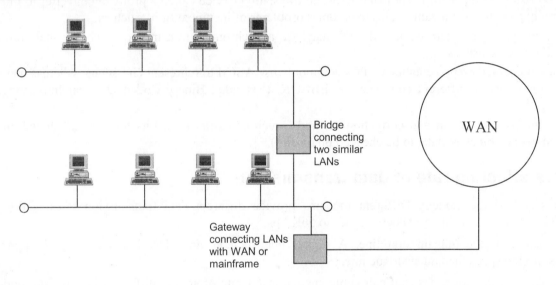

Figure 29.3: Local area networks connected to a central computer

Modems

Telephone lines were originally designed for speech, which is transmitted in analogue or wave form. In order for digital data to be sent over a telephone line, it must first be converted to analogue form and then converted back to digital at the other end. This is achieved by means of a modem (MOdulator/ DEModulator) at either end of the line.

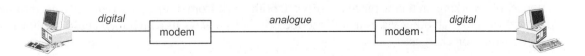

Figure 29.4: A modem converts digital signals to analogue and vice versa

Synchronous and asynchronous transmission

With **asynchronous** transmission, one character at a time is sent, with each character being preceded by a start bit and followed by a stop bit. A parity bit is also usually included as a check against incorrect transmission. This type of transmission is usually used by PCs, and is fast and economical for relatively small amounts of data.

In **synchronous** transmission mode, timing signals (usually the computer's internal clock) control the rate of transmission and there is no need for start and stop bits to accompany each character. Mainframe computers usually use synchronous transmission. It is less error-prone than asynchronous transmission.

Protocol

In order to allow equipment from different suppliers to be networked, a strict set of rules (**protocols**) has been devised covering standards for physical connections, cabling, mode of transmission, speed, data format, error detection and correction. Any equipment which uses the same communication protocol can be linked together.

It is also possible to link equipment using a special translation device called a protocol converter to link, for example, a PC to a mainframe. This overcomes problems of incompatibility such as:

- different types of transmission – the PC may use asynchronous transmission, and the mainframe synchronous transmission;

- different character representations – PCs commonly use ASCII to represent characters, whereas many mainframes use a different code such as EBCDIC (Extended Binary Coded Decimal Interchange Code);

- different error detection and correction methods (such as extra check bits that are calculated and added to each block of data, to be checked on receipt).

Factors affecting rate of data transmission

- The speed of the modem. Different modems provide different data transmission rates, varying typically between 9K bps (bits per second) to 56K bps.

- The nature of the transmission line. A digital line such as an ISDN line has a much higher transmission speed than an analogue line.

- The type of cable used. Twisted pair cable has a transfer rate of about 10Mbps, whereas fibre optic cable is about 10 times as fast.

- The type of transmission, synchronous or asynchronous.

Exercises

1. A local surgery uses a number of stand-alone computer systems to manage patient records, appointments, staff pay and all financial accounts. The surgery manager is considering changing to a local area network.

    Compare the relative advantages of stand-alone and local area network systems. (6)

    NEAB IT02 Qu 9 1996

2. Two people working on a new piece of software both work from home, and frequently need to send data and files to each other via e-mail. Describe briefly **two** ways in which they could minimise the data transmission charges. (4)

    New question

Chapter 30 – User Interfaces

Introduction

The '**human-computer interface**' is a term used to describe the interaction between a user and a computer; in other words, the method by which the user tells the computer what to do, and the responses which the computer makes.

It's important not to allow the word 'computer' to limit your vision to a PC sitting on an office desk. You also need to think in terms of a person getting cash from a cash machine, a pilot of a jumbo jet checking his instrument panels, the operator of a high-volume heavy duty photocopier, a scientist monitoring a chemical reaction, a musician composing a symphony using appropriate hardware and software.

> ➢ **Discussion: Name some other tasks for which computers are used, and for which special purpose interfaces are required.**

The importance of good interface design

A good interface design can help to ensure that users carry out their tasks:

- **Safely** (in the case of a jumbo jet pilot, for example);
- **Effectively** (users don't find they have video'd two hours of Bulgarian clog dancing instead of the Cup Final);
- **Efficiently** (users do not spend five minutes trying to find the correct way to insert their cash card and type in their PIN and the amount of cash they want, and then leave without remembering to extract their card);
- **Enjoyably** (a primary school pupil using a program to teach multiplication tables).

Well designed systems can improve the output of employees, improve the quality of life and make the world a safer and more enjoyable place to live in.

> ➢ **Discussion: In the early days of cash machines, it was found that users sometimes forgot to remove their cards after withdrawing their cash. What simple change was made to eliminate this fault?**

Designing usable systems

In order to design a usable interface, the designer has to take into consideration:

- **Who** will use the system. For example, will the users be computer professionals or members of the general public who may be wary of computers? For an educational program, will the users be young, for example primary school children, or teenagers on an A Level course? Will the system have to cater for both beginners and experienced users?
- **What tasks** the computer is performing. Is the task very repetitive, does the task require skill and knowledge? Do tasks vary greatly from one occasion to the next? A travel agent who spends most of the day making holiday bookings will require a different interface from an office worker who needs to be able to switch between word processing, accounts and accessing the company database.

- **The environment** in which the computer is used. Will the environment be hazardous (in a lifeboat setting out to rescue a stricken vessel), noisy (in a factory full of machinery), or calm and quiet (some offices)?

- **What is techologically feasible** (is it possible to simply dictate a letter to a word processor instead of typing it in?)

Interface styles

There are a number of common interface styles including:

- Command line interface;
- Menus;
- Natural language;
- Forms and dialogue boxes;
- Graphical user interface (GUI).

Command-line interface

The command-line interface was the first interactive dialogue style and is still widely used in spite of the availability of menu-driven interfaces. It provides a means of expressing instructions to the computer directly using single characters, whole word commands or abbreviations.

With this type of interface very little help is given to the user, who has to type a command such as, for example, **Format a:** to format a disk. Commands enable a user to quickly and concisely instruct the computer what to do, but they do require the user to have a knowledge of the commands available and the syntax for using them. How for example do you format a double density disk rather than a high density disk? *(Answer: **Format a:/n:9/T:80**)*

> ➤ **Discussion: Identify TWO situations in which a command-driven interface would be appropriate.**

Menus

There are several different types of menu interface, outlined below.

1. **Full screen menu.** This type of menu is often used as the 'front end' of an application. It stays on screen until the user makes a choice.

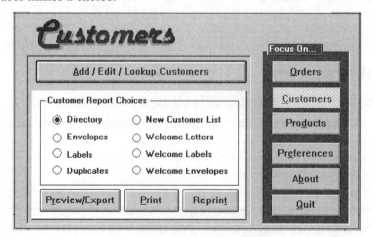

Figure 30.1: Full screen menu

2. **Pull-down menu.** This type of menu is displayed along the top of the screen, and when the user clicks on an item, a submenu appears. The menu is always present whatever screen the user is looking at in the application.

Figure 30.2: Pull-down menu

3. **Pop-up menu.** The menu pops up in response to, say, a click of the right mouse button on a particular area of the screen.

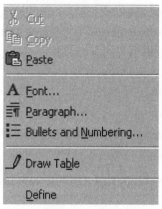

Figure 30.3: Pop-up menu

Natural language

It is a very attractive idea to have a computer which can understand natural language – 'plain English' in other words. *'Please, dear computer, format this double-density disk for me and don't give me obscure error messages which I can't understand'* seems an eminently civilised way of communicating with a PC. Unfortunately, the ambiguity of natural language makes it very difficult for a machine to understand. Language is ambiguous in a number of different ways. Firstly, the syntax, or structure of a sentence may not be clear – for example consider the sentences

James and Henrietta are married.

A salesman visited every house in the area.

The man hit the dog with the stick.

Are James and Henrietta married to each other? Was there only one salesman involved in the house-to-house sales operation?

Secondly, many English words have more than one meaning. How many ways can the word 'match' be interpreted?

Advantages and disadvantages of natural language dialogue

Advantages:

- Most natural form of dialogue for humans — no need for training in a specialised command language;
- Extremely flexible and powerful;
- The user is free to construct his own commands, frame his own questions, etc.

Disadvantages:

- People find it difficult to stick to strictly grammatical English;
- A well designed 'artificial language' can often say the same thing more concisely than 'natural language';
- A smooth, natural language can easily mislead the naive user into believing the computer is much more intelligent than it actually is.

Forms and dialogue boxes

When a user is required to enter data such as, for example, sales invoices or customer names and addresses, it is common to have a 'form' displayed on the screen for the user to fill in. The following points should be noted when designing forms of this type:

- The display should be given a title to identify it;
- The form should not be too cluttered – spaces and blanks in a display are important;
- It should give some indication of how many characters can be entered in each field of data;
- The user should be given a chance to go back and correct any field before the data is accepted;
- Items should appear in a logical sequence to assist the user;
- Default values should wherever possible be prewritten onto the form so that a minimum of data entry is required;
- Full exit and 'help' facilities should be provided – for example, users could enter '**?**' in a field if they require more information;
- Lower case in a display is neater and easier to read than upper-case;
- 'Attention-getting' devices such as blinking cursors, high-intensity, reverse video, underlining etc should not be over-used.

Dialogue boxes are a special type of form often associated with the Windows environment; an example shown below is the dialogue box which appears when the instruction to *Print* is given in Word 2000.

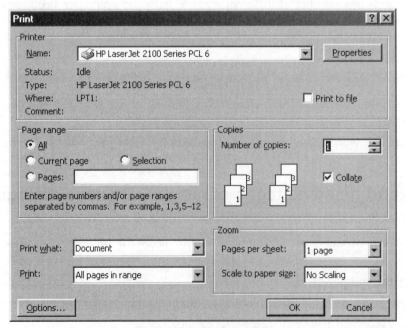

Figure 30.4: Dialogue box

The WIMP interface

WIMP stands for Windows, Icons, Mouse and Pull-down menus.

A **window** is an area on the screen through which a particular piece of software or a data file may be viewed. The window may occupy the whole screen, or the user can choose to have several windows on the screen with a different application running in each one. Windows can be moved, sized, stacked one on top of the other, opened and closed. A Windows environment mimics a desktop on which a worker may have several books or pieces of paper spread out for reference.

An **icon** is a small picture representing an item such as a piece of software, a file, storage medium (such as disk or tape) or command. By pointing with a mouse at a particular icon and clicking the mouse button the user can select it.

Microsoft Windows enables the user to run several different software packages such as MS Word (a word processor), MS Excel (a spreadsheet), MS Paint (a graphics package) simultaneously and to move data and graphics from one package to another. Software packages written by other manufacturers, such as Aldus PageMaker, have been written to run under Windows because of the convenience to the user of this easy-to-use environment.

Advantages of a common user interface

All the software packages mentioned above use a consistent interface and have a similar 'look and feel' so that a user familiar with one package can quickly learn a second. For example, in each package a single click of the mouse button **selects** an item, and a double click **activates** the item. In each package, the methods for opening, closing, sizing and moving windows is identical. The advantages can be summarised as:

- Increased speed of learning;
- Ease of use;
- Confidence building for novice users;
- Increased range of tasks solvable by experienced users;
- A greater range of software accessible to the average user.

Speech input (voice recognition)

The ultimate in user-friendly interfaces would probably be one in which you could simply tell your computer what to do in ordinary speech. Two distinct types of voice recognition system are emerging; small vocabulary command and control systems and large vocabulary dictation systems.

- **Command and control systems** can be relatively small and cheap because they need only a small, tightly defined vocabulary of technical terms. Such systems are coming rapidly into use as automatic call-handling systems for applications such as bank account enquiries. In PC systems, voice command can be used to bring up files, control printing and so on, effectively replacing the mouse. In some systems the computer is 'trained' by an individual user pronouncing a given vocabulary of words; it then stores a recording of the user's speech pattern for each word or syllable.

- **Large vocabulary dictation systems** can handle whole sentences and extensive vocabularies but need much greater processing power and memory space. These systems use elaborate probability distributions to estimate which word the accoustic pattern it has picked up is most likely to be, partly by looking at other words in the developing sentence and predicting what sort of word (noun or verb, for example) is likely to be used. Various voice recognition packages after suitable 'training' will take dictation at 70 words per minute and get about 97% of them correct. Voice recognition is however still an expensive technology and widespread use is some way off.

> ➤ **Discussion: Name some other situations in which voice input would be appropriate.**

Speech/sound output

A speech synthesis system works as follows:

Individual words and sounds are spoken into a microphone by a human being and recorded by the system, thereby training it to speak. Output that would normally be printed can then be spoken, so long as the word is contained in its vocabulary. Sometimes words which are not recognised are spelt out.

Such a system has limited use but could for example be used by a bank computer connected by telephone line to customers' homes and offices. The customer could key in his account number using the telephone keypad, and the computer could then access his account and speak out the customer's account balance.

Exercises

1. *see case study below*

Case study: Putting patients in the picture

New software is about to go on trial in doctors' surgeries to enable patients to see a picture of their condition on screen. An attractive interface features drawings of the human body overlaid with 'hotspots'. The cursor can be moved to the part of the body under investigation and clicked to reveal information. If for example the patient has a problem in the knee, the doctor clicks on the appropriate spot and a menu of options is displayed on the screen. Information can then be obtained on medical history, examinations, investigations, diagnosis, referrals and procedures.

The interface was designed to salvage a £19m coding system for the health service, whereby 245,000 medical conditions were given unique computer codes. The system was difficult to use because in order to do a keyboard search for a particular condition, everything including spaces and syntax had to be typed in with 100% accuracy. With the new system a complete list of possible diagnoses and treatments is available at the touch of a button. In addition, patients are much better informed because they can see a picture of the problem.

Three doctors and two programmers have worked on the interface, called Visual Read, for two years in their spare time.

> ➤ **Questions:**
> a. What name would you give to this type of interface? (1)
> b. Describe **one** advantage of the software to   (i) the doctor;
>   (ii) the patient. (2)
> c. Why do you think the NHS spent £19m on a coding system for medical conditions? What use could such a scheme be put to, apart from the one described in the case study? (4)
> d. Describe briefly **two** possible problems with the software that may come to light during testing in surgeries. (2)
> e. The development team consisted of three doctors and two programmers. Identify the likely strengths and weaknesses of such a team. (4)
> f. "If the system works as well as it is supposed to, the doctor will be superfluous." State whether you agree or disagree with this statement, giving **two** reasons to support your answer. (2)

2. A college uses a range of software packages from different suppliers. Each package has a different user interface. The college is considering changing its software to one supplier and to a common user interface.

   (a) Give **four** advantages of having a common user interface. (4)

   (b) Describe **four** specific features of a user interface which would benefit from being common between packages. (4)

   (c) Discuss the issues involved, apart from user interfaces, in the college changing or upgrading software packages. (8)

   NEAB IT02 Qu 8 1997

3. A railway station has a computer-based timetable enquiry system for use by passengers. Enquiries are entered from a keyboard and displayed on the screen-based form illustrated below.

   ```
   Destination:
   Date of Travel:
   Latest arrival time:
   ```

   Details of the train times are displayed at the bottom of the screen.

   (a) The exact format of the input required for this system is not clear. Redesign the form to make it clear. (4)

   (b) Some users of the enquiry system find it difficult to use. Suggest **three** ways in which it could be made easier to use. (3)

   London Computing Paper 2 Qu 4 1995

4. Briefly describe **three** important features of a well-designed user interface. (6)

   NISEAC Paper 2 Qu 7 1996

5. A different human-machine interface would be needed for each of the following users:

   (i) a young child in a primary school;

   (ii) a blind person;

   (iii) a graphic artist.

   For each user describe and justify an appropriate human-machine interface. (9)

   NEAB Computing Paper 1 Qu 9 1994

IT02 – Sample Questions and Answers

1. SupaGoods is a home sales company. Catalogues are left at people's homes. A local agent calls two days later to take orders and collect the catalogues. The agent sends the details of the goods ordered to the Head Office where they are processed. The completed order is returned to the agent who distributes the goods and collects payment.

    (a) Describe two distinct methods of data capture for the agent. State one advantage and one disadvantage of each method. (6)

    (b) The orders are validated at Head Office.

       (i) Explain what is meant by validation. (2)

       (ii) Describe briefly two validation checks that might be carried out on an agent's order. (2)

    NEAB IT02 Qu 5 1998

Notes:

Think carefully what the question is asking – in general it was answered badly in 1998 by the majority of candidates, who misinterpreted what was being asked. Do you get catalogues left on the doorstep? Take a look at the order form inside. What happens – does the householder fill the order form in and hand it to the agent when he returns, or does he stand in the pouring rain typing the order into his laptop as Mrs Bloggs dictates her requirements for a new potato peeler, a set of nylon sieves and a doormat saying 'Beware of the cat'?

What is meant by 'data capture'? Generally it means the method by which the data is entered into the computer system. In the situation described there are basically two possibilities: the agent enters the data himself, either on the doorstep or later that day, and transmits it to Head Office, or he sends the completed forms to Head Office where they are entered by some means. Once you have thought the question through to this point you should be able to describe two different methods of data capture applicable to one or other scenario.

'Validation' is covered in Chapter 16.

Suggested answer

   (a)   The paper order forms could be collected by the agent and sent to the Head Office where the data could be keyed in using a key-to-disk system. The advantage of this method is that it is economical for high volume data entry and as the data is verified (i.e. entered a second time by a different operator) the chances of data entry errors are much reduced. The disadvantage is that keying in data is very time-consuming.

   Alternatively the forms could be preprinted with the householder's account number and the form designed in such a way that if carefully filled in it can be read using OCR (optical character recognition). The forms would again be transmitted to Head Office and put through an optical character reader, so no manual data entry would be required. The advantage of this method is that it saves time on data entry and transcription errors do not arise. The disadvantage is that if the forms are not carefully and legibly filled in they will be rejected by the optical character reader and have to be manually keyed.

   (You could also describe Optical mark recognition, or barcoding.)

   (b) (i) Validation is the use of computer software to detect data which is missing or unreasonable.

(ii) Validation checks: Check digit on the agent's number or customer code. An extra digit calculated from the code is added to the end of the code, making it self-checking.
A presence check could be carried out on several fields such as agent's code, or quantity of an item ordered.
(Could also mention range check or format check on catalogue numbers etc.)

---

2. The manager of a video hire shop uses a relational database management system to operate the business. Separate database files hold details of customers, video films and loans. Customers can hire as many films as they wish.

   (a) For each of the files mentioned above identify the key fields and list other appropriate fields that would be required to enable this system to be maintained with minimum redundancy. (6)

   (b) Describe **three** advantages of using a relational database rather than a flat-file information storage system.

   (6)
   NEAB IT02 Qu 7 1996

Notes:

You need to show primary keys and foreign keys, i.e. the fields that will link the three tables together. Do NOT put 'Age' as a field on the customer file – age is never an appropriate field as it changes all the time. DateOfBirth would be acceptable. You will lose marks for naming inappropriate fields so don't just put down anything in the hope of scoring a few hits – think carefully. You can use standard database notation to answer this question (see Chapter 18.) You will find the answers to part (b) in Chapter 17.

Suggested answer:

   (a) CUSTOMER(<u>CustomerNumber</u>, Surname, FirstName, Address, Telephone)
   VIDEO_FILM(<u>VideoNumber</u>, VideoName, Category, DateProduced)
   LOAN(<u>CustomerNumber, VideoNumber</u>, DateDue)

   (b) **Data independence** – the structure of the database does not affect programs which access it so for example an extra field could be added to the CUSTOMER table without needing to change programs not directly affected by the new field.
   Control over redundancy (less data duplication. i.e. the same data is not stored several times on different files, so for example the video name and customer name are not stored on the LOAN table, as they can be looked up from the relevant table.
   Consistency of data – because data is not duplicated there is no possibility of holding inconsistent data on different files, for example if a customer changes address.

---

3. A spreadsheet package is described as having a macro facility. Describe what is meant by the term 'macro' and suggest a situation in which the use of a macro would be appropriate. (4)
   NEAB IT02 Qu 1 1997

Notes:

It will be much easier to answer this question if you have done some practical work with spreadsheets and created your own macros. Don't just rely on your textbook to pass this exam – practical work, work experience, watching appropriate TV documentaries, reading relevant newspaper articles, noticing how computers are used in different situations or businesses and just plain old common sense are vital ingredients for success!

Suggested answer:

> A macro is a sequence of instructions stored with the spreadsheet or other application, and activated by a keystroke, clicking a command button or icon, selecting from a menu etc.

> A macro would be appropriate to automate a task which has to be frequently or regularly repeated, and which takes several steps to perform, thus helping to provide a customised user environment. For example a macro might be used to display a data entry form, clear any existing data, put today's date at the top and position the cursor ready for the user to start entering data.

---

4. You have installed a new piece of applications software onto a stand-alone PC. You then find that the printer attached to the PC fails to produce what can be seen on screen in that package.

   Explain clearly why this might happen. (2)

   NEAB IT02 Qu 2 1998

Notes:

> There are some fairly obvious reasons why the printer may not print what is on your screen, for example your screen is showing a full colour image and the printer is not a colour printer. Will that answer score you a mark? Hard to say – I would be inclined to throw it in as a third answer just in case the examiner does not like your first two. Something more technical is probably required.

Suggested answer:

> If you try to send a very long document, the printer may not have sufficient memory to hold the output and it may not print anything at all.

> The correct printer driver may not be installed – this is the software that translates the information about fonts, formatting etc into a form that the printer can understand. If you are using an older version of the printer driver with a new version of the software it may not be compatible.

---

5. A computer system can be described as being a "pseudo real-time system".
   (i) State clearly what is meant by pseudo real-time. (2)
   (ii) Give a situation where pseudo real-time is essential, stating a reason why it is needed. (2)

Notes:

> Be sure you understand the difference between genuine real-time processing (where for example an aircraft must respond instantly to an instruction to gain height) and pseudo real-time where a delay of a few seconds does not matter (for example in displaying your bank balance at a cash machine).

Suggested answer:

> (i) A pseudo real-time system is one which accepts transactions from outside sources and processes each transaction more or less immediately, before the next transaction is accepted.

> (ii) A theatre booking system would require this type of processing so that as soon as a booking is made the file will show that the seats have been sold, to prevent double-booking.

---

6. Articles in the media referring to computer software which fails to work properly are commonplace. Discuss the difficulties facing software companies when testing and implementing complex software, and the measures that software providers could take to minimise these problems. (6)

   NEAB IT02 Qu 8 1996

Notes:

In the second part of the question you should discuss different types of testing that the developer should carry out. 'Alpha' and 'Beta' testing are not directly on the specification but from your general knowledge you may be aware of how software such as a new version of Windows is tested. Chapter 23 describes the difficulties of testing software.

Suggested answer:

In a GUI interface, there is no single, well-defined sequence of events and therefore it is difficult to test for every combination of events.

Users often use software in ways which were not predicted by the developers.

Software may work well with a limited volume of test data but it may be difficult to simulate the actual volume of data or users in a working version. Performance testing involving say 1000 users may be impossible to set up.

The pressure to get a new version on the market and the pace of change of the hardware may mean that there is insufficient time for thorough testing.

Software developers can minimise the problems of buggy software by formulating an effective test strategy, using different types of testing such as testing each module, testing the system as a whole, and then involving the users in testing. Software such as Windows is often issued as a 'beta' version or test version, to a group of users who then use it over a period of months and report any difficulties encountered.

---

7. A publishing company administers its business by using a database system running on a network of PCs. The main uses are to process customer orders and to log payments. You have been asked about backup strategies and their importance.

    (a) Give **two** reasons why it is essential that this company has a workable backup strategy. (2)

    (b) State five factors that should be considered in a backup strategy, illustrating each factor with an example. (10)

    (c) Despite all the precautions, some data might still be lost if there was a system failure. Give two reasons why this might be the case. (2)

    NEAB IT02 Qu 6 1998

Notes:

Avoid giving one word answers which will probably not score full marks. Be sure to justify or explain any points you make. Very many candidates scored only 5 marks, not 10, in part (b) although they probably thought they had gained full marks.

Suggested answer:

    (a) The company needs a workable backup strategy (i) to ensure that no data is lost in the event of a catastrophe such as a fire or flood; (ii) to ensure that if errors are made which compromise the integrity of the data, (i.e. the data becomes completely wrong or unreadable) the files can be recreated from the backups.

    (b) **Frequency of backups.** Many organisations, such as a school or college, find it sufficient to back up data once or twice a day. On-line databases (for example in a hospital or airline booking system) need to be backed up constantly to prevent any loss of data.

    Backup medium. Magnetic tape is cheap, compact and can store large amounts of data, and is used by many organisations to back up data from hard disks every night. Smaller amounts of data may be backed up on removable disks using a Zip drive.

Location of backup storage. The data needs to be held in a secure location in case of fire or burglary. Many organisations have a fireproof safe for the latest backups, with another set of backups being stored off-site.

Number of generations to be kept. A typical strategy is to:

keep the daily backups for a week;

keep Friday's backup for a month;

keep one backup each month for a year;

give each tape or disk a serial number and keep a log book, to prevent mix-ups.

Responsibility for implementing the backup strategy. Although the regular backup routine may be performed by a computer operator or an office worker, a senior manager should have overall responsibility for ensuring that all aspects of the backup strategy are properly implemented.

Testing of recovery procedures. At regular intervals the effectiveness of the backup strategy needs to be tested to ensure that the organisation can recover quickly from loss of data.

---

8.   (a)   Give two differences between a Local Area Network (LAN) and a Wide Area Network (WAN).   (2)

       (b)   Discuss the relative merits of server based networks and peer to peer networks.   (6)

NEAB IT02 Qu 5 1997

Notes:

A fairly straightforward question if you have done your homework! Refer to Chapter 29. You will get no marks for answers such as 'A server-based system needs a server and a peer to peer system does not', or 'A peer to peer network is cheaper'.

Suggested Answer:

       (a)   A LAN connects computers within the same building or site, whereas a WAN connects computers over a wide geographical area , in different towns or countries. A LAN connects computers via cables but computers on a WAN are connected via modems and a telecommunications link such as a telephone line or satellite link.

       (b)   A server-based network has a central backing store available to all users whereas on a peer-to-peer network the storage facilities, although available to all users, are distributed among the computers on the network. The central backing store makes it simpler for backups to be done by the systems manager.

              On a server based network only one copy of the software needs to be held on the server, which can be used by all users on the network. On a peer to peer network each computer may have its own copy of the software. This means that upgrades have to be installed on all computers instead of on only one.

              A peer to peer network is simpler to install and maintain and does not need a systems manager to control and look after it.

---

9. A large entertainment and leisure complex has a wide range of facilities available including a cinema, live entertainment, indoor sports and exhibition facilities. They have made use of computer systems since it opened, but due to the popularity of the complex, and the wide range of activities available, they are considering introducing a computer based information system. This system will be used by the general public who visit the complex.

    Discuss how such a system would operate in practice. Particular attention should be paid to the following issues:

    - the dialogue between the user and the computer;
    - the types of interface suitable for this system;
    - the hardware required;
    - the timeliness and accuracy of the information displayed.

Quality of language will be assessed in this question.

(20)

NEAB IT02 Qu 11 1998

Notes:

It is extremely important to write down only relevant points in this type of question, and not to waffle. Do make notes first of the points you consider relevant. Some students write up to 4 pages and score virtually no marks, whereas a good candidate can get almost full marks in a single page of well-written prose. There will be up to 4 marks allocated to each point mentioned in the question and another 4 for quality of language. (See IT01 question 9 for mark allocation on QOL.)

Suggested answer:

The complex could have touch screens located at various points in the complex, displaying an opening screen with a menu of options and an instruction to touch the relevant box on the screen to go to the desired option. e.g. Options for Cinema, Live Entertainment, Sports, Exhibitions. Once the user touches, say, Cinema, the next screen would display all the films showing in each cinema with times. Each screen would have an option to return to the main menu, and a 'Help' option to give further guidance where required. There could be an option to print out hard copy of the information shown on screen.

The most appropriate interface would be a menu-driven interface, with full-screen menus activated by touching the selected item. The advantage of this is that it would be very simple for members of the public to use – many people might not be confident using a keyboard, and it is far more robust than using, say, a mouse to select options. There is no possibility of entering a 'wrong' command and getting a puzzling error message. The disadvantage of this type of interface is that the number of options that can be displayed is quite limited and of course the screen might get quite dirty.

The hardware required would be a number of touch screens connected to a central processor, cabling to connect them a keyboard in the main office so that data and programs could be loaded onto the system and updated, hard disk storage to store the programs and data, and a printer in the office. If hard copy was available to the public, special printers would be needed at each kiosk.

The information on films would have to be updated every time the film changed. If the system gave seat availability, it would have to be online to the booking system and updated in real-time as seats were sold. This would ensure that the information was up to date and accurate. The information on sports facilities, exhibitions, etc would probably not have to be changed more than once a week and could be entered via a keyboard in the office. The data entered could have some validation checks applied to it, to ensure that valid dates and times were entered, but it is quite likely that spelling errors would occur. I saw the film 'Rouge Trader' not long ago. The public is probably fairly tolerant of such errors if they even spot them.

Section 3

Coursework:

The Use of Generic Application Software for Task Solution

In this section:

Chapter 31 – Tackling a Minor Project

Syllabus requirements

At the time of writing, the AQA Information and Communications Technology specification requires candidates to undertake a project for Module 3. For the project, you are expected to tackle a task-related problem of limited scope, which in general can be implemented using a single piece of generic applications software such as a database, spreadsheet or desktop publishing package. You are, however, encouraged to use other software tools and objects as appropriate to complete the solution.

There are certain expectations from each type of software, for example:

Word processing software

Remember that the emphasis for the project is on *developing a solution* to a reasonably substantial problem posed by an end-user. You need to select a problem that can be broken down into subtasks, each of which can be implemented using your chosen package. You will need to use a powerful word processing package such as Word 7, 97 or 2000 that has sufficient advanced facilities to carry out some non-trivial tasks. For example, your project could be to produce all the templates needed for a club or a small business to send out letters and invoices to members or customers. The project might also involve holding a list of names and addresses so that you could send a mail shot to a selected group, for example a reminder notice to people who had not paid their subscriptions or invoices.

Automating the processes using the macro language might be demonstrated using a User Data Entry form, with macros attached on entry and exit. Finally, the project might attempt to fully customise the solution by tailoring the toolbars and drop-down menus.

You can use a word processing package to:

- Create a company 'ident'; that is, a logo and typeface for letter headings, invoices, fax cover sheets, With Compliments slips and business cards which gives the company or club a recognisable identity.

- Create templates for some/all of the above. Templates can be set to be read-only so that data is added to a document based on the template and not stored with the template itself.

- Create an internal data source containing names and addresses, subscriptions due, whether paid, etc.

- Create a mail-merge letter containing fields. You should explore the advanced features of the software that allow you to insert formulas and IF fields.

- Insert FILLIN fields to enable the user to fill in, say, a subscription rate (Family, Adult or Junior) for each member of a club.

- Insert a table into a document that contains formulae – for example, to add up the individual lines in an invoice, add VAT and calculate a total amount due.

The important thing is to be aware that all these things can be done in Word, and then to carefully analyse the user's requirements and use whatever features of the software are required to perform the tasks involved.

A word of warning – a simple mail-merge letter using a single file of data just won't make the grade, and nor will an application to allow a user to print out business cards.

Steer clear of word-processing software except to write up your project documentation, unless you have a good idea from a real user with a genuine need that can be broken down into several subtasks.

Database software

Databases must be relational and used in a fully relational manner. This implies that your system must contain at least two related tables. Typically, you should choose a project which gives you scope to perform some or all of the following tasks:

- Draw an entity-relationship diagram;

- Normalise your data;

- Design your table structures, giving due consideration to field lengths and types, validation and default values;

- Create relationships which enforce referential integrity;

- Create and tailor forms and subforms to provide a pleasing and easy-to-use interface for the user;

- Perform multi-table queries;

- Perform some processing or calculation on the input data to produce information;

- Display or print reports, perhaps summarising data or displaying data that has been calculated, sorted or processed in some way;

- Write macros and code modules to customise your database;

- Provide a menu of options (a 'switchboard') as a front end to your application;

- Provide the user with on-line help.

Software such as Works is not suitable for a minor project, since it does not have a full range of advanced facilities available.

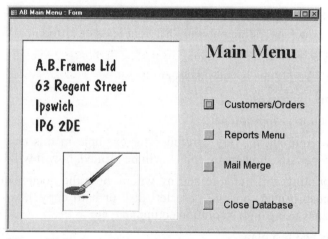

Figure 31.1: A sample opening menu for a database project

Spreadsheet software

A spreadsheet application must consist of more than a single sheet containing labels, numbers and formulae into which the user types data. It could well involve the use of:

- A template which can only be altered by an authorised user, while other users would load the template, enter their own data and save the spreadsheet as a worksheet rather than altering the original template;

- A separate area of the spreadsheet set aside for data entry, making use of a User Input dialogue box and validation of input data. Data would then be automatically transferred to a different area for processing;

- Pivot tables for management analysis;

- Multiple scenarios of best, likely and worst case;

- Use of Goal Seek and solver;

- Locking sheets (with some cells unprotected) to prevent unwanted modification;

- Outlining and other auditing tools;

- Table lookup functions;

- Cell naming. Rather than having formulas such *as =D2*E2*, it is more meaningful to have a formula such as *=Qty*Unit_Price*;

- Macros to control input, processing and output. Auto Open and Close macros;

- A front-end menu to allow the user to select different options;

- Command buttons to perform various tasks;

- Use of control boxes such as list box, check box and option buttons;

- On-line help for the user.

Desktop publishing

It is difficult to score good marks using a desktop publishing package. The essence of the project is that it should not be simply a passive document, for example a beautifully produced newsletter or theatre program. It should have some element of interactivity with an end-user – for example, a template which a user can use over and over again with different text and graphics. The project needs to make use of advanced features of the package and must give scope for the full range of activities (Analysis, Design, Testing etc.)

A DTP project needs to be based on a repeatable need and must not be a one-off. This then gives you the scope to provide test data, such as testing out with different texts or different articles.

It is extremely important to:

- Have a real end-user (even if this is your teacher);

- Establish the aims and objectives;

- State why a DTP solution is appropriate;

- Consider the user's requirements very carefully; for example in this case the layout, appearance, colour restrictions, paper size, how many copies will be printed, how it will be folded;

- Establish how the printing will be done and by whom, how the document will be supplied to the printers (i.e. the human printer, not the LaserJet! disk or hard copy?), whether the printer will be scanning in photographs using high resolution equipment, etc.

- Design a test strategy and test plan;

- Evaluate the final solution against the objectives;

- Write technical and user manuals on how to use your template – NOT on how to use desktop publishing software.

Presentation packages

In the main, packages such as PowerPoint are unsuitable for a project at this level. There is simply not enough scope for a high-scoring project.

Authoring packages

A package such as Authorware can be used to produce an interactive tutorial, and has plenty of scope for advanced features to be used but as the package costs around £800 for a single copy probably very few centres or candidates would have access to such software.

If you have used sound, video or animation in your project and it is hard to show evidence of how it works in the report, you may as a last resort include a video with the project. Do NOT send a disk.

Internet Web pages

It is relatively easy to produce a Web page using Microsoft software, and so unless you can develop a functional site on the Internet that records hits and collects e-mail responses or answers to on-line questionnaires, this is likely to score only low marks.

Planning the time schedule

Once you have decided on a project, one of the first things you should do is draw up a timetable of when each stage is going to be done and completed, so as to ensure it is handed in before the deadline.

There are many different possible schedules. If your teacher has more or less suspended theory classes to allow you to work flat out on your project, it should be possible to complete it within 6 to 8 weeks. This assumes that you will have 3-5 hours per week of class time, and at least as much again outside class. Even if you don't have a computer at home, and the open-access facilities at school or college are limited, do remember that there is a huge amount of work to be done away from the computer. You can:

- plan your schedule;
- interview the user;
- design the application;
- draw data flow diagrams (Context Level 0 and Level 1);
- read books to find out about the advanced features of the software;
- design your test strategy and test plan.

The project requirements

Your project should include:

- A clear statement of the problem;
- An appropriate specification, reflecting the end-user's requirements of the solution, the desired outcomes and any constraints or limitations on the development of the solution, e.g. human or physical resources.
- Input, processing and output needs matching the requirements specification. The format of this section will vary according to the software solution available. For example, a database solution will need a database design from which to complete the project.
- A test strategy, test plan and test results cross-referenced to the test plan;
- An implementation using a software package;
- An evaluation of how well the final system met the objectives and performance criteria;
- Documentation showing how all the above were achieved;
- A user guide.

In the next few chapters each of these aspects will be tackled in more detail. The AQA project mark scheme is given in Appendix B.

Chapter 32 – Specification and Analysis

Selecting a project

For the AS Module 3 project it is acceptable for your teacher to identify a problem for computerisation and act as the end-user. However you are very strongly encouraged to find your own project since this is much more likely to give you the opportunity to show your capabilities in a clearly original way. It's very important that the project is not teacher-led, with the whole class ending up with more or less identical solutions. Even if you find a particularly good way of overcoming some problem encountered in a class project, you're not likely to get any credit if the rest of the class has copied your techniques.

Try and find an application that you have personal knowledge of, or that you can investigate further. Parents can be a good source of ideas, or perhaps you belong to a club of some kind that could use a computerised membership system. The lab technician might like a computerised stock control system, or the school librarian may have an idea for computerising some aspect of the library. Do not be too ambitious – don't try and redo Tesco's stock control or the payroll system for British Gas. It is perfectly acceptable to ask the end-user for their priorities, be selective and model just a small slice of the user's problem.

Investigating the user's requirements

Analysis involves finding out:

- How the current system works;
- What the problems are with the current system, including any client dissatisfaction;
- What the user's requirements are for a new system;
- What constraints there are on hardware, software, time-scale.

In order to do this, you need to prepare a list of questions and interview the user. Ask to see any (source) documents that are currently used, and if possible include a copy of them in an Appendix.

Establishing the objectives

It is a good idea to write a clear statement of the objectives, both **qualitative** and **quantitative**. An example of a qualitative objective is:

"It should be easy for the user to locate a particular customer invoice".

An example of a quantitative objective is:

"It should be possible to locate any customer invoice in under 30 seconds".

Having a clear list of objectives will not only make the design of the system more straightforward, it will also enable you to evaluate the implementation by comparing its performance point-by-point with the objectives.

Writing up the specification

A possible framework for the specification is given below:

---

1. Introduction

    1.1   Background
Describe and name the user and/or type of organisation (club, library, garage, etc) the project is to be written for and give some background information about the organisation.

    1.2   Statement of the problem
Give an overview of the problem that you intend to solve.

2. Investigation

    2.1   The current system
Include a summary of the main points of an interview if appropriate. Identify the data flows and tasks being performed, and summarise these in a data flow diagram.

    2.2   Problems with the current system

3. Requirements of the new system

    3.1   General objectives

    3.2   Specific objectives – quantitative

    3.3   Specific objectives – qualitative

4. Constraints

    4.1   Hardware
Describe the hardware that is available both for development and at the end-user's organisation, or wherever the system is to be implemented.

    4.2   Software
Name the software you have available to use (including the version number) and briefly describe its main capabilities.

    4.3   User's I.T. skills and knowledge
Give some indication of the level of the end-user's I.T. skills, and what possible effects this could have on the design.

Do vary this format according to the demands of your own particular project – don't try and force it into a format which does not fit. This is only a starting point from which you can branch out.

Chapter 33 – Design

Design tasks

Designing a system involves the following tasks:

- Identifying the required output from the system;
- Identifying the input data;
- Specifying the processing that needs to be carried out;
- Devising a test strategy and test plan;
- Planning a schedule of activities to ensure that the project is finished by the deadline – and sticking to it!

As this is likely to be the first substantial project you have attempted, it may be very difficult for you to produce a complete design before you start the implementation, especially if you are learning about the software as you go along. The AQA Exam Board recognizes this and does not expect you to produce complete design documentation. Rather, you should make what notes you can on design before starting the implementation, and as you implement the project and discover better ways of doing things, or extra features that you can incorporate, document these. Keep a project log and make notes as you proceed through the project.

Database design (for a database project)

Identify the entities involved and the relationships between the entities and draw an entity-relationship diagram. A database project should involve at least three related tables. A sample entity-relationship diagram is shown below. The meaning of the 'crow's feet' pointing in the direction that they do below is:

One customer places many orders   (a one-to-many relationship)

One order consists of many line items (a one-to-many relationship)

Figure 33.1: An entity-relationship diagram

Data descriptions

For each item of data you should specify:

- Name;
- Data type (integer, real, text etc);
- Length (if text);
- Default value (if any);
- Validation.

For a database project, you can use a form with headings similar to those shown below for each table in the database.

TABLE NAME:

Attribute name	Data type	Length	Default value	Description, validation, comments

Figure 33.2: Suggested headings for a table layout form in a database project

For a spreadsheet project, you should specify the purpose and contents of each sheet:

SHEET NAME:

Row/Column heading	Data description and format	Comment	Example
Book code	Unique 6 character code	Acts as a link between sheets "Book" and "Sales"	AC0073, CM0021
Total sales	The total month's sales of a book		=sum (d5..d11)

Figure 33.3: Designing a spreadsheet

Input

In a database project you may well design your screens with the help of 'wizards'. Try to maintain a consistent style and position for headings and buttons – for example buttons on each screen which return a user to the Main Menu or Switchboard should all be placed in the same position in every form.

For each sheet in a spreadsheet project show:

- General layout;
- Which cells will be locked or protected;
- Links to other sheets;
- Fonts, shading etc.

Output

List the reports or other output (e.g. mailing labels, information available on screen). You should design each report or screen on paper, listing the data items that will appear. It does not have to be done on squared paper with every character shown, but you should give thought to whether a report is to be tabular or not, whether labels are to be printed 2 or 3 across the page, and so on. You can always change the design if you later find you have made some mistakes – such changes can be documented and justified as part of your report.

Menu design

If your system has a menu structure, draw a chart showing how various submenus relate to each other. An example is shown below.

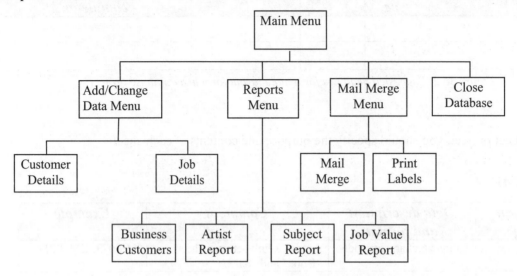

Figure 33.4: A sample menu structure chart

Test plan

The test plan may be included here or in the Testing section. It will be discussed in the next chapter.

Writing up the design and implementation

A possible framework for the design and implementation documentation is given below:

---

1. **Database/Spreadsheet design**

    1.1   Entity-relationship diagram (for a database)

    1.2   Data descriptions

2. **Input**

    Design of input forms and screens. (These may develop as the project progresses, and you can show what improvements you have made to original designs)

3. **Output**

    Design of reports and other output.

4. **Menu design**

5. **Test plan**

6. **Project log**

    A log describing progress and improvements made to the implementation and further tests that were made.

Chapter 34 – Implementation and Testing

Organisation is the key

You will almost certainly be learning more about the software as you go along. There are many things you can do to ensure a successful implementation.

1. Buy a binder to hold everything to do with your project, divided into sections so that you can quickly find what you are looking for. A floppy plastic binder of the type that holds papers securely through punched holes is most suitable.

2. Have your design documentation in front of you and follow it; if you find it needs to be adjusted, remember to do so, and make a note of why this was necessary.

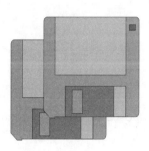

3. Have at least two spare floppy disks and make a backup after every session at the computer. Having 2 backup disks means that you can leave the most recent backup alone and overwrite the previous 'generation'. It is impossible to be too conscientious about backups; sooner or later you will lose the current version, quite possibly through no fault of your own – but blaming the dog, Microsoft or the school network won't bring your project back!

4. Keep a diary and leave 15 minutes at the end of every class to write up what you did and what problems you encountered. This will help you at the beginning of the next class.

5. Test each form, report, macro etc. thoroughly as you go, and make a note of these tests for your test plan.

6. Buy a good book on the software you are using, and spend time actually READING it. Try out the exercises and improve your knowledge of the advanced features of the software.

The implementation

The implementation is the actual software solution that you create, using whichever package you have chosen to use. It is very tempting to proceed straight to the implementation stage without doing any design work first, but try not to do this. *Write down* the menu structure, *design* the data structures/fields/tables, the input and the output screens or reports. *Construct a list* of subtasks. Then you will be able to see what parts of your project you need help with. It is very hard for a teacher to help students who have nothing written down and have only the vaguest idea of what they are trying to achieve.

If you are using the computer facilities at school or college, there is a lot of work you can do at home. You can:

- Read software guides to learn how to overcome any problems you have encountered;
- Refine your design;
- Create sets of test data;
- Draw up a test plan;
- Work on your documentation;
- Plan how you are going to make the best use of your next practical session.

If you are using computer facilities at home, then all these tasks can be done during practical sessions. If you can plan your time effectively, you will be able to complete the project in the time allowed.

Testing objectives

The objectives of testing are to prove that:

- All parts of the system work correctly, no matter what data is input;
- All parts of the system as originally specified are present.

In drawing up a test plan, you should bear in mind the following rules proposed by Glen Myers in his book 'The Art of Software Testing'.

1. **Testing is a process of executing a program with the intent of finding an error.**
2. **A good test case is one that has a high probability of finding an as yet undiscovered error.**
3. **A successful test is one that uncovers an as yet undiscovered error.**

In other words, it is not sufficient to think up a few tests which you are fairly sure will not make your program crash or give a wrong result; you must use tests and test data which have been carefully thought out to test all parts of the program.

Steps in software testing

1. Module testing

As you complete each module of your program, it needs to be thoroughly tested. Even if you can't test every combination of paths, you can test the important paths, the extreme cases, valid and invalid data, and so on. For the purposes of your project, you should aim to demonstrate that you have tested systematically and that your testing is **reasonably** exhaustive. A maximum of 20 to 30 pages of actual test runs which cover major processes and show a variety of test data (i.e. extreme, correct, incorrect) is quite sufficient.

2. System (or integrated) testing

When all the modules have been written and the whole system put together, system testing can begin.

At this stage, you should ideally test your system with a realistic volume of data. If the system is designed to hold details of 5000 stock items, and you have never tested it with more than 8, there is no way of knowing how it will perform after installation unless you test it. Obviously, you will not have the time to enter 5000 different records, but it would be reasonable to enter about 20 items of data.

Drawing up a test plan

For the module testing, draw up a test plan of preferably no more than two or three pages which shows that you have chosen your test data carefully, tested each module, and know what the results ought to be. A suggested table for a test plan is given below.

Test No	Test Data	Purpose	Expected Result	Comment /Verified
1	Enter incorrect password 'ABC'	Test password	Only password 'ABF' accepted	
2	Enter Customer ID abc	Test invalid digits	Not accepted	
3	Enter new customer with ID 456, 'Jones K.'	Test 'Add new customer' function	Jones added to database	

Figure 34.1: A suggested format for a test plan

Sometimes it is impossible to show evidence that a test works correctly; in those cases, have your supervisor carry out the test and authenticate the result in the 'Comments/Verified' column. You could also use this column to reference the page number on which your test evidence is shown, or to make notes to yourself of any tests that did not work correctly.

Selecting tests for the test plan

Try to choose tests that test the more complex aspects of your system, such as calculations, command buttons that perform updating or open up a form with data already in it, and so on. Masses of tests for really trivial validations that are performed automatically by Access (such as a date in the correct format) are fairly pointless.

If, for example, you are testing a mail-merge, it is not necessary to include all the printouts as evidence. A better test would be to see whether your system can insert a new name into the list and then just print out one more letter, rather than printing the whole lot again.

You may well have to amend or add to your initial test plan as the program develops, but you will find it very helpful to have a written plan at all stages, even if you keep adjusting it.

Similarly, if you design your system tests **before** you start coding, you will be forced to think about how this phase will be carried out, what will have to be done to make system testing possible, and how to ensure that it will be successful. The earlier you can foresee any problems, the easier they will be to solve.

Presenting the test results

Your test results should be presented in an Appendix, and cross-referenced to your test plan. They will normally take the form of test runs, screen dumps and file dumps. You may need to explain exactly what data was input. Use a highlighter pen to emphasise the key point about a screenshot, and annotate the output by hand to show what the test proves. Be selective, and consider it a challenge to make it as easy as possible for a reader to confirm that test results were as expected. As a general rule, include the absolute minimum essential to get the point across.

Test runs and screenshots with no annotation and no cross-referencing to the test plan are virtually useless!

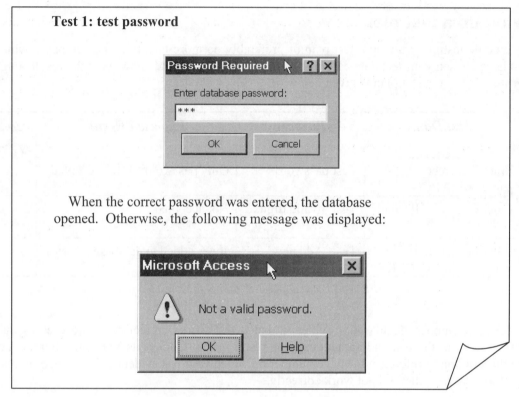

Figure 34.2: Presenting the test results

Chapter 35 – Documentation

Introduction

The report that you hand in at the end of your project contains all the evidence of the work you have done over the past few months. No matter how careful your analysis, how appropriate the design, how clever the macros or modules and how thorough the testing; if the written evidence is not there to prove it, you will not achieve a good mark.

It will take longer than you expect to complete the documentation. It will pay you to write the documentation in parallel with the other stages of the project and not leave it all to the end. Then, when you have finished the implementation and testing, you will be able to go through it all, proof reading, adding a table of contents, page numbers, and appendices.

Remember that the project is going to be seen by a reader who may have no knowledge of the background to the project. Try to be highly aware of the reader when writing the documentation.

Should the documentation be word-processed?

The short answer is YES. It should also be thoroughly spell-checked, both using the spell-checking facility provided by the word processor, and by reading it through slowly and carefully.

> They're know miss steaks in my project report cause I used special soft wear witch checked my spelling. However it cannot correct arrows inn punctuation and it will not fined words witch are miss used but spelled rite. An it wont catch the sentence fragments witch you have forgotten to.

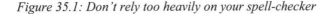

Figure 35.1: Don't rely too heavily on your spell-checker

Word processing skills

There are some crucial word-processing skills which you need to acquire in order to present a really professional-looking final report. This document must do justice to the effort you have so far put into your project; it is all that the examiner will see, and even if you feel you have perhaps not achieved as much as you could have, a well-presented report will help.

Use the Help system to learn new skills, including:

- **Setting styles for the various level of headings and text in your document.** (All the tips below apply to MS Word.) The 'Normal' template comes with built-in styles for Heading 1, Heading 2, Heading 3 and Normal text. You may like to alter the font, size, style and justification of these, or set up new styles of your own.

- **Creating a Table of Contents.** If you have used styles consistently throughout your document, you can create a Table of Contents automatically. Put your cursor where you want the Table of Contents to appear, select Insert, Index and Tables from the menu bar and then select Table of Contents. It can be updated at any time by selecting it and pressing F9.

- **Inserting headers and footers.** The project title and the page number can be placed in either a header or footer. Select View, Header and Footer from the menu bar.

- **Inserting a page break whenever you want one.** Press Ctrl-Enter.
- **Using numbered points and bullet points.** Use the tools on the toolbar.
- **Creating tab stops.** Never use the space bar to indent; nothing will line up when you print the document. Learn to use the tab stops on the ruler line, and the Tab key (above Caps Lock on the keyboard) to tab.
- **Inserting tables.** Use the Table menu.
- **Inserting screenshots.** When you want to take a screenshot to include in your User Manual, for example, press Alt-Print Screen to copy the current window to the clipboard. Then switch to your Word document and use Edit, Paste. A better way is to use a screen capture utility program to copy your screens to a file, from where they can be linked to your document using Insert, Picture, From File. Screen capture utilities are available as shareware.

Putting it all together

Your project documentation should be neatly bound in such a manner that it can be read without a major unbinding job. A ring binder is too large and heavy to be conveniently posted, so investigate the shelves of W.H.Smith or any stationery shop to find something suitable.

Do not put each page (or several pages together) in a plastic sleeve; it makes the project report heavy, expensive to post, and inconvenient for marking.

The title page

The title page should include the title of the project, your name and centre, school or college. It could also include the date you submitted the project and your candidate number, if appropriate.

Table of contents

This is a must. Include in it the sections and numbered subsections, together with page numbers. Every page in your project should be numbered for easy reference; you can add page numbers by hand at the end to pages of test data, for example.

Specification

A suggested framework for the Specification section is given at the end of Chapter 32. You need to make a clear statement of the problem to be solved, with background information.

Design and Implementation

Headings for the design section are given in Chapter 33. Your design may change as you learn more about the software you are using, and your documentation needs to reflect this, through the Project Log. Your test strategy should be included in this section. You must aim to show that you have worked out what tests need to be performed and what results you expect. If you number the tests, it will make it easier to cross-reference them to the actual test runs.

Testing

Testing is a vitally important part of the project. The test data and test plan should all be included in this section. The Testing Section should also contain a test plan analysis to show that it does test all parts of the system. Test runs may be included in an Appendix. **The test runs should be cross-referenced clearly to the test plan**, and be presented in such a way that the reader can see at once what a specific page of output is designed to show. Devising appropriate tests, organising and cross-referencing screen dumps and printed output can take a great deal of time and ingenuity. There is no point including several pages of output with no explanation of what test it relates to or how the output proves that a certain section of the program is working correctly. Make hand-written annotations on the output and use highlighter pen to show significant results.

There is a great temptation to skimp on this section of the project; the feeling is "Right! I've finished the programming and I'm pretty sure it all works. Here's a disk – you try it...". Unfortunately the devising and implementation of the test plan is your job, not the examiner's!

You will also be awarded marks in this section for macro code, if your project has involved writing macros, SQL or other code as part of the customisation of a software package. The listing should be a genuine printout rather than a word-processed document, and should be clearly annotated by hand wherever this helps to explain what is happening. It needs to be made easily understandable, for example by:

- using meaningful variable names;
- stating the purpose of each variable unless it is self-explanatory;
- using comments to state the purpose of each procedure;
- using comments where necessary to explain the logic of a particular section;
- grouping procedures in a logical order so that it is easy to find your way around a long program;
- using indentation to clarify the extent of loops and condition statements;
- using blank lines between procedures to separate them.

System-generated code such as that produced by wizards or recorded macros should be clearly labelled as such.

User manual

This section is aimed entirely at a non-technical user and should use ordinary English rather than 'computer-speak'. For example, do not say 'Boot up the system' when 'Switch on the computer' will achieve the same result.

Presentation is all-important here. Use whatever facilities your word processor has to enhance the appearance of the document, spell-check it carefully and read it through to make sure it flows well and makes sense. It should be a 'stand-alone' document and could even be bound separately from the rest of the project.

Your user manual should include:

- a table of contents;
- an introduction, stating what the system is about and who it is for;
- examples of actual screen displays such as menus, data input screens and output screens;
- samples of printed output;
- an explanation of what each option on a menu does;
- any special instructions on how to input data – for example the format of a date field, or the range of accepted values in an amount field;
- an explanation of any manual procedures such as batching or recording data manually;
- error messages that may be displayed and what to do in that event;
- error recovery procedures – for example what to do if you realise you have made a wrong data entry, or the power goes off in the middle of an update;
- perhaps a hot-line help number.

If you have used a package, explain how to use the system you have created, rather than explaining how to use the software package in general terms. It is a good idea to test out your user manual on the user or a colleague to see if they can follow your instructions without any extra help from you.

Evaluation

The evaluation is an important part of the project accounting for some 10% of the total mark. It should be clearly related to the list of specific objectives written in the Analysis section. The more clearly you have stated the objectives, the easier it will be to evaluate how well your system achieved them.

If the project has been written for a real user, it is a good idea to include the user's comments in this section, perhaps in the form of a letter written on official headed paper and signed by the user. If any suggestions have been made for amendment or improvement, include these as well, whether or not you have managed to incorporate the suggestions. Add your own suggestions for improvement and possibilities for future development. Do take note that a fake letter from your best friend or a glowing letter from an uncritical parent stating how marvellous your system is, flying in the face of all the evidence, is not likely to gain you any marks.

Be honest about the shortcomings of the project; if it is not complete, maybe this is because it was over-ambitious and you should say so. You will not, however, score many marks for criticising the hardware, software, staff or lack of time. One of the skills to be learned in writing a project is to finish it on time in spite of all the difficulties you may encounter!

Honesty pays – if the project has some apparent failures, turn these into successes and gain credit showing what was learnt, documenting what was being attempted, what the outcome was and what difficulties were experienced. Your teacher can authenticate hardware and software difficulties that were beyond your control.

Section 4

Information Systems in Organisations

In this section:

Chapter 36 – Organisational Structure

How organisations work

Organisations are entities comprising a range of human and technological resources which are managed, organised and coordinated to accomplish goals. The goal of a business organisation is usually to generate a profit; other types of organisation may have quite different objectives such as the preservation of the environment, military conquest or gaining religious converts.

> ➤ **Discussion: What are the goals of the following organisations? A College of Further Education, a hospital, the BBC, McDonald's, Greenpeace?**

The three fundamental resources of any organisation are

- People;
- Organisation;
- Technology.

The success of an organisation is determined by how well it manages and controls these three resources (the 'pillars' of an organisation), the components of which include the following:

People	*Organisation*	*Technology*
Career	Strategy	Hardware
Education	Policy	Software
Training	Mission Statement	Telecommunications
Employee Attitudes	Culture	Information Systems
Employee Participation	Management	
Employee Monitoring	Bureaucracy	
Work Environment	Competition	
	Environment	

Figure 36.1: The three pillars of an organisation

Ingredients for success

A survey commissioned by the Department of Trade and Industry in 1997 came to the following conclusions about the most successful UK companies.

Winning UK companies:

- Are led by visionary, enthusiastic champions of change;
- Unlock the potential of their people
  - Creating a culture in which employees are genuinely empowered and focused on the customer;

- Investing in people through good communications, teamwork and training;
- Flattening and inverting the organisational pyramid;
- Know their customers
  - Constantly learning from others;
  - Welcoming the challenge of demanding customers to drive innovation and competitiveness;
- Constantly introduce new, differentiated products and services
  - By deep knowledge of their competitors;
  - Encouraging innovation to successfully exploit new ideas;
  - Focusing on core businesses complemented by strategic alliances;
- Exceed their customers' expectations with new products and services.

Nine out of ten of the winning UK companies studied exhibited these characteristics of innovation best practice.
Source: DTI 'Winning' Report 1997

Focus on people

Successful companies view people as a key resource rather than simply as a cost - the competition may copy the product but it cannot copy the people. One of the main tasks of management, therefore, is to enable each person in an organisation to fulfil his or her full potential.

As one MD puts it, "motivated staff will be ten times more productive than unmotivated staff". There is a clear recognition that it is employees who most often meet with the company's customers and that "when customers meet an employee they meet the whole organisation and often judge the whole on that basis".

Training is seen as a key component in achieving empowerment of the individual and in maintaining focus on the customer in order to remain competitive. Not only is training "the epicentre of empowerment", with as much as 100% of employees' time spent on it, but successful companies "use education as a competitive weapon".

Focus on organisation

Business organisations have four internal functions which they must manage and control:
- The **Production** group produces the goods or services;
- The **Sales and Marketing** group sells the product;
- The **Personnel** or **Human Resources** group hires and trains workers;
- The **Finance and Accounting** group seeks funds to pay for all these activities and keeps track of the accounts.

Traditionally, an organisation is structured in a pyramid fashion, as in Figure 36.2.

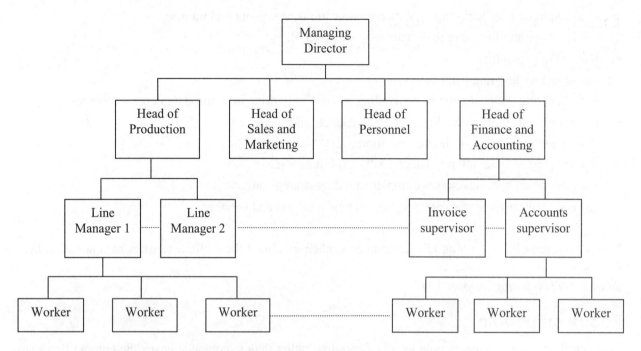

Figure 36.2: The traditional organisational structure

In the late 1990s, changes in working practices resulted in 'flatter' organisations, with layers of middle management disappearing in an effort to eliminate the stifling effects of hierarchy and bureaucracy. As the DTI 'Winning' report says:

"Five years ago the corporate structure was like a pyramid with very steep sides, in fact one could say a stalactite. Now it is more like a plate of peas. The number of levels in an organisation is cut to as few as possible. In some instances there are only three levels within the organisation: Directors, Managers and People".

Turning the organisational pyramid upside down emphasises that customers, markets and competition are crucial to business success, and employees are in the front line, being the major point of contact between the organisation and the customers.

Inverting the organisational pyramid

Customers/markets/competition

Technology Legislation

Employees

Economy/ finance

Management

Champions of Change

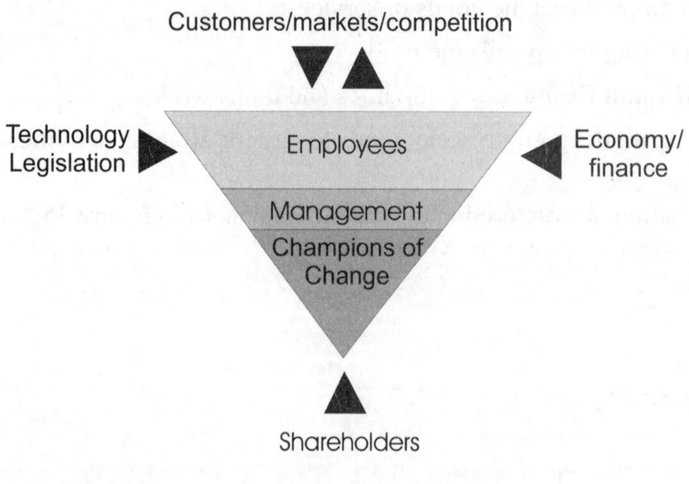

Source: DTI 'Winning' Report 1997

Shareholders

Figure 36.3: A different view of organisational structure

External pressures on an organisation

Surrounding the organisation is an environment of customers, competitors, government regulators, pressure groups and other interested parties, all of which have an influence on how the business is run and what policy decisions are made. (See Figure 36.4.)

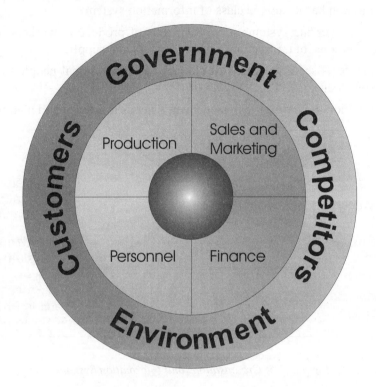

Figure 36.4: The activities of a business organisation

Case study: Preservation vs. the people

In November 1997 the Guardian carried an article describing the four-year battle over local authority plans to replace the chairlift serving the ski centre of Aviemore with a funicular railway. Conservationists compare it with driving a motorway through Stonehenge while local people say it will bring much-needed jobs and money to the area. The RSPB together with the World Wide Fund for Nature (WWF) have fought the plan to develop a glen that offers one of the most breathtaking views in Scotland, home to the rare black grouse and scene of Landseer's famous tribute to the stag, "Monarch of the Glen". For the people of Strathspey, the funicular railway holds the key to their economic future, and the Government is prepared to contribute £9 million to the £17 million scheme.

➤ **Discussion: This is a good illustration of the external pressures that can be brought to bear on the decision-making process within an organisation. Anyone with an interest in a business is called a "stakeholder". Who are the stakeholders in this case?**

Focus on technology

In the first year of this course you learned about various computer technologies. In this module, you'll learn how technology can be used in building and using information systems in organisations. Technology is the third 'pillar' of a successful organisation.

Organisations and information systems

Most organisations are hierarchical; they are arranged in ascending order of power, pay and privilege. The three major levels in an organisation are production workers, information workers and management workers.

Each level in an organisation has its unique class of information system:

- Data or transaction processing systems serve the needs of production workers who must deal with thousands, or even millions, of transactions with customers and suppliers.

- Knowledge work systems serve the needs of clerical and professional people to process and create information and knowledge.

- Management information systems serve management's needs to control and plan the organisation.

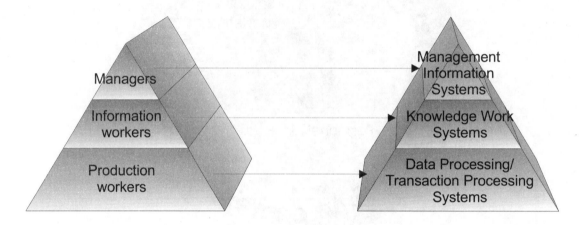

Figure 36.5: Organisations and Information Systems

Organisations, then, do not have just one information system; they may have hundreds. Each of the basic types of systems is described below.

Data processing systems

A data processing system is also known as a **transaction processing system**. Every time you buy an item in a supermarket, withdraw some cash from your bank account, make a hospital appointment or sign up for a college course, a **transaction** has occurred. Transactions are all the events that are recorded when goods or services are bought, sold, distributed or dealt with in some manner.

There are two kinds of transaction processing system:

- Batch systems, whereby transactions are collected over a period of time (say a day or a week) and processed together;

- On-line systems where the data is processed as soon as it is collected.

When there is no immediate urgency for a response or up-to-the-minute information, a batch processing system is often suitable. The TV Licensing Authority, for example, may collect requests for TV licences and process them in batches of 50 or 100 at a time. An airline reservation system, on the other hand, requires up-to-date information on what seats are available, so an on-line system must be used. Such a system is also known as a 'pseudo real-time' system. The word 'pseudo' indicates that processing takes place effectively but not absolutely immediately: a delay of a couple of minutes is normally acceptable.

> ➤ **Discussion: What type of transaction processing (batch or on-line) would be suitable for the following?**
> **A mail-order company taking orders by telephone or mail;**
> **A credit-card company processing sales transactions;**
> **A bookshop using electronic point-of-sale tills to keep track of sales and stock;**
> **A hospital appointment system.**

Knowledge work systems

'Information workers' are of two general types: office clerical workers and sales personnel, and behind-the-scenes professionals such as accountants, lawyers, doctors and engineers.

Knowledge work systems are used by information workers to help deal with problems requiring knowledge or technical expertise. Word processing programs, spreadsheets, databases, computer-aided design packages and project management software all fall into this category. In addition, software and hardware that enables groups of people to find out information, communicate or work together as a team, even though they are geographically separated, is of vital importance in large organisations. Networks, web browsers, e-mail facilities and the use of video conferencing are examples of such technology.

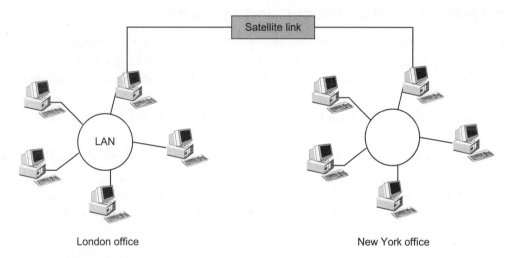

London office   New York office

Figure 36.6: Global communications network

Management information systems

Management information systems are designed to help managers monitor and control organisational performance and plan for the future. This type of information system is discussed in more detail in the next chapter.

Exercises

1. What are the major functions and levels in an organisation? How do the information systems used in an organisation relate to those functions and levels?   (6)

   New question

2. An organisation generally consists of different levels, employing production workers, knowledge workers and management.

   Give an example of each of these types of worker in a named organisation.   (4)

   New question

Chapter 37 – Management Information Systems

Introduction

Over the past two decades, a transformation to an information society has been taking place, and computers and telecommunications technologies have revolutionised the way that organisations operate. We live in an information age, and no business of any size can survive and compete without embracing information technology. Information has come to be recognised as a resource of fundamental importance to an organisation, in the same way as the more traditional resources of people, materials and finance.

It is not enough to be merely 'computer-literate' in order to become an expert in information systems. It is also necessary to understand how to apply modern technology in a business, commercial or other environment to achieve the goals of the organisation.

Information systems vs. data processing systems

In the last chapter we looked at the different levels of information system in an organisation.

Remember that a data processing system is simply one which records the day-to-day transactions taking place within an organisation. An information system is one which uses this data and turns it into useful information. For example:

- Data on items sold is collected by the **data processing system**, using a barcode scanner and an EPOS system, and stored on a computer file;

- An **operational information system** then reads this data and produces a list of items that need reordering;

- A **management information system** may analyse the sales data to highlight sales trends and use this information to plan a new marketing campaign, adjust price levels or plan an increase or reduction in production facilities.

Internal and external information

Much of the information used by management concerns the **internal** operations of the company. However, **external** information about the environment in which the organisation exists is crucial to all organisations. This may include

- Intelligence gathering about competitors' activities;

- Information about population shifts;

- Economic and social factors;

- Government legislation.

This type of information is of great importance to managers who are trying to shave production costs, find new markets, develop new products, or have strategic decisions to make about the future direction of the company. Information is collected in many ways – through conversations and interpersonal 'networking', reading newspapers, trade reviews and magazines, attending conferences and meetings, browsing the Internet. A **formal information system** relies on procedures for the collecting, storing, processing and accessing of data in order to obtain information.

> ➤ An international car manufacturing company maintains a database holding details of every car that will be made over the next ten years by every other car manufacturer in the world. This data is collected through agencies specialising in information gathering, through trade fairs and reviews, 'leaks' and even industrial espionage.
>
> A special department exists to collect and collate this information. One of the manager's jobs is to read every relevant magazine, newspaper article and communication every morning, highlight anything of importance and pass the pile of paper round the department for the others to read prior to the database being updated.

Information flow

Information flows through an organisation through both formal and informal information systems. Informal ways of gathering information include face-to-face conversations, meetings, telephone conversations, reading newspapers and magazines, listening to radio and television and surfing the Internet.

Information is also circulated through company newsletters, memos and notice boards. The problem with newsletters and memos is that readers often have so much information to absorb that they quickly forget it.

Formal methods of disseminating information around an organisation include the following:

- Computerised information systems which allow users to query databases over a company-wide network. Internal data is often collected in the first instance through transaction processing systems. External data can be collected, for example, through agencies such as Dun and Bradstreet which produces an on-line electronic data service called 'DataStream' to both business and academic organisations.

- Software packages such as Lotus Notes enable people at different locations to have the same document on their screens and work on it together. Appointments can be held on the systems so that meetings can be arranged at a time when everyone is free.

- E-mail allows correspondence and files to be transmitted throughout an organisation as well as to others outside the organisation.

- Company-wide Intranets are networks which work on the same principle as the Internet but are for use within the organisation. Information can be disseminated throughout an organisation via the Intranet rather than in the form of written memos and newsletters.

The role of a management information system

The role of a management information system is to convert data from internal and external sources into information that can be used to aid in making effective decisions for planning, directing and controlling the activities for which they are responsible. An organisation may have dozens of different information systems, some of which are useful for the day-to-day operational decisions, and some of which are used in making tactical and strategic decisions.

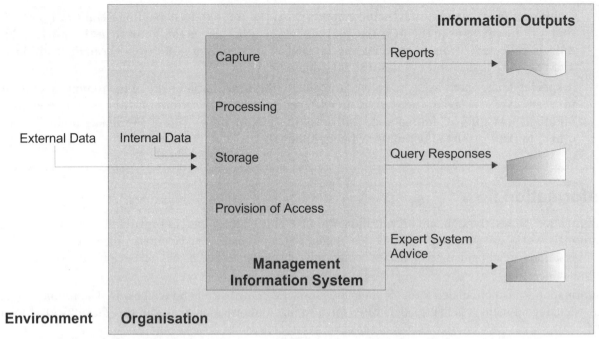

Figure 37.1: The role of a Management Information System

What managers do

To understand how information systems can benefit managers, we first need to examine what the functions of management are and the kind of information they need for decision-making.

The five classical functions of managers (described more than 70 years ago) are:

1. **Planning.** Managers plan the direction a company is to take, whether to diversify, which areas of the world to operate in, how to maximise profit.

2. **Organising**. Resources such as people, space, equipment and services must be organised.

3. **Coordinating**. Managers coordinate the activities of various departments.

4. **Decision-making**. Managers make decisions about the organisation, the products or services made or sold, the employees, the use of information technology.

5. **Controlling**. This involves monitoring and supervising the activities of others.

Management information systems must be designed to support managers in as many of these functions as possible, at different levels (operational, tactical, strategic) of an organisation.

> ➤ **Discussion: How could a MIS help college managers at various levels to carry out activities of planning, organising, coordinating, decision-making and controlling?**

A study in 1973 by Henry Mintzberg found that managers divided up their time as shown in the pie chart below. He described the work of a manager as consisting of hundreds of brief activities of great variety, requiring rapid shifts of attention from one issue to another, very often initiated by emerging problems. Half of the activities of chief executives lasted less than 9 minutes.

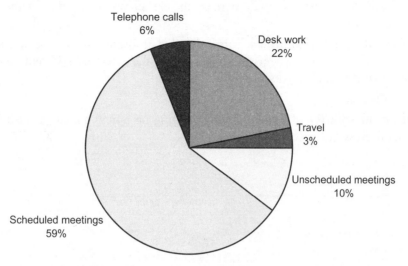

Figure 37.2: How managers spent their time in 1973

> ➤ **Discussion: Today's managers still spend their time divided between many activities. Do you think there are any activities which managers spend more time on than they did in 1973?**

Types of decision

Management decisions can be classified into two types – *structured* and *unstructured*. Structured decisions are repetitive, routine and involve a definite procedure for handling them. Unstructured decisions on the other hand are decisions which require judgement, insight and evaluation. They are often important decisions and there is no set procedure for making them.

> ➤ **Discussion: Categorise the following decisions to be made by a department store manager as structured or unstructured:**
>
> **In which town shall we open the next branch?**
>
> **How many extra staff shall we hire to cope with the Christmas rush?**
>
> **What shall we do about an employee who has had 30 sick days in the last 6 months?**
>
> **Should we try and increase the number of customers who hold a store card?**

Stages of decision-making

Making unstructured, non-routine decisions is a process that takes place over a period of time, and consists of several stages. Think of any important decision that you may have to make, like whether to go on to University or get a job, which college or University to attend, what course or career to follow. You will probably reach any of these decisions over a period of time, having gathered together information from various sources and listened to friends, parents or careers advisers.

The manager who has non-routine decisions to make typically goes through the following stages:

1. **Recognition that there is a problem.** An information system is useful at this stage to keep managers informed of how well the department or organisation is performing and to let them know where problems exist. The principle of exception reporting is especially important in this stage – in other

words, only situations which need some action are reported. (For example, customers with outstanding accounts, a sudden drop or increase in sales compared with the same period last year or a rash of staff resignations.)

2. **Consideration of possible solutions.** More detailed information may be needed at this stage, or possibly tools such as a spreadsheet which can model the effect of different solutions such as price increases or decreases, staff pay increases etc.

3. **Choosing a solution.**

4. **Implementing the solution**. This may involve setting up a new management information system to report on the progress of the solution.

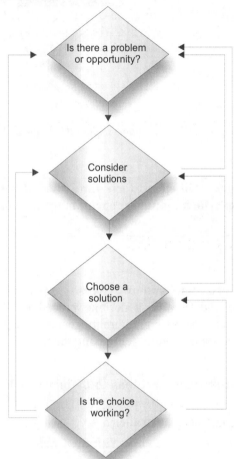

Figure 37.3: The decision-making process

Most decisions do not proceed smoothly from one stage to the next, and backtracking to a previous stage is often required if a chosen solution turns out to be impossible or new information comes to light which offers alternative choices.

Making structured decisions – often of an operational nature – is made easier by having an information system which provides the information necessary to make the correct decisions.

> ➤ **Discussion: A car company gathers information about its customer base through many sources, including market research surveys. One company has discovered that it has relatively few customers in the 18-30 age range. How can this information be used by the company to improve its sales?**

Case study: Buying a new car

If you want to purchase a new car from a Ford dealer, chances are that the make and model you want, in the right colour with the right accessories, is not in stock. It's just too expensive to have cars with every possible combination of options sitting in the parking lot waiting for a customer. In the past, it's been almost impossible for dealers to track down exactly the model that a customer wants.

With the new information system, the dealer can type the details of the required car into a terminal connected to the main Ford plant at Dagenham. The information will then come back to tell the dealer whether there are any cars available of that specification, and exactly where they are. They may be on the Ford parking lot, or there may be only two available, one at a dealer's in Perth and the other in Bournemouth. There may be none available – in which case Ford will make one for you, though this may take some time.

Plant production managers are also connected to the system, and so they know exactly what cars have been ordered and can adjust production to reflect demand every day.

➢ **Discussion: This is an example of a management information system. How does it help**
   – the dealer?
   – the customer?
   – the manufacturer?

Desirable characteristics of a MIS

Formal information systems are useful at every level of an organisation. Operational systems provide answers to specific, routine questions on screen or through regular daily, weekly or monthly reports. A senior manager is likely to need information which comes to light from a new way of analysing the available data, or information from external sources.

Systems designers need to try to design management information systems which have the following characteristics:

- They are flexible, allowing for many different ways of analysing data and evaluating information;
- They are capable of supporting a range of skills and knowledge;
- They help managers get things done through interpersonal communication with other members of the organisation;
- Because managers are busy people who switch rapidly between different tasks, they should not require extensive periods of concentration;
- They should make it easy to interrupt the work and return to it at a later time;
- They should protect a manager, as far as possible, from information overload.

Factors influencing success or failure of MIS

Management information systems are generally enormously complex, and their selection, design and implementation will involve dozens of people from both within and outside the organisation. The managers and directors who are ultimately responsible for ensuring the success of the system need to have not only an intimate knowledge and appreciation of exactly what they want out of the system. They must be aware of the possibilities that ICT systems can offer, the difficulties that may be encountered and the importance of having in place the proper procedures to ensure the smooth functioning of the system.

Failure of management information systems can attributed to a number of reasons such as:

- **Inadequate analysis.** The potential problems, exact needs and constraints are not fully understood before the design or selection of a new system;

- **Lack of management involvement in design.** It is essential that all those expecting and needing to benefit from a new system are involved in its design. Without this involvement, any system is doomed to failure either by providing information which nobody needs (or, worse still, nobody understands) or management having expectations from a new system which cannot be delivered.

- **Emphasis on the computer system.** Selecting the right hardware and software is clearly essential as the basis for a modern computer system but appropriate procedures for handling both data input and output must be established before a system is implemented. The objectives of the new system need to be clearly thought out. Users often request the population of fields on a database for no explained reason and often request management reports which are neither useful nor read!

- **Concentration on low-level data processing.** One of the fundamental functions of a system within a company is the day-to-day processing of transactions, including sales and purchase orders, invoices, goods receipts and credit notes. When designing a basic system, the management information available from the system must be both easily accessible and easily understandable by users who may be neither computer literate nor managers.

- **Lack of management knowledge of ICT systems and their capabilities.** Managers require information for running companies or departments, and among other things, for producing budgets and forecasts. Managers must know what they want from a system but it cannot be assumed that these same managers have a full (or even a slight) grasp of the technology which will provide the information they need.

- **Lack of teamwork.** The needs of the accounts department, the marketing department, the sales department (home and export), and the storage and despatch departments are all likely to differ and an ICT manager needs not only to lead his team but also to be able to take on board the whole company's requirements. Teamwork needs leadership and a good leader is one who can convince all the members of a company team that the ICT system being designed is going to meet everybody's needs – but not necessarily in quite the way that the different players may have pictured.

- **Lack of professional standards.** Clear documentation written in a language that not only the ICT manager can understand is essential for training, implementation and daily use of a new system. Operators need to know exactly what to do in their work (including what to do if they need to undo some action); managers need to feel reassured that, if necessary, explanations are available to help them to interrogate the system for the information they require, and all people using the system must feel confident enough to be able to help others.

(Thanks to John Walsh of BEBC for contributing these thoughts after the installation of their new computer system – which, I hasten to add, is a complete success!)

Exercises

1. (a) What is the purpose of a Management Information System? (1)

    (b) Why is such a system required by managers of an organisation? (1)

    (c) Give **one** example of the use of a Management Information System within an organisation, clearly stating its purpose. (2)

    NEAB IT04 Qu 1 1997

2. List **three** desirable features of a management information system, stating in each case why the feature you have specified is useful. (6)

    New question

3. A school is planning the introduction of a computer-based attendance system for classes and registration groups. The purpose of the system is to produce information for the following end-users:
    *   Class teachers
    *   Tutors/Head of Year
    *   Senior managers (e.g. Deputy Head)

    (a) Describe **three** alternative ways of collecting the information for the system. (6)

    (b) For each of the different end-users describe, with the aid of an example, information that the system might produce in relation to their requirements. (6)

    NEAB IT04 Qu 3 1997

4. With the aid of appropriate examples, explain the difference between formal and informal information flows. (6)

    NEAB IT04 Qu 2 1998

Chapter 38 – The Information Systems Life Cycle

Overview of the systems life cycle

Large systems development projects may involve dozens of people working over several months or even years, so they cannot be allowed to proceed in a haphazard fashion. The goals of an information system must be thoroughly understood, and formal procedures and methods applied to ensure that the project is delivered on time and to the required specification.

The systems life cycle methodology approaches the development of information systems in a very methodical and sequential manner. Each stage is composed of certain well-defined activities and responsibilities, and is completed before the next stage begins. This approach was popular in the 1960s and 70s, when systems were largely transaction-processing systems and had a much heavier reliance on programming than most modern information systems, which are database-oriented.

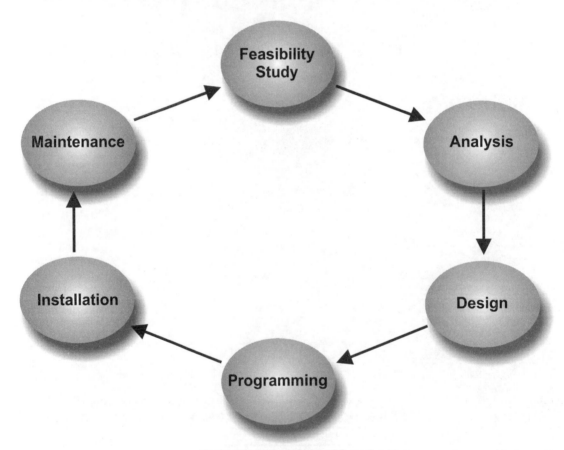

Figure 38.1: The systems life cycle

> ➢ **Discussion: In your experience of practical work on information technology projects, is this a good representation of the process of implementing a system from scratch? If not, why not?**

The waterfall model

The systems life cycle approach to development is also known as the 'waterfall model', and a variation on the basic diagram of 38.1 is shown in Figure 38.2.

Note that the arrows go up and down the 'waterfall', reflecting the fact that developers often have to rework earlier stages in the light of experience gained as development progresses.

A project milestone terminates each stage of a life-cycle-oriented approach. At this stage, the 'deliverable' resulting from that stage – such as the documentation for the analysis or the design, or the program code or finished database application, is *signed off* by all concerned parties and approval is given to proceed. The 'concerned parties' usually include the end-users, the management and the developers, as well as other experts such as database administration personnel. This sequence continues until the evaluation stage has been completed and the finished system is delivered to the end-users.

In this model, the end-user has very little say in the development process, which is carried out by technical specialists such as systems analysts and programmers. He or she is presented with the finished system at the end of the development cycle and if it is not quite what was wanted, it is generally too late to make changes. Therefore, it is extremely important that the system requirements are very clearly specified and understood by all parties before being signed off.

Such levels of certainty are difficult to achieve and this is one of the major drawbacks of the 'waterfall model'.

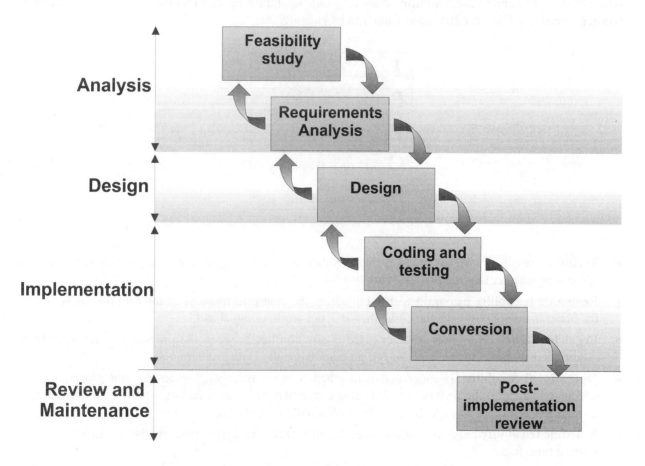

Figure 38.2: Systems development life cycle (the 'Waterfall model')

What prompts a new system?

The development of a new information system is a major undertaking and not one to be undertaken lightly. Wal-Mart, an American discount store, spent $700m on its new computerised distribution system in the 1980s. Tesco, Sainsbury's and Marks and Spencer have spent massive sums of money on their computer systems in the past decade. Businesses must adapt to remain competitive. Some of the reasons for introducing a new system may be:

1. **The current system may no longer be suitable for its purpose**. Changes in work processes, expansion of the business, changes in business requirements or the environment in which the organisation operates may all lead to a reassessment of information system requirements.

2. **Technological developments may have made the current system redundant or outdated**. Advances in hardware, software and telecommunications bring new opportunities which an organisation cannot ignore if it is to keep ahead of its rivals.

3. **The current system may be too inflexible or expensive to maintain**, or may reduce the organisation's ability to respond quickly enough to customer's demands.

Feasibility study

This is the first stage of the systems life cycle. The **scope** and **objectives** of the proposed system must be written down. The aim of the feasibility study is to understand the problem and to determine whether it is worth proceeding. There are five main factors to be considered:

Technical feasibility

Economic feasibility

Legal feasibility

Operational feasibility

Schedule feasibility

Figure 38.3: TELOS – a mnemonic for the five feasibility factors

- **Technical feasibility** means investigating whether the technology exists to implement the proposed system, or whether this is a practical proposition.

- **Economic feasibility** has to do with establishing the cost-effectiveness of the proposed system – if the benefits do not outweigh the costs, then it is not worth going ahead.

- **Legal feasibility** determines whether there is any conflict between the proposed system and legal requirements – for example, will the system contravene the Data Protection Act?

- **Operational feasibility** is concerned with whether the current work practices and procedures are adequate to support the new system. It is also concerned with social factors – how the organisational change will affect the working lives of those affected by the system.

- **Schedule feasibility** looks at how long the system will take to develop, or whether it can be done in a desired time-frame.

The completion of this stage is marked by the production of a feasibility report produced by the systems analyst. If the report concludes that the project should go ahead, and this is agreed by senior managers, detailed requirements analysis will proceed.

Requirements analysis

The second phase of systems analysis is a more detailed investigation into the current system and the requirements of the new system.

Gathering details about the current system will involve:

- Interviewing staff at different levels of the organisation from the end-users to senior management.

- Examining current business and systems documents and output. These may include current order documents, computer systems procedures and reports used by operations and senior management.

- Sending out questionnaires and analysing responses. The questions have to be carefully constructed to elicit unambiguous answers.

- Observation of current procedures, by spending time in various departments. A time and motion study can be carried out to see where procedures could be made more efficient, or to detect where bottlenecks occur.

The systems analyst's report will examine how data and information flow around the organisation, and may use **data flow diagrams** to document the flow. It will also establish precisely and in considerable detail exactly what the proposed system will do (as opposed to how it will do it). It will include an in-depth analysis of the costs and benefits, and outline the process of system implementation, including the organisational change required. It must establish who the end-users are, what information they should get and in what form and how it will be obtained.

Alternative options for the implementation of the project will be suggested. These could include suggestions for:

- Whether development should be done in-house or using consultants;

- What hardware configurations could be considered;

- What the software options are.

The report will conclude with a recommendation to either proceed or abandon the project.

Case study: Computer-dating the customer

When it started a century ago, marketing treated all customers the same. By the 1960s, marketers were able to break that anonymous mass into segments. Now customer databases allow them to treat customers as individuals. They may know consumers' names and addresses, what they buy, what they have stopped buying and even how they respond to a rise in the price of dog food.

For big multinational retailers, this is the equivalent of going back to the days of the individual store owner who knew and greeted each customer personally. The benefits are potentially huge: instead of spending millions on advertising beamed at people who may be indifferent or even hostile to it, retailers can use databases to help them hang on to their existing customers and persuade them to buy more. But it is not trouble-free: databases are expensive to collect and analyse, and some customers may see such individual marketing as an invasion of their privacy.

Talbot's, a 385-store women's clothing chain based in Massachusetts, has compiled a database of 7m names that includes information about customers' sizes. This has enabled them to forecast more accurately which sizes will sell in particular stores. It also asks all customers for their post codes when they pay, to help it plan new store openings. The effort seems to be paying off. For the past five years the company has been opening around 50 new stores a year.

Source: The Economist 4 March 1995

➤ **Discussion: A system like the one above would have cost millions of dollars to install. What were the major costs? What were the benefits?**

System design

The design specifies the following aspects of a system:

- The hardware platform – which type of computer, network capabilities, input, storage and output devices;
- The software – programming language, package or database;
- The outputs – report layouts and screen designs;
- The inputs – documents, screen layouts and validation procedures;
- The user interface – how users will interact with the computer system;
- The modular design of each program in the application;
- The test plan and test data;
- Conversion plan – how the new system is to be implemented;
- Documentation including systems and operations documentation. Later, a user manual will be produced.

Implementation

This phase includes both the coding and testing of the system, the acquisition of hardware and software and the installation of the new system or conversion of the old system to the new one.

The installation phase can include:

- Installing the new hardware, which may involve extensive recabling and changes in office layouts;
- Training the users on the new system;
- Conversion of master files to the new system, or creation of new master files.

Methods of conversion

There are several different methods of conversion:

- **Direct changeover.** The user stops using the old system one day and starts using the new system the next — usually over a weekend or during a slack period. The advantage of this system is that it is fast and efficient, with minimum duplication of work involved. The disadvantage is that normal operations could be seriously disrupted if the new system has errors in it or does not work quite as expected.
- **Parallel conversion.** The old system continues alongside the new system for a few weeks or months. The advantage is that results from the new system can be checked against known results, and if any difficulties occur, operations can continue under the old system while the errors or omissions are sorted out. The disadvantage of parallel conversion is the duplication of effort required to keep both systems running, which may put a strain on personnel.
- **Phased conversion**. This is used with larger systems that can be broken down into individual modules that can be implemented separately at different times. It could also be used where for example only a few customer accounts are processed using the new system, while the rest remain for a time on the old system. Phased conversion could be direct or parallel.
- **Pilot conversion.** This means that the new system will be used first by only a portion of the organisation, for example at one branch or factory.

> ➤ **Discussion: For each of the following examples, state with reasons what type of conversion method would be suitable.**

(a) A bakery is introducing a system to input orders from each salesperson and use this data to calculate how much of each product to bake each day, and also to calculate the salesperson's commission.

(b) A chain store is introducing EPOS terminals connected to a mainframe computer which holds details of stock levels and prices.

(c) A public library is introducing a computerised system for the lending and return of books.

(d) A large hospital is introducing a computerised system for keeping patient records and appointments.

(e) A College is introducing a computerised timetabling and room allocation system.

(f) A Company manufacturing electronic components is introducing an integrated system for production control, stock control and order processing.

(g) A Local Authority is introducing a computerised system for the collection of a new type of tax.

Post-implementation review

An important part of the implementation is a review of how the new system is performing, once it has been up and running for a period of time. Minor programming errors may have to be corrected, clerical procedures amended, or modifications made to the design of reports or screen layouts. Often it is only when people start to use a new system that they realise its shortcomings! In some cases they may realise that it would be possible to get even more useful information from the system than they realised, and more programs may be requested. The process of **system maintenance**, in fact, has already begun, and the life cycle is complete.

System maintenance

All software systems require maintenance, and in fact the vast majority of programmers are employed to maintain existing programs rather than to write new ones. There are differing reasons for this, and different types of maintenance.

- **Perfective maintenance**. This implies that while the system runs satisfactorily, there is still room for improvement. For example, extra management information may be needed so that new report programs have to be written. Database queries may be very slow, and a change in a program may be able to improve response time.

- **Adaptive maintenance**. All systems will need to adapt to changing needs within a company. As a business expands, for example, there may be a requirement to convert a standalone system to a multi-user system. New and better hardware may become available, and changes to the software may be necessary to take advantage of this. New government legislation may mean that different methods of calculating tax, for example, are required. Competition from other firms may mean that systems have to be upgraded in order to maintain a competitive edge.

- **Corrective maintenance**. Problems frequently surface after a system has been in use for a short time, however thoroughly it was tested. Some part of the system may not function as expected, or a report might be wrong in some way; totals missing at the bottom, incorrect sequence of data, wrong headings, etc. Frequently errors will be hard to trace, if for example a file appears to have been wrongly updated.

Prototyping

The waterfall model of the system life cycle has major shortcomings and often bears little relation to what happens in practice. One reason for this is that it doesn't allow for modifications to the design as the project proceeds, with both user and developer learning as they go along. Users frequently have difficulty in explaining their requirements at the start of a proposed system since they do not know what is possible and cannot visualise how the final system will work. This can result in a system which does not really match their requirements. (See Figure 39.2.)

Using the **prototyping** approach, a model of a new system is built in order to evaluate it or have it approved before building the production model. Applied to software projects, this means, for example, using special software to quickly design input screens and create a program to input and validate data. This gives the user a chance to experience the 'look and feel' of the input process and suggest alterations before going any further. The earlier a user is involved, the easier it will be to make changes.

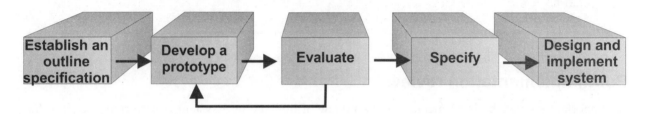

Figure 38.4: The prototyping approach

Benefits of prototyping

The benefits of prototyping are:

- Misunderstandings between software developers and users can be identified when the prototype is demonstrated;

- Missing functions may be detected;

- Incomplete or inconsistent user requirements may be detected and can be completed or corrected;

- A prototype version will be quickly available to demonstrate the feasibility and usefulness of the proposed system to management;

- The prototype can sometimes be used for training before the final system is delivered.

Prototyping may be used in a number of different ways, and various terms have been coined to describe them:

- **Piloting** – using a prototype to test the feasibility of a design proposal;

- **Modelling** – building to develop an understanding of the user's requirements;

- **Throw-away prototyping** – both piloting and modelling are 'throw-away prototypes': once they have achieved their purpose the real system is built;

- **Evolutionary prototyping** – each prototype built represents a step closer to the final solution.

Exercises

1. A feasibility study will often be carried out at an early stage of system development. As well as finding out if the proposal is technically possible the study will also consider economic and social feasibility.

    In the context of a feasibility study describe **one** cost, **one** benefit and **three** possible social effects that would be considered. (5)
    AEB AS Computing Qu 7 1996

2. Often the most critical phase in the systems life cycle is the changeover from the old system to the new one. This may be implemented by *parallel running* or by *pilot running*. Briefly describe these installation methods. (3)
    AEB AS Computing Qu 4 1997

3. State **three** different methods of fact finding available during the systems analysis stage of the systems life cycle, and for **each** of these three methods, give **one** reason for its use. (6)
    AEB Computing Paper 1 Qu 11 1996

4. State and briefly describe **two** different types of program maintenance. (2)
    NEAB Computing Paper 2 Qu 1 1995

5. Describe **five** main stages in the full life cycle of a computerised system. (10)
    NEAB Computing Paper 1 Qu 11 1995

6. Some of the steps in computerising an existing manual system are:
    *   systems analysis
    *   systems design
    *   programming
    *   testing
    *   changeover to the new system
    *   operation and maintenance.

    (a) Describe **three** aspects of the existing manual system which would have to be investigated so that the analysis could be carried out. (3)

    (b) Briefly describe **four** tasks which will be performed during the design process. (4)

    (c) Explain how it is possible for all the individual component modules to pass their tests and yet for the system still to fail. (3)

    (d) The changeover to the new system from the manual system can be achieved in three ways:
    (i)   immediate change;
    (ii) running the manual and computerised systems in parallel;
    (iii) gradually introducing the new system a subsystem at a time.
    In **each** case, state an application for which the technique is most appropriate. (3)

    (e) Briefly describe the responsibilities of the systems analyst once the system is operational. (2)
    London Paper 1 Qu 13 1994

Chapter 39 – Implementation of Information Systems

What is implementation?

Implementation is the process of preparing people for the introduction of a new system and actually introducing it. Preparation work can start early in the systems development life cycle, even preceding the development stage. A major new system runs a high risk of failure if its implementation is not very carefully planned and the organisational changes that will be required not fully recognised and allowed for. A fully developed system may be regarded by its developers as a success because it 'works', and yet never become operational, or fall into disuse after a short trial period.

Successful implementation

As part of your course you will probably analyse, design and develop an information system for a real user. This will include scheduling the various stages of implementation, and evaluating its success. You are in fact doing on a small scale what the developers of any system, large or small, have to do. So what are the criteria for judging the success of a system? Here are some possible measures:

- **High level of use**. Is the new system actually used? New systems for recording student results, registering students' presence using swipe cards, or constructing timetables and scheduling classroom use may all be introduced but not be widely accepted. A new customer information system may never become operational because users discover it simply takes too long to enter the data.

- **High level of user satisfaction.** Do users like the system? Large companies may identify products and services provided by the information systems unit (such as e-mail or Intranet services, network services, new software) and ask users to fill in questionnaires to gauge their level of satisfaction with each product or service.

- **Accomplishment of original objectives.** A comprehensive list of objectives should have been stated in the Analysis stage of system development. Have these objectives been satisfactorily achieved? The objectives may be, for example, to perform certain tasks such as recording student grades or sending out invoices in a shorter time than before, to increase market share of a particular product or to produce more accurate estimates of building costs.

- **Appropriate nature of use.** A high level of use is not always an indication that a system is a complete success. Witness the man who called a PC manufacturer to complain that his coffee-mug holder had broken. The puzzled service engineer, on quizzing the customer, finally realised he was referring to the CD drive. Software, too, can be used inappropriately if training is not given.

- **Institutionalisation of the system**. A successful system will be taken on board enthusiastically by users and used in new and changing ways, evolving to meet new demands.

> ➤ **Discussion: Think of some large-scale information systems that have been successfully implemented. What makes these systems so successful?**

Why do information systems fail?

Information systems fail for many reasons at any stage of the systems life cycle.

1. **Analysis**

   - Not enough time and money is spent researching the problem, and objectives are poorly defined, so that benefits will be hard to measure.

   - The project team is not properly staffed, with team members being allocated only when available so that they cannot dedicate themselves to the task, resulting in a lack of continuity and commitment.

   - Users are not sufficiently involved.

   - Analysts have poor communication skills and do not ask the right questions or extract the necessary information to establish what the problems are with the current system or what the requirements of the new system are.

2. **Design**

   - Users have little involvement and the design therefore does not reflect their requirements.

   - The system is designed to meet current needs but is not flexible enough to respond to changes in the business environment.

   - Management is not involved in the design, or makes excessive and inappropriate demands with no real understanding of information technology and its capabilities.

   - Major changes to clerical procedures are planned with no regard to the impact on staffing or the organisation.

3. **Programming**

   - The amount of time required for programming is grossly underestimated.

   - Programmers lack the necessary skills: too much time is spent on coding and not enough on proper program design.

   - Programs are not properly documented and so disruption occurs when any of the team leaves.

   - Not enough resources such as computer time are allocated.

4. **Testing**

   - The project team does not develop a proper test plan.

   - Users are not sufficiently involved in testing. They do not help by creating test data and tests with expected results specified.

   - Acceptance tests are not devised, conducted and signed off by management.

5. **Conversion**

   - Insufficient time and money is allocated for converting the data to the new system.

   - Training is not given to the users, or is only started when the system is installed.

   - User documentation is inadequate.

   - Performance evaluations are not conducted.

With so much to go wrong, it seems quite amazing that so many systems are successfully implemented! The key lies in careful planning and heavy involvement from both users and management combined with technological expertise.

Case study: Tiptree Book Distributors

Tiptree is a book distributor holding books from many different publishers in its huge warehouse and distributing them to bookshops and libraries around the country as orders come in. One of the largest distributors in Britain, it has 10 acres of warehousing and 25 million books in the warehouse, and in 1994 won the British Book Awards Distributor of the Year. It was able to guarantee that any order received would be dispatched by the following day.

Tiptree wanted to ensure that it stayed at the top – and had plans to put in place a computerised warehousing system that would be so much more efficient that all orders would be filled the same day. Under the manual system, when an order was received from a bookshop, warehouse staff would have to travel all over the warehouse finding the correct titles to put in the box. Then to fill the next order they might have to go right to the far end of the warehouse again.

The new computerised system would hold a map of where every book was positioned in the warehouse. The orders would be entered into the computer, which would work out the most efficient way for books to be picked off the shelves and put onto a new conveyor belt system. The system automatically issued an invoice, advising if books were out of stock. The dimensions and weight of each book were entered so that the computer could automatically pick the right sized box to pack the books in, and double-check the consignment was correct by weighing the box before heat-sealing it and dispatching it.

The system worked perfectly during trials. Tests were carried out with every aspect of the hardware, software and warehouse equipment functioning as they would when the system went live. Tiptree's management was so confident of success that they decided to use a 'direct conversion' method of implementation – stop using the old system one day, and start up the new system the next.

Almost immediately, things started to go wrong.

The warehouse staff did not appreciate the need to pick the books off the shelves exactly as instructed by the computer. If the books were awkward to reach, they would take them from a more convenient shelf. This meant that the computer's map showed the correct pallet of books as being out of stock and in need of replenishment, and the incorrectly dispatched pallet as being still on the shelf when in fact it had gone.

After a few weeks, the computer's map became hopelessly inaccurate. The problem was made worse because as the system deteriorated and customers began to complain about books not being delivered, warehouse staff started to circumvent the computer system and take books off the shelf themselves for immediate dispatch. At this point there were no reliable manual stock records for backup, and it also transpired that the map had not been completely accurate in the first place because staff hadn't transferred data from the old manual system to the new computerised system completely accurately.

With the stock records now corrupted, staff were unable to find books to put onto the conveyor belt within the two-hour period allotted by the computer. After this time the books were marked out of stock and the customers did not receive their orders. Meanwhile, some perfectly packed orders were rejected by the computer system because they were underweight. This turned out to be because the programmers had not allowed for the fact that paperback books lose moisture in a warehouse and so weigh a few grams less. Also, some warehouse staff had mistakenly keyed in the dimensions of the box instead of the book, so the computer thought that only one book would fit into a large box. To add to the problem, the computer would allocate a box to be filled with books it thought were in stock but which could not be found anywhere.

One retailer received six pallets of one title, another received three beautifully packed, heat-sealed boxes which contained no books at all. Waterstone's in Croydon opened a large box that should have contained many titles to find inside a single book: *Chaos* by James Gleick.

As the managing director of Tiptree said: "It took 27 years to build up a reputation as the best distributor in the country, and 7 weeks to lose it".

The story has a happy ending – by 1995 the system was yielding the promised rewards and 98% of orders were dispatched the same day as they were received, and the systems have become a model for the book trade.

(Adapted from Tony Collins' account of this implementation in his book 'Crash')

> **Discussion: What were the major errors in the implementation of Tiptree's system? Could these have been avoided? Think of at least three things they could have done differently in order to ensure a smooth changeover from the old system to the new one.**

Factors in successful implementation

Some recognised factors in successful system implementation are shown in Figure 39.1.

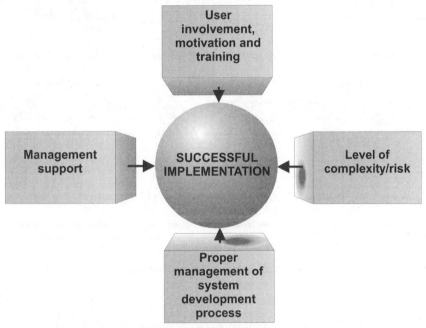

Figure 39.1: Factors in successful system implementation

These factors are considered in more detail below:

1. **User involvement, motivation and training.** If users are involved right from the start of a project, they have more opportunity to state their priorities and have some influence on the end result. Their expertise may lead to a better system being developed. Secondly, they are more likely to react positively to the finished system if they have had an active part in its development.

2. **Level of complexity and risk.** The larger the project, the greater the risk. Some projects are relatively straightforward and others are so highly complex that the requirements may change even before the project is completed. If the implementation team is inexperienced or lacks the required technical expertise, this adds to the likelihood of failure.

3. **Proper management of the system development process.** A project that is not properly managed is likely to suffer from:

   - Cost overruns;
   - Delays in completion;
   - Technical problems resulting in poor performance;
   - Failure to achieve expected benefits.

4. **Management support**. New systems that have the backing of management are more likely to succeed because they are more likely to be positively perceived by both users and technical staff. Also, sufficient funds are more likely to be made available. Changes in work habits and any organisational realignment associated with the new system are likely to be implemented more successfully with management backing.

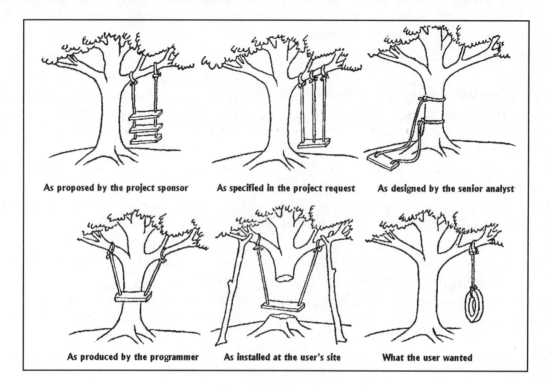

As proposed by the project sponsor   As specified in the project request   As designed by the senior analyst

As produced by the programmer   As installed at the user's site   What the user wanted

Figure 39.2: Problems of communication

Exercises

1. The management of a company wishes to introduce a computerised diary/scheduling package which is known to be compatible with the existing software base. With the aid of examples, give **three** factors which could influence the success or failure of this exercise. (6)

   NEAB IT04 Qu 2 1997

2. A theatre plans to introduce a computerised booking system. Apart from the ability to take bookings and print tickets, describe **two** other possible benefits to the theatre management. Describe briefly three ways in which the success of the new system can be measured. (5)

   New question

3. (a) Name **five** stages of the systems life cycle. (5)

   (b) At each stage of the cycle, things can go wrong which ultimately mean that the system is not successfully implemented. Describe briefly **one** possible cause of failure at **each** stage of the life cycle. (5)

   New question

4. Give **two** reasons why major information system projects which are scheduled to take several years to develop have a higher risk of failure than smaller ICT projects. (2)

   New question

Chapter 40 – Information Systems Strategy

Introduction

All businesses, from the smallest sole trader to the largest multi-national concern, need to have a long-term plan of where they are headed – a business strategy, in other words. Over the next few years, will the business expand or stay the same size? Will it develop new markets for existing products, or expand its product line? Should it aim to take over one or more of its supplier's or customer's businesses, or sell part of the business to a competitor?

Without a business strategy, a business may drift along for some time but it is unlikely to be successful in the long term. A strategy is needed for the following reasons:

- There needs to be an agreed set of objectives for the whole company so that the activities of individual departments are coordinated to serve these objectives.

- Resources have to be allocated to departments to buy new equipment, property and machinery, or to allow new products to be developed or advertised. Such expenditure can only be made effectively if there is an overall plan for the direction the business is moving in.

- Organisations have responsibilities to their 'stakeholders' – for example employees, owners, shareholders, banks and customers. The stakeholders will have a particular interest in seeing that the corporate strategy takes into account their interests.

A SWOT analysis (Strengths, Weaknesses, Opportunities, and Threats) may be used to identify internal and external factors that will have an impact on the business. (Figure 40.1)

Figure 40.1: Formulating a business strategy

Formulating an information system strategy

An information systems strategy is just one part of the overall business strategy and must be developed within the context of the overall corporate objectives, which it will be designed to support. Expansion or development of an information system will inevitably involve:

- The allocation of significant resources;
- Changes in the way that certain parts of the business operate.

The emphasis in formulating the strategy is on determining the information needs of the business, rather than on how the information is to be provided. It must be led by the needs of the business and not by technology. However, an awareness of developments in technology will enable a business to find new ways of gaining competitive advantage.

The general organisational structure, the personalities of managers and other employees and the technology available will all play a part in determining the information system strategy.

Figure 40.2: Factors influencing an information systems strategy

The following is an extract from Ford's Graduate Recruitment brochure in 1998:

> **'Ford is looking for quantum improvements in cost, timing, productivity and customer satisfaction. The way to achieve this is through people, processes and technology. Most important are the people, because without a highly motivated workforce, willing to embrace change, none of this will happen. We need processes that are lean, robust and nimble, changing the way we do business, and we need leading edge technology to implement these processes.**
>
> **Our manufacturing and product engineering operations are two areas of the business undergoing significant change and Advanced Information Technology is the key to enabling that change. It is reducing cycle times, improving quality standards, and allowing us to respond more flexibly to changing customer needs.'**

> ➢ **Discussion: What impact does Ford's information systems strategy have on their recruitment strategy? What sort of people are they looking for in their Business Systems Department?**
> ➢ **What benefits do they hope that ICT will bring to the organisation?**

End-user computing

The 'end-user' is the person who uses the information produced by a management information system. Traditionally, the MIS professionals developed all the computer applications, and end-users were provided with the output in the form of reports. Today's computing environment is very different: end-users now typically develop systems themselves to satisfy a large proportion of their own informational requirements. For example, a manager may use a spreadsheet to work out the forecast for the next quarter. A marketing manager may develop a database application to help plan a marketing strategy for a new product. Teachers develop their own applications to track students' progress and print out results.

The management of end-user computing is one aspect of the overall MIS strategy of an organisation. The dividing line between what systems should be developed by the MIS professionals and what is more efficiently developed by the end-users themselves is not at all well-defined. Some managers think the best strategy is to exert strict control over end-user development (the 'monopolist' approach), while others see benefits in encouraging it to expand (the 'laissez-faire' approach). This allows the creativity and capabilities of end-users to be exploited to their full potential, and means that users' needs can be met without having to wait for funds or time to become available for a professional to develop or upgrade a system, or add a much-needed function to an existing system.

The policy also has major disadvantages:

- **Ineffective use of resources.** Many organisations spend more than half their total ICT budget on end-user computing, so cost-justification is essential.

- **Incompatible hardware and software between departments.** Hardware and software may be incompatible between departments. It is generally more economical to purchase a site licence for software than to have individual departments buying their own packages.

- **Poorly designed and documented systems.** Some systems may be developed by people who are less than expert in analysis, design and implementation, leading to systems which are difficult to use or allow invalid data to be input. Such systems may fall into disuse when the developer leaves.

- **Threats to data security and privacy.** Controls over what data is held, and who has access to it, may be missing.

ICT for competitive advantage

There are four major forces exerting pressure on a business:

- Bargaining power of customers;
- Bargaining power of suppliers;
- New and better products appearing which make the organisation's product obsolete;
- New competitors entering the market.

Figure 40.3: Pressures on an organisation

Strategies can be adopted to counteract these pressures, and maintain competitive advantage, for example by:

- Keeping costs lower than those of competitors;

- Producing better products than competitors;

- Creating new or different products that no one else produces;

- Locking suppliers or customers in to the organisation's products or services, for example by supplying excellent after-sales service.

> **Discussion: Information technology can help in all these aspects. Think of some examples of how technology can be used to keep costs down (see also case study below), or how it has been used in new products over the past ten years.**

Case study: Just-in-time at Wal-Mart's

Wal-Mart's is an American discount store that was among the first to use I.T. for competitive advantage in the 1980s. Many of Wal-Mart's strategies were born of necessity. 'Sometimes it was difficult getting the bigger companies – Proctor and Gamble, Kodak, whoever – to deliver to us, and when they did, they would dictate how much they would sell us and at what price', Walton said later. This forced him to set up his own distribution system. In 1969, with just 32 stores, he built his first warehouse so he could buy goods in volume.

In the past each store manager would order goods to replace those sold, relying on suppliers to deliver them direct to the shop – a hit-and-miss system that took up potential selling space for storage and often left shops out of stock. As Wal-Mart developed its distribution centres in the 1970s, it introduced two innovations. The first was 'cross-docking': goods were centrally ordered, delivered to one side of the distribution centre, and then transferred to the other side for delivery to an individual shop, along with the other goods the shop had ordered. This meant that one full lorry would make frequent trips to each store, instead of several half-empty ones visiting less often. To make this system work well, the firm had to keep track of thousands of cases and packages, making sure they were delivered to the right shop at the right time.

That was where computers came in. By the early 1980s Wal-Mart had not only set up computer links between each store and the distribution warehouse; through a system called EDI (electronic data interchange), it also hooked up with the computers of the firm's main suppliers. The distribution centres themselves were equipped with miles of laser-guided conveyor belts that could read the bar codes on incoming cases and direct them to the right truck for their onward journey. The final step was to buy a satellite to transmit the firm's enormous data load. The whole system covering all the firm's warehouses, cost at least $700m, but it quickly paid for itself.

The first benefit was just-in-time replenishment across hundreds of stores. This has since been refined further, using computer modelling programs to anticipate sales patterns. The second benefit was cost. According to Walton, Wal-Mart's distribution costs in 1992 were under 3% of sales, compared with 4.5 - 5% for the firm's competitors – a saving of close to $750m in that year alone.

Source: The Economist 4 March 1995

> **Discussion: Note how Wal-Mart's I.T. strategy was driven by its business strategies. What problems did Wal-Mart need to overcome to gain competitive advantage? In what ways does information technology help them?**

Exercises

1. Name **three** major resources of an organisation that will influence its business information strategy.

    (3)
    New question

2. An educational publishing company publishes about 100 different titles which are sold by direct mail and through bookshops. Describe briefly **three** alternative strategies which the company might adopt to increase its profit. For **each** of these strategies, show how information technology could help to carry them out.

    (6)
    New question

3. Describe briefly **three** factors within an organisation that can contribute to the successful implementation of an information system strategy.

    (3)
    New question

4. A national charity which provides housing for homeless people has a Head Office in London and 12 branch offices in other parts of the country. The management is currently developing an information systems strategy to help them achieve their objectives, which are to increase donations and ensure that the money raised is spent effectively. Describe briefly **four** ways in which information technology could be used to help them achieve their objectives.

    (8)
    New question

5. Name **four** external 'threats' to a commercial organisation, giving an example of each. Describe with the aid of an example in each case how information technology can be used to counteract these threats.

    (8)
    New question

6. The recruitment department of a large company has an MS Access database which was developed by an information systems professional, to help them keep track of students on sponsorship schemes.

    A student on the scheme is currently spending 3 months in the department and has found that there is a need for some extra reports, and that it would also be useful to keep details of sponsored students' 'mentors' on the database. As she recently gained a Grade A in Advanced Level ICT and acquired a good knowledge of Access in the process, she is able to add some extra options to the main menu, and also correct some minor bugs which have annoyed the recruitment personnel for some time.

    Describe, with reference to the above scenario, **two** advantages and **two** disadvantages of a management strategy that allows users a large degree of freedom to develop their own applications.

    (8)
    New question

Chapter 41 – Expert Systems

Definition

An expert system is a computer program that attempts to replicate the performance of a human expert at some specialised reasoning task. Also known as **knowledge-based systems**, expert systems are able to store and manipulate knowledge so that they can help a user to solve a problem or make a decision.

The main features of an expert system are:

- It is limited to a specific domain (area of expertise);
- It is typically rule-based;
- It can reason with uncertain data (the user can respond "don't know" to a question);
- It delivers advice;
- It explains its reasoning to the user.

An expert system has the following constituents:

- The 'knowledge base' that contains the facts and rules provided by a human expert;
- Some means of using the knowledge (the computer program, commonly known as the 'inference engine');
- A means of communicating with the user (the 'human-computer interface').

Case study: ELSIE the expert system

ELSIE is an expert system that was built in the 1980s for use in the construction industry, is still in widespread use today, and is continually being refined and improved. It is designed to take over many of the more mundane aspects of the job of a quantity surveyor. When a customer approaches a construction company to have, say, a new office block built, hundreds of questions first have to be answered with regard to the size of the building, the number of storeys, the type of central heating required, the number of elevators, the type of cladding (e.g. brick or stone), the state of the proposed building site (level or sloping, wet or dry, clay or rock etc.) The quantity surveyor then takes all these factors into consideration and comes up with an estimate.

ELSIE is an expert system that runs on a PC and is organised in a simple menu-driven format with well-presented screen layouts. It can be used by people with no previous computer experience, and takes the form of a question-and-answer session. When the user has input the answers to all the questions, the system gives a total cost for the building, with a detailed breakdown. The user can then go back and change the answers to certain questions to see what the effects would be of selecting, for example, a less expensive form of heating, or having an extra storey and more car-parking space on the site. The knowledge base also contains current building regulations for all areas of the country to ensure that the proposed building stays within the law.

ELSIE can perform calculations in a matter of seconds that would previously have taken days or even weeks of a quantity surveyor's time.

Expert system shells

An expert system shell is a special software program that allows a user to build an expert system without having to learn a programming language. It provides a straightforward user interface both for the expert to enter the facts and rules, and for the end-user to use the completed expert system to solve a problem.

A shell is basically an expert system without a knowledge base. It provides the developer with the inference engine (i.e. the program that sorts through the facts and rules and produces the answer), the user interface and the means of inputting the 'knowledge'. Many shells enable the developer to present examples with the correct conclusions and the system automatically builds the rules. Thus, for example, a medical team building an expert system could type in the symptoms of hundreds of patients with 'upper abdominal pain' with a known diagnosis of kidney stones, gallstones, stomach ulcers, cancer and so on for each one. The software will then calculate the significance of each symptom so that presented with a new case, it can give one or more diagnoses with an indication of the probability of each being correct.

> ➤ **Discussion: Many expert systems have been developed for medical diagnosis (see 'Expert systems in Medical Diagnosis' in Chapter 4). What are the advantages and disadvantages of such systems?**

Uses of expert systems

Expert systems are used in a wide range of applications such as:

- **Medical diagnosis.**
- **Fault diagnosis** of all kinds – gas boilers, computers, power stations, railway locomotives. If your gas boiler breaks down, the service engineer may well arrive with a laptop computer and type in all the symptoms to arrive at a diagnosis, and then use the system to find out the exact part numbers of any replacement parts required for your particular model of boiler.
- **Geological surveys** to find oil and mineral deposits.
- **Financial services** to predict stock market movement or to recommend an investment strategy.
- **Social services** to calculate the benefits due to claimants.
- **Industrial uses** such as the expert system ELSIE described above.

Benefits of expert systems in organisations

Expert systems can be used to assist decision-makers in much the same way as an experienced colleague. They cannot entirely replace the decision-maker but they can dramatically reduce the amount of work that a person has to do to solve a problem.

Some of the *organisational* benefits of expert systems are:

- An expert system can complete some tasks much faster than a human – for example performing all the calculations required to estimate the costs of a construction project – which will enable an immediate response to be made to a client.
- A reduction in the downtime of an expensive piece of equipment when an expert system is able to quickly diagnose the fault.
- The error rate in successful systems is often very low and may be lower than that of a human being.
- Recommendations will be consistent: given the same facts, the recommendation will always be the same and completely impartial.

- An expert system can capture the scarce expertise of a well-qualified professional who may leave or retire, and can be used at locations where the human expert is not available – say, for geological surveys or medical expertise in remote areas.

- An expert system can be used as a repository for organisational knowledge – the combined knowledge of all the qualified experts in an organisation – which makes the organisation less dependent on an individual's knowledge, which may be lost when they leave.

- Expert systems can be useful for training employees.

Limitations of expert systems

- Expert systems can make mistakes, just as humans do, but even a low error rate in the diagnosis of a disease, for example, may cause people to mistrust a computer system.

- Expert systems do not 'learn from their mistakes' – new knowledge has to be entered into the knowledge base as it becomes available.

- It can be difficult to acquire all the required knowledge from the human experts in order to build the expert system. Expert systems work best when the problem is very well defined and the facts and rules associated with the problem can be clearly stated.

- The use of expert systems within an organisation can result in a decline in the skill level of some of the people using the systems. If a large part of the task is handled by an expert system, employees may not acquire the experience or knowledge that gives them a 'feel' for the task.

- Over-reliance on an expert system may stifle creative thinking and lead to the advice delivered being slavishly followed. For example an expert system which delivers advice on whether a client should be given a loan may come to a different conclusion from a human adviser who can spot exceptional circumstances that the expert system does not take into account.

> ➢ **Discussion: Southampton Football Club is experimenting with an expert system to decide on the monetary value of each player in the Club, based on number of goals, assists, contacts with the ball, age etc. It has been found to give a largely accurate estimate of the value of players who have been transferred in the past.**
>
> ➢ **What are the benefits to the management of using such a system? What factors are not likely to be taken into account by this system in assessing the desirability of selling or buying a player?**

Exercises

1. *(see case study below)*

Case study: Protecting endangered species

The annual turnover in live animals, skins and animal products of endangered species is astonishingly even greater than the money made from the illegal arms trade, amounting to £3 billion per year – second only to illegal drugs trading.

At airports such as Heathrow, Customs Officers are often faced with the task of identifying the particular species of animal or reptile that, say, a handbag has been made from – not an easy task when there are over 35,000 different species of snake alone, each with a different level of protection. The item often has to be sent to a Zoo or Natural History Museum, where an expert counts the number of scales and other features and cross checks this with reference material, a process which can take up to 3 weeks.

Help is now at hand in the form of 'Nemesis', a computer system that can identify the species that a product is made from. A camera attached to a computer takes a photograph of the product, and the computer program compares the features with its database and displays the name of the species on the screen. The more skins it sees, the more accurate it becomes, a process known as 'training' the system.

At the moment, it only stores information on the 15 most traded snake skins, but the developers hope that it will eventually be able to identify all species, and will also be used on furs.

➢ **Questions:**

    (a) The system described could be said to be an 'artificially intelligent' system, performing a task that would require intelligence if performed by a human. What distinguishes an 'artificially intelligent' system from an 'expert system'? (2)

    (b) Give another example of an 'artificially intelligent system'. (1)

    (c) What does 'training' an artificially intelligent system involve? (2)

    (d) What are the likely consequences of the use of a fully developed system of this kind? (3)

2. Expert systems are suitable for many different categories of application. Give **two** different categories and, for each category, **one** typical application. (4)

    AEB Computing Paper 1 Qu 8 1996

3. One of the essential components of an expert system is a knowledge base.

    Using suitable examples, describe the nature and structure of the data held within a knowledge base. (4)

    London Computing Paper 2 Qu 8 1997

Chapter 42 – Information

Introduction

The theme running through this entire course is information: ways of acquiring it, distributing it and using it at the various different levels of an organisation. In this chapter we'll take a closer look at the characteristics of information.

Sources of information

Information can be gathered from a number of different sources. It may be:

- Internal information produced by processing transactions within the organisation;

- External information collected by buying it from agencies or other organisations, reading trade magazines and newspapers, visiting trade shows, Internet databases, government and other statistics.

Levels of information

In the 1960s and 70s, computers were largely used for applications such as payroll, or for scientific and engineering applications where their ability to perform rapid and accurate calculations was an obvious benefit. But today, computers are invaluable because of the information that they can provide to assist and improve decision-making. There are three main reasons why information is needed in organisations:

1. A record of daily events and transactions must be kept so that the company can operate. For example, employees must be paid and records kept of gross pay, tax paid, pension payments and so on; customer orders must be recorded, invoices must be sent out and payments recorded, stock levels must be adjusted. This type of information is called **operational information**.

2. Middle managers in an organisation need information to help them manage effectively. For example, a supermarket manager needs to know how fast particular items move, how quickly stock can be replenished, how well a particular new product is selling, at what times of day or week the store is most crowded. This type of information is referred to as **tactical information**.

3. Historical information, environmental information and information about new businesses moving into the area may be used to build computer 'models' which help to forecast future changes or needs. For example, if a new car manufacturing plant is to open in a particular area, this may have an impact on local supermarkets because more workers and their families may move into that area. This type of information is referred to as **strategic information**.

Quality of information

Useful information should have certain attributes. It should be:

- **Brief.** The information needs to be as concise as possible: too much detail can result in overlooking vital facts. A stock report giving the amount sold and quantity in stock of every one of a hundred thousand items is not useful to a manager who needs to know which are the top selling items or the items which are not selling enough; a summary or aggregate of data is needed. Reports which only list items on which some action may be required are known as **exception reports**.

- **Accurate.** Information which is inaccurate is likely to lead to poor decisions being made and a loss of confidence in the source of the information. Sometimes information can only be given with a certain probability that it will be correct: for example, a farmer may rely on the weather forecast to plan when to harvest a field of wheat, but the forecast is unlikely to be 100% accurate.

- **Up-to-date.** Sometimes information needs to be up to the minute, for example in a booking system or ordering system where a customer needs to know whether a certain item is available. In other cases, it may not matter if the information is not up to the minute; a theatre manager reviewing the season's ticket sales does not necessarily need the figures for last night's performance.

- **Timely.** Reports must reach the right person at the right time.

- **Right level of detail.** Information is sometimes too detailed for a manager to be able to make sense of it. The principle of reporting by exception is very important in management information – in other words, only items that need some action on them are reported.
  Conversely, if not enough information is given it can be misleading. One of the criticisms leveled at the school League tables which are regularly published in newspapers is that they do not show how well a school performs in areas other than exam results – for example in creating a happy environment where each child fulfils his or her potential.

- **In an appropriate format.** Information can be useless if presented in a format which managers cannot understand. Sometimes a graph or chart may be a better way of presenting information than giving a list of figures.

> **Discussion: A manager in a fast food store wants to know how many days of sickness employees have had over the past 3 months. The data is available in the following form:**

REPORT FOR WEEK ENDING 13/12/97

Employee Name	Date	Hrs Scheduled	Hrs Worked	Reason for Absence
Andrews, M	10/12/97	7	7	
Andrews, M	11/12/97	5	4.5	
...				
...				
Goode, L	12/12/97	7	7.5	
Goode, L	13/12/97	8	0	Sick
...				

(rest of records for Goode, L followed by other employee records in alphabetical order)

> **Would this be a suitable report to present to the manager? What are its faults? Check the list given above for 'characteristics of good information' and suggest improvements.**

Case study: Clearing off to College

Every year thousands of students who fail to get the required grades for their chosen University place have to go through 'Clearing' to find a suitable place. This process is made infinitely easier by being able to look up information on the web site www.ucas.ac.uk . In 1999 between August 19 and September 8th the site received a mammoth 1.97 million hits, with over 20,000 students using the course search function to find places.

The key advantage online clearing has to offer is that information is constantly updated as course vacancies fill up and admissions grades alter.

Channels of communication

Formal information systems at an operational level are categorised by having well-defined procedures for the flow of data and information between the people who need it, often in the form of reports or other documents produced by the system. Sales orders in a manufacturing company, for example, may come in to the Sales Department, copies are passed to the Production Department, who will order parts from the Stock Department, who may need to order parts from a supplier, and so on.

How well data and information flows through an organisation will depend on several factors, including:

- The nature of the information – whether it is routine operational information or 'ad hoc' information requested intermittently by managers;

- The organisational structure – for example, the size of the organisation and the number of management 'layers';

- The amount of processing that has to be carried out on the data, and the frequency of processing;

- The geographical distance between the different parts of an organisation.

Case study: Guides need information

The Guide Association is a voluntary organisation with 700,000 members, one tenth of whom are adult leaders. Leaders are registered as members at one of nine regional offices in the UK Each region is responsible for the registration process, and each has a different PC custom-built member registration database system. There is a head office for the UK where programmes of activities and international events are developed for guides throughout the UK, and from which training for leaders is co-ordinated. This central office has no information on the membership because they are registered regionally.

The central office wants to provide more exciting opportunities to more members, and to be able to consult more widely with the membership at large. In order to achieve this and to plan for the future, there is a need to be able to access the regions' information.

Currently the central office has a Novell network, and is currently installing e-mail links to the regional offices. The regional offices have historically paid for their own ICT equipment, and therefore having taken advice locally, have all installed different hardware and software.

An ICT strategy is being developed which aims to improve communication and data sharing within the Association, and to enhance the management information available.

➢ **Discussion: What are the problems in getting the information to the Head Office of the Guide organisation? How can these problems be solved?**

➢ **Think of some ways in which the Head Office will be able to make use of the information it can access once the new system is in place.**

Presenting management information

The way that information is presented can be almost as important as the information itself. Information can be presented in numerous different ways:

- On computer printouts, using the principle of exception reporting for brevity and clarity;

- On a VDU. It could take the form of a report or a 'slide show' produced using a presentation graphics package, for example;

- Desktop published, incorporating company logo, graphs, diagrams, photographs etc;

- Orally – 'over the grapevine', by telephone or in formal presentations;

- Using videoconferencing to enable several people at separate locations to participate in meetings and information exchange;

- Over a company-wide intranet – an internal network which all employees have access to and on which important information can be posted.

> ➤ **Discussion: Think of other ways in which information can be disseminated to employees in an organisation.**

The intended audience

The way that information is presented will depend to a large extent on who it is intended to reach. Information on products and sales intended for customers will be presented in a different way from information intended for wholesalers or the company accountant.

Graphs and charts

Graphs and charts are an effective way of presenting information and highlighting problems or trends. A **bar chart**, for example, shows a trend at a glance. (Figure 42.1.)

Figure 42.1: Bar charts are often used in newspapers

A **line graph** may be a good way to highlight seasonal sales figures.

A **pie chart** can be a good way of showing how a total is made up, but is not effective if there are too many segments. The one shown in Figure 42.2 could be used to emphasise the amount of money spent on domestic services at Oxford Colleges.

Oxford Colleges		
Expenditure 1995/96		
	£m	%
Academic	33	29
Catering	10	8
Domestic services	30	27
Administration	13	12
Buildings	22	19
Other	6	5

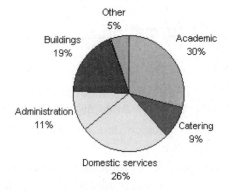

Source: Oxford Magazine

Figure 42.2: A pie chart illustrating a table of figures

Guidelines for presentations

A presentation could for example take the form of a talk accompanied by overhead projector transparencies or slides, or a slide show prepared in PowerPoint or a similar graphics package. Either way, the information on each screen or slide should be:

- Simple – no more than 5 or 6 clearly legible lines, in clear English;
- Brief – bullet points are a good communication tool;
- Visually appealing – don't use too many different fonts, or all uppercase letters. Graphs and charts are useful where numeric information has to be imparted.

Keeping everyone informed

The Department of Trade and Industry (DTI) commissioned a survey in 1997 of 'best practices' in over 100 different 'winning UK companies'. They note that in these organisations:

> 'Communication takes place in many directions throughout an organisation, and is always a two-way process. Just as the leaders of a company communicate their vision of where the company is going, they welcome and encourage feedback and ideas from all their employees, for they recognise that all have something to offer: "one proposal from each of our 100 employees is better than 100 proposals from one super boss". Communication takes the form of regular team briefings, frequent internal newsletters and regular contact with customers. In addition, senior management frequently gets out to meet employees by walking around the organisation and talking with individuals, encouraging the team concept of "us" rather than the divisive "them" and "us".'

Source: 'Winning' (A DTI report 1997)

The bar chart below summarises the different ways that information is disseminated around the organisations surveyed.

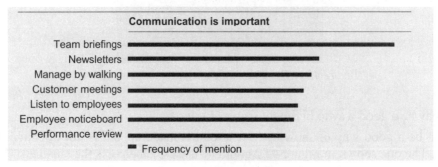

Figure 42.3: Methods of communication

Marketing information

One of the most valuable assets that many companies hold is the information they have collected about their customers. As well as names and addresses, they may collect information about their incomes, their professions, how much they spend, what products they are most likely to be interested in and so on. There are several ways this information can be collected:

- Every time a customer makes a purchase or orders a catalogue, their name and details are added to a customer database.
- When customers make a purchase and fill in a guarantee card, they are frequently asked to provide a lot of information about products they own, their income group, number of children and so on.

- People visiting a company's Web site can be asked to 'register' by providing a lot of personal information before gaining access to the site.
- Companies may buy mailing lists from other companies selling related products. For example, a company selling seeds, bulbs and shrubs may buy a list from a manufacturer of garden furniture.

Keeping a mailing list up-to-date is a major task – it is estimated that companies in the UK waste over £37m a year on 'gone-aways' – people who have died or moved with no forwarding address, and whose letters are returned. Companies do not usually remove 'gone-aways' from their lists: they mark them as such, and leave them on the database. If they subsequently buy a list from another organisation, they can run a program to identify names which appear on both lists, and thus avoid the problem of reinserting names they had previously deleted.

Some people object to their names being passed on, and questionnaires usually include a box to tick if the customer does not want this to happen. However, the data is often collected without the customer's knowledge, simply by making a purchase in a shop, so there is no guarantee that your name, address and purchasing habits are not on databases all over the world.

Exercises

1. The management of a company complains that the Management Information System (M.I.S.) continually fails to produce the appropriate information at the right time. The person responsible for the M.I.S. responds by blaming the 'inadequate data and information flow' within the company and requests a review of 'data and information flows'.
   (a) State **six** factors which influence the flow of information and data within an organisation. (6)
   (b) With the aid of examples, describe **three** techniques which could be used to review the current information flows. (6)

   NEAB IT04 Qu 8 1997

2. "The quality of management information is directly related to its timing."
   (a) Discuss this statement paying particular reference to:
   - The different purposes for which the information may be required;
   - The relative merits of speed versus accuracy. (6)
   (b) In planning the information flow within a system, where are the delays likely to occur and why? (6)

   NEAB IT04 Qu 9 Sample Paper

3. Many retail organisations have developed large databases of customer information by buying data from each other.
   (a) Describe **two** possible uses these organisations could make of the data they purchase. (4)
   (b) Some customers may object to data held on them by one organisation being sold to another organisation. Describe some of the arguments which either of these retail organisations may use to justify this practice. (4)

   NEAB IT04 Qu 2 Sample Paper

4. A manufacturing company intends to use an information system to store details of its products and sales. The information system must be capable of presenting the stored information in a variety of ways. Explain, using **three** distinct examples, why this capability is needed. (6)

   NEAB IT02 Qu 4 1997

Chapter 43 – Data

Data capture

Data may be entered into a computer system by a variety of different methods depending on the quantity of data and the circumstances in which it is captured. Wherever practical, methods of direct data entry (without having to key data in) will be used to avoid the possibility of entering the data wrongly. Common methods of data include:

- bar code readers;
- magnetic stripe cards;
- smart cards;
- magnetic ink character recognition (for reading information from cheques – the amount still has to be keyed in);
- keyboard.

It is in some cases possible to avoid having to re-enter data that has already been captured by sending it from one organisation to another via Electronic Data Interchange.

Using bar codes

Bar coding is one of the most popular ways of capturing data, with the most common application being in shops and supermarkets where all items are bar coded. In spite of the high initial investment, it is estimated that a 2% investment of costs in information technology leads to a 6% saving in costs.

The major benefit of using bar codes at point of sale is that management is provided with very detailed up-to-date information on key aspects of the business, enabling decisions to be made quicker and with more confidence. For example:

- Fast-selling items can be identified quickly and automatically reordered to meet demand;
- Slow-selling items can be identified, preventing a build-up of unwanted stock;
- The effects of repositioning a given product within a store can be monitored, allowing fast-moving more profitable items to occupy the best space;
- Historical data can be used to predict seasonal fluctuations very accurately.

Bar code scanners are relatively low cost and extremely accurate: only about one in 100,000 entries will be wrong.

Photograph courtesy of Scanner Technologies

Figure 43.1: A bar code scanner

Other uses of bar codes

Bar codes can be used in a wide range of applications that require fast and accurate data entry. These include:

- **Warehousing**. Bar coded containers of raw materials are stored in racks of bins which are also bar coded. When goods are put into the warehouse, the computer system instructs an automatic crane to retrieve the nearest available empty bin. The filled bin is then returned to an empty location. The crane relies entirely on bar codes to move goods in and out.

- **Transport and distribution**. All major road freight carriers now use bar codes. Individual packages are bar coded as are depot consignments. The exact location of any package is known at any one time together with details of the type of service used. Individual customers can be billed quickly and missing parcels traced more easily.

- **Manufacturing**. Very accurate data relating to work in progress can be obtained using bar codes as the data entry method. Management can obtain up to date data on the progress of unfinished goods, enabling bottlenecks and over-production to be reduced and production efficiency to improve.

- **Marketing**. Many polling companies now use bar coded multiple choice questionnaires to enter data quickly and accurately. Survey times can be dramatically reduced.

- **Medical**. Bar codes are commonly used to identify blood and other samples. Hospital patients' and outpatients' records are increasingly bar coded for fast retrieval and better accuracy.

- **Libraries**. Bar codes are used to record loans and provide more information on stock.

- **Banking, insurance and local government**. Bar codes are used extensively for accurate document control and retrieval. Many cheque book covers, insurance claim files and council tax forms are bar coded.

Magnetic stripe cards

Cards with a magnetic stripe are widely used for applications ranging from railway cards to customer loyalty cards. The information provided when someone signs up for a loyalty card with Sainsbury's, Tesco, Boots or W.H.Smith, for example, plus a few months of shopping records, can provide a detailed portrait of customers' habits.

The day is not far off when you will be able to wake up on Saturday morning (or whichever is your regular shopping day) to an e-mail from Sainsbury's suggesting what you need to buy this week.

Linking customers and suppliers through EDI

Electronic data interchange (EDI) is the electronic transmission of business data, such as purchase orders and invoices, from one firm's computerised information to that of another firm. Since EDI transmission is virtually instantaneous, the supplier's computer system can check for availability and respond quickly with a confirmation.

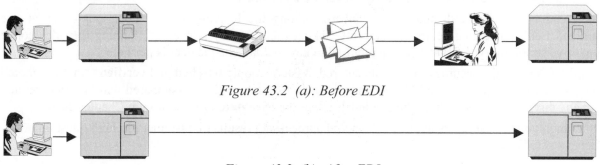

Figure 43.2 (a): Before EDI

Figure 43.2 (b): After EDI

Speed and reliability are major advantages of EDI. It does away with re-keying data, increases accuracy and eliminates delays. Data such as 'A' Level results are now commonly transmitted direct to schools and colleges rather than being sent by mail. Using a service such as BT's CampusConnect, schools and colleges are able to download the results in encrypted form up to two days before their official release date; at one minute past midnight on results day, they are sent a password which allows them to decode the results. Having the results on computer also makes it far easier for the schools and colleges to collate exam results and produce the various statistics and performance indicators required by the DfEE for national league tables.

Smart cards

Smart cards containing a microchip are likely to replace cash over the next five years. Cash-loaded smart cards are already undergoing trials in several British cities and university campuses.

Case study: A smarter way to pay

Students at Aston University are all issued with a plastic smart card. That one card gets the students through security checks into any area they need to visit. It can also be used to buy lunch at any one of the campus refectories or bars and acts as a student ID and library card.

If a student's cash balance gets low, it can be replenished at a bank or through a hole-in-the-wall machine that acts like a cashless ATM. There is a £5 minimum and £100 maximum cash capacity on the card.

➢ **Discussion: As students move around the campus, data can be collected about where they have been, what they have bought, what books they have borrowed from the library and so on. This data could be processed in many different ways to provide all sorts of management information. Think of some useful reports that could be produced, and ways in which this information could be used.**

➢ **What would be the benefits and drawbacks of smart cards replacing cash in the UK? It would theoretically be possible to know exactly how much cash each individual spent – would this be desirable, or an invasion of privacy?**

Keying in data

The keyboard is still widely used for data input in spite of the drawbacks of inaccurate data transcription (copying from a paper form), comparatively slow data entry and the risk to the health of employees who spend all day at a keyboard.

Banks, for example, no longer process routine transactions (such as paying in cheques) in branches. Instead, the work is sent to giant processing centres where the staff do nothing but key in data.

"It's like a factory", said one Barclay's worker. "There's just crates and crates of work everywhere. They call them customer service centres, but you never see a customer".

The trend is raising health and safety concerns among the banking unions. Four employees at one Midland Bank processing centre are currently taking their employer to court claiming they developed repetitive strain injury (RSI) after being required to key in 2000 cheque details per hour.

In order to ensure the accuracy of the data entered, it is commonly **batched** and **verified** – that is, entered twice by different operators with the second version being automatically compared with the first version and any discrepancies brought to the operator's attention. (See **batch processing** in Chapter 24.)

Other high volume data entry applications include processing results of customer research questionnaires. (See case study below).

Case study: Bradford & Bingley

In January 1998 the Bradford and Bingley, Britain's second biggest Building Society, mailed a questionnaire to its two million members asking them for personal details about their employment status, financial position and so on. Customers were also asked whether they agreed or disagreed with the statement "I appreciate the value of the long-term benefits provided by a mutual building society as against a one-off windfall from a converting society."

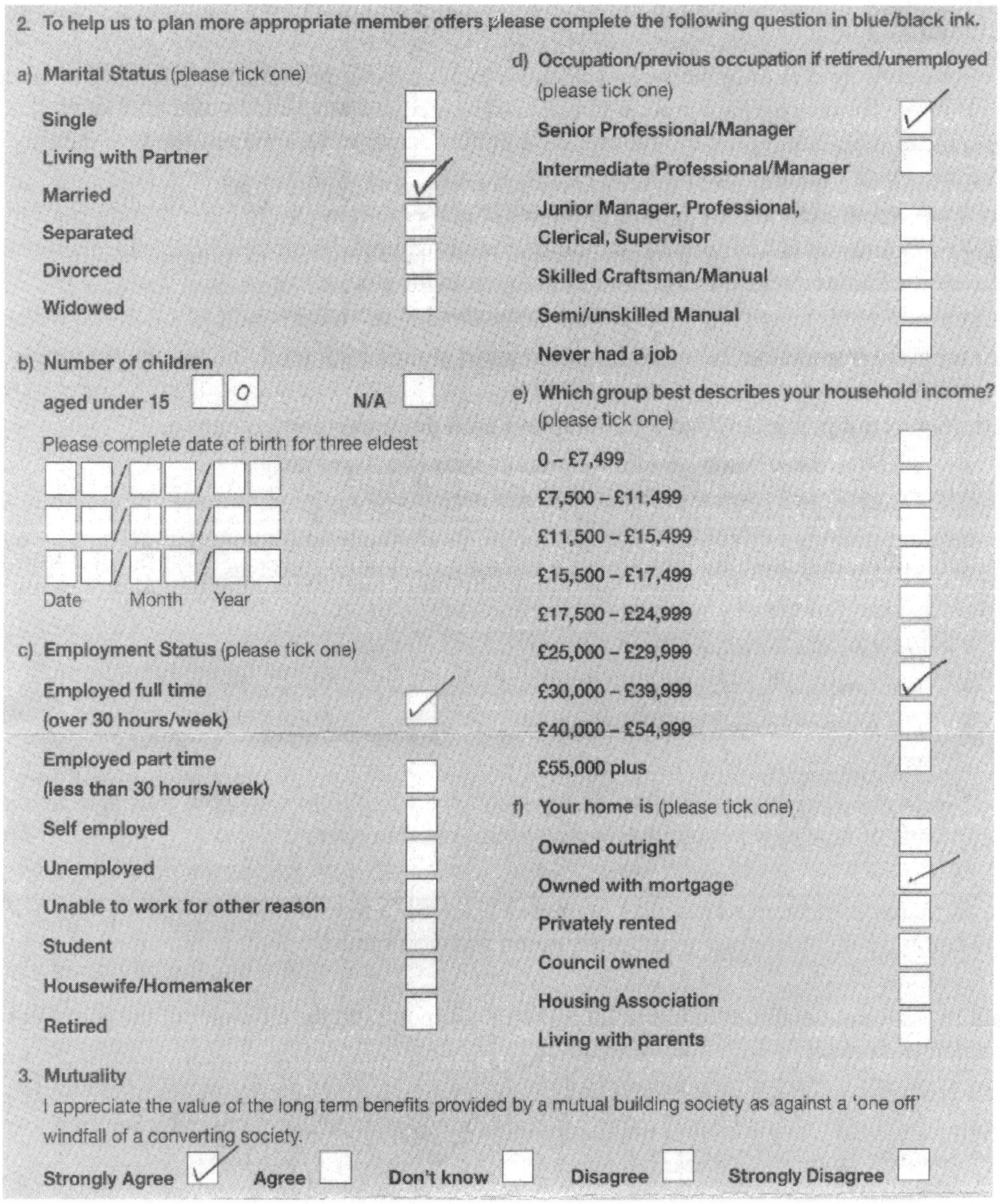

2. To help us to plan more appropriate member offers please complete the following question in blue/black ink.

a) Marital Status (please tick one)

- Single
- Living with Partner
- Married
- Separated
- Divorced
- Widowed

b) Number of children aged under 15 — N/A

Please complete date of birth for three eldest

Date / Month / Year

c) Employment Status (please tick one)

- Employed full time (over 30 hours/week)
- Employed part time (less than 30 hours/week)
- Self employed
- Unemployed
- Unable to work for other reason
- Student
- Housewife/Homemaker
- Retired

d) Occupation/previous occupation if retired/unemployed (please tick one)

- Senior Professional/Manager
- Intermediate Professional/Manager
- Junior Manager, Professional, Clerical, Supervisor
- Skilled Craftsman/Manual
- Semi/unskilled Manual
- Never had a job

e) Which group best describes your household income? (please tick one)

- 0 – £7,499
- £7,500 – £11,499
- £11,500 – £15,499
- £15,500 – £17,499
- £17,500 – £24,999
- £25,000 – £29,999
- £30,000 – £39,999
- £40,000 – £54,999
- £55,000 plus

f) Your home is (please tick one)

- Owned outright
- Owned with mortgage
- Privately rented
- Council owned
- Housing Association
- Living with parents

3. Mutuality

I appreciate the value of the long term benefits provided by a mutual building society as against a 'one off' windfall of a converting society.

Strongly Agree — Agree — Don't know — Disagree — Strongly Disagree

Figure 43.3: A customer research questionnaire

(Reproduced with permission from Bradford & Bingley Building Society)

> ➤ **Discussion: What would be the best method of inputting data from the returned questionnaires?**
>
> ➤ **Studies have shown that on average one error occurs every 300 key presses. If the data is keyed in, approximately what percentage of forms will contain an error? Do these errors matter? How can they be spotted and corrected?**
>
> ➤ **What sort of analyses could be performed on the data to provide management with useful information about their customers? How could the management use this information?**

Exercises

1. A college collects data from incoming students which includes the students' subjects and grades at GCSE level. These grades are processed and used to predict an expected grade at A level. It is found that some of the grades given by students are less than accurate. Describe methods of data capture and entry which minimise this problem. (6)

   NEAB IT04 Qu 5 Sample Paper

2. A large supermarket has fifty checkout points. Each is equipped with a point of sale incorporating a bar code reading device and is linked to a computer in the stock room.

   The supermarket is one of a number of similar supermarkets, all supplied from a central warehouse.

   Each night the supermarket's computer is connected to the computer in the warehouse to pass on the requirements for the supply of stock.

   Fresh food is ordered direct from local suppliers each day according to demand.

   (a) (i) Identify **three** points at which data is captured for this system.

   (ii) Describe **two** methods of capturing this data. (5)

   (b) Explain why the supermarket management might encounter difficulties if it relies only on sales data captured at the point of sale, as a basis for restocking the shelves. (2)

   (c) Occasional failures of equipment occur which might affect:

   - Point of sale terminals;
   - The supermarket computer;
   - The communication links;
   - The warehouse computer.

   Discuss how the system could be designed to cope with failures, without causing a serious loss of data, or making it impossible for the supermarkets to operate. (8)

   London Computing Paper 1 Qu 9 1997

3. In a particular computerised payroll system data is keyed in from timesheets. In the context of this application distinguish between data verification and data validation. (4)

   NISEAC Computing Paper 1 Qu 1 1997

4. State **two** advantages to the supermarket and **two** advantages to the customer of the use of bar code scanning equipment. (4)

   NISEAC Computing Paper 1 Qu 1 1996

5. Briefly describe **two** direct data capture methods stating one application for which each is appropriate. (6)

   NISEAC Computing Paper 1 Qu 7 1995

Chapter 44 – The Management of Change

Outcomes from ICT investments

A study carried out in the UK in 1996 by OASIG, a special interest group concerned with the organisational aspects of ICT, came to the following alarming conclusions:

- 80-90% of systems do not meet their performance goals;
- About 80% of systems are delivered late and over budget;
- Around 40% of developments fail or are abandoned;
- Fewer than 40% fully address training and skills requirements;
- Fewer than 25% properly integrate business and technology objectives;
- Just 10-20% meet all their success criteria.

Source: OASIG Study 1996

This study drew on the expertise of leading management and organisational consultants and researchers, and covered approximately 14,000 organisations in all major sections of the economy, including a comprehensive range of ICT systems.

Valuing the workforce

The increasing complexity of interactions between business, work and technological changes is a source of an immensely difficult set of problems for everyone who manages, uses and develops ICT systems. These complexities are made even more difficult to resolve when organisations are faced with competitive and economic pressures. The emphasis on minimising costs and increasing efficiency sometimes means that not enough weight is given to other values and goals, and insufficient attention is given to human and organisational factors.

When cost savings are the dominant criteria on which ICT investments are judged, people become perceived as costs rather than as assets; as units of production rather than motivated beings who add value to products and services; as sources of error rather than assets whose experience and creativity differentiate one organisation from another.

Job cuts, described euphemistically as 'downsizing' or 'delayering' are often perceived as a major goal of a new ICT project. Naturally, employees are unlikely to participate enthusiastically in a new system that they perceive is a one-way ticket to unemployment.

Reasons why ICT systems fail

Common causes of the failure of new ICT systems are:

- There is too much emphasis on technological factors and the capabilities of the latest hardware. Trying to use the latest hardware, unproven by time and the experience of other organisations, is very risky.
- Senior managers are often vague about exactly what the objectives of a new system are. They may fail to understand fully the business opportunities and the difficulties arising from new ICT systems, justifying the investment on the grounds of cost reduction alone.

- This narrow viewpoint means human and organisational factors are often ignored. The way things are done and the jobs of individual users will be changed and this needs to be carefully explained and managed. Most senior managers do not have a good enough understanding of the links between technological and organisational change.

- Users are often not involved or invited to participate in the design or development of a new system and as a result are resentful and obstructive when they could make the difference between success and failure.

- Users may have been given unrealistic expectations of the new system so that even if it is a success judged by the performance criteria, they may be disappointed and feel that the effort was a waste of time. The benefits to the business may be overestimated by management, unintentionally or for political reasons.

- Costs are often underestimated.

- The time that the new system will take to develop is often underestimated.

- The new system may be over-ambitious. The more complex the system, the greater the risk of failure.

Case study: London Ambulance Service

It was never going to be easy computerising the largest ambulance service in the world, while at the same time profoundly changing an organisation that had existed since before the Second World War. Today, the service covers about 600 square miles with a population of 6.8 million residents, increasing steeply during the daytime. In January 1993 it employed 22,700 people including 200 managers and 326 paramedics. 300 emergency ambulances and over 400 patient transport vehicles struggled to cope with between 1,300 and 1,600 emergency calls a day.

In the early 1990s, the service was experiencing internal problems, with the staff resenting management's imperious attitude towards them, and management resenting the staff's resistance to change. In 1990 there was a major pay dispute and, in preparation for government health reforms, 53 senior and middle managers were made redundant. It was against this background of instability, organisational change and employee resentment that plans for a new computerised system were made. It was claimed that "it would be the first of its kind in the UK", and would involve "a quantum leap in the use of technology" – two phrases that should have caused a chill of foreboding in anyone remotely connected with ICT projects.

The objectives of the new system included the following:

1. Call-taking, accepting and verifying incident details, including location;
2. Determining which ambulance to send;
3. Communicating details of an incident to the chosen ambulance;
4. Positioning suitably equipped and staffed vehicles in places where they were most likely to be needed, so minimising response times to calls.

Under the manual process, when a 999 call was received the details were written down together with the location and a map reference. The form was put on a conveyor belt by one of the 200 people working in the department, and at the other end a resource allocator identified duplicate calls and, taking into account the location of ambulances from information radioed in, dispatched the nearest or most suitable one. The whole process took about 3 minutes.

Much of this process could be computerised, but part of the process depended on the judgement and experience of the dispatcher. But the end-users were not involved in the computerisation – there was little consultation of employees and many saw it as a way of downgrading their jobs and forcing them to accept unwelcome changes. They regarded it with distrust from the start. Training on the new system was given, but so far in advance of implementation (as the deadlines for implementation slipped) that many had forgotten how to use it by the time it was introduced.

In January 1992 a limited trial took place, which demonstrated a number of problems.

- Ambulance crews did not always report where they were and what call they were handling, and the computer required a perfect knowledge of where every vehicle was.

- Transmission blackspots and software error resulted in inaccurate location fixes of ambulances.

- The system could not cope with established working practices such as an operator allocating a different vehicle from the one allocated by the system.

- Problems with hardware, especially slow system response times during busy periods.

Despite recognition of all these problems, deployment of the full system went ahead on October 26 1992, with disastrous consequences. As the hours went by, the system knew the correct location of fewer and fewer ambulances. Neither did it know what equipment they carried or the particular skills of the crew on board. Several ambulances were dispatched to single minor incidents, and real emergencies were ignored. The staff had been told to minimise voice communications and lost complete control of the system. During the three-week period which followed, an eleven year-old girl died of renal failure after waiting 53 minutes for an ambulance. The irony was that she lived only two minutes from a hospital where she was a regular patient, and the only available ambulance was sent to a caller who turned out to have a headache.

The 80-page report which was produced after a three-month enquiry stressed that:

- such a system needs to be fully resilient and reliable, with fully tested levels of backup;

- the system must have total ownership by both management and staff, and staff must have confidence in its reliability;

- the system must be developed in a time scale and at a cost that allow for consultation, quality assurance and testing;

- the system should be introduced in a stepwise, modular approach;

- retraining of staff should be carried out thoroughly on the system, and the timing of the training should be such that 'skills decay' does not occur;

- a suitably qualified and experienced project manager should be appointed to ensure the close control and coordination of all parts of the system.

A full and fascinating account of this disaster is given in 'Crash' by Tony Collins. (See booklist in Appendix C.)

> **Discussion: Change needs to be properly managed. What could the management have done differently to avoid this disastrous computerisation?**

Managing change successfully

Generally, the introduction of a major new ICT system needs to be preceded by a review of the organisational structure and current working practices. Trying to change too much at once is a sure step to disaster – and change cannot be successfully managed by imposing it on a reluctant organisation.

All the users of a proposed new system, from the shop-floor workers through to senior management, need to be involved and included in consultations. Ideas and misgivings should be listened to and proposed changes explained.

The benefits of a new system should be explained but not exaggerated – unrealistic expectations of what a new computerised system will do can lead to disappointment.

Training must be given to all those involved, not only in how to use the technology but also in the new organisational procedures and the consequences of not using the new system correctly.

Case study: Pindar

Andrew Pindar is the fourth-generation chairman of Pindar, a printing firm recently nominated as one of Britain's finest users of best-practice management. Pindar's main business is printing BT phone directories and industrial catalogues. Pindar described his early problems:

"Walking around Pindar, I encountered a feeling of frustration and dissatisfaction among the workforce. One could almost feel a certain hostility in the air, born no doubt out of a resentment and a feeling that management just did not understand the everyday issues and pressures heaped upon them by a hierarchy that never bothered to explain the logic behind directives. On the other hand, we had a management that could not understand why the workforce was not satisfied, in fact grateful, for being employed."

Andrew concluded that Pindar had to change, and he hired Time Manager International to put in place its Putting People First programme. Early enthusiasm soon dissipated, however. "I had a romantic notion that people would come along with me", he says, "and understand what we'd agreed at board and strategy meetings. I never appreciated that obstacles could be put in place, not by worker-bees, but by senior managers. They felt territory-threatened."

Pindar redoubled his efforts "My resolve was greater than their resistance." He staged the first of several all-worker conferences, and described how Pindar were putting in place foundations that would create maximum understanding, which would create commitment as their core philosophy.

The directories' workforce is a mixture of typesetters and graphic-arts graduates. Its database had a £1.5m upgrade a year ago, and now stores 300 billion bytes. "We are looking to replace it in October, with a £3m or £4m facility," says Rick Lumby, managing director of the Directories division. This will enable customers to dial into the Internet to amend ads.

Lumby says "When Pindar first got involved in technology in the early 50s, we had 20 employees. Now we have almost 1000. Has technology done us out of business? When we started doing telephone directories, we had 17 people working on them. We now have more than 200. Along the way, certain jobs have been automated out of existence. We've always changed for the sake of improving the job we do – because if we don't do it, somebody else will."

Source: John Lawless, Sunday Times 25 January 1998

➢ **Discussion: What factors contribute to the successful management of change at Pindar?**

Today's leaders, tomorrow's dinosaurs?

The coming of age of the Internet has posed enormous challenges to existing companies. At the same time it has given exciting opportunities to new companies which have been able to build up from scratch using the new technology. Thus it is not Waterstone's or WH Smith which is transforming the book business, but new companies such as Amazon and BOL. It is much harder for an established company to change because if they start to sell books over the Internet, this will adversely affect their High Street stores. Grabbing new opportunities threatens the value of their existing investments. On the other hand, if they do not change, they may be put out of business. So it was the newcomer, Direct Line, which transformed the insurance market rather than Guardian Royal or General Accident. These companies did not want to upset the insurance brokers who account for most of their business.

Many established companies are vulnerable: who needs banks, travel agents and shops like Marks and Spencer or Debenhams when you can get lower prices, better information and more choice from your armchair? Last year, for example, 11% of all new cars in the US were bought on the Internet. To many US car buyers, dealers are becoming simply pick-up points.

Managers have to adapt to this revolution or they will soon be logging on to www.unemployment.com.

Implications of change

The introduction of new technology or a change in the way an organisation does business will inevitably impact upon everyone in the organisation. Consideration will have to be given to:

- Possible redundancies and the effect of this on the rest of the workforce;
- Teaching and learning new skills;
- A change in organisational structure;
- Changes in employment patterns and conditions;
- Changes in internal procedures.

Exercises

1. An information system was introduced into an organisation and was considered a failure. The failure was due to the inability of the organisation to manage the change rather than for technical reasons.

    With the aid of examples describe **three** factors which influence the management of change within an organisation. (6)

    NEAB IT04 Qu 10 1997

2. It is not uncommon for designers involved in the introduction of information systems to encounter resentment and opposition from existing employees.

    Discuss the reasons for this response and describe steps that can be taken by the system designer to reduce this resistance. (10)

    NEAB IT04 Qu 10 Sample Paper

3. A small firm of solicitors is considering the introduction of an Information Technology system to improve the efficiency of its operations. One of the directors of the firm has expressed some concerns over the effects on the organisation of the introduction of the system.

    Describe **five** possible concerns the director may have, and the arguments that may be used to persuade her to accept the new system. (10)

    NEAB IT04 Qu 7 Sample Paper

4. "Companies must adapt to new technology, or go out of business." Discuss this statement, with the aid of examples. (6)

    New question

Chapter 45 – Security Policies

Threats to security and integrity

Today's organisations are dependent on their information systems, and most could not survive the devastating effects of their destruction. Threats to information systems include human error, computer crime, natural disasters, war or terrorist activities and hardware failure. (See Table 45.1)

Threat to security/integrity	*Example*
Human error	Mistakes in data entry
	Program errors
	Operator errors (e.g. loading wrong tape)
Computer crime	Hacking (unauthorised access) and stealing data
	Modifying data illegally
	Planting viruses or 'logic bombs' (code which remains inactive until triggered by an event such as a certain date becoming current, or an employee's record being marked 'Fired'.
Natural disasters	Fire, earthquake, hurricane, flood
War and terrorist activity	Bombs, fire
Hardware failure	Power failure
	Disk head crash
	Network failure

Table 45.1: Threats to security of information systems

Risk analysis

"Those who think they have no time for bodily exercise will sooner or later have to find time for illness", said Edward Stanley, the 15th Earl of Derby. This quote could be paraphrased:

"Those who think they have no time or money to put in place a security policy will sooner or later have to find both the time and money for unplanned disaster recovery – and it will cost a lot more."

A corporate ICT security policy is a strategic issue, and as such is for company directors and senior managers to sort out, rather than something which can be left to technical staff. The first step in defining a security policy is to establish a clear picture of what the risks are and what the company stands to lose if disaster strikes. This **risk analysis** could include finding answers to questions such as:

- What is the nature of the data being stored in the system?
- How is the data used?
- Who has access to the system?
- How much money does the company stand to lose if the data is lost, corrupted or stolen?

Layers of control

Computer systems must be made secure to protect valuable data, and different 'layers' of security can be implemented, as shown in Figure 45.2.

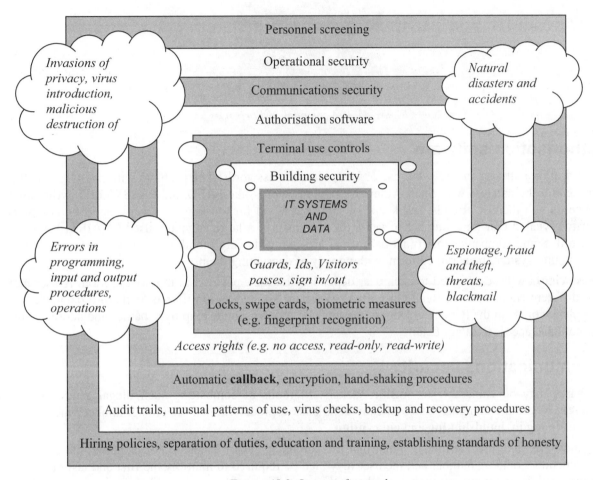

Figure 45.2: Layers of control

Building and equipment security

Building security can include measures to protect the premises from break-ins or unauthorised visitors, as well as from natural disasters such as fire and flood. Locks and window grilles, guards on the gate, rottweilers patrolling the fences, earthquake-proof construction, smoke alarms and automatic fire extinguishers are all possibilities.

Once in the building, even genuine employees and visitors may be restricted as to the areas they are permitted to visit. Employees may have ID cards with a bar code, magnetic strip or chip which allow access to particular areas. Visitors may be issued with passes. The visitor's pass shown in Figure 45.3 uses special ink which becomes visible 12 hours or so after being issued, and then displays 'EXPIRED' in red ink all over the card.

Biometric methods include fingerprint, handprint and iris recognition. These can be used to gain access either to a room or to a particular terminal. The Chancellor of the Exchequer, Gordon Brown, was presented in 1997 with a new dispatch box containing a laptop computer which required him to register a fingerprint before he could sign on. History does not relate whether he actually uses it.

Figure 45.3: A company visitor's pass

Authorisation software

Authorisation software includes the use of User Ids and passwords. The problem with passwords is that users tend to be careless with them – they use obvious words like FRED and PASSWORD, write down passwords, tell them to friends, and keep the same password for too long. A recent report on computer security revealed that for a number of years the chairman of a large company used CHAIRMAN as his password. Some companies insist that passwords are changed every month or so. Passwords are held on the computer system in encrypted form, with no way of decrypting them.

Access rights will be assigned to each user depending on their position in the organisation. A user may have different rights such as Read Only, Read-Write or No Access to different parts of a database. For example a worker in the Personnel Department may be able to change employee names and addresses but may not have access to salary details.

Communications security

Databases may be vulnerable to outside hackers. Methods of combatting such illegal access include **callback**, where the computer automatically calls back a predetermined telephone number when a user attempts to log in, **handshaking** and **encryption**.

A 'handshake' is a predetermined signal that the computer must recognise. For example, the computer may generate a random number and the user may then be required to multiply the first and last digits and add the product to the current month number. Of course this could pose a problem to people with shaky mathematical skills but it is generally more secure than a simple password, because it is never the same twice, and every user has their own algorithm.

Operational security

During daily operations, careful checks of logs showing terminal usage and any unusual behaviour should be regularly carried out. Many PC LAN security packages now include **audit controls**. Audit controls track what happens on a network, for example:

- which users have logged on, where from and for how long;
- how many times a server has been accessed;
- what software has been used;
- which files have been accessed by which users;
- how many unsuccessful attempts were made to log on from any terminal (to detect hackers trying to guess the password).

Anti-virus software can be installed on all PCs, and employees forbidden to bring in disks from outside the organisation. Viruses can also be introduced by downloading files from the Internet, so to guard against spreading a virus from one of these files, many firms run anti-virus software every night. This isolates all files containing a virus in a special directory and leaves a warning message on the screen.

Backup and recovery procedures form part of disaster planning which is discussed in the next chapter.

Audit trail

An **audit trail** is a record that allows a transaction to be traced through all the stages of processing, starting with its appearance as a source document and ending with its transformation into output.

Public companies have to have all financial records audited by external accountants every year, and the system must create an audit trail that makes it possible to see how each figure on a report is arrived at. No accounting system allows a financial record simply to be altered without a transaction being stored which can be checked. The auditor typically selects source documents, traces associated entries through intermediate computer printouts, and examines the resultant entries in summary accounts.

It is not only financial systems that have a use for audit trails, as the case study below illustrates.

Case study: Harold Shipman, GP and serial killer

Harold Shipman, a trusted family GP from Mottram, near Hyde, Greater Manchester was convicted in January 2000 of murdering 15 of his elderly female patients. This is a transcript of part of an interview between Dr Shipman and the detective at the police station after he was arrested.

"You attended that house at three o'clock and that's when you murdered this lady, and so much was your rush to get back that you went back to the surgery and immediately started altering this lady's medical records; we can prove that only minutes after three o'clock on that date you are fabricating that false medical history for this woman. You tell me why you needed to do that?"

"There's no answer."

"Well there is, there is a very clear answer because you've been up to her house, rolled her sleeve up, administered morphine, killed her and you were covering up what you were doing. That's what happened, isn't it, doctor?

"No."

"I am now showing you .. an exhibit .. from your computer which shows what's placed in, when and what's removed…"

The doctor examines the document. It shows that a patient record from August 1, 1997, a woman complaining of chest pains, accompanied by a doctor's note "?? angina", was actually typed into the computer three minutes and 39 seconds after the doctor had left the woman's house following her death on May 11, 1998.

"I'll ask you again, doctor, Where's that information come from?"

"I've no recollection of me putting that on the machine… I still have no recollection of entering that onto the computer… I'm well aware that that's how an audit trail works … there's no argument about that…"

Shipman has no answers now, except to say that the clock on his computer is not set for summer time and must be out by one hour.

The computer's audit trail helped to provide enough evidence to charge Shipman eventually with 15 murders – leaving another 131 other suspicious deaths to be investigated.

Source: David James Smith, The Sunday Times 6 February 2000

Personnel safeguards

Many studies show that users and computer personnel within an organisation are far more likely to breach security than outsiders. Security may potentially be breached by anyone from computer operators and programmers right up to company directors. Motivated by revenge, financial gain, fanaticism or irrational behaviour, employees are sometimes well-placed to plant a virus, steal or corrupt data, set up false accounts or attempt to extract money by extortion by threatening to destroy vital files.

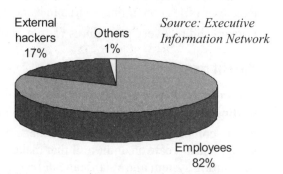

Figure 45.4: Who commits computer crime?

Motivating employees to be alert to security breaches and giving publicity to security measures may serve as a deterrent to computer crime.

Separation of duties is an important principle in maintaining security of data – no employee should perform all the steps in a single transaction. This makes it more difficult for a single individual to perpetrate fraud or theft.

Corporate ICT security policy

Once the risks to ICT systems and data have been established, policies can be determined which will be effective without costly overkill. There is often a conflict between wanting to make systems as secure as possible, but at the same time accessible to authorised users. For this reason university, college and school systems tend to be relatively insecure, because one of their most important requirements is to be easily accessible by students.

Once policies have been developed, they need to be implemented. The best security policy in the world is no use if people do not abide by it, and the key here is education – all employees should be made aware of the security policies and mechanisms put in place to ensure that they are adhered to. Instilling norms of ethical behaviour with respect to the use of information and information systems is an important management responsibility.

A typical security policy will cover the following aspects:

- **Awareness and education;**

    Training and education requirements

    Timetable for training/education

- **Administrative controls;**

    Formal procedures and standards are defined for all ICT systems

    Careful screening of personnel during the hiring process

    Separation of duties to ensure that it would take collusion between at least two employees to perpetrate fraud

    Disciplinary procedures in the event of security breaches

- **Operations controls;**

    Backup procedures

    Control of access to data centres by means of smart cards, ID badges, sign-in/sign-out registers

- **Physical protection of data;**

    Controlled access to sensitive areas

Protection against fire and flood

Uninterruptible power supplies

- **Access controls to the system and information;**

   Identification and authentication of users

   Password protection

   Different levels of access for different users according to their needs

   Different access rights, e.g. read only, read-write, read-write-update, etc.

   Encryption of sensitive data

   Detection of misuse using, for example, audit control software which detects multiple attempts to get a password correct.

- **Disaster recovery plan;**

   (See next chapter.)

Exercises

1.   A particular organisation uses a computerised stock control system. On performing the half-yearly stock check it is discovered that the actual stock levels of some of the items are below that shown on the system.

   (a)   Describe the functionality which should have been built into the software to minimise the possibility of this happening.   (2)

   (b)   Explain why this functionality is required.   (2)

   NEAB IT04 Qu 5 1997

2.   Some software packages can be set up to monitor and record their use. This is often stored in an access log.

   Name **four** items you would expect to be stored in such a log.   (4)

   NEAB IT04 Qu 1 Sample Paper

3.   Many accounts packages have an audit trail facility. Explain why such a facility is necessary, what data is logged and how this information can be used.   (6)

   NEAB IT04 Qu 6 Sample Paper

4.   Describe briefly **four** areas you would expect to be covered in a company's security policy.   (4)

   New question

Chapter 46 – Disaster recovery

Effects of negligence

The risks to businesses from computer disaster range from spilling a cup of coffee into the computer file server or a workman drilling through a cable to a fire or bomb which completely destroys the building. The results of such an incidence may be catastrophic: a recent survey showed that about 90% of companies which suffered a significant loss of data went out of business within two years. Of these, 43% went out of business almost immediately.

After working for 1 day without essential business data, a company operates at about 96% of its capability. By the tenth day, it is operating at only about 10% of its capability (Figure 46.1).

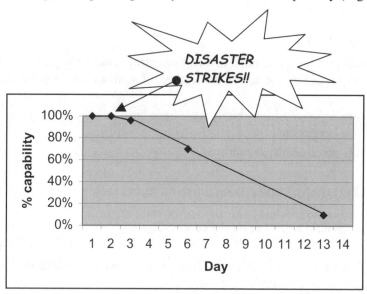

Figure 46.1: Effect of disaster

In the UK, the company and the directors may be prosecuted by the Health and Safety Executive if loss of essential business data or safety data adversely affects the health and safety of the public or the environment. In the case of banking, financial, insurance and related services, loss of essential business data which adversely affects the customer could bring about very costly litigation and fines.

> ➤ **Discussion: Suppose that a supermarket had all its data stored on disks and tapes in a computer room which was destroyed by a small localised fire one night. What sort of data would it have lost? Can you imagine the consequences? How long could it continue to operate?**

Stages in disaster planning

However many precautions are taken, no company can protect themselves completely against a disaster which will wipe out their computer system. What they must do is to ensure that if this happens, they can be up and running again in the shortest possible time. In disaster recovery planning, an essential task is to identify the most critical business functions to be supported by the plan, since covering less vital functions is, in general, too costly.

Contents of a security plan

The first step in solving any problem is understanding and defining it, and then assessing how it may affect the company. A security officer may be appointed who has both the technical and organisational skills to implement a security plan. The key elements of such a plan include:

- A list of the most critical business functions;

- A list of the facilities, hardware, software, data, personnel and other equipment that are necessary to support those functions;

- A method for securing access to all necessary resources;

- A method for getting in touch with all key personnel;

- A step-by-step course of action to follow to implement the plan;

- Education and training of personnel involved in implementing the plan;

- Regular drills to test the effectiveness of the plan.

Disaster recovery plan

Two 'controls of last resort' can be put in place to guard against the failure of a business after a catastrophe – adequate insurance and a disaster recovery plan.

Insurance is not a substitute for loss prevention, and it cannot lessen the likelihood of loss – it can only help to reduce the financial impact of such a loss when it does occur. Insurance premiums will be based in part on the precautions that the company has taken to protect itself against disaster.

A disaster recovery plan has to contain provision for backup facilities which can be used in the event of disaster. Three alternatives are:

- A company-owned backup facility, geographically distant from the main site, known as a 'cold-standby' site.

- A reciprocal agreement with another company that runs a compatible computer system.

- A subscription to a disaster recovery service, such as the one described in the case study below.

Case study: Trust in the Virtual World

Ron Hixon says of his workforce: "I trust them, that's the key." Yet none of those 70 employees has turned up at the office. They will not be in the office tomorrow, either. As he looks round his 6000sq ft of almost deserted premises in Woking, Surrey, he is untroubled.

His staff are computer technicians who work from home. With a modem and a laptop, they are connected to the rest of the company as surely as if they were in the room next door. Mr Hixon's company, Catalyst Technology Solutions, is a service provider to the service sector, providing disaster recovery services for businesses. If a client is hit by fire or flood, or a computer malfunction, they can reload their companies' data onto the Catalyst system and continue to operate as if the crisis had never happened.

The Woking office stands empty, so if a client's premises have been destroyed, they can move in their whole operation. The paradox of running a company with 30,000sq ft of empty office space on three separate sites, and 70-plus employees who work from home appeals to Mr Hixon, who has further plans for revolutionising Catalyst. A new telephone system will soon automatically route calls to workers' home numbers or another location, and divert them to a secretary if the call is unanswered.

"Customers will think they are talking to an office full of people, whereas in fact we could be anywhere."

Meanwhile the offices stay empty, waiting for disaster to strike, while the virtual workforce talk to each other through the ether.

Source: Charlotte Denny, The Guardian 25 August 1997

> ➤ **Discussion: Can you think of some local organisations which would need to make use of a disaster recovery service such as this if they experienced a catastrophe?**

Criteria used to select a contingency plan

The choice of contingency plan will be based upon the costs of the extra provision vs. the potential cost of disaster. Factors which will be taken into account include:

- The scale of the organisation and its ICT systems;

- The nature of the operation: an on-line system may need to be restored within hours, whereas a customer billing operation may not be unduly harmed by a few day's delay, so long as no data is lost;

- The relative costs of different options: a company with several sites linked by telecommunications may be able to formulate a disaster recovery plan which temporarily moves operations to an alternative site, but need not involve a special 'cold-standby' site, or a 'hot' site provided by a third party;

- The perceived likelihood of disaster occurring: companies in the earthquake zone around San Francisco, for example, are likely to invest more in a disaster recovery service than the average firm in Ipswich.

> ➤ **Discussion: What are the most critical ICT functions at your school or college? What would be the consequences of a disaster such as fire or theft of computer equipment? What sort of contingency plan would be appropriate?**

Exercises

1. A small company runs a network of 4 PCs on which it keeps records of stock, customer accounts, a mailing list and a multitude of word-processed documents. Draw up a security plan for this company to ensure that it will be able to continue operating normally within a day or so of a disaster such as a fire.
(20)
New question

2. Describe **five** facilities that may be provided by a Disaster Recovery Service to which a major bank may subscribe.
(5)
New question

3. Describe **two** ways in which a company may raise the awareness of personnel to its security policy.
(4)
New question

4. Briefly describe the safeguards a company could use for each of the following threats to its computer system.
   (i) Terrorist bomb;
   (ii) Accidental overwriting of a master file;
   (iii) Hackers outside the organisation;
   (iv) A corrupt employee perpetrating fraud;
   (v) The millennium bug.
(5)
New question

Chapter 47 – Implementation of Legislation

Laws relating to ICT

Legislation governs many aspects of the use of computers within organisations, and it is the responsibility of organisations to ensure that the legislation is implemented. The laws include:

- The Data Protection Acts of 1984 and 1998. (see Chapter 12);
- Copyright Designs and Patents Act of 1988 (see Chapter 10);
- The Health and Safety (Display Screen Equipment) Regulations of 1992 (see Chapter 13).

The Data Protection Act

The Data Protection Act exists to protect the privacy of individuals, its main areas of concern being that:

- Data and information should be *secure;*
- Private, personal or other data should be *accurate;*
- Data stored should not be *misused.*

Organisations should develop their own privacy policies to ensure that the law on Data Protection is upheld. A policy might typically contain two sections, one focussing on the customers and the other on the organisation itself.

A data protection policy

Section 1: Customer Service

1. The policy on data privacy should be publicized, and customers given a copy on request.
2. Customers should be told why their personal information is needed and what use it will be put to. No more data than is necessary should be collected.
3. Data should be obtained directly from the customer, to ensure as far as possible that it is accurate.
4. No data should be used for any purpose other than that which it was collected for, without the customer's consent. This includes selling the data to a third party.
5. Consent should be obtained by providing a clear opt-out check box on any form used to collect data.
6. Customers should be given easy access to files containing their own personal information.
7. Any errors in personal data should be corrected immediately.
8. Customers' concerns should be listened to and acted upon.

Section 2: Organisational culture

1. The company's policy should be clearly communicated to all staff. The policy may form part of a company handbook, form part of a training program, or be posted on notice boards or an Intranet.
2. An awareness of the issue of privacy should be fostered among all employees.
3. Staff should be held accountable for the company's privacy policy. It should be emphasised that if an individual acts contrary to a clause of the Data Protection Act, the individual is personally liable.
4. The effect on privacy of any new proposed system or service should be assessed before it is developed.

5. Reasonable steps should be taken to ensure that all data stored or used is accurate and up-to-date.

6. A schedule should be kept of how long data can be stored before it should be destroyed.

7. A security policy should be developed and enforced to ensure that all data is kept secure from accidental or malicious damage and from unauthorised people looking at it.

8. A senior manager should be designated to be responsible for seeing that the security policy is enforced.

9. All staff should be made aware of their responsibilities to keep data secure by keeping passwords secret, changing them regularly, maintaining physical security of disks, performing scheduled backups etc.

10. Periodic checks should be made to ensure that the policy is being adhered to.

Software copyright

Under the terms of the Copyright Designs and Patents Act of 1988, it is illegal to copy software or run pirated software. The Business Software Alliance (BSA) exists to make organisations and their employees aware of the Law and steps they should take to ensure that it is implemented.

Figure 47.1: The Business Software Alliance provides guidance to companies

The BSA has prepared a step-by-step guide to software management which includes the following advice:

- **Conduct an audit.** Prepare an inventory of your current software situation by conducting an audit using a commercially available audit tool or commissioning an audit service provider. Any illegal software discovered during the audits should be deleted immediately.

- **Purchasing.** Purchase licences for enough copies of each program to meet your current needs. Network operators should consider purchasing a network metering package to restrict the number of users according to the number of licences.

- **Procedures.** Demonstrate your organisation's commitment to using legal software by adopting the following procedures:

    - Appoint a Software Manager to ensure that all appropriate software analysis and management functions are conducted efficiently.

    - Arrange an audit of all machines on a regular basis.

    - Send a memo to all staff reiterating your organisation's concerns about software duplication and advising them of the forthcoming audit. (See Figure 47.2)

- Channel software requirements/purchases through a single point. One of the main entry points for unscrupulous resellers is through a fragmented purchasing system in which various personnel are ordering software.

- Make regular checks on software suppliers and software entering your company.

- Send a memo to staff, and add a note within your company policy and employee handbook, that illegal software copying is a disciplinary offence and that piracy should be reported.

- Request your staff to sign an employee agreement verifying their understanding of the organisation's policy regarding the use of illegal software.

SUGGESTED MEMORANDUM TO EMPLOYEES

To: *(Specify distribution)*

From: *(Senior management official or CEO)*

Subject: *PC software and the law*

Date: *(insert)*

The purpose of this memorandum is to remind you of (name of organisation)'s policy concerning copying and use of software.

Unlicensed duplication or use of any pirated software program is illegal and can expose you and the company to civil and criminal liability under copyright law.

In order to ensure that you do not intentionally or inadvertently violate copyright, you should not copy any program installed on your computer for any purpose without permission from (insert reference to responsible manager or department). Likewise, you should not install any program onto your computer without such permission, in order to verify that a licence is held to cover such installation.

- *The company will not tolerate any employee making unauthorised copies of software.*

- *Any employee found copying software illegally is subject to termination from the company.*

- *Any employee copying software to give to any outside third party, including clients and customers, is also subject to termination.*

- *If you want to use software licensed by the company at home, you must consult with (insert name of manager) in order to make sure such use is permitted by the publisher's licence.*

Figure 47.2: A sample memo to staff

Education of employees and a raising of awareness of the problems and consequences of software piracy is a major step in controlling software misuse.

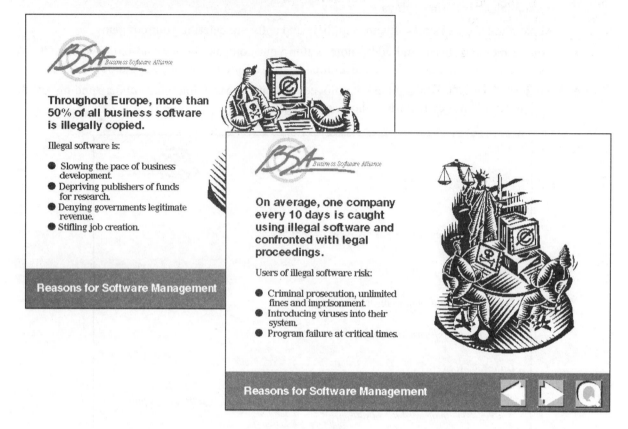

Figure 47.3: Part of a BSA presentation

Health and Safety

Where health is concerned, prevention is always better than cure and the first step is to understand why and how health complaints associated with computer use begin. Measures can then be taken to avoid the bad habits, unsuitable equipment and furniture and poor working environments that are frequently to blame.

Whether people are using computers at home or at the office, the way they interact with their computer affects their physical and mental health. Educating employees and instilling good working practices is one way of preventing problems such as backache, eyestrain and repetitive strain injury (RSI).

Employers should avoid incentive schemes designed to increase the rate of data entry, as applying pressure of this sort has been shown to contribute to the onset of RSI (see case study "Bank staff driven to injury" in Chapter 13).

Encouraging 'ownership' of workspace

Under the Health and Safety at Work Act, employees have a responsibility to use workstations and equipment correctly in accordance with training provided. They are also required to bring any problems to the attention of their employers and cooperate in their correction. One way that employers can help to ensure that employees heed this directive is to involve them in the choice of furniture, hardware and software, as well as in the arrangement of the office space. People generally are better motivated and take a more responsible attitude if they are consulted and allowed to define their own workspace.

Taking regular breaks

Specialists recommend thirty-second 'micropauses' every five to ten minutes, with longer pauses of ten to fifteen minutes every hour or so. Providing regular breaks and coffee-making facilities, as well as varying tasks, can help prevent health problems. Employers who provide this kind of environment are also likely to end up with happier and more productive employees.

Providing the right equipment

There are regulations concerning the type of computer equipment and furniture that must be provided for people who spend a lot of time in front of a VDU. Refer back to Chapter 13 for guidelines on the ergonomic environment.

The employer's responsibility

Employers are responsible for the health and safety of their employees, and they are obliged to demonstrate this responsibility by carrying out a formal evaluation of the working environment and acting on any feedback from the evaluation. This evaluation should either be carried out by an employee whom the Health and Safety Executive recognises as competent, or by an independent professional ergonomist, and it will cover workplace design, including computer hardware, lighting, cooling, humidity and software.

The bottom line is that ignorance of the law is no defence, and sooner or later all organisations will have to invest some money in ergonomics. Companies who disregard their obligations may be successfully sued by injured employees.

> ➢ **Discussion: Does your computer classroom satisfy the ergonomic requirements of the Health and Safety legislation? Does the school or College have an obligation to comply with the terms of the Directive?**

Exercises

1. A Company uses a computer network for storing details of its staff and for managing its finances. The network manager is concerned that some members of staff may install unauthorised software onto the network.

   (a) Give reasons why it is necessary for some software to be designated as unauthorised. (2)

   (b) What guidelines should the network manager issue to prevent the installation of unauthorised software onto the network? (2)

   (c) What procedures might be available to the company to enforce the guidelines? (2)
   NEAB IT04 Qu 6 1997

2. A particular college uses a computer network for storing details of its staff and students and for managing its finances. Network stations are provided for the Principal, Vice-Principal, Finance Officer, clerical staff and teaching staff. Only certain designated staff have authority to change data or to authorise payments.

   (a) What are the legal implications of storing personal data on the computer system? (4)

   (b) What measures should be taken to ensure that the staff understand the legal implications? (3)
   NEAB IT03 Qu 3 Sample paper

Chapter 48 – User Support

The need for support

As computers become more and more powerful, the software that runs on them becomes more and more sophisticated. The 'ease of use' promised by graphical user interfaces like Microsoft Windows has made PCs accessible to more and more non-technical users, so that paradoxically the need for user support is set to continue growing, rather than the reverse. The nature of the support services required by users has also changed since the days of terminals running a single, character-based application: the more features and complexities there are built into the software, the more expertise is required to solve users' problems.

Software companies which create tailor-made ICT solutions for companies, as well as manufacturers of software packages, all provide user support, though users are normally expected to pay an annual fee for this service, whether or not they use it.

The help desk

User support may be provided in a number of ways, from a simple help desk to a user support centre. The person sitting at the help desk answers telephone queries during office hours and depending on their skill level, attempts to solve the problem or passes it over to an expert. There may be other ways of contacting the help desk such as fax or e-mail, but essentially this is a receive-only service, existing to take queries and resolve them.

The help desk offers a single point of contact for customers, and a good rapport can be built up between the person on the help desk and the customers. All the questions asked by different customers can be stored on a database and this can provide useful information about the usability of the software. The information can then be used to improve future versions of the software or plan training courses.

On the other hand, the work can be demoralising for the person at the help desk, especially if they generally have to pass the problem on to someone else to solve. People typically only call a help desk as a last resort, by which time they are probably quite frustrated and angry and ready to take it out on whoever picks up the phone. Communication can be a problem when the help desk tries to explain the problem to a third party, and quite probably the problem solver will not see the problem as a top priority so that the service may not be very fast or efficient.

The help desk will typically log:

- The user's name and telephone number or postcode;
- Version number of the software;
- Serial number of the software (to ensure that the user has a legitimate copy);
- The nature of the enquiry;
- The time and date of the call.

Using e-mail rather than the telephone is sometimes cheaper and avoids the problem of a telephone line that is constantly busy. Being held in a queue of callers for half an hour or more is not uncommon on the average help line, and it's bad luck if you don't like the music they've chosen to play you while you wait.

Technical support

Technical support exists to solve technical problems and tends to be staffed by specialists who perhaps had some hand in writing the software, but have very little idea of how the software is used in a business context. There may be problems of communication between the expert spouting technical jargon and the business user who wants to know how to get the package to allocate, say, a different level of discount to a particular customer.

Help desk software

Special help desk software such as McAfee's HelpDesk Suite is available for large and small organisations running a help desk.

This software comes with an Expert System database of answers to over 25,000 different hardware and software problems, which enables the staff at the help desk to ask the right questions and let the software diagnose the problem. It also allows the helper to take over the user's computer and screen, calling it up on his own screen and typing in the necessary fix. A 'whiteboard' facility allows all users within an organisation to be notified of a particular problem – say, the printer in a particular area is not functioning, or the network will go down between 5pm and 7pm on Tuesday. Numerous reports are available, for example to track service levels in order to help ensure that service level agreements are being kept.

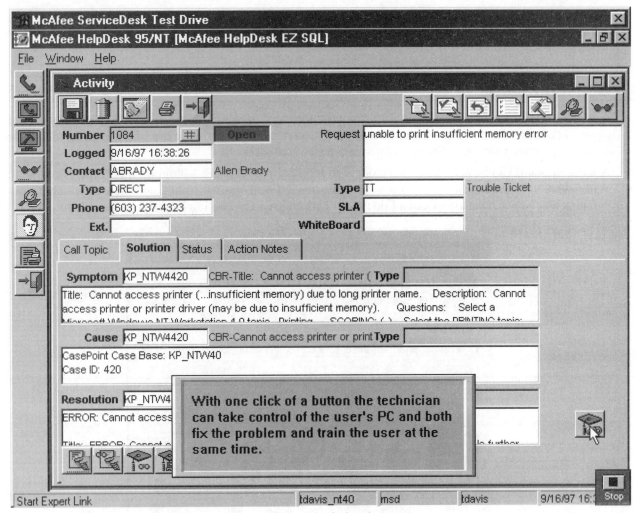

Figure 48.1: Help desk software

> ➤ **Discussion: What other reports would be useful in assessing the efficiency of the help desk service?**

Case study: Call centres

By the year 2001, one in fifty of us will be working in a call centre where hundreds of people take calls on their behalf: the Scottish Highlands, for example, are already dotted with them, including centres for Virgin, the London boroughs and M&G. This 2% of the population will do nothing but answer a telephone all day.

If you have a PC and telephone a number in Watford for technical support, you are quite likely to be rerouted to someone in Dublin, Edinburgh or even Hamburg. The person who answers your call sits in front of a computer, which recommends the questions he asks, and he then searches a database to see if anyone else has ever had the same problem. In other words, your problem is solved by someone who doesn't work for the company you bought your PC from, who wasn't at the number you called, who doesn't even work in the same country, and didn't solve the problem himself!

Source: Tim Phillips, The Guardian 11 December 1997

➢ **Discussion: What are the advantages and disadvantages to an organisation of using a call centre compared with internal help desks using special help desk software?**

Bulletin boards

A bulletin board system (BBS) is an electronic noticeboard to which items of interest, notes, hints and requests for assistance and so on can be pinned. The concept predates wide use of the Internet and some do not require users to subscribe to an Internet Service provider.

A bulletin board can be accessed via a modem in terminal mode, using a program like HyperTerminal in Windows 95. Selecting Start, Programs, Accessories, HyperTerminal brings up a screen which allows you to select New Connection from a File menu. This opens a Connection Description box (Figure 48.2).

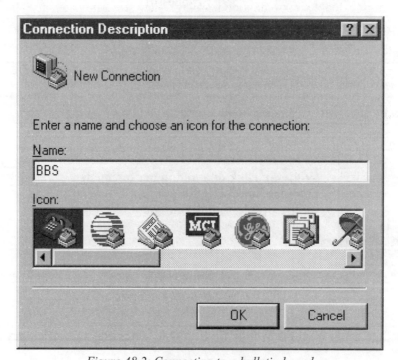

Figure 48.2: Connecting to a bulletin board

After selecting OK and on the next screen, typing in the phone number provided in the software user manual, some user identification and password, a menu of options is displayed and the user can access advice on how to solve their problem.

Various other types of bulletin board serviced by software manufacturers can be accessed via the Internet. These often list 'frequently asked questions' (FAQs) and their answers, as well as providing a forum for users to solve each other's problems or refer them to the software manufacturer's experts.

User booklets

Some software support departments issue new users with an introductory guide to things they might need to know about the product they have purchased. The information given might include:

- Instructions to change the password after logging on for the first time;
- The name and address of their local contact;
- The hours that User Support is open;
- How to get printer paper, toner and other consumables;
- Where to go for training.

Newsletters and support articles

Many software companies produce their own regular newsletters. This typically contains tips on how to get the most out of the software, details of forthcoming support meetings and conferences, FAQs, articles and letters sent in by users describing how they have cleverly solved some obscure problem and previews of the inevitable forthcoming upgrade. Computer magazines also regularly have articles on similar topics.

On-line help

On-line help can be an invaluable aid to anyone learning a new software package. This typically contains an index of topics and a tutorial for beginners. Microsoft Help has a link to a Web site offering various options (Figure 48.3).

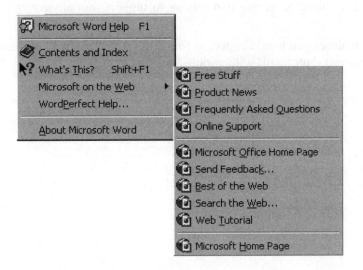

Figure 48.3: On-line help with Internet links

Documentation

Users need different levels of documentation depending on how they are using the software and how expert they are. Clerical workers may need an introductory tutorial, whereas 'knowledge workers' will probably need a reference manual as they use the software for increasingly complex tasks.

> ➤ **Discussion: What are the relative advantages of on-line help and user manuals?**

Exercises

1. (a) Describe **three** items of information a user support line would log when taking a call from a user.
    (3)

    (b) Many user support lines need to share problems and potential solutions between a number of operators who are answering calls. Describe **one** method of achieving this. (3)

    (b) Some user support lines also offer a mailbox facility to enable users to log their problems using e-mail. What advantages does this have for
    (i) the software user;
    (ii) the user support staff. (4)
    NEAB IT04 Qu 8 1997

2. Each day a software house logs a large number of calls from its users to its support desk.
    (a) Describe how the support desk might manage these requests to provide an effective service. (3)
    (b) Describe **three** items of information the support desk would require to assist in resolving a user's problem. (3)
    (c) The software house receives complaints from its users that the support desk is providing a poor service. Describe **three** reports that the software house could produce in order to combat the validity of this claim. (6)
    NEAB IT04 Qu 7 Sample paper

3. "As software becomes increasingly easy to use, the need for user support will decline."
    State whether you agree or disagree, giving **two** reasons to support your answer. (4)
    New question

4. Describe briefly **four** features you would expect to find in help desk software designed to be used by a call centre diagnosing users' problems with various software packages. (4)
    New question

Chapter 49 – Training

The need for training

Companies in industrialised countries spend huge amounts of money, often several million pounds a year, on training their employees. There are numerous different reasons why companies perceive training to be a valuable investment.

- Employees need training to give them the skills, attitude and knowledge required to do their jobs safely and well. This is true at all levels in a company, from the new recruit in a supermarket learning how to use the till and interact with customers, to the manager who needs to learn how to motivate the staff and to make effective decisions.

- New employees often need training before they can be reasonably effective within a company. They may need to be trained in the use of hardware or software they have not used before, or on the operational procedures that have to be followed.

- Existing employees require retraining because companies and jobs are constantly changing, new technologies are installed and new procedures are introduced.

- Well-trained employees are likely to be better motivated and have a better chance of promotion on a well-defined career path.

- Training can lead to increased sales, a better service to customers, better quality products, good safety records, and lower staff turnover.

> ➤ **Discussion: Have you worked in an organisation where you were given training? What were the benefits? Have you been in a situation where training was needed but not given?**

Training in the use of information technology

Training staff in the use of new technology is crucial to the success of any computer system. Unless staff at all levels of an organisation know how to use the new technology effectively, investment in a computer system can be a waste of money.

Training for senior managers

Managers who understand fully the benefits and problems associated with the use of information technology are likely to make better decisions than less well-informed colleagues when:

- establishing a corporate information systems strategy;
- appraising advice from ICT professionals either within or outside the organisation;
- allocating resources to information systems.

Training for middle managers

Middle management will be responsible for ensuring that computer systems are correctly used, and that accurate, timely and useful information reaches the right people at the right time. They will also be responsible for the organisation's computer security policy. Therefore, they will need training in how to define information requirements, how to integrate systems and how to realise the potential of a new computer system. They will also need training in the use of software such as spreadsheets, communications software, word processing and specialised software needed for their particular job.

Training for users

When a new software package is introduced into a company, users at different levels of the company may require different levels of training. At the lowest level, for example, a clerical worker may need to know how to load a spreadsheet package, enter the daily or weekly sales figures and print a report. A member of the sales staff in an electrical retailer's may need to know how to enter a customer's details to check their credit rating, and put through a sale. A secretary may need to know how to use a word processor to write and print letters and reports, and how to use function keys to activate macros. These activities are **task-based**.

A middle manager or 'knowledge worker', on the other hand, may need **skill-based** rather than task-based knowledge. A marketing manager who has to give a presentation on the expected sales of a new product may need to use a spreadsheet to analyse and graph actual and projected figures and insert the results into a word processed report for the managing director. An office supervisor may design a style for all internal memos and reports, and create a template and macros to automate certain functions, using a word processing package.

> ➢ **Discussion: A company uses a database package to develop a customer invoicing and information system. Identify the different functions that this system could be used for, and different levels of training that would be required by the people using the package.**

Methods of training

There are several different methods by which users can gain expertise in the use of software packages. These include:

- Computer-based training;
- Watching a video training course;
- Interactive video training;
- On-line tutorials supplied with the software;
- Step-through guides;
- Formal, instructor-led training courses.

Computer-based training

Computer-based training has several benefits.

- For an employer, a major benefit is cost. Training courses can easily cost £500 per day per employee, with accommodation costs as an added extra. The investment in a suitable training package can quickly pay for itself if there are large numbers of employees requiring training.
- Staff can do the training at times which fit in with their workload, causing the least amount of disruption. During a slack period a member of staff can be sent to a training room on the premises to do an hour or two of training, or it may take place at the employee's own computer at their desk.
- Employees can study at their own pace and repeat sections which are difficult or which they have forgotten.

- Standardised training. Instructor-led training varies with the trainer and the training centre, whereas computer-aided training offers standardisation. However it cannot guarantee that all employees will gain the same benefit; it is very easy to keep pressing the 'Next' button without taking anything in!

> ➤ **Discussion: Have you ever used an on-line tutorial or other form of computer-based tutorial? What are the disadvantages of this method of learning?**

Instructor-led courses

For some, nothing can replace a good instructor. As one trainer said, "We are not very keen on computer-assisted learning because it is too impersonal. The best training results from the personal inspiration of a good trainer, from his or her ability to communicate with the trainee and whet the appetite for further knowledge and the ways to use that knowledge to good effect." Other advantages of classroom learning include the following:

- Learning is essentially a communal activity and students learn a lot from debate and discussion in the class.

- Peer collaboration in learning can help to develop general problem-solving skills. Learning together has the potential to produce gains superior to learning alone.

- Individuals often have a valuable store of personal knowledge which they can share with a group.

- Many jobs involve working together in teams and rely on successful collaboration with colleagues: formal education in a classroom can help prepare people to work together in groups.

Skills updating

Employees do not need training only when they start a new job, or when new technology is introduced; there is an ongoing need for skills updating and refreshing. An initial training course may be given in the rudiments of the software, which employees need to practice before they can take in new information. Some functions may not be introduced initially; for example year-end procedures may not be taught to everyone, but extra training may be needed for those who need to use these functions. As the new system becomes better understood, managers may want to learn new skills using advanced features. Employees who have been or are about to be promoted may need to learn new aspects of an information system.

Corporate training strategy

Companies with a commitment to training generally have well thought out objectives in their training programmes, and a clear idea of the benefits of training. The primary goal of training in one large company, for example, is stated as "to produce outstanding quality and service, to achieve total customer satisfaction, aggressive sales growth and optimum profits."

Without a training policy, companies can quickly lose their competitive edge. Experience shows that an unable, unwilling unresponsive or unskilled workforce can undermine or negate even the best strategies. On the other hand, companies which are managing the development of their people show enhanced performance because the employees are able, consistent, co-operative, responsible and solvers of problems.

The Department of Trade and Industry has published a booklet entitled 'Partnerships with People' which suggests ideas for a corporate training strategy. (Figure 49.1.)

Ideas worth trying

Develop appraisal systems which focus on individual development. Look at other jobs in the organisation that an individual may aspire to, encourage the development of necessary attributes to take them on.

Seek advice from the TEC/LEC or specialist training adviser to design a development programme for managers.

Provide business training for supervisors, technical managers, union representatives.

Investigate NVQs and encourage staff to take relevant qualifications.

Encourage key staff to develop training skills so they can pass on knowledge.

Make booklets and other self-help learning packages available to staff.

Develop links with local FE colleges – reimburse college fees in full or in part, to encourage people to get into the learning habit.

Encourage relevant people to take HND, degree or professional qualifications.

(Partnerships with People – a DTI booklet)

Figure 49.1: Points to consider in a corporate training strategy

Exercises

1. You are asked to advise an organisation on the introduction of a new software package.
   (a) With the aid of **three** examples, explain why different users may require different levels of training. (6)
   (b) Following the initial training you advise subsequent training for users. Give **two** reasons why this may be required, other than financial gain for the agency. (4)

   NEAB IT04 Qu 9 1997

2. Describe briefly **five** facilities you would expect to find in an on-line tutorial for a spreadsheet package. (5)

   New question

3. Describe briefly **three** different methods of training that may be used to train staff in aspects of information technology, explaining **one** relative advantage of each method. (6)

   New question

4. Why should a corporation have a training strategy for staff? (3)
   Give **three** points that could be included in such a strategy. (3)

   New question

Chapter 50 – Project Management

Introduction

A **project** is a short-term activity bringing together people with different skills, equipment and resources to achieve specified objectives. Project management often begins with the selection of a project manager and a project team. The project itself must be broken down into tasks, whose sequence and estimated time for completion is calculated and documented. Projects usually have the following characteristics:

- They have a specific objective – for example, the networking of all the computers in a college, or the introduction of a new computerised enrolment system;
- They must be developed within a specified time period;
- They must be developed within a given budget;
- A team of people is brought together temporarily from different areas to work on the project. When the project is finished, the team will be disbanded.

Selection of a project manager

Once a project has been given the go-ahead by senior management, the first step is the appointment of a project manager. The project manager needs to have the necessary technical skills, but just as important are the managerial skills needed to be able to lead and motivate a group of people from different departments and different levels within the organisation. Good interpersonal skills and business experience are also essential assets.

The tasks of a project manager

The project manager must:

- Plan and staff the project;
- Analyse risk;
- Monitor progress;
- Adjust schedules;
- Report project status;
- Control budgets and salaries;
- Prepare performance appraisals;
- Interact with users, corporate management and project personnel.

Courses in project management are offered by many educational and training establishments.

The project team

One of the first tasks of the project manager may be to pick the project development team. Studies have shown that an ideal team size is between 5 and 7 members, and that as the team size increases, level of job satisfaction drops, absenteeism and turnover rise, and the project may start to miss deadlines. Some projects, of course, are far too large and complex to have such a small team.

> ➢ **Discussion: Adding more people to a team which is behind schedule often has the effect of putting it even further behind schedule. Why?**

Regardless of the size of the project team, it should have a balance of theoreticians and practitioners, idealists and realists, technical and business specialists. Boehm in his book *Software Engineering Economics* (Prentice Hall 1981) listed five principles of software staffing:

1. **Principle of top talent**. Employ fewer but better people.

2. **Principle of job matching**. Match skills and motivations available to the task at hand.

3. **Principle of team balance**. There needs to be a balance between the technical skills, knowledge and personality characteristics of team members.

4. **Principle of phase out**. There will inevitably be a misfit on the team resulting in "unhealthy results in the long run". Getting the misfit out may not be easy but must be done with adequate thought, time and sympathy.

5. **Principle of career progression**. Bring out the best in people by enabling them to work on tasks that will help them to progress.

Project planning and scheduling

The project manager will divide up the project into phases and the phases into tasks. This may be done by identifying *milestones* which represent significant progress towards completion. Next, the skills that are needed for each of these tasks are identified and the time required for completion of each task calculated, based on the skills and availability of staff. A team leader may be appointed for each of these tasks, and the cost of completion of each task calculated.

Task definition forms the basis of the overall project plan, on which schedules and budgets are based. It is also used to track the progress of a project. Overlooking tasks is a common cause of cost and time overruns in projects, so it is very important to define all the tasks that need to be completed. Tasks that are commonly overlooked include training (or learning new skills), production of reports, project reviews, correction of errors and omissions.

Example: It is proposed to install a new computer network in the 6ᵗʰ form block of a school. What are the tasks involved in completing this project?

Tasks:

1. Carry out initial feasibility study
2. Invite tenders from suppliers
3. Choose a supplier
4. Purchase computers
5. Recable the building
6. Draw up plans for new classroom layout
7. Convert classroom
8. Install computers
9. Purchase network software
10. Install hardware and network software
11. Test network
12. Install end-user software

> ➤ **Discussion: Is this list complete? Can any of the tasks be carried out simultaneously?**

Many project managers keep a day-by-day log of the progress and difficulties encountered in a project, which can be an invaluable aid to planning the project schedule of future projects.

Project reviews

Most project schedules need constant updating and revision during the course of the project. It is important to have a formal *review process* to monitor and control the progress of a project. Review sessions every few weeks or so may be held in order to:

- Compare progress against the project schedule;

- Keep management informed and involved in the progress of the project;

- Reconfirm that current task lists and schedules are correct and on target;

- Identify any problems or slippage and come up with solutions;

- Encourage team spirit and communication between team members.

In spite of regular reviews and reports, many projects fail to meet deadlines and cost considerably over budget. Some projects may be so innovative that it is difficult to make accurate estimates. Sometimes excessive pressure on team members to keep to deadlines makes them hesitant to report problems, and sometimes the requirements of the project are changed in midstream. The larger and more complex the project, the more room there is for error. Louis Fried, a project manager, had a number of rules for project management including one which read "Any task that requires more than 10 people can't be done". ("The Rules of Project Management", *Journal of Information Systems Management Summer 1992*)

Characteristics of a good team

A good team requires:

- leadership – someone who can inspire and keep the team motivated, and who understands exactly what has to be achieved;

- appropriate allocation of tasks – the best person for the particular job;

- adherence to standards – proper procedures carried out, documentation kept up to date, etc;

- monitoring, costing, controlling – progress must be monitored, schedules adjusted, costs kept within agreed limits and not allowed to spiral out of control.

Exercises

1. A project team has been appointed by a firm of consultants to write a tailor-made customer billing and accounts system for a medium-sized business. The project team consists of a project leader (the systems analyst), two programmers and a technician. The project is falling behind schedule and the managing director of the company decides to allocate two more programmers to the team. The project continues to fall further behind.
   Give **three** reasons why this might be so. (6)
   New question

2. The management of a college decides that a college-wide network should be installed to link together all the computers in the college. The estimated cost of the project is £1 million. What factors should the project manager take into account when planning the estimated time to completion of the project? (6)
   New question

3. A firm is creating a team to plan, design and implement an IT project. Describe **four** characteristics of a good IT project team. (8)
   NEAB IT05 Qu 7 1998

Chapter 51 – Codes of Practice

Ethics and computing

Ethics is the science of morals; the study of ethics is the study of how to make choices between right and wrong. Why should we care about ethics? The number of ethical decisions of one kind or another that we face in our personal and professional lives makes it imperative that we care. Some unethical decisions may be illegal; others may have drastic consequences for our lives or careers. Therefore, each of us must care about ethics as a matter of self-interest. In addition, we are all members of society, and ethical decision-making is vital to creating the sort of world in which we want to live.

> ➤ **Discussion: Is 'computer ethics' any different from other kinds of ethics? Is there a difference between**
>
>   – **browsing through files on someone's PC, and rummaging through their locker?**
>
>   – **sending obscene messages over a computer network, and writing anonymous obscene notes on paper to someone?**
>
>   – **using unlicensed software and travelling on a train without paying?**

Factors in ethical decision-making

Ethical decisions, whether or not they involve information technology, are rarely straightforward. There is often not a straight choice between right and wrong – rather, the choice lies between the lesser of two evils. Of course, it is wrong to lie, cheat or steal – but is it wrong to steal food if your child is starving, lie to a friend about how good they look, give a fellow student a helping hand by writing most of his program or essay for him? A poor decision can have a number of undesirable consequences. People may be left hurt or offended, employee morale may be adversely affected, customers may be lost, a company may go bankrupt.

Sometimes the law prescribes whether a certain action is legal. Often an ethical principle is the basis of the Law; for example, the recognition that an individual has the right to ownership of an original work has led to copyright laws being enacted. In other cases, the law does not provide an answer and it is then useful to have a set of guidelines for how to act.

Formal guidelines in the computing industry

When a person accepts employment in any company, he or she accepts moral responsibilities that define appropriate behaviour in that job – responsibilities referred to as professional ethics. Two factors apply to all professionals and influence their actions: professional relationships and professional efficacy ('doing a good job'). Most professions have ethical codes or standards that explain appropriate professional behaviour and efficacious behaviour in various situations, and the computing profession is no exception. Various professional bodies such as the British Computer Society (BCS) and the Association for Computing Machinery (ACM) produce their own Code of Ethics and Professional Conduct. (You can look up the BCS Code of Conduct on the Internet, using the web address www.bcs.org.uk, and then searching for Code of Conduct using the index, or the ACM code of ethics on www.cs.orst.edu/~cook/acm.html .)

The ACM Code of Conduct is shown below:

ACM Code of Ethics

ACM* Code of Ethics and Professional Conduct

1. GENERAL MORAL IMPERATIVES
As an ACM member I will ..

1.1	Contribute to society and human well-being
1.2	Avoid harm to others
1.3	Be honest and trustworthy
1.4	Be fair and take action not to discriminate
1.5	Honour property rights including copyrights and patents
1.6	Give proper credit for intellectual property
1.7	Respect the privacy of others
1.8	Honour confidentiality

2. MORE SPECIFIC PROFESSIONAL RESPONSIBILITIES
As an ACM computing professional I will ..

2.1	Strive to achieve the highest quality, effectiveness and dignity in both the process and products of professional work
2.2	Acquire and maintain professional competence
2.3	Know and respect existing laws pertaining to professional work
2.4	Accept and provide appropriate professional review
2.5	Give comprehensive and thorough evaluations of computer systems and their impacts, including analysis of possible risks
2.6	Honour contracts, agreements, and assigned responsibilities
2.7	Improve public understanding of computing and its consequences
2.8	Access computing and communication resources only when authorised to do so

3. ORGANIZATION LEADERSHIP IMPERATIVES
As an ACM member and an organisational leader I will ..

3.1	Articulate social responsibilities of members of an organisational unit and encourage full acceptance of those responsibilities
3.2	Manage personnel and resources to design and build information systems that enhance the quality of working life
3.3	Acknowledge and support proper and authorised uses of an organisation's computing and communications resources
3.4	Ensure that users and those who will be affected by a system have their needs clearly articulated during the assessment and design of requirements. Later the system must be validated to meet user requirements.
3.5	Articulate and support policies that protect the dignity of users and others affected by a computing system
3.6	Create opportunities for members of the organisation to learn the principles and limitations of computer systems

4. COMPLIANCE WITH THE CODE
As an ACM member I will ..

4.1	Uphold and promote the principles of this Code
4.2	Treat violations of this Code as inconsistent with membership of the ACM

Figure 51.1: The ACM Code of Ethics and Professional Conduct

Codes of practice

The ACM code of Ethics and Professional Conduct above lays out a general code of practice for ICT professionals. Here is a summary of some of the main points:

1. **Contribute to society and human well-being**. Share your expert knowledge freely with others, and be prepared to help colleagues and others when needed.
2. **Avoid harm to others**. This could include passing on a virus through carelessness or not following company procedures.
3. **Be honest and trustworthy**.
4. **Honour property rights including copyrights and patents**.
5. **Give proper credit for intellectual property**. Do not try and pass off another person's work as your own.
6. **Respect the privacy of others**. For example, if you have authorised access to confidential files of information, do not 'gossip' about this information, or pass on other people's personal information. Do not read other people's e-mail.

Employee code of conduct

An employee code of conduct can be an effective measure against computer misuse and abuse. Potential employees need to be checked out carefully before they are hired and, once hired, required to sign an employment contract which sets out the types of misconduct, including computer abuse, which will result in dismissal without notice.

Once new employees actually join, they should be given training which includes a general awareness of computer crime and misuse, the company's policy on security, the use of illegal software, the introduction of viruses, reading other people's e-mail and privacy issues including the Data Protection Act. They should be instructed to change their password frequently and to refer to the company's security manual from time to time. Their responsibilities and authorisation for specific duties should be clearly specified.

> ➤ **Discussion: What sort of 'rules' would you expect to find in an employee code of conduct? Draw up a 'code of conduct' for students using school or college computers.**

Using informal guidelines to make ethical decisions

Informal guidelines can be useful in reaching an ethical decision. Here are some long-standing, broad-based ethical principles to help decide between conflicting demands:

*   **The Golden Rule.** Do unto others as you would have them do unto you. Think about the effects of your actions, and put yourself in the position of someone who would be affected.
*   **The Greatest Good/Least Harm**. When choosing between courses of action, choose the one which achieves the greatest good for the greatest number of people, and causes the least harm.
*   **Kant's Categorical Imperative**. If the action is not right for everyone to take, then it's not right for anyone to take. Think about what would happen if everyone acted as you propose to do.
*   **The Slippery Slope Rule**. Actions that bring about a small, acceptable change but that, if taken repeatedly, would lead to unacceptable changes, should not be taken in the first place.

Case study 1

Staff working for a large company called Cyber Electronics frequently complain of various faults on their PCs. Printers that fail to print, software that won't load, files going missing and dollar signs appearing instead of pound signs are among countless faults commonly reported.

Until recently Ben, the software support analyst, was difficult to track down as he was always roaming from room to room, building to building, fixing problems of one sort or another. Recently, however, the company has invested in a software package called ScreenScape which enables the computer support staff to view anyone's screen from their own PC. Ben is now able to spend almost all of his time at his desk, taking calls from users, calling up their screens and advising the user what to do or fixing the problem himself. Users are delighted with the improved service.

One day he happens to mention the improvement to a Senior Manager in the Accounts Department, who is instantly interested. He asks "You mean you can see exactly what any member of staff is doing on his PC at any time?" "That's right", replies Ben. "Well, I'd like a copy of that software installed on my PC. Can you fix that for me? I have a suspicion that one of my staff is involved in something illegal which could be potentially disastrous for this company, but I've never been able to catch her at it. This could be very useful."

Ben is taken aback. "I'm not sure I can do that. I'll have to let you know."

➤ **What is the ethical dilemma facing Ben? Should he supply the software to the Senior Manager? What are the conflicting issues here?**

Case study 2

Programs which can read and sift 10 CVs in less than a minute and a half are increasingly replacing humans as the first screening stage in the recruitment process, particularly for big companies which receive hundreds of CVs each week. If you've recently applied for a job with Cable and Wireless, Mercury, ICL or Sainsbury's, chances are it was a computer which determined whether you advanced to the next round in the job hunt.

The simplest programs work by searching for key words, so if the job requires knowledge of a particular software package, the computer will pick out applications which mention this word.

➤ **What are the advantages and disadvantages to the employer, and the prospective employee, of using a computer to sift applications? Do you think this is an ethical procedure? Justify your answer.**

Case study 3

Times are bad at B.G. Computer Consultants, with some employees facing redundancy and others who have already been made redundant. Only last week Tom was given 15 minutes to clear his desk before being escorted from the building and his User ID and password removed from the company network. Helen and Ian are fairly confident, however, that their jobs as systems analysts are secure, since they are both working on large contracts. Ian in fact is on the verge of taking out a huge mortgage on a new house. He has often told Helen that if the company ever 'did the dirty on him' as he put it, he would get his own back in no uncertain terms.

One day Helen is working on a presentation. The figures she needs are in a file on the boss's computer, and he is out to lunch. She happens to know his password (unbeknownst to him) and decides to look for the file. Purely accidentally she comes across a memo indicating that Ian is to be made redundant as soon as the contract is completed.

➤ **Should Helen warn Ian about his forthcoming redundancy before he commits himself to a mortgage that he won't be able to afford? Who benefits? Who is harmed?**

➤ **What changes to company policies are needed to prevent such a situation arising in the future?**

Exercises

1. Use the Internet to look up the British Computer Society's Code of Practice. Describe briefly **four** general areas that you would expect such a Code of Practice to cover. (8)

    New question

2. Describe briefly a situation within an Information Technology environment which could pose a moral or ethical dilemma. Describe briefly **three** informal rules which could help in reaching an ethical decision in how to deal with the situation. (5)

    New question

3. As the IT manager for a large company, you have been asked to develop an employee code of conduct. Describe four issues which might be included in such a code. (8)

    NEAB IT05 Qu 4 1998

IT04 – Sample Questions and Answers

1. (a) What is meant by a Management Information System? (4)

   (b) State **four** factors which could contribute to the success or failure of a Management Information System. (4)

   NEAB IT04 Qu 3 1998

Notes:

Unless you have memorised answers from the textbook (always dangerous) to questions such as this one, it helps to have an example of a MIS in mind, if possible from your own experience, or one that you have studied. For revision purposes, you should always try and write down an answer before consulting the textbook or looking at the suggested answer. Then at least you know what you don't know.

OK, so a MIS is a system which provides information to management (0 marks so far). Try carrying on… in order to help them do what? What sort of managers – managing directors, or shop floor managers? Where does the data come from that is turned into useful information? What form does this information take? A string of numbers, or a bar chart?

The answers to part (b) are very clearly laid out in Chapter 37 and are summarised in the AQA Specification for IT04. You would be well advised to read very carefully through the specification and use it as basis for revision.

Suggested Answer:

(a) A Management Information System is a system to convert data from internal and external sources into information in an appropriate format. The information produced will be used by managers at different levels of an organisation to help them to plan, control and make effective decisions.

(b) Any of the following can lead to the failure of a MIS:

Inadequate analysis – the problems and exact needs of managers are not fully understood when the system is designed.

Excessive management demands – managers sometimes ask for information which is hard to extract from the system and which they do not in the end even need.

Lack of teamwork – a good team requires a good leader, and the ICT manager must lead, motivate and control his team effectively, and also take on board the whole company's requirements.

Lack of professional standards – systems must be developed using agreed standards for each stage from analysis to the final user documentation. Poorly documented systems are difficult to amend and maintain. Users need clear documentation so that they know exactly what to do.

2. Information systems are capable of producing strategic and operational information. With the aid of examples, explain the difference between these two levels of information, clearly stating the level of personnel involved in using each one. (6)

   NEAB IT04 Qu 3 1999

Notes:

Here you have to alternately imagine yourself as the managing director of a company, producing anything from cars to hamburgers, and one of the workers engaged in, say, chasing up customers who have not paid for goods received. What sort of information would you need in each case?

Suggested answer:

Strategic information is used to inform senior managers at Board level to assist in planning or budgeting, or deciding in which direction the company should expand. For example statistics on the success of a new online shopping facility may be important in deciding whether to expand that side of the business. Operational level information is used by middle management or clerical workers to assist in daily tasks such as 'When was the order dispatched to Henry VII school?' or 'How many customers have debts of over £250 outstanding over more than 30 days?'

---

3. A particular organisation is upgrading its computer-based stock control system. The previous data collection system was OMR based.

    One function of the system is to allow stock levels to be monitored on a regular basis.

    (a) State **three** other alternative methods of collecting stock control data. (3)

    (b) What factors, other than cost, will determine the method of data collection? (4)

    (c) The software used to control the system must support an audit trail. Explain what is meant by the term 'audit trail', and state why this functionality is necessary. (6)

    NEAB IT04 Qu 5 1999

Notes:

You have to be very clear in your mind what sort of stock control system is being described here. For example if you are selling books in a bookshop, the quantity in stock is automatically adjusted every time you sell a book so there would be no need to monitor stock regularly by actually counting what was on the shelves. However if you are selling meals in a restaurant, you might very well want to check stocks of basic items on a daily or weekly basis. How will this be done? In this question, I think you can assume that you are to describe methods *either* of collecting data about stock that is actually physically counted on the shelves of the stockroom or warehouse, *or* through sales at the till or invoicing system.

Parts (b) and (c) are fairly standard questions with fairly standard answers. The main thing to understand about audit trails is that they provide a means of checking all the transactions that have been processed. You can't have a system which simply tells you that you have 4,168 mobile phones in stock but does not explain how this figure is arrived at when you started 3 months ago with 10,000 being delivered.

Suggested answer:

(a) Stock control data may be collected at the tills with a bar code reader by scanning each item as it is sold. The stock level will be automatically adjusted by the system.
    Alternatively the stock on the shelves may be barcoded and using a hand-held laser gun the bar codes can be read and the data transferred later electronically to the main computer system.
    Data at a till may be collected using a special 'touch till' where, for example, the staff touch a symbol for each drink or food item ordered in a restaurant. The stock information will then be automatically updated.

(b) Factors which determine the method of data collection include:

    •   The volume of stock and the number of transactions performed daily;

    •   The need to have completely up-to-date information on stock levels;

- The diversity of stock. Not everything can be bar-coded, for example portions of vegetables.

(c) An audit trail provides a means of tracking every transaction that has been entered into the system so that it is possible to see how a particular figure was arrived at. It is possible to get a printout of all transactions which affect one particular line of stock, for example. Some systems record who has used the system, when and for how long, which enables any unauthorised or suspicious use to be monitored.

It is essential to maintain an audit trail in order to meet legal requirements to do so, as every business must produce a set of accounts based on verifiable facts. Also, an audit trail is a protection against fraud and against theft of stock.

---

4. A multi-site college is considering the introduction of an IT based system to log visitors. The current system is based on a manual log at reception. The new system will capture visual images of visitors together with details of their visit. The introduction of this system will cause considerable change for staff and visitors.

   In the context of this example describe **four** factors that the management should consider when introducing this change. (8)

   NEAB IT05 Qu 4 1998

Notes:

The key word here is *change* which if you have done your revision should set bells ringing and remind you to look again at the topic 'The Management of Change' (Chapter 44). However failing that, use some imagination and common sense. You can think of some aspects that will affect visitors and some that will affect staff at various levels. (This system seems pretty pointless to me, how is the management going to convince lecturers who have no money for textbooks that it is worth the expense? Will some anarchic Computing lecturer smash the camera at the end of his evening session?)

Suggested answer:

The management should consider how the change will affect the staff at reception and whether they will object to the change. Their support should be gained by explaining the benefits of the new system and involving them in planning details. Training for staff to operate the new system will be required. It is possible that some visitors may object to having their photographs taken, and this needs to be investigated. The management should also consider whether such a plan is cost-effective and whether the information captured by the new system will actually be used by anyone. Involvement of those who are likely to use the information is essential to determine their requirements and to gain their support. Ideas and misgivings should be listened to and taken into consideration when planning the system.

---

5. The Head of a school decides to adopt an IT package to maintain pupils' records of attainment. The package will be used throughout the school.

   (a) (i) Identify three potential users of this package. (3)

       (ii) With the aid of examples, describe the different types of documentation that each user will require. (6)

   (b) Training in the use of this package may be provided by a variety of methods other than formal training courses. Describe **two** possible alternative methods. (4)

   NEAB IT04 Qu 5 1998

Notes:

Note that the potential *users of the IT package* will be within the school, even though the documents produced may be bound in a folder and used by a potential employer. So confine your answers to users within the school. Part (a) (ii) is at first sight open to misinterpretation – does it mean the documentation that would be needed to use the system, for example to input data or customise reports, or the output that would be produced by the system in the form of reports? Just be sure you know which you are talking about.

Suggested answer:

(a) The package will be used by the **Form Tutor** to enter data regarding individual pupils' progress and levels of attainment. User documentation would be required to show a teacher how to log on to the system, input student data and print out reports for each student or for a whole class.

Management would use the system to produce school statistics on achievement for the school prospectus etc. The results might of course be produced by the **clerical support staff** using the system rather than the Head Teacher. The documentation required would be advice on how to perform queries, sorts, etc to produce the required statistics.

Technical Support Staff would be required to customise reports, install the system on new computers, respond to error messages, perform backups etc. They would need technical documentation on how to perform these functions.

(b) Training could be provided by:

An on-line tutorial so that the user can sit at the computer they are actually going to use and go through the steps to input data, select reports etc;

A video which has a tutor explaining how to perform all the tasks, the advantage being that the video can be watched anywhere, even at home at the end of an exhausting day coping with Year 10;

A step-by-step user guide can be used by following it through while trying out each step on a computer;

(Could also mention: One person can go for formal training and then show relevant parts of the system to smaller groups or individuals on an informal basis.)

---

6. A software house has a user support department that provides a range of services to customers including telephone advice and the supply of data fixes for corrupt files. The department uses a computer-based logging system to store details of incoming telephone calls from users (a call management system). The system is capable of producing a variety of reports via a report generator.

(a) The software house receives complaints from its users that this department is providing a poor service. Describe three reports that the software house could produce to examine the validity of this claim. (6)

(b) The department uses traditional mail to receive disks containing corrupt files and to return them with the data fixed. However, the department now wishes to use electronic communications based on ISDN. Describe **two** potential advantages and **one** potential disadvantage to the customer of this proposed change. (6)

NEAB IT04 Qu 7 1999

Notes:

Think what would constitute a poor service. Not being there to answer the call, taking too long to answer, not being able to fix the problem, etc. This should give you some ideas for reports that could monitor these events. Be aware that you will get *one* mark for writing, for example, 'a report which logs the response time to a customer call'. For the second mark, you will have to give more detail.

In part (b) avoid answers such as quicker, cheaper, more convenient unless you can fully justify your answer. You will get no marks for suggesting that the user may not be connected to the Internet, because for heaven's sake, they should be! And no marks for suggesting they will save the cost of a stamp by not having to post a disk.

Suggested answer:

(a) One problem with help lines from software houses is that they are often inundated with calls at busy periods of the day and the user is held in a queue, for periods of up to half an hour or more. A report which logs the number of calls taken per hour, and the actual response time until the user gets to speak to a member of the user support staff, will show whether waiting times are acceptable.

When a user calls they are usually asked for their software serial number and the nature of their problem. The time spent on the phone explaining how to solve the problem is also logged. Therefore a report analysing the amount of time solving each different type of problem, and which member of staff fielded the call, would show whether there was consistency in the amount of time spent by different staff members on solving similar types of problem.

A third report might show the number of problems that could not be resolved by the staff at the help desk, or which had to be passed to someone else to solve, and compare this figure to the number of problems that were solved satisfactorily the first time.

(b) Advantages to customer: Many data files are too large to fit on a floppy disk and zip disks are expensive, and not all users will have a zip drive, so it is impractical to copy large data files to disk.

It would be possible for a user at the Help desk to take over the user's screen remotely, calling it up on their own screen to solve the problem or provide the fix immediately.

A disadvantage could be that the service could be more expensive, and the client would also have to bear the cost of an ISDN line.

---

7. A company has three departments to handle finance, buildings and equipment maintenance. Each department currently operates a separate IT system. The company wishes to improve the efficiency of the operations by implementing a common corporate system across all three departments. In order to achieve this improvement, the company has decided to select members of staff from each department to form a project team to plan, design and implement the new system.

    (a) Describe three corporate level factors the team should consider when planning the new system.
    (6)

    (b) At their first meeting the team decide to sub-divide the project into a series of tasks. Describe **two** advantages of this approach.
    (4)

    NEAB IT05 Qu 8 1999

Notes:

Remember the factors that affect the success or failure of a Management Information System? Time to dust them off again. Also, the new system implies *change*, so the implications of change could form part of your answer.

In part (b), you should be able to call on your own experience of group assignments, but you must make sure you relate them to an ICT project.

Suggested answer:

(a) It is essential that the management from each department is involved in the planning stages to ensure that the new system meets their requirements and will have their support. Employees at all levels of the organisation are likely to be affected by the new system and they should also be informed and their views taken into account. A proper training program will have to be worked out for both operations staff and management. The implications of the change on employment conditions and practices need to be considered. It is possible that some jobs may disappear or that staff may need to be redeployed when the new system becomes operational.

(b) All ICT projects of this nature will break down into various phases such as Analysis, Design, Implementation etc. Within these phases there will be subtasks such as designing the user interface, writing programs, writing user documentation etc. By breaking down the project into subtasks each member of the team can be allocated tasks that play to their strengths – one may be a good analyst and communicator, one a good programmer etc. A project that consists of a number of clearly defined tasks is very much easier to control as it is clear when one task such as 'Set up the database table' has been completed. It also means that if someone leaves the team before the project is completed, their tasks can more easily be re-allocated as it is clear what needs to be done and what sort of person is needed, e.g. a good technical person or someone who has a good understanding of the business etc.

---

8. Organisations and IT professionals are required to comply with a legal framework when introducing and using IT systems. In addition there will normally be a code of practice.

    (a) Define what is meant by a 'code of practice'. (2)

    (b) Describe **two** ways in which institutions, such as the British Computer Society, promote professionalism for individuals within the IT industry. (2)

    NEAB IT01 Qu 5 1998

Notes:

No getting away from it, you probably need to have attended the lecture on this one or at least read through Chapter 51 if you were unable to drag yourself out of bed on the day.

Suggested answer:

(a) A code of practice lays out the general 'rules' that an ICT professional should follow, though it does not have the force of law. It will lay down the standard of behaviour and actions expected of an employee within an organisation. For example, employees may be forbidden by the code of practice to send e-mails containing inflammatory / derogatory material or jokes in questionable taste.

(b) The BCS has its own code of ethics which members are expected to abide by. Membership is by examination or professional status within the industry. It also holds seminars, meetings and lectures which enable professionals to get together, exchange ideas and learn from each other.

---

9. "Information systems are mission critical, the consequences of failure could prove disastrous." Discuss this statement, including in your discussion:

    - the potential threats to the system
    - the concept of risk analysis
    - the corporate consequences of system failure
    - the factors which should be considered when designing the 'contingency plan' to enable a recovery from disaster. (20)

    Quality of language will be assessed in this question

    NEAB IT04 Qu 9 1998

Notes:

There will be 4 marks allocated to each of the bullet points and 4 marks for 'quality of language'. (See the advice for question 9 at the end of IT01 for more detail on how marks are allocated for this, and also advice on how to construct your essay.)

Try to make 2 or 3 good points for each part of the question and then *discuss* these points. You will not get 4 marks for simply listing 4 potential threats to a system – you'll get 2 marks if you're lucky. The intelligent, analytical discussion is an essential ingredient of the essay question, which is why it is a good discriminator between strong and weak candidates. But at least if you know what is expected you can give it your best shot!

Suggested answer:

One potential threat to a system is the occurrence of a 'natural' disaster such as a fire, flood or earthquake. The likelihood of earthquakes or hurricanes may be low in some areas but every organisation must make provision for the physical destruction of its hardware, software or data. Hardware failure such as a hard disk crash could destroy vital data in a fraction of a second.

A second threat to an information system is the corruption of data, whether accidentally or deliberately. This could happen because it has been infected by a virus, because an operator has followed the wrong procedure when inputting data, or because of a program error. A disgruntled employee could deliberately cause data to be corrupted by hacking into a database and altering or deleting data, for example.

Risk analysis is the process of weighing up the threats to the computer system and the likely consequences of data loss against the cost of protecting the system. First of all the possible threats to information systems within the company must be established. There may be many information systems and some may be more at risk than others, and some may be more 'mission-critical' than others. It may be a disaster for an online system to be out of action for more than an hour or two – for example on a Stock Exchange or a computerised Ambulance information system, or even the EPOS system at a supermarket. On the other hand some systems such as a mail order invoicing system may not be critically affected if it is out of action for a day, but it is crucial that data is not lost.

Most businesses will not survive the loss of their data files. The loss of customer records, supplier records, accounts and stock control records would make it difficult to continue in business. Surveys show that a significant number of businesses collapse within a short time of a significant data loss. Moreover, the directors of a company may be prosecuted by the Health and Safety Executive if loss of essential business data or safety data adversely affects the health and safety of the public (for example, by losing medical records) or the environment. Under the Data Protection Act, companies have a legal obligation to keep data safe and secure.

When designing a contingency plan to enable recovery from disaster, key elements will include

- A list of the most critical business functions;
- A list of the facilities, hardware, software, data, personnel and other equipment that are necessary to support those functions;
- A method for securing access to all necessary resources;
- A method for getting in touch with all key personnel;
- A step-by-step course of action to follow to implement the plan;
- Education and training of personnel involved in implementing the plan;
- Regular drills to test the effectiveness of the plan.

Section 5

Information: Policy, Strategy and Systems

In this section:

Chapter 52 – Policy and Strategy

The challenge of information management

Within the space of a few decades, businesses have moved from having one mainframe computer to process data for payroll, stock control and customer accounts to having company-wide, often worldwide networks of computers affecting and controlling every aspect of their business. Computers are no longer a centralised resource operated and understood by a few knowledgeable experts: at every level of a company, employees will be interacting with and using computers to perform a huge variety of tasks. Customers may also be interacting with the company's computers through the Internet, cash machines, touch screens in shopping malls and so on.

'Information' is a resource, but one that has completely different properties from other resources such as raw materials or stock. For one thing, it is not depleted when it is used. For another, it is difficult and usually undesirable to keep exclusive ownership of information. It is usually regarded as a shared resource within a company.

The challenge for management is to formulate an information management policy that will help them manage computing resources in an effective and profitable way, and maximise the benefits of information.

We'll look at four different strategic planning issues related to information systems:

- Consistency with business priorities;
- Centralisation vs. decentralisation;
- Different user needs;
- Hardware and software choices.

Consistency with business priorities

A company's information system strategy should be linked to its business plan. This may seem obvious, but in practice, it does not always happen. One method used to try and ensure that it does is to use an approach called the **critical success factors** (CSF) method. This encourages senior executives to identify the company's primary goals and what things must go right for the business to succeed. They then identify measures of performance for each of these CSFs and make sure that the information systems are in place to collect and use this information.

> ➤ **Discussion: Typical example of CSFs include improving customer service, improving supplier relationships, holding the right stock at the right time in the right quantity, and using human resources efficiently.**
>
> ➤ **What performance indicators could be used to measure better customer service?**
>
> ➤ **What are the critical success factors in your school, college or department? How are information systems used to collect information about performance indicators?**

Centralisation vs. decentralisation

Most organisations today retain a department for computing services known for example as the 'Information Systems Department'. This department will have the responsibility for the planning and control of processing, the maintenance of hardware and software and the development of new computerised information systems.

In some organisations, the various tasks connected with managing computer resources are all performed centrally by the Information Systems Department. In other organisations, many tasks are performed by individual departments in a so-called decentralised or 'distributed' system. A centralised system has the advantage of providing a centralised pool of expertise and better control over what hardware and software is purchased. A distributed system, however, allows users in individual departments to develop their own applications and lessens dependence on the central resource.

Different user needs

A typical medium- to large-sized organisation using computers will have a number of different types of users, each with their own different requirements, as shown in Figure 52.1.

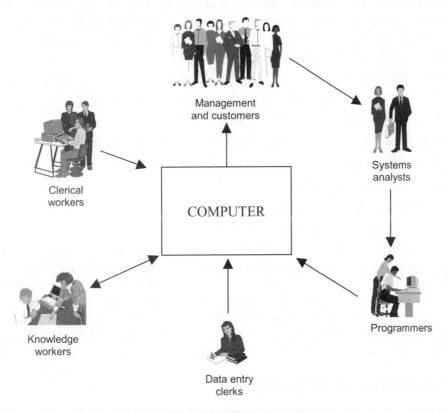

Figure 52.1: Different users in an organisation

Systems analysts, programmers and data entry clerks are computer users who interact with the computer system, but are distinct from 'end-users' who are the ultimate consumers of computer processing and information. Information systems fall into three major categories, each of which has different end-users:

- **Transaction processing systems**. Users: Clerical workers, salespeople, data entry clerks and customers.
- **Knowledge work systems**. Users: Middle managers, professional people such as accountants, engineers and graphic designers.
- **Management support systems**. Users: Senior managers.

End-users require software that is easy to use and which has enough features to help them to get their jobs done as efficiently as possible. They need hardware that is sufficiently powerful to run the software without frustrating delays.

> ➤ **A personnel manager in a large engineering company has asked one of her staff to produce a report showing which Universities they recruited from in the past five years, the proportion of those accepted out of the total interviewed, the proportion of men and women, and various other statistics. What software would be helpful in compiling this report?**

Hardware and software choices

With the trend towards distributed systems, there is a choice between allowing each department to purchase the hardware and software it considers most suitable for its own applications, or controlling all purchases from a central Information Systems Department. Generally the advantages of centralised control outweigh the disadvantages, and include the following:

- All hardware within the company will be compatible and can be linked in a company-wide network;

- Purchasing power is increased if high volumes are ordered by an organisation;

- The organisation is likely to get a better deal on maintenance contracts;

- Employees will not have to learn new systems if they move to another department;

- Training courses can be organised for people using the same software from many departments;

- Site licences can be purchased for software;

- There is better control over the use of unlicensed software;

- Data can be exchanged more easily between similar types of computer.

The term **platform** is used to describe the basic type of computer that an information system uses. A small business might for example choose between a platform based on an Intel chip (used on PCs) or a Motorola Power PC chip (used in Apple computers). The decision would depend on the characteristics of the application and the availability of software that runs on a particular platform. Upgrading to a more powerful computer in the same family costs money but in principle causes few technical difficulties, but moving between platforms is usually more complex because software written for one type of computer will generally not run on another.

Upgrading hardware and software

Many firms face a crucial challenge in the form of **legacy systems**: systems that have been passed down to the current users and IS staff. They are old, often technically obsolete systems that perform essential data processing such as accounting and customer billing. Many of these systems, written in COBOL in the 1960s and 70s, have been upgraded time and time again, using programming methods that are years out of date, and are technically fragile, difficult to maintain and impossible to understand. Because they still work, however, it may be difficult to get the funds to start from scratch with a new system.

Even companies with relatively new information systems face the constant problem of upgrades. Nothing stands still in computing – sometimes it seems as though no sooner have you bought a brand new PC to run your software than a new, better software version comes out that requires an even more powerful processor and twice as much memory to run it. When a company has upwards of a thousand PCs, the problem of upgrading becomes immense. Should everyone upgrade? Should no-one upgrade? Should selected departments upgrade?

Very likely some people would really benefit from the new features of upgraded software. On the other hand, documents created on the latest version of Word, for example, cannot be read in a previous version. This will inevitably cause problems.

> ➤ **Discussion: A school has the funds to equip a classroom with a new set of computers running the latest version of Windows. However, the other computers in the school are not powerful enough to run this version. What factors should the computer manager take into account when deciding what to do?**
> ➤ **What would you do if you were the computer manager?**

Future proofing

Is it possible to make such a shrewd choice of hardware and software that there will be no need to change it for years to come – to 'future proof' your purchases? Experience says a firm No. With processors still doubling in power every 18 months or so, and new versions of software appearing with monotonous regularity every year or two, most individuals and organisations resign themselves to the fact that regular upgrades will be necessary. The best strategy may be to buy hardware that has far more capability than is currently needed in anticipation of future need.

> ➤ **Discussion: What are the drawbacks of this strategy?**

Offers from TIME computer systems: Future proof?

Below are some offers from Time Computer Systems advertised over a four-year period:

Date	Processor	RAM	Disk	Price
January 1996	75MHz Pentium	8Mb	850Mb	£1666
May 1996	100MHz Pentium	16Mb	850Mb	£1291
April 1997	166MHz Pentium	32Mb	2.1Gb	£1291
February 1998	233MHz Pentium	64Mb	6.4Gb	£1099
January 2000	500MHz Pentium	128Mb	20Gb	£1096

> ➤ **Discussion: Look up the latest offer from TIME Computer Sytems. (Try the back of Thursday's OnLine section of the Guardian, or Wednesday's edition of the Interface section of the Times)**

Exercises

1. 'If I need an I.T. system I buy whatever hardware and software I want without any regard to anyone.'
   This statement was made by a manager of a department in a company.
   Why is this an inappropriate approach in a large organisation? (6)
   NEAB IT05 Qu 7 Sample paper

Chapter 53 – Security and Backup Policies

Introduction

There are two main ways to ensure that ICT systems, once up and running, are protected from disaster, misuse or abuse. These are:

- Security measures;
- A personnel policy which covers data security and employee codes of conduct.

Under UK law, the responsibility for the security of the ICT assets of a company, including its hardware, networks, software, databases and so on lies not with the ICT department or the security officer, but with the company directors. They are *personally* responsible for the security of these assets. For this reason, they can be expected to give unequivocal support to the formulation and enforcement of an effective security policy.

Security policies were covered in Chapter 45. In this chapter we'll take a closer look at backup strategies.

Backup strategies

Some key questions need to be addressed when planning a backup strategy:

- How often should backups be done?
- What should be backed up?
- Where should the backups be stored?

In devising a backup plan, several factors need to be taken into account such as:

- The value of the data;
- The amount of data stored on the computer;
- The frequency with which the data changes;
- The type of backup equipment.

Proper backup procedures are the first line of defence against disaster. Both software and data need to be backed up and stored safely, off-site or in a fire-proof safe. Data may need to be backed up at least once a day and taken off-site. Software only needs to be backed up when a change is made or a new version installed.

Many organisations, from hospitals and government departments to banks and manufacturers, are totally dependent on the data held in databases which are continually being updated. A comprehensive backup strategy is required.

Full backup

A full backup is a copy of all the files on a disk. This is a very safe strategy because it ensures that you have a copy of every program and every data file on the disk, and it is easy to restore if it ever becomes necessary. However a full backup takes a long time to complete and the computer cannot be used for anything else while it in progress.

Example: A large organisation holds all the data on its database on a 10Gb file server in the office. It uses the following backup strategy:

- The organisation has a service agreement with a local company under which engineers will be at the office in under two hours in the event of any problem.

- The file server contains two disk drives, 'mirrored disks' containing identical data. All transactions are written simultaneously to both disks, so that if one disk crashes, the other disk drive contains all the data. No further transactions are accepted until the disk drive is repaired or replaced by the Service Agency.

- Four backup tapes marked **Monday, Tuesday, Wednesday, Thursday** are stored in a fireproof safe in the office. Each night, the relevant day's tape is loaded, a backup program starts automatically at midnight and backs up the entire contents of the hard disk, which takes several hours. One person in the office (a young Business Studies graduate whose main job is Marketing) is in charge of checking the on-screen messages in the morning to ensure that the backup has completed successfully, and if not, the Service Agency is notified.

- Every Friday, the person responsible for the backup procedures takes the **Friday** tape home, and on Monday, brings back the tape from two Fridays ago to be overwritten the following Friday.

- The Service Agency is responsible for maintaining the hardware and replacing, say, a worn tape drive.

- Occasionally, the tape is tested by restoring it onto a spare machine provided by the agency to check that the data is in fact being correctly backed up and that the hard disk can be correctly restored to its previous state.

Incremental backup

With this type of backup, a full backup of the entire hard disk is made say once a week on Monday. On Tuesday, only those files which have been created or changed during the day are backed up. This backup tape or disk is carefully labelled 'Tuesday'. On Wednesday, only the files which have been changed or created on Wednesday are backed up, and so on.

This backup strategy is less time-consuming but more complex to restore, as all the backups have to be restored in the correct sequence.

Hardware for backups

- For small quantities of data, removable disks are the simplest. Iomega's Zip drive sells for under £100 and takes 100Mb disks similar to floppy disks (£10 each). It can copy 100Mb of data in about 5 minutes.

Figure 53.1: Iomega Zip drive

- For larger backups, tape is the preferred medium. A DAT tape drive with a capacity ranging from 2-24Gb costs about £600 and tape cartridges cost from about £5 to £50 depending on capacity.

- A CD-ROM drive using rewritable optical disks costs about £280. The 650Mb disks cost about £20 each.

Case study: Back up that data

The simplest backup strategy is to copy the contents of your hard disk at the end of each day to a tape or removable disk. Keep Friday's backup for a month, and one backup each month for a year. To prevent mix-ups, give each tape or disk a serial number, and keep a log book. Once done, the backup tape or disk should be stored in a safe place.

You can reduce the volume and time by using 'compression' software, which comes with the tape or disk drive, and by only backing up data files. Software programs do not need to be backed up except when they are changed. If the backup is still unmanageable, you can reduce it by backing up only files which have changed since you last did a backup – an 'incremental' backup. A typical strategy would be to do a full backup on a Monday, and incrementals Tuesday to Friday.

"One small business did backups every day and stored them in a fireproof safe", says Colin Pearson, I.T. adviser at Business Link Staffordshire. "Then some thieves stole the computer and the safe, so they lost the lot."

Once the backup is made, your worries are not entirely over, as self-employed public relations consultant David Bridson discovered. He religiously backs up his data every night onto a removable optical disk. But some months ago he moved his e-mail database to a different directory on his hard disk, and forgot to tell the backup software. Recently, seeing that his hard disk was getting full, he deleted some redundant files.

"Of course, the directories I cleared out were the ones I'd moved all this valuable information to", he says. "I went to each of my five backups and found that none of them contained my up-to-date e-mail list."

Source: Paul Bray, Sunday Times 19 October 1997

On-line backup (RAID)

Thousands of organisations such as hospitals, banks, airlines, supermarkets etc. as well as smaller organisations cannot afford to lose even a few second's worth of data. How can they protect against disaster? The answer is that each transaction is written simultaneously to at least two and probably three different disks. Such a system is known as a drive array or RAID system (Redundant Array of Inexpensive Drives). The system is usually accompanied by software which gives the operator the option of switching over to the second disk automatically in the event of the first one failing. A third disk drive at some geographically remote location also records the data so that if one building is bombed the data is still safe.

Grandfather-father-son backups

Not all organisations use on-line databases. Many companies do their processing in 'batch mode', collecting transactions over a period of time and batching them into sets of say 50 documents. These can then be checked, control totals calculated and entered on a batch header record, and the data entered using a key-to-disk system. (Chapter 15).

> **Discussion: What sort of organisation might use a batch processing system? Why?**

When batch processing is used, it is not necessary to back up all the data every night. The system uses 'generations' of master files, automatically creating a new 'generation' of master file each time the day's transactions are processed. To understand this process, imagine an equivalent manual system.

A class register for Lower VIa is written out in a register book in alphabetical order of students' names. Halfway through the term, it is decided to combine three classes into two, so a list of 5 extra students is given to the teacher of Lower VIa, who has to write out a brand new register. Unfortunately, three days later, the register disappears. Luckily, however, the teacher still has the old register and the list of names that were to be added, so the new register can be recreated.

In batch processing, transactions are typically processed once a day. A block diagram of the process is shown in Figure 53.2.

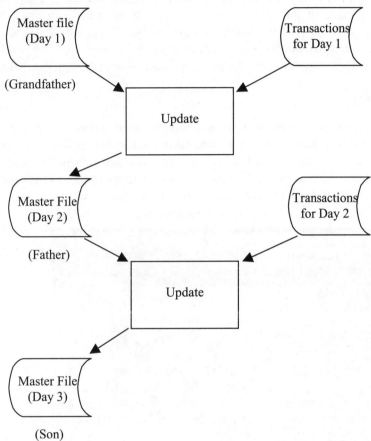

Figure 53.2: Grandfather-Father-Son method of update

When this method of processing is used, it is common to keep at least four generations of the master file along with the transactions that were used to update each generation. On the fifth day, the oldest generation of the master file (the 'grandfather') can be overwritten. Thus, there is always at least one generation of the master file and the corresponding transactions stored off-line in a secure fire-proof safe, with at least one pair off-site.

Exercises

1.   A hospital information system holds program files which are rarely changed and large database files which are constantly changing.

     Describe a suitable backup strategy for this system, explaining what is backed up and when, together with the media and hardware involved. (8)

     NEAB IT05 Qu 8 1997

Chapter 54 – Software Evaluation

Introduction

When a decision is made to computerise some aspect of the business, a feasibility study is carried out and then a detailed analysis is made of the user requirements. At some stage a decision has to be made whether to buy a software package 'off the shelf' or have software specially designed and developed either in-house or by outside consultants. In this chapter we'll be looking at methods of evaluating software packages to assess their suitability for the proposed task, and writing an evaluation report.

Choosing software

Suppose that you work for a small business that needs a computerised accounting system. You have been given the task of evaluating accounting packages and making a recommendation. Where do you start? Perhaps you may have heard the names of a few accounting packages, or can find out some names by browsing round PC World or asking a friend. The next thing you might try is to look up a supplier on the Internet – Sage, for example, has a well-known range of accounting packages.

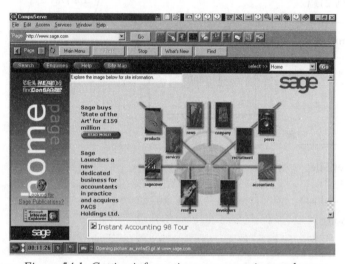

Figure 54.1: Getting information on accounting packages

Exploring a little further in the Sage site will bring up a guide which provides useful advice on finding a suitable package:

- DON'T walk into a shop or dealership and buy the cheapest thing on offer. Remember, it is not the PC that does the real work, it is the software and if you buy a system that is not suited to your business it could cost you a lot of time, money and effort later on. You should make this decision with great care because effectively, you will be running your business on the accounting system.

- DO start to collect some information on accounting software products and PCs and read some of the reviews published in computer magazines.

- DO talk to your accountant, who may be able to advise you about some packages. Information may also be available from professional bodies such as the Institute of Chartered Accountants.

- DO define what it is that you need an accounting software package to do. Do you want to run your whole system on it or just do some sales invoicing? Will you need to automate just the main ledgers or would you like to put sales order processing, purchase order processing and stock control onto the computer? Do you have any special procedures or requirements that you must stick to, whatever the system? Will you want to extract management information for use in decision-making?

When you have answered these questions, you can begin your search in earnest.

(Reproduced with permission from Sagesoft Ltd)

Tailoring the software

Sage emphasises that the first crucial step in selecting a suitable software package is to define exactly what the system must do to fulfil the requirements of the business. Cheaper packages bought off the shelf generally cannot be tailored to individual requirements. More expensive packages can often be configured to match user needs. It is no good buying a standard package that meets 80% of the user's needs but can't cope with the other, crucial, 20%.

Some software houses will be able to tailor an existing package to provide the extra functionality required. However, this is a dangerous option – Tony Collins in his book 'Crash' advises:

"With a standard package there is no such thing as a 'minor' code change. It is like trying to add an appendage to a human being. Imperfect as we are, we are tried and tested and are unlikely to work better with two hearts, or run faster with three legs. If you want to keep the project really simple, buy a package but *don't modify it.*"

Upgradability

A small business trying to keep a tight rein on overheads may be tempted to go for a good, simple and inexpensive package that serves their current needs. As the business expands, the package may no longer be adequate, and the pain of changing to a completely new system can be considerable. Therefore, it is desirable to choose a package that has a clear 'upgrade path' – many companies offer a range of upwardly-compatible packages so that data can easily be transferred to a more powerful package. The upgrades are offered at a special price to existing customers.

Other evaluation criteria

Several other factors need to be considered:

- **Compatibility with existing hardware and software**. Will the package run on existing hardware? Can files be easily transferred from existing systems without re-keying? Can files created in the package be exported to other systems in use in the company?

- **Resource requirements**. Will the system require expenditure on more powerful hardware, or extra staff to key in data?

- **Quality of documentation**. Are manuals supplied? Is there a good on-line help system?

- **Ease of learning**. Are tutorials supplied? Are books on the software available in bookshops? Are training courses available?

- **Ease of use**. Is it easy to use, for example using pull-down menus, icons, helpful error messages when you do something wrong?

- **Technical support**. Is support available? Is it very costly? Often, a technical support contract can add 50% or more to the price of a package, but without it no support at all will be given by the manufacturer.

- **Cost**. This includes the original cost of the package, technical support, and upgrades.

- **Speed**. The speed at which the package carries out critical operations can be measured using benchmark tests (see below).

Benchmark tests

A benchmark test, or performance test, can help determine the efficiency of the product. These tests involve comparing several different software packages by measuring the time that each one takes to perform various tasks. Computer magazines regularly publish the results of benchmark tests on different types of software.

Checking out the manufacturer

An important criterion in selecting a software package is the reputation of the manufacturer and the supplier: the relationship with the supplier can be crucial in getting the right package. It is important that the supplier understands how your business works and what the requirements are, and to provide support when problems arise. Consulting other users, reading magazine articles and visiting suppliers to discuss requirements are all ways of finding out who you can rely on.

Evaluation report

Once a thorough evaluation of possible software options has been made, an evaluation report may be written to document the performance of the software examined, and to make recommendations so that a decision can be made on what software to purchase.

The report will typically contain:

- An introduction stating the purpose of the report;
- The methodology used to evaluate the software options;
- The actual evaluation, including the capabilities of the software, results of benchmark tests, upgrade facilities, compatibility with existing software base etc.
- Recommendations;
- Justifications for the recommended purchase.

Exercises

1. In groups of two or three students, carry out an evaluation of several similar packages e.g. word processing packages, spreadsheets, databases or graphics packages. Write an evaluation report and give a presentation of your recommendations for which package the school/college should invest in.

   New question

2. You are asked to evaluate a software package and produce an evaluation report.
   (a) Describe **four** criteria you would use to evaluate the package. (8)
   (b) What is the function and content of an evaluation report? (4)

   NEAB IT05 Qu 4 Sample paper

3. A company is about to change its accounting software. In order to evaluate the different packages available to them, they have drawn up a number of evaluation criteria.
   (a) Why are such evaluation criteria needed? (2)
   (b) Explain the issues involved with each of the **three** evaluation criteria given below:
      Functionality
      User Support
      Hardware Resource Requirements. (6)
   (c) Identify and describe three additional evaluation criteria that you might expect the company to include. (6)

   NEAB IT05 Qu 8 1998

4. A system for the production of about one hundred thousand electricity bills per day is required. A number of alternative systems are available for purchase.

    The following features of each alternative system have been given numerical weightings to reflect their relative importance:

Feature	Weighting
A: purchase cost	5
B: maintenance and running costs	10
C: user friendliness of the software	3
D: bill printing speed	12
E: quality of printed output	8

    The required system is selected as follows:

Step 1	Rank each feature of each alternative system in order of merit.	For example, with regard to feature A, purchase cost, the most expensive system would be given a ranking of 1, the second most expensive a ranking of 2, and so on.
Step 2	Multiply each of these rankings by its respective weighting.	For example, with regard to feature E, which has a weighting of 8, the system with the worst printed output would have a computed value of (1 x 8), the system with the second worst printed output a computed value of (2 x 8) and so on.
Step 3	For each alternative system calculate a total of these computer values. The system with the largest total should be selected.	

    (a) Suggest a possible consequence of feature C being given a low weighting. (2)

    (b) Comment on the relative size of the weighting given to feature D in comparison to the other features. (2)

    (c) State **three** advantages of this method of selecting a computer system. (3)

    (d) Identify **four** factors other than those listed which should be taken into account before a system is purchased. Justify your suggestions. (8)

    London Computing Paper 2 Qu 12 1997

Chapter 55 – Data Modelling

Traditional file approach

Most organisations began information processing on a small scale, buying a computer for perhaps one or two individual applications, and then computerising other departments one by one. Applications were developed independently, and files of information relevant to one particular department were created and processed by dozens or even hundreds of separate programs. This situation led to several problems:

- **Data redundancy**. The same data was duplicated in many different files. For example, details of a salesman's name, address and pay rate might be held on a payroll file for calculating the payroll. The same data may be held on a file in the Personnel department along with a lot of other personal data, and in the Sales Department which has a program to keep track of each salesman's record and performance.

- **Data inconsistency**. When the same items of data are held in several different files, the data has to be updated in each separate file when it changes. The Payroll Department, for example, may change the commission rates paid to salesmen but the Sales Department file may fail to update its files and so be producing reports calculated with out-of-date figures.

- **Program-data dependence**. Every computer program in each department has to specify exactly what data fields constitute a record in the file being processed. Any change to the format of the data fields – for example, adding a new field or changing the length of a field – means that every program which uses that file has to be changed, since the file format is specified within each program.

- **Lack of flexibility**. In such a system, when information of a non-routine nature is needed, it can take weeks to assemble the data from the various files and write new programs to produce the required reports.

- **Data was not shareable**. If one department had data that was required by another department, it was awkward to obtain it. A second copy of the file could be made, but this would obviously soon lead to problems of inconsistency. If the same file was used, it would almost certainly be necessary to add extra fields for the new application, and that would mean the original programs would have to be changed to reflect the new file structure.

The database approach

In an attempt to solve these problems, the concept of a database was born.

A **database** is defined as a collection of non-redundant data shareable between different applications.

All the data belonging to the entire organisation would be centralised in a common pool of data, accessible by all applications. This solved the problems of redundancy and inconsistency, but two major problems remained to be addressed.

- **Unproductive maintenance**. Programs were still dependent on the structure of the data, so that when one department needed to add a new field to a particular file, all other programs accessing that file had to be changed.

- **Lack of security**. All the data in the database, even confidential or commercially sensitive data, was accessible by all applications.

The Database Management System (DBMS)

A DBMS is a layer of software inserted between the applications and the data, which attempts to solve these problems. Two essential features of the DBMS are:

- Program-data independence, whereby the storage structure of the data is hidden from each application/user;

- Restricted user access to the data – each user is given a limited view of the data according to need.

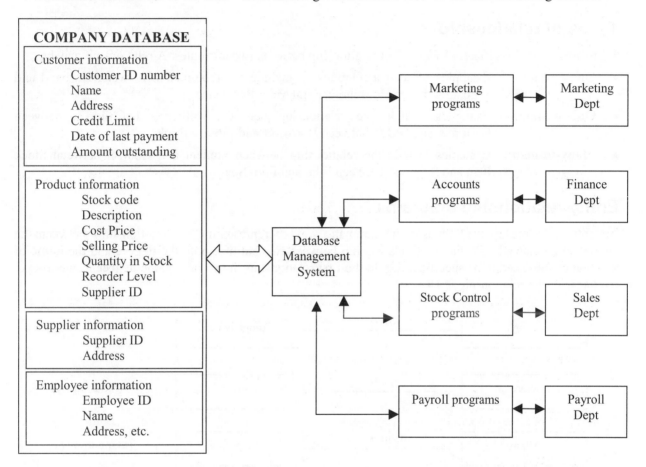

Figure 55.1: The DBMS acts as an interface between application programs and data

The conceptual data model

The first stage in designing a database is to identify and state what data needs to be held. Figure 55.1 shows some of the data items that may be required for some of the applications required by an organisation such as a Department store.

From the statement of data requirements a **conceptual data model** is produced. This describes how the data elements in the database are to be grouped. Three terms are used in building a picture of the data requirements.

1. An **entity** is a thing of interest to an organisation about which data is to be held. Examples of entities include Customer, Employee, Stock Item, Supplier.

2. An **attribute** is a property or characteristic of an entity. Examples of attributes associated with a Customer include Customer ID, Surname, Initials, Title, Address, Credit Limit.

3. A **relationship** is a link or association between entities. An example is the link between Dentist and Patient; one dentist has many patients, but each patient only has one dentist.

This conceptual data model is created without specifying what type of database system will eventually be used to implement the system.

Types of relationship

There are only three different 'degrees' of relationship between two attributes. A relationship may be

- **One-to-one**   Examples of such a relationship include the relationship between Husband and Wife, or between Householder and Main Residence.

- **One-to-many**   Examples include the relationship between Mother and Children, between Customer and Order, between Borrower and Library Book.

- **Many-to-many**   Examples include the relationship between Student and Course, between Stock Item and Supplier, between Film and Film Star.

Entity-relationship diagrams

An entity-relationship diagram is a diagrammatic way of representing the relationships between the entities in a database. To show the relationship between two entities, both the **degree** and the **name** of the relationship need to be specified. E.g. In the first relationship shown below, the **degree** is one-to-one, the **name** of the relationship is *Drives*:

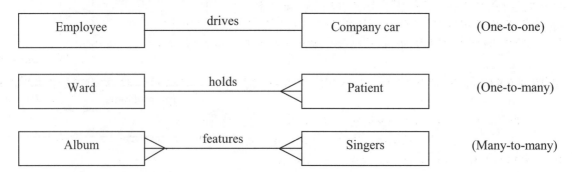

Figure 55.2: Entity-relationships

Sometimes it can be tricky to establish the degree of the relationship. For example, several employees may use the same company car at different times. A single employee may change the company car that he uses. The relationship will depend upon whether the data held refers to the current situation, or whether it is a historical record. The assumption has been made above that the database is to record the current car driven by an employee.

Example:

The data requirements for a hospital in-patient system are defined as follows:

A hospital is organised into a number of wards. Each ward has a ward number and a name recorded, along with a number of beds in that ward. Each ward is staffed by nurses. Nurses have their staff number and name recorded, and are assigned to a single ward.

Each patient in the hospital has a patient identification number, and their name, address and date of birth are recorded. Each patient is under the care of a single consultant and is assigned to a single ward. Each

302

consultant is responsible for a number of patients. Consultants have their staff number, name and specialism recorded.

State four entities for the hospital in-patient system and suggest an identifier for each of these entities.

Draw an entity-relationship diagram to show the relationship between the entities.

Answer:

Entity	Identifier
WARD	Ward number
NURSE	Staff number
PATIENT	Patient identification number
CONSULTANT	Staff number

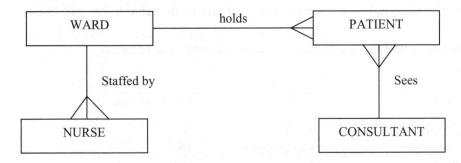

Exercises

1. A library plans to set up a database to keep track of its members, stock and loans.
   (a) State an identifier for each of the entities MEMBER, STOCK and LOAN. (3)
   (b) Draw an entity-relationship diagram showing the relationships between the entities. (3)
   (New question)

2. What is meant by program-data independence in the context of a database management system? (2)
   AEB Computing Paper 2 Qu 2 1994

3. A vet has a database to keep track of the animals seen at the surgery.
   (a) Name two entities in this database, and suggest an identifier for each one. (2)
   (b) Name FOUR attributes for each of the entities. (4)
   (c) What is the relationship between the two entities? (You may use a diagram). (2)
   (New question)

Chapter 56 – Relational Database Design

What is a relational database?

There are several different types of Database Management System available. The most common type of DBMS is the **relational database**, widely used on all systems from micros to mainframes. In a relational database, data is held in tables (also called relations) and the tables are linked by means of common fields.

Conceptually then, one row of a table holds one record. Each column in the table holds one field or attribute.

e.g. A table holding data about an entity BOOK may have the following rows and columns:

BOOK

Accession Number	DeweyCode	Title	Author	DatePublished
88	121.9	Let's Cook!	Chan, C	1992
123	345.440	Electricity	Glendenning, V	1995
300	345.440	Riders	Cooper,J	1995
657	200.00	Greek in 3 weeks	Stavros,G	1990
777	001.602	I.T. in Society	Laudon, K	1994
etc				

Figure 56.1: A table in a relational database

There is a standard notation for describing a table in a relational database. For example, to describe the table shown above, you would write

> BOOK (<u>AccessionNumber</u>, DeweyCode, Title, Author, DatePublished)

Note that:

> The entity name is shown in uppercase letters;
>
> The key field (unique identifier) is underlined;
>
> The attributes are shown in brackets, separated by commas.

Linking database tables

Tables may be linked through the use of a common field. This field must be a key field of one of the tables, and is known as a **foreign key** in the second table. An example best illustrates this.

In a library database, two entities named BOOK and BORROWER have been identified. An entity-relationship diagram may be used to describe the relationship between these two entities.

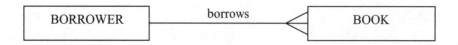

Figure 56.2: One-to-many relationship between BORROWER and BOOK

The BORROWER table can be described using standard notation as follows:

BORROWER (<u>BorrowerID</u>, name, address)

In order to link the two entities, the key field Borrower ID needs to be added to the BOOK table as a *foreign key*. The BOOK table can be described as

BOOK (<u>AccessionNumber</u>, DeweyCode, Title, Author, DatePublished, *BorrowerID*, DateDue)

Note that a foreign key is shown in italics.

In practice, since only a very small proportion of books are on loan at any one time, it would be sensible to have a third table holding data about books on loan, who had borrowed them and when they were due back. The three tables would then look like this:

BORROWER (<u>BorrowerID</u>, name, address)

BOOK (<u>AccessionNumber</u>, DeweyCode, Title, Author, DatePublished)

LOAN (<u>AccessionNumber</u>, *BorrowerID*, DateDue)

The entity-relationship diagram would then look like this:

Figure 56.3: Entity-relationship diagram for a library database

> ➢ **Discussion: The model above assumes that the LOAN record will be deleted when a book is returned. If this is not going to be done, what adjustments will have to be made to the entity-relationship diagram and LOAN table?**

Normalisation

Normalisation is a process used to come up with the best possible design for a relational database. Tables should be organised in such a way that:

- No data is unnecessarily duplicated (i.e. the same data held on more than one table).
- Data is consistent throughout the database (e.g. Mr Bradley's address is not recorded as The White House, Sproughton on one table and as 32 Star Lane in another. Consistency should be an automatic consequence of not holding any duplicated data.)
- The structure of each table is flexible enough to allow you to enter as many or as few items (for example, books borrowed by a particular person) as you want to.
- The structure should enable a user to make all kinds of complex queries relating data from different tables.

We will look at three stages of normalisation known as first, second and third normal form.

First normal form

Definition: A table is in first normal form if it contains no repeating attributes or groups of attributes.

Let's look at a simple example of two entities STUDENT and COURSE. A student can take several courses, and each course has several students attending. The relationship can be represented by the entity-relationship diagram.

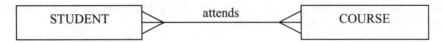

Figure 56.4: The many-to-many relationship between entities STUDENT and COURSE

Sample data to be held in the database is shown in the table below:

STUDENT

student number	student name	date of birth	sex	course number	course name	lecturer number	lecturer name
12345	Heathcote,R	20-08-77	M	EC6654	A-Level Computing	T345267	Glover,T
22433	Head,J	13-02-77	F	EC6654	A-Level Computing	T345267	Glover,T
				HM7756	A-Level Music	T773351	Reader,B
				AD1121	Pottery	T876541	
66688	Hargrave,R	13-09-54	M	BM3390	HNC Business	T666758	Newman,P
				HM7756	A-Level Music	T773351	Reader,B

The two tables STUDENT and COURSE will be represented in standard notation as

STUDENT (<u>student number</u>, student name, date of birth, sex)

COURSE (<u>course number</u>, course name, lecturer number, lecturer name)

The question now is, how can the relationship between these two tables be shown? How can we hold the information about which students are doing which courses?

The two tables need to be linked by means of a common field, but the problem is that because this is a many-to-many relationship, whichever table we put the link field into, there needs to be *more than one field*.

e.g.   STUDENT (<u>student number</u>, student name, date of birth, sex, *course number*)

is no good because the student is doing several courses, so which one would be mentioned?

Similarly,   COURSE (<u>course number</u>, course name, lecturer number, lecturer name, *student number*)

is no good either because each course has a number of students taking it.

One obvious solution (and unfortunately a bad one) springs to mind. How about allowing space for 3 courses on each student record?

STUDENT (<u>student number</u>, student name, date of birth, sex, *course1, course2, course3*)

> **Discussion: Why is this not a good idea?**

What we have engineered is a repeating attribute - anathema in 1st normal form. In other words, the field course number is repeated 3 times. The table is therefore NOT in first normal form.

It would be represented in standard notation with a line over the repeating attribute:

STUDENT (<u>student number</u>, student name, date of birth, sex, $\overline{course\ number}$)

To put the data into first normal form, the repeating attribute must be removed. In its place, the field course number becomes part of the primary key in the student table. The tables are now as follows:

STUDENT (<u>student number</u>, student name, date of birth, sex, <u>course number</u>)

COURSE (<u>course number</u>, course name, lecturer number, lecturer name)

> ➢ **Discussion: What is a primary key? Why does course number have to be part of the primary key?**

The two tables STUDENT and COURSE now in first normal form, look like this:

STUDENT

student number	student name	date of birth	sex	course number
12345	Heathcote,R	20-08-77	M	EC6654
22433	Head,J	13-02-77	F	EC6654
22433	Head,J	13-02-77	F	HM7756
22433	Head,J	13-02-77	F	AD1121
66688	Hargrave,R	13-09-54	M	BM3390
66688	Hargrave,R	13-09-54	M	HM7756

COURSE

course number	course name	lecturer number	lecturer name
EC6654	A-Level Computing	T345267	Glover,T
HM7756	A-Level Music	T773351	Reader,B
AD1121	Pottery	T876541	
BM3390	HNC Business	T666758	Newman,P

> ➢ **Discussion: Why is this a better way of holding the data than having one table with the following structure?**
>
> **STUDENT (student number, student name, date of birth, sex, *course1, course2, course3*)**
>
> **If student Head, J decides to take up A Level Art, what changes need to be made to the data?**
>
> **How will we find the names of all students doing A-Level Computing?**
>
> **What are the weaknesses of this table structure?**

Second normal form – Partial key dependence test

Definition: A table is in second normal form (2NF) if it is in first normal form and no column that is not part of a primary key is dependent on only a portion of the primary key.

This is sometimes expressed by saying that a table in second normal form contains no partial dependencies.

The tables above are not in second normal form. For example, Student name is dependent only on Student number and not on Course number. To put the tables into second normal form, we need to introduce a third table (relation) that acts as a link between the entities Student and Course.

The tables are now as follows:

STUDENT (student number, student name, date of birth, sex)

STUDENT_TAKES(student number, course number)

COURSE (course number, course name, lecturer number, lecturer name)

Dealing with a Many-to-Many relationship

As you get more practice in database design, you will notice that *whenever* two entities have a many-to-many relationship, you will *always* need a link table 'in the middle'. Thus

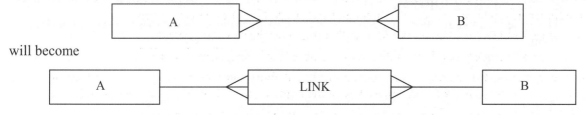

will become

Figure 56.5: A 'link' table is needed in a many-to-many relationship

Third normal form – Non-key dependence test

Definition: A table in third normal form contains no 'non-key dependencies'.

Looking at the COURSE table, the lecturer name is dependent on the lecturer number, not on the course number. It therefore needs to be removed from this relation and a new relation created:

LECTURER (<u>lecturer number</u>, lecturer name)

The database, now in third normal form, consists of the following tables:

STUDENT (<u>student number</u>, student name, date of birth, sex)

STUDENT_TAKES (<u>student number</u>, <u>course number</u>)

COURSE (<u>course number</u>, course name, lecturer number)

LECTURER (<u>lecturer number</u>, lecturer name)

This is the optimum way of holding the data, with no attributes being duplicated anywhere. In any database work that you do, you should always make sure you have designed the tables in such a way that they are in THIRD NORMAL FORM.

Comparing a flat-file system with a relational database

From the example above you will have seen that a relational database is able to create **links** between tables representing different entities such as STUDENT and COURSE, through the use of **foreign keys.** *A flat-file system is not able to create links between tables* and is therefore only useful for very simple databases which contain information about just one entity. It is impossible to 'normalise' a database in a flat-file system, since this involves correctly establishing links between tables.

Flat-file systems do not have any of the sophisticated features of a full DBMS such as the ability to set individual user access rights, or allow several people to access the database at the same time.

Exercises

1. Data on patient prescriptions are held by a GP's surgery in the following form:

PRESCRIPTION

Patient ID	Patient Name	Date of Birth	Address	Date of prescription	Drug ID	Drug Name	Dosage	Manufacturer
111	Naylor E	12-9-76	76 Church St, Hull	2-9-96 5-12-96 3-4-97	AS12 AS12 BS03	Aspirin Aspirin Migril	2 tablets 3 tablets 2 tablets	Bayer Bayer Wellcome
123	Jones R	23-9-55	23 Bay Ave Hull	5-12-96	AR14	Arnica	2 tablets	Boots
234	Leech M	4-8-77	Reckitt Hall Cottingham	3-5-97	AS12	Aspirin	2 tablets	Bayer

(a) Draw an entity-relationship diagram showing the relationships between the entities PATIENT, DRUG and PRESCRIPTION. (3)

(b) Describe the three relations needed to hold the data in a relational database in second normal form. (7)

New question

2. The manager of a video hire shop uses a relational database management system to operate the business. Separate database files hold details of customers, video films and loans. Customers can hire as many films as they wish.

   (a) For each of the files mentioned above identify the key fields and list other appropriate fields that would be required to enable this system to be maintained with minimum redundancy. (6)

   (b) Describe **three** advantages of using a relational database rather than a flat-file information storage system. (6)

   NEAB IT02 Qu 7 1996

3. The data requirements for a booking system are defined as follows.

   An agency arranges booking of live bands for a number of clubs. Each band is registered with the agency and has its name (unique) recorded, together with the number of musicians, the type of music played and hiring fee. Each band is managed by a manager. A manager may manage several bands. Each manager is assigned an identification number and managers have their name, address and telephone number recorded. Each club is assigned an identification number and clubs have their name, address and telephone number recorded.

   The agency records details of each booking made between a band and a club for a given date. A band will never have more than one booking on any particular date.

   (a) In database modelling, what is:

      (i) an attribute; (1)

      (ii) a relationship? (1)

   (b) Four entities for the booking system are Manager, Club, Band and Booking.

      (i) Suggest an identifier, with justification, for **each** of the entities Manager, Club and Band. (3)

      (ii) Describe **four** relationships involving the entities Manager, Club, Band and Booking that can be inferred from the given data requirements. (4)

   (c) A relational database is to be used. Describe tables for the following entities underlining the primary key in each case:

      (i) Manager; (2)

      (ii) Band; (4)

      (iii) Booking. (5)

   AEB Computing Paper 2 Qu 12 1996

4. A company sports centre uses a database management system to operate a membership and fixture system. Normally members register for at least three sports, although they can play any of the sports offered by the centre. Fixtures against many other organisations are arranged in a wide range of sports involving a large number of teams.

   (a) Name three database files you would expect to find in this system. (3)

   (b) For each of the database files you have named, list the fields required to enable this system to be maintained with minimum redundancy. (6)

   (c) Draw a diagram to show the relationship between the database files named in part (a). (3)

   (d) Describe three reports that the system might be required to produce. (3)

   (e) The manager of the centre intends to send out personalised letters to each of the members. This is to be done using the mail-merge facility offered by a word-processor in conjunction with the database. Explain how this is achieved. (4)

   NEAB IT02 Specimen Paper Qu 10

Chapter 57 – Database Management

Introduction

The pooling of information, software, and computer power is very useful but it does involve potential problems. There is the danger that one user will damage or change data used by other people without their knowledge; there is the question of how to protect confidential information; there may be problems if more than one person tries to change the same item of data at the same time. If a hardware failure occurs, everyone using the database is affected, and recovery procedures must ensure that no data is lost.

In order to minimise the potential hazards, a group known as **database administration** (or a person in charge of the group, known as the **database administrator**) is responsible for supervising both the database and the use of the DBMS.

Database Administration (DBA)

The DBA's tasks will include the following:

10. The design of the database. After the initial design, the DBA must monitor the performance of the database, and if problems surface (such as a particular report taking an unacceptably long time to produce), appropriate changes must be made to the database structure.

11. Keeping users informed of changes in the database structure that will affect them; for example, if the size or format of a particular field is altered or additional fields added.

12. Maintenance of the **data dictionary** (see below) for the database, and responsibility for establishing conventions for naming tables, columns, indexes and so on.

13. Implementing access privileges for all users of the database; that is, specifying which items can be accessed and/or changed by each user.

14. Allocating passwords to each user.

15. Providing training to users in how to access and use the database.

The data dictionary

The data dictionary is a 'database about the database'. It will contain information such as:

- What tables and columns are included in the present structure;
- The names of the current tables and columns;
- The characteristics of each item of data, such as its length and data type;
- Any restrictions on the value of certain columns;
- The meaning of any data fields that are not self-evident; for example, a field such as 'course type';
- The relationships between items of data;
- Which programs access which items of data, and whether they merely read the data or change it.

The Database Management System (DBMS)

The DBMS is an application program that provides an interface between the operating system and the user in order to make access to the data as simple as possible. It has several other functions as well, and these are described below.

1. **Data storage, retrieval and update.** The DBMS must allow users to store, retrieve and update information as easily as possible, without having to be aware of the internal structure of the database.
2. **Creation and maintenance of the data dictionary**.
3. **Managing the facilities for sharing the database.** The DBMS has to ensure that problems do not arise when two people simultaneously access a record and try to update it.
4. **Backup and recovery.** The DBMS must provide the ability to recover the database in the event of system failure.
5. **Security.** The DBMS must handle password allocation and checking, and the 'view' of the database that a given user is allowed.

Querying the database

Different database systems all have their own way of performing **queries** to extract data from the database. However all perform similar functions, allowing the user to:

*   Combine into one table the information from two or more related tables;
*   Select the fields that are to be shown in the 'Answer' table;
*   Specify criteria for searching on; e.g. find the names and addresses of all club members whose subscriptions are due;
*   Save the query so that it can be executed whenever necessary;
*   Save the 'Answer' table so that it can be displayed or used as the basis for a report or a mail shot, for example.

The figure below shows a **query by example** window in the Access database.

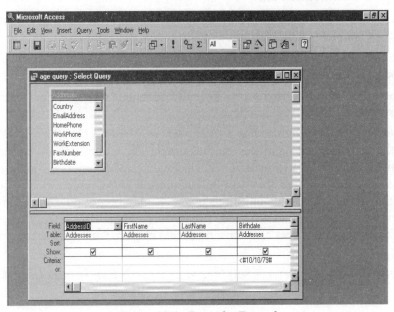

Figure 57.1: Query by Example

Using SQL

When a user constructs a query using a **query by example** form like the one shown above, the resultant query is automatically coded by Access into statements in **SQL**, or **Structured Query Language**. This is a data manipulation language that has been supported by many mainframe and minicomputers and more recently by PCs as well. The SQL for the query performed above, for example, can be viewed using a menu option in Access and is as shown below:

```
SELECT Addresses.AddressID, Addresses.FirstName, Addresses.LastName,
Addresses.Birthdate
FROM Addresses
WHERE (((Addresses.Birthdate)<#10/10/79#));
```

Client-server database

Many modern databases management systems provide an option for **client-server** operation. Using a client/server DBMS on a network, **DBMS server software** runs on the network server. This server software processes requests for data searches, sorts and reports that originate from the **DBMS client software** running on individual workstations. For example, a car dealer might want to search the manufacturer's database to find out whether there are any cars of a particular specification available. The DBMS client refers this request to the DBMS server, which searches for the information and sends it back to the client workstation. Once the information is at the workstation, the dealer can sort the list and produce his own customised report. If the DBMS did not have client-server capability, the entire database would be copied to the workstation and software held on the workstation would search for the requested data – involving a large amount of time being spent on transmitting irrelevant data and probably a longer search using a less powerful machine.

The advantages of a client-server database are, therefore:

- an expensive resource (powerful computer and large database) can be made available to a large number of users;

- client stations can, if authorised, update the database rather than just view the data;

- the consistency of the database is maintained because only one copy of the data is held (on the server) rather than a copy at each workstation;

- the database processing is normally carried out by the server, with the query being sent by a client station to the server and the results assembled by the server and returned to the client station;

- communication time between client and server is minimised because only the results of a query, not the entire database, is transmitted between the server and client;

- relevant programs and report formats can be held on client workstations and customised for a particular department.

Sage Accounting software, for example, has a client-server version. The Server Network Installation procedure installs the software and data files on the server. The Client version of the software is then installed at each workstation. Report formats for Stock, Invoices, Customers etc can be stored locally on the relevant client workstations where they can be customised and altered. Each client workstation is allocated access rights to particular files on the database; it may be possible for example to view stock levels, but not alter them from one workstation, ('read only access') to make stock adjustments from another workstation, ('read-write access'), or have no access at all to Customer account records from, say, a workstation in the warehouse.

Exercises

1. A college library uses a relational database management system to operate a membership and loans system. Staff and students can borrow as many books as they wish at any given time.
    (a) Name three database tables that you would expect to find in this system. In each case, identify the columns and keys required to enable this system to be maintained with minimum redundancy. (6)
    (b) Draw an entity-relationship diagram to show the links between the database tables named in part (a). (3)
    (c) Describe the capabilities of the relational database management system that might be used to identify and output details of overdue loans. (6)
    NEAB IT02 Qu 7 1997

2. (a) Briefly explain the principal differences between a relational database and a flat-file system. (4)
    (b) What is meant by data consistency, data redundancy and data independence? (3)
    (c) Describe two distinct security procedures you would expect to find in relational database management systems. (2)
    (d) Describe the function of a database administrator. (3)
    New question

Chapter 58 – Communication and Information Systems

Centralised processing systems

Until the 1970s, most organisations using computers were using **centralised** computer systems, with a mainframe computer doing all the processing for the whole company. Sometimes, on-line access to the mainframe computer would be possible from distant 'dumb' terminals – so-called because the terminals consisted of just a screen and a keyboard and no processor of their own. A similar type of centralised processing is still in use for some applications: banks, for example, use ATMs (Automated Teller Machines), a form of terminal containing a microprocessor which dispenses cash and enables customers to query their accounts. The ATMs are connected to a remote central computer which can be accessed from any ATM in the country.

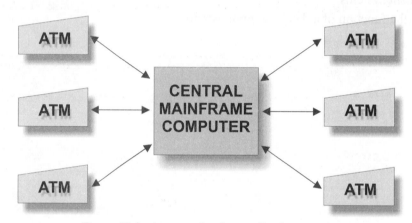

Figure 58.1: An example of centralised processing

Dispersed systems

As the price of hardware dropped, it became more cost-effective to move the processing power to where it was needed, often on individual users' desks. At first, as applications such as spreadsheets and word processors led to an explosion in the popularity of microcomputers, large numbers of standalone computers were to be found throughout an organisation, each running software suitable for a particular application or department but without the ability to communicate with one another. This arrangement could be termed a 'dispersed system'. The shortcomings of this arrangement soon became apparent, however.

> ➢ **Discussion: What were the advantages of having a number of standalone computers instead of having all the processing done on a central mainframe computer with remote terminals connected to it?**
>
> ➢ **What are the drawbacks of this arrangement?**
>
> ➢ **How can these drawbacks be overcome?**

Today, these microcomputers are commonly linked by means of cables and telecommunications into one or more types of **network**, allowing what is known as a 'distributed' system. There is a great variety of different types of network, and they can be categorised broadly into local, wide area and public networks.

Local area networks (LANs)

A local area network consists of a number of computers in the same building or site, connected by cables. No telecommunications lines are needed. Such an arrangement has many advantages over standalone computers:

- It permits the shared use of facilities such as printers, scanners and hard disk space.
- Communication between users becomes possible and, using software such as Lotus Notes, many workers can work on the same document at the same time.
- Software can be loaded on the file server and used by everyone on the network. When it is upgraded, new software has to be loaded only once instead of onto every machine.
- All users can have access to a database.
- Backup of all data held on a central file server can be done automatically every night.

Frequently, one of the facilities of a LAN is a **gateway** – hardware and software which gives all network users access to other networks.

> **Discussion: Is data MORE or LESS secure on a network than on standalone computers? Why?**

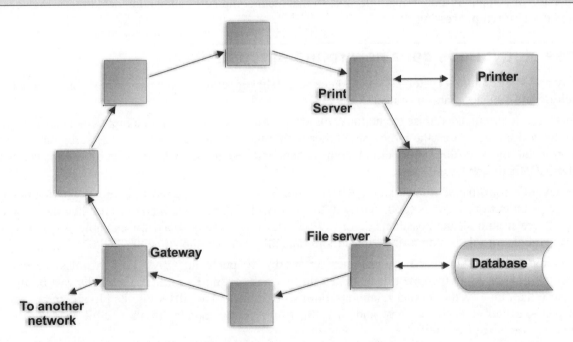

Figure 58.2: A local area network

Client-server and peer-to-peer networks

Most networks, except very small ones, operate on a client-server system. The 'clients' are normally microcomputers with their own processing power, connected to the file server which holds software and data. When a client wants to use a word processing package or a CAD package, for example, the software is downloaded into the client's RAM. Printing tasks may be handled by a print server, which queues the output from all the machines in the network and passes it to the printer. Both processing power and data may be distributed between the various machines on the network. Backup and security will be handled by the server.

Small networks of no more than 10 computers may use a peer-to-peer configuration, with none of the computers being in control of the network. Software may be held on any of the computers and made available to any other machine on the network. This does have the effect of slowing down the speed at which the software runs, but enables computer users in a small office to share disk space, software and data.

The relative benefits of client-server and peer-to-peer networks are summarised in Table 29.1 in Chapter 29.

Wide area networks (WANs)

Large organisations rely on wide area networks for communication and data exchange, not only between branches within the organisation but also between organisations. Booking an airline ticket or paying for goods by credit card are just two examples of transactions that would be impossible without wide area networks.

Distributed processing

With the growth of powerful telecommunications networks, organisations moved away from having a central mainframe to installing minicomputers and microcomputers at remote sites. These distributed processors directly serve local and regional branches and are generally linked together in networks. The dispersion of computers among multiple sites so that local computers can handle local processing needs is called **distributed processing**.

Case study: Pubs get a new round of touch tills

Many pub and restaurant customers can soon expect a slicker service as a new wave of computerised tills reach Britain's busiest bars and cafes.

Touch screen terminals promise to end those minor irritations which can spoil a night out, such as waiting ages for a drink or getting the wrong side order with a meal. Greenalls, a leading leisure company, has begun installing 1,000 InnTouch terminals in its bars and restaurants, which include the Henry's chain, Millers Kitchens and Bygone Inns.

The new tills allow bar staff to simply touch a symbol for each drink ordered and quickly provide the total cost. When a customer orders food, staff will touch a symbol for the main course and then move on to a second screen with all the possible side orders. If a customer orders steak, for example, the screen will show symbols for salads, onion rings, mushrooms and all other accompaniments.

"We expect the tills to speed up customer service by 40 per cent," says Tim Kowalski, Greenalls' financial director. With the new tills and back-up services costing £3 million, Greenalls will be looking for more than improved customer relations from its investment. The tills are linked to a computer in the manager's office at each property and that PC is linked by modem to the 32-bit Windows-based Innmaster system at Head Office.

The system will enable the company to gather immediate information about food and drinks sales, and this will inform decisions on changing menus or launching promotions. "While analysing food sales, for example, we noticed that Wall Street, a busy young persons' pub in Preston, was selling an average of only ten rounds of garlic bread per week," reports Kowalski. "This was at odds with sales in similar houses. We phoned the manager who hadn't realised this shortfall and he was able to brief waiters and waitresses. Consequently, sales increased by 40 to 50 rounds a week which, at a retail price of £1.20 per portion, could add £2,500 to annual sales."

The system also enables managers to monitor staff performance. Gail Pritchard, manager of Off the Wall, Chester, says: "We ran a promotion on Miller Draught with a £10 incentive to the staff member turning in the best performance each shift, and I was able to get an instant printout of everyone's performance.

Touch screens are logical and incredibly fast. They are a huge asset for us, and the staff like them."

Source: Tony Dawe, The Times 18 February 1998

> **Discussion: Is this a distributed or a centralised system? Where is the processing performed at each stage?**

> **Describe some of the advantages of the new system.**

Distributed systems may be organised in many different ways. Decisions have to be made on where to locate both the processing power and the databases, and how to connect the nodes (host computers and workstations) of the network. Distributed systems may extend over several levels, with some processing taking place at many different levels. In the case study above, processing is taking place at only two levels: local managers' offices and Head Office. In a large organisation such as for example Ford Motor Company which has offices and sites all over the world, there may be six or more levels over which processing is distributed, as shown in Figure 58.3.

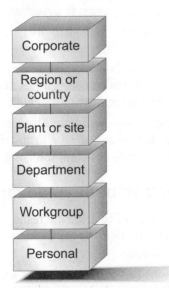

Figure 58.3: Possible distribution of systems in an organisation

Distributed databases

Although early distributed systems generally worked with a single centralised database, over time the smaller local systems began to store local databases as well. However, local branches frequently still need access to the main company database, which may be held in a different country altogether. Maintaining on-line access to a central database from all over the world can be very expensive – and so the next logical step was to distribute the central database to local processors. A mechanism is then needed to ensure the several versions of the database are properly updated, that the integrity of data is maintained (i.e. that different versions of the data are not held in different places) and that security is maintained.

A **distributed database** is one that is stored in more than one physical location. There are three main ways of distributing a database.

1. The central database can be partitioned so that each remote processor has the data on its own customers, stock, etc.

2. The entire database is duplicated at each remote site.

In both these cases, the two databases have to be reconciled with each other. This is usually done by updating the central database each night to reflect local changes made the previous day.

3. The central database contains only an index to entries which are held on local databases. This system is used for very large databases like the FBI's National Crime Information Centre. A query to the central database identifies the location where the full record is held. The National Westminster Bank uses a similar system to hold details on all its customers.

A variation of this system is not to hold an index, and to simply poll all remote databases until the required record is found. The complete record is then transferred to the local computer that requests it.

> ➢ **Discussion: What sort of organisation could use**
>   **(a) the first type of distributed database?**
>   **(b) the second type of database?**

Advantages and limitations of distributed databases

Distributed systems reduce the dependence on a single, massive central database. They increase responsiveness to local users' and customers' needs. They can provide a better response rate to queries which are handled locally.

Depending on how the distributed database is held, however, it can be highly dependent on powerful and reliable telecommunications systems. Local databases can sometimes depart from central data definitions and standards, and security can be compromised when distribution widens access to sensitive data.

Despite these drawbacks, distributed processing is growing rapidly. For large organisations operating on several sites, the question is not *whether* to distribute but *how* to distribute in order to minimise costs, increase efficiency and provide the best service while not compromising data integrity and security.

Using telecommunications for competitive advantage

The use of telecommunications is increasingly being used to reshape the way that organisations do business, increasing the efficiency and speed of operations, making management more effective and providing better services to customers. For example:

- A large publisher has a telecommunications link to its distributor's warehouse. Under the old system, when an order was received from a bookshop or wholesaler, invoices were printed and sent by post to the warehouse where one copy was sent with the box of books and a second copy retained for reference. Under the new system the invoice is transferred electronically and printed at the warehouse, enabling books to be shipped out at least 24 hours earlier.

- Yalplay, the Internet Music and Video store, takes orders from customers over the Internet. Orders to suppliers are then placed by Yalplay electronically in a 'just-in-time' system and the CD or video normally shipped within 48 hours. Confirmation of the order is sent by e-mail to the customer, and in the case of delays, the customer can find out via the Internet where the order has got to.

- Yellow Pages has equipped its sales force with laptop computers from which they can initiate a phone call by clicking a phone number displayed in the database. Instead of faxing sales enquiries and mock-ups for advertisements, mobile staff can now access a fully automated sales system and query the corporate database direct. When an advertisement is approved, it can be sent from the salesperson's home computer to the production department at head office via ISDN.

- SMI, an advertising agency, uses a company-wide internal network (an 'Intranet') to share documents though a single viewing interface, Lotus Notes. Through a password-protected front end, customers can access and inspect prospective campaigns the moment they come off the digital drawing board, and comment on them, sending their text straight into SMI's Notes system. A proposed radio advertisement could be put on the system and a client in Timbuktu could listen to it a minute later.

Case study: United Parcel Service (UPS)

UPS is a major package delivery and shipping company which does a large part of its business over the Internet. When a manufacturer has products to sell to a customer, they use a service like UPS to deliver the goods.

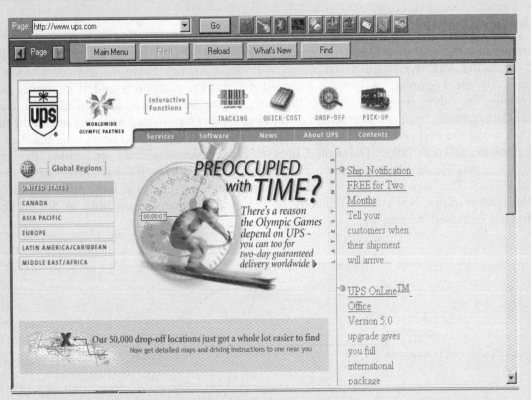

UPS uses a nationwide cellular system called TotalTrack to provide information at any time, day or night, on the status of a parcel. When the driver picks up a package, it is immediately logged using a portable hand-held computer containing a barcode reader for capturing the barcode identification on the package, and a keyboard for entering additional information such as the destination's area code. On returning to the truck, the driver inserts the hand-held computer into a small computer that transmits the data to the local dispatch centre, where it is recorded on a database. The location data is updated automatically as the package moves through each step on the way to its destination. The combination of telecommunications and computing permits UPS to know the location of every package at any time.

When the package is delivered to the customer, the customer signs for it using a pen-based computer and delivery confirmation is transmitted back to UPS.

Both sender and receiver of the package can track the status of the parcel at any time, day or night, via the Internet using UPS's OnLineTM Office software.

As UPS says: "After placing an order with you most customers have just one question on their minds: When will my shipment arrive? With just one click you can give them the answer! Just go to the UPS

OnLineTM Office software and click on Ship Notification. From there, you can send consignees a detailed fax report showing who sent the shipment, where the shipment was sent, and when it's scheduled for delivery. All with no phone calls to make and no calls to answer. There's just no easier way to keep customers satisfied.

➢ **Discussion: This is an example of a highly distributed system, with data about each parcel being held at local dispatch centres, accessible from all over the world. What are the advantages of this system to UPS, the consigner of the parcel, and the recipient?**

➢ **Apart from knowing where the parcel is, could UPS use this system to provide other services to its customers?**

The Internet and the World Wide Web

The Internet is a network of networks, connecting computers all over the globe. In 1969, the Internet started life as the ARPANET (Advanced Research Projects Agency Network) and consisted of just 4 computers. By the beginning of 1997, it included 1.7 million computers and it continues to grow exponentially. The cables, wires and satellites that carry Internet data form an interlinked communications network. Data traveling from one Internet computer to another is transmitted from one link in the network to another, along the best possible route. If some links are overloaded or out of service, the data can be routed through different links. The major Internet communications links are called the **Internet backbone**. A handful of network service providers (NSPs) such as BT each maintain a series of nationwide links. The links are like pipes – data flows through the pipes and large pipes can carry more data than smaller pipes. NSPs are continually adding new communications links to the backbone to accommodate increased Internet use.

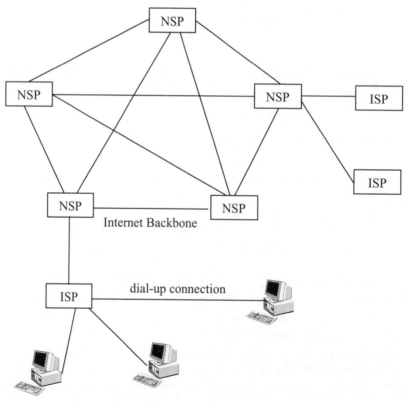

Figure 58.4: Structure of the Internet

When you connect your computer to the Internet, you do not connect directly to the backbone. Instead, you connect to an ISP (Internet Service Provider) that in turn connects to the backbone.

An ISP generally charges you a monthly fee for Internet access (though many such as Freeserve are free) and provides you with communications software and a user account. You need a computer with a modem to connect your computer to a phone line, and when you log on, your computer dials the ISP and establishes a connection over the phone line. Once you are connected, the ISP routes data between your computer and the Internet backbone. A phone line provides a very narrow pipe for transmitting data, having a typical capacity of 56 thousand bits per second. Using a phone line, the time taken to transfer the contents of a 680Mb CD-ROM would be over 26 hours!

The World Wide Web is a special part of the Internet which allows people to view information stored on participating computers. It is an easy-to-use, graphical source of information which has opened the Internet to millions of people interested in finding out information. It consists of documents called pages that contain information on a particular topic, and links to other Web pages, which could be stored on other computers in different countries.

Exercises

1. (a) What is meant by distributed processing? (2)
   (b) With the aid of an example, describe how distributed processing may be implemented in an organisation which has a Head Office, and several sites each with a number of different departments. (5)
   New question

2. (a) Describe how a distributed database may be implemented. (3)
   (b) Give an example of an organisation that might hold its data in this way. (1)
   (c) What are the advantages and disadvantages of such a distributed database to this organisation? (4)
   New question

3. A supermarket has direct links to some of its major suppliers so that orders can be sent electronically each day for 'just-in-time' delivery of goods that need replenishing. What are the advantages to
   (a) the supermarket
   (b) the suppliers
   of this arrangement (4)
   New question

4. A large national charity holds a central database of donors and recipients. Branch offices equipped with PCs and modems are able to dial in over a telephone line to get lists of members living locally to inform them of local fund-raising events. What would be the advantages to the charity of a distributed system? How would distributed databases be kept in the same state as the central database? (6)
   New question

5.

> *Networks are the future!*

Explain why computer networking has developed rapidly over the past 15 years. Your answer should discuss **three** factors which have stimulated this development and **three** implications for society. (6)
SEB Paper 2 Qu 10 1994

Chapter 59 – Network Security and Accounting

Introduction

Computer networks bring their own particular security problems. One of the great advantages of networks is that data held on databases can be accessed by people from all over the world – but clearly, this poses the threat that the data may be accessed, stolen, altered or deleted by unauthorised people – or even by authorised employees with criminal tendencies. In this chapter we'll look at methods used to help keep data held on networked computers secure, as far as possible. *(No system is completely foolproof!)*

Training users about security

Every employee should be made aware of the company's security policy and of the risks to data held on networks. The importance of following rules and procedures, and of being alert to possible breaches of security, need to be emphasised and understood. Downloading programs from the Internet, for example, can introduce viruses on to a computer network, and so all such files should be virus-checked before use. All employees should be made aware of their responsibilities not to allow strangers access to restricted areas, not to leave machines logged on while they go to lunch and not to write their password down.

Access privileges

The main method of controlling access to data held on a network is by defining **access privileges** for each user. These define for each user exactly which computers and what data he or she is allowed to access, and what they are allowed to do with data they can access. Typical access levels include:

- No access;
- Read only;
- Read and copy;
- Read and update.

Junior nursing staff, for example, might be able to access a patient's medical record in a hospital but not to update it. A doctor from another hospital might be able to read and copy it, and the patient's own doctor would be able to read and update the record.

Access controls can be applied to software as well as data, so that users have access to software needed for their particular tasks, but not to other software.

Access control

Access control may be based on:

- **What you know** – for example a password or PIN number. These suffer from many shortcomings, as users tend to be careless about using obvious words or names, or writing their passwords down. Many computer system break-ins occur because a password has been divulged to someone who appeared to be authorised to know it – for example a repairman. The fraudster can, for example, run a program which appears to be a login procedure but which simply writes a password to a file. The unsuspecting user is then requested to type in their password as part of the 'repair'.

- **What you have** – for example, an ID card perhaps in the form of a smart card or magnetic stripe card.

- **Where you are** – you may be able to gain entry to a computer system only from a specified location or telephone number. Using a **callback system**, the user dials in and enters an ID number and password, and is then automatically disconnected. The computer checks the ID and password and if these are correct, the user is called back at a predetermined telephone number.

- **Who you are** – specialised equipment can check your handprint, retinal image or voice print. These are all forms of **biometric identification**.

All these methods of identifying authorised users can be made less effective if users are careless about leaving terminals unattended when they are logged on. Some systems automatically log off if there is no activity at a terminal for a specified period, say 10 minutes.

Firewalls

Linking to the Internet or transmitting information via Intranets requires special security measures. A **firewall** is software that prevents unauthorised communication into or out of the network, allowing the organisation to enforce a security policy on traffic flowing between its network and the Internet. The firewall is generally placed between internal LANs and WANs and external networks such as the Internet.

Various different types of firewall products are available, such as:

- A router which examines each incoming packet of data, checking its source or destination address. Access rules must identify every type of packet that the organisation does not want to admit;

- Special software that restricts traffic to a particular application such as e-mail or Lotus Notes groupware;

- A 'proxy server' that maintains replicated copies of Web pages for easy access by a designated class of users. Outside visitors to the Web site can be routed to this information while being denied access to more sensitive information.

Audit controls

Audit controls track all activity on a network – for example:

- What programs have been used;
- What files have been opened;
- How many reads and writes have been executed;
- How many times a server has been accessed.

Special monitoring software can also be used to produce statistical profiles and store statistics about the behaviour of each user with respect to objects such as data files or programs. The program can then detect statistically abnormal behaviour of users.

Performance management

Network monitoring software will collect data and statistics on all aspects of network use to help with the management and planning of a network. Data may be collected on:

- Network availability (i.e. switched on and not working);
- Response time (time between making a query and receiving a response);
- Utilisation of hardware resources (CPU, disks, bridges, repeaters, clients and servers);
- Utilisation of software;
- Traffic density in each segment of a network.

These statistics can help to identify bottlenecks and potential problems and aid in planning future developments. By monitoring software usage, it is possible to detect if there are more copies of any particular software package being used than the company has a licence for, and take action.

> ➤ **Discussion: What action should the Computer Centre management take if it detects illegal use of software?**
>
> ➤ **In what other ways could it be useful to monitor software usage?**

Data encryption

Data on a network is vulnerable to wire-tapping when it is being transmitted over a network, and one method of preventing confidential data from being read by unauthorised hackers is to **encrypt** it, making it incomprehensible to anyone who does not hold the 'key' to decode it.

There are many ways of encrypting data, often based on either **transposition** (where characters are switched around) or substitution (where characters are replaced by other characters).

Figure 59.1: Data encryption

In a **transposition** cipher, the message could be written in a grid row by row and transmitted column by column. The sentence 'Here is the exam paper' could be written in a 5 x 5 grid:

```
H E R E *
I S * T H
E * E X A
M * P A P
E R * * *
```

And transmitted as HIEMEES**RR*EP*ETHXA**HAP*

> ➤ **Using the same grid, decode the message ITT*O*E*HRWDNIYA*OS*NITT***

Using a substitution cipher, a 'key' that is known to both sender and receiver is used to code the message. A very simple example is to substitute each letter with the next one in the alphabet.

In practice, since the key must be difficult to break, a much more sophisticated algorithm must be used, with frequent changes of key.

Cryptography serves three purposes:

- It helps to identify authentic users ;
- It prevents alteration of the message;
- It prevents unauthorised users from reading the message.

Exercises

1. A university provides staff and students with access to its computer network.

    (a) Activity on the university's networking system is monitored and an accounting log is automatically produced. Suggest what this log might include and explain why it is useful.   (8)

    (b) Appropriate staff have access to personal and financial data. What steps should be taken to preserve the security of the data in such a system?   (4)

    NEAB IT05 Qu 4 1997

2. One method of encryption used in transmitting data requires data to be placed in a grid with 4 rows and 5 columns. The data enters row by row and is transmitted column by column.

    (a) Show that the data string "THE*EXAM*BEGINS*AT*9" would be sent as

    "TXE*HAGAEMIT**N*EBS9"

    (b) Decode the following received message using the same grid, showing how you obtain your answer.

    "TIS*HSSFI*AOSMGU*EER"   (4)

    London Computing Paper 1 Qu 2 1996

3. The IT manager of a large college is about to change the software that is used to record student attendance in classes. Given that this new software must provide different access permissions and types of report, what capabilities and restrictions should the IT manager allocate in order to satisfy the needs of each of the following groups of users?

    * students
    * teaching staff
    * office staff
    * senior managers   (8)

    NEAB IT05 Qu 4 1999

Chapter 60 – Data Communications and Standards

Communications software

Communications software enables computers to communicate with each other, controlling transmission by specifying:

- Speed of transmission;
- Direction of data flow;
- Method of transmission;
- Which computer code is used (e.g. ASCII, EBCDIC);
- Type of parity used (e.g. odd or even).

The rules and procedures for allowing computers to communicate with each other is called the **communications protocol**.

Speed of transmission

Transmission speed is related to the bandwidth of the communications channel. A communications 'channel' is the link between two computers and could be, for example, a telephone line, a fibre-optic or coaxial cable, a microwave or satellite link.

There are two common types of bandwidth called *baseband* and *broadband*.

- **Baseband** carries one signal at a time. A bit value of 0 or 1 is sent by the presence or absence of a voltage in the cable. Baseband signals can travel very fast but can only be sent over short distances. Over about 1000 feet special booster equipment is needed.

- **Broadband** can carry multiple signals on a fixed carrier wave, with the signals for 0 and 1 sent as variations on this wave. Data, audio and video transmission can take place simultaneously.

The speed at which data is sent is expressed as the baud rate, measured in bits per second (bps). The computer code for a single character typically uses 7 or 8 bits, and in addition a start and stop bit and/or a parity bit is added to this, so that each character requires say 10 bits. Thus a speed of 56,000bps means that about 5,600 characters a second can be transmitted.

Modems

Telephone lines were originally designed for speech, which is transmitted in analogue or wave form. In order for digital data to be sent along a telephone line, it must first be converted to analogue form and then converted back at the other end, hence the need for a MOdulator/DEModulator. Modems typically transmit data at rates of between 9,600 and 56,600bps.

Figure 60.1: Modem

Direction of transmission

Communications software sets the transmission protocols that indicate the way that data will flow over the communications channel, which will be one of:

- **Simplex** – data can flow in one direction only. Electronic 'notice-boards' that receive and display information about, for example, train arrival times could use a simplex line, since communication is one-way only;

- **Half-duplex** – data can flow in both directions, but not at the same time, like a CB radio;

- **Full-duplex** – data can flow in both directions at the same time, like a telephone line where two people can both be talking at once.

Serial and parallel transmission

In serial transmission, each bit is transmitted one at a time over a single channel. There are two types of serial mode for sending data – synchronous and asynchronous. In asynchronous transmission, one character at a time is transmitted, with a start and stop bit sent with each character. This is generally used for lower speed transmission, for example on a local area network. Synchronous transmission enables whole blocks of data to be sent in timed sequences, and is much faster.

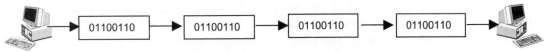

Figure 60.2: Serial transmission

In parallel transmission, all the bits making up a character, together with a parity bit (if used) are transmitted simultaneously. Parallel transmission is limited to communications over short distances of a few metres, for example between a computer and a printer.

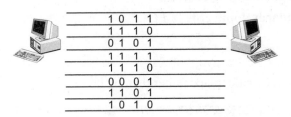

Figure 60.3: Parallel transmission

Telecommunications standards and protocols

In order to allow machines from different manufacturers to communicate with each other over local or wide area networks, standards covering all aspects of communication from the number of pins on connectors to how a particular software package displays a menu at a user's terminal need to be defined.

Although having standards makes it possible to create networks containing hardware from different vendors (such as Apple and IBM), there are tradeoffs. Standards may disallow certain features or capabilities that are valuable in a particular situation but inconsistent with the standard. Standards may also prohibit features which certain vendors have built into their hardware in order to steal a march on the competition – something that is better than other architectures but will not work with other hardware. In spite of this, most people would rather have hardware that has less than the maximum capabilities but is compatible with their other hardware, and welcome the introduction of standards.

Standards can be divided into de facto standards and de jure standards. **De facto standards** are established by the fact that a particular product dominates the market, like Intel microprocessors or Microsoft's products. **De jure standards** are defined by industry groups or by government.

The **OSI** (Open System Interface) was created to guide the development of standards for communications between networked systems, regardless of technology, vendor or country of origin. The standards have been developed by an industry consortium called the International Standards Organisation, and they cover all aspects of network operations and management.

Other standards and protocols such as IBM's Systems Network Architecture, and standards set up by other manufacturers, exist but there is a strong desire to have just one international standard which will provide a seamless system of communication between any type of network. The OSI model protocol will be the principal means of ensuring this.

The development of de facto standards

Some technologies don't depend on widespread acceptance for their value. A device that automatically opens a garage door when you point at it and press a button may be very useful even if you're the only person in the world who has one. But for products that depend on communications or collaboration between different organisations, much of a product's value comes from its widespread acceptance. There is no point owning a new type of CD player that plays full-length videos on a TV screen, if no one has recorded the videos that you want to watch. Likewise, there is no point buying a computer that is much faster than any other, and has a better user interface, unless it will run the software that you want to use. You're better off with the slower one that will do the job.

> ➢ **Discussion: Why do all keyboards have the same layout of letters, i.e. QWERTY along the top line? Would it be a good idea to adopt a new standard?**
>
> ➢ **In England we push a light switch down to turn the light on. In the US, 'Up' is On. These are 'de facto' standards – standards that have evolved.**
>
> ➢ **Think of some 'de facto' standards applicable to PCs.**

De facto standards are developed by the marketplace rather than by law.

Case study: Microsoft's MS-DOS

In the summer of 1980 two emissaries from IBM came to Microsoft – then a tiny, unknown company – to discuss a personal computer they said IBM might or might not build. Working with the IBM design team Microsoft encouraged IBM to build one of the first computers to use the 16-bit microprocessor chip, the Intel 8088. The move from 8 bits to 16 bits meant that the PC would be able to support up to one full megabyte of memory – 256 times as much as an 8-bit computer. Microsoft granted IBM the royalty-free right to use their MS-DOS operating system for a one-time fee of about $80,000. In other words, they practically gave it away – but their goal was not to make money from IBM but to license the operating system software to other companies who made IBM-compatible machines.

Consumers bought the IBM PC with confidence, and by 1982 third party software developers began turning out applications to run on it. Each new customer and each new application added to the IBM PC's strength as a de facto standard for the industry, until almost all of the newest and best software was written for PCs running MS-DOS. A positive-feedback cycle began to drive the PC market, so that within three years, almost all other personal computers (Apple being the main exception) had disappeared. Many new companies such as Eagle and Northstar (ever heard of them?) thought people would buy their new computers because they offered something different and slightly better than the IBM PC. They were wrong. The IBM PC had become the hardware standard.

Internet protocol

Communication between computers connected to the Internet is governed by a protocol named TCP/IP (Transport Control Protocol/Internet Protocol), which has become a *de facto* standard. By following this standard set of communications rules, Internet computers can efficiently control and route data between your computer and the Internet computers maintained by ISPs and NSPs.

Addressing mechanisms on the World Wide Web

Every host computer (e.g. Internet Service Provider) connected to the Internet has a unique IP (Internet Protocol) address. This is a collection of four numbers separated by full stops, (e.g. 123.456.789.852). There are plans to extend and expand this system since the net will shortly run out of available addresses.

As these numbers are impossible to memorise, the **Domain Name System** translates these numbers into a domain name which identifies the organisation and often the country in which the computer is located (e.g. amazon.com, guardian.co.uk).

A **URL** (Uniform Resource Locator) is the standard address used to find a page, Web server or other device on the Web or the Internet. A Web site has a Home Page and usually links to several other pages on the site. Each page has its own unique case-sensitive URL.

For example, the Payne-Gallway Web site home page has the address

http://www.payne-gallway.co.uk/

The first part of the address (http://)

specifies the protocol used for connection to the server. http stands for Hypertext Transfer Protocol, which is used for Web sites. Other kinds of protocols include

https://   'Hypertext Transfer Protocol, Secure' for a Web site with security features. Credit card numbers should be safer here.

ftp://   'File Transfer Protocol' for an FTP site. FTP software allows you to upload and download files from computers throughout the world.

The second part of the address (www)

indicates which part of the Internet is being addressed, in this case the World Wide Web.

The third part of the address (payne-gallway)

is the first part of the **domain name**, called the 'sub-domain'. This comprises the name of the institution or people running the site or the computer which it is stored on, for example *payne-gallway*.

The fourth part of the address (.co)

is known as the 'top level domain'. It tells you what sort of institution is behind the site. For example:

    .ac or .edu   an academic institution

    .co   a company that trades in a single country

.com	a commercial organisation that trades internationally
.gov	a government department or other related facility
.org	a non-commercial organisation such as a charity
.sch	a school (this code is specific to the UK)

There are plans to extend the number of top level domains. The seven new top level domains will be:

.firm	for businesses, or firms
.store	for businesses offering goods to purchase
.web	for entities emphasizing activities related to the WWW
.arts	for entities emphasizing cultural and entertainment activities
.rec	for entities emphasizing recreation/entertainment activities
.info	for entities providing information services
.nom	for those wishing individual or personal nomenclature

The fifth part of the address (.uk)

specifies the country in which the site is located, .jp for Japan, .de for Germany, .sg for Singapore etc.

Note that a URL, like a domain name, is an Internet address. A URL is the address of a *document* on the computer, whereas a domain name represents the IP address of a *computer*.

Each page at a website is a file with the extension .htm, written in HTML (Hypertext Markup Language). If you click on the catalogue link on the payne-gallway site, for example, you will be taken to another page with a URL http://www.payne-gallway.co.uk/Products/cat.htm

To find out more about domain names – how to register them, how to sell them, who runs them etc., try either of the following sites: http://www.igoldrush.com or http://www.netnames.co.uk. The first is a very informative, clear and entertaining guide to the whole business of domain names and well worth a visit. The second is less funky but gives plenty of information, useful especially if you want to register a domain name of your own.

Exercises

1. (a) What is meant by the term wide area network? (1)
    (b) Explain the term protocol in the context of transmission over a wide area network. (2)
    (c) Why is a protocol needed for a wide area network? (1)

    AEB Computing Paper 3 Qu 2 1999

2. With the growth in computer systems being purchased for use on networks, there is a greater need for manufacturers to conform to standard protocols.
    (a) What are protocols and why are they required? (4)
    (b) The application layer is one of seven layers in the OSI model. Name **three** other layers. (3)
    (c) Briefly describe the role of the application layer in this model. (3)

    NEAB IT05 Qu 6 1997

3. Explain what is meant by the terms
    IP (Internet Protocol) address, domain name, URL (Uniform Resource Locator). (3)

    New question

Chapter 61 – Human-Computer Interaction

Computers in the workplace

'Ergonomics' – the design and functionality of the environment – was discussed briefly in Chapter 13 (Health and Safety). Applying ergonomics successfully means studying the whole office environment to see how it can be made into a comfortable, safe and productive place in which to work. To begin with, simple measures such as persuading staff to tidy their desks or reorganise the office furniture so that people are not in danger of tripping over telephone and computer cables can achieve a great deal.

Lighting should be carefully chosen so that the office is neither overlit nor underlit, avoiding excessive contrast between lit and unlit areas, or patches of shadow falling on work areas. Computers should not face windows, as the glare will be unbearable, and nor should users be forced to sit facing a window with the sun in their eyes. The optimal position for computer monitors is side on to a window. Windows should have adjustable blinds so that the changing light from the sun can be controlled.

Furniture must be comfortable and adjustable. Poorly designed chairs are responsible for back trouble, and chairs at the wrong height can contribute to the onset of repetitive strain injury (RSI), an affliction which affects people who spend too many hours at a keyboard without breaks and in uncomfortable positions. Short people may need a footrest, and are now legally entitled to ask for one.

Environmental considerations have led to more manufacturers producing energy-efficient computer systems. It is estimated that the electricity used by computers accounts for between 5 and 10% of the USA's annual total commercial electricity bill. Research suggests that computers are used for only a tiny proportion of the time that they are switched on, with over a quarter of the nation's computers running overnight and at weekends. Energy-efficient computers and printers which go into 'sleep' mode, a low-power state, when the unit is inactive, stand to save US businesses $2 billion per year. Apart from the money, the use of energy-efficient products will reduce emission of carbon dioxide by 20 million tonnes, roughly comparable to the emissions of 5 million cars.

Psychological factors

Apart from the physical factors, there are numerous psychological factors which affect our interaction with computers. An understanding of how we receive, process and store information can be used to design effective, user-friendly interactive systems.

Information is received through senses, and a knowledge of human senses and skills is used by interface designers.

- **Vision**. Research has shown, for example, that the eye is less sensitive to blue light than to red or green, and therefore important information should not be displayed in blue text. Also, 8% of males and 1% of females are colour-blind, most commonly being unable to distinguish between red and green. Therefore, no interface should depend on everyone being able to distinguish colours.

- **Hearing**. Sound is commonly used for warning sounds in interfaces, for example to tell the user that they have tried to perform an illegal operation – humans can distinguish between a wide range of sounds and can react faster to auditory stimuli than to visual ones. The SonicFinder for the Macintosh uses auditory icons to represent desktop objects and actions. Copying is indicated by the sound of pouring liquid into a bottle. A file arriving in a mailbox sounds like a large parcel if it is very large, or a light packet if it is small.

- **Touch**. Touch is an important in keyboard and mouse design. The feeling of a button being depressed is an important part of the task of pressing it.

- **Movement**. Speed and accuracy are measures of motor skills and are important considerations in interface design. Users may find it difficult to manipulate small objects and so targets should generally be reasonably large.

Short-term memory

We have two main types of memory: short-term memory and long-term memory. Short-term memory is used for example to remember a telephone number for the length of time it takes to dial it after looking it up. The average person can remember 7 plus or minus 2 digits. Look at the number sequence

472081325

Now write it down. Did you get it right? Now try the sequence

649 723 106

Grouping the digits can increase short-term memory. It is also much easier to remember information that you can find a pattern in. For example, you probably won't be able to remember the sequence of letters

AST NIG HTW EWE NTT OTH ECI NEM AL

However, if you notice that by moving the last character to the first position, you will get a sentence by reblocking the letters into words instead of groups of three, you should have no trouble in being able to reproduce the letters.

Long-term memory

Long-term memory is used for the long-term storage of information – factual information, experiential knowledge and 'rules' about behaviour and procedures are stored here. It differs from short-term memory in a number of respects. Firstly, it has an almost limitless capacity. Secondly, it has a relatively slow access time of approximately a tenth of a second. Thirdly, forgetting occurs much more slowly in long-term memory.

Information can be moved from short-term memory to long-term memory by rehearsal or repetition. In addition, information is easier to remember if it is meaningful. Thus, it is difficult to remember a series of unconnected words such as

Violet hope see gannet builder green yesterday new sadly may

but much easier to memorise a sentence such as

I'll have a crocodile sandwich and make it snappy.

In other words, learning is aided by structure and familiarity.

We all carry around with us a mental picture of how the world works, put together from experiences stored in long-term memory. Consider the sentences:

Richard took his cat to the surgery. After seeing the vet he took the cat home.

You will probably assume from this that Richard consulted the vet, the cat was treated, Richard paid the bill and they left – rather than assuming that Richard took one look at the vet and took the cat home immediately.

Principles and results from research in psychology have been distilled into guidelines for designing user interfaces.

> ➤ **Discussion: One guiding principle for interface design is that you should never use an image which contradicts our mental image of how things are – for example, Red means Stop, Green means Go. Can you think of other examples?**

Designing good software

Interacting with computers can be a daunting, frightening and incomprehensible business to novices, and on occasion an infuriating experience for experts. Repeated failure with a new software package is frustrating and depressing and soon becomes boring. Researchers into human-computer interaction (HCI) study good software design to see what makes it good, and observe people interacting with computers to find out what they find easy, and which parts of the software lead them to make more errors than necessary, or what difficulties they encounter.

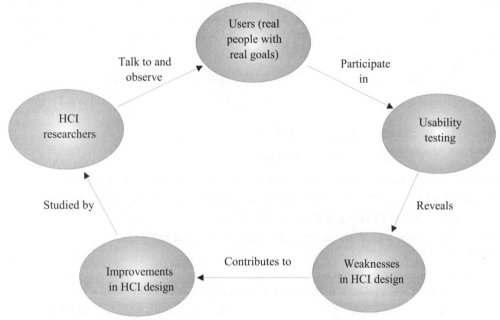

Figure 61.1: HCI design cycle

The best user interfaces provide:

- Help for novice users;
- Short cuts for experts;
- 'Metaphors' or images which are meaningful, such as the letter *W* on the icon for Word, or a picture of a printer for a print tool;
- Consistent behaviour which makes use of long-term memory, such as always using the function key F1 for Help, or the Escape key to get out of trouble;
- Clear, helpful error messages;
- Uncluttered screens with effective use of colour, with text that is easy to read.

Text versus graphics

The graphical user interface is appealing and generally far easier to use than a command interface, but sometimes icons cannot express an abstract concept and menus of one kind or another are essential.

Specialist products such as a travel agent's package may use a command interface in preference to a GUI because graphical interfaces generally:

- Occupy more memory;
- Need more space on disk;
- Run more slowly if complex graphics and many windows are open;
- Can be more time-consuming for an experienced operator than simply typing in a command.

Exercises

1. A new shopping centre requires a computerised interactive information system. The system is to have a number of information points distributed throughout the centre. The diagram below shows a plan of the centre.

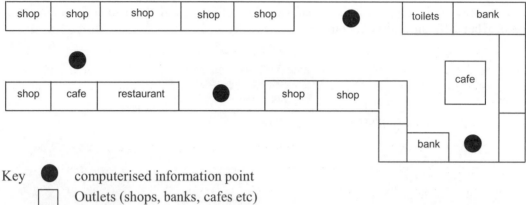

Key ● computerised information point
☐ Outlets (shops, banks, cafes etc)

The computerised information points have to provide information on each of the following:

Shops; Restaurants; Toilets; Disabled facilities; Advertising; A map of the centre; Banking services.

   (a) The system has to have a suitable user interface.

   Describe aspects which should be considered when designing the user interface. (4)

   (b) Individual outlets will have the facility to use the system to provide up-to-the-minute details of special offers, opening hours, etc.

   Describe the hardware and software that would be necessary to implement this facility. (3)

SEB Paper 1 Qu 11 1995

2. (a) Give **six** of the physical and psychological factors which govern how people interact with computer systems. (6)

   (b) Give **three** factors which should be considered when providing a sophisticated human-computer interface, explaining the impact of each one on the system's resources. (6)

NEAB IT05 Qu 7 1997

3. (a) What are the factors you need to take into account when designing a screen layout for a database application? (6)

   (b) What are the resource implications for providing a sophisticated human/computer interface? (4)

NEAB IT05 Qu 9 Sample Paper

4. The term 'human-computer interface' is used to describe the means of interaction between a computer and its human user. Since microcomputers were first introduced, the design of suitable human-computer interfaces has presented a number of problems.

   (a) Name and briefly describe **four** distinct solutions which have been developed by software writers to address these problems. (4)

   (b) Discuss an advantage and disadvantage to each of the solutions which you have given in your answer to part (a). (8)

   (c) Describe how each solution would detect and deal with an invalid input from the user. (4)

   (d) The aim of a human-computer interface is to make interaction with a computer as efficient and effective as possible. Describe **four** criteria which could be used to judge the 'user-friendliness' of any piece of software. (4)

London Computing AS Paper 1 Qu 9 1997

Chapter 62 – Software Acquisition and Testing

Make or buy?

At the start of the systems life cycle, a new computer project is proposed and a feasibility study is carried out to examine the economic, technical and social feasibility of the project. If a decision is made to go ahead, one of the major decisions that will have to be made is how to acquire the software. There are several options:

- The software may be written by the end-user;

- A specialist department within the organisation may design, write, test and document the software;

- External consultants may be called in to write and test the software;

- An off-the-shelf package may be bought, and possibly customised;

- Software may be leased rather than purchased, with the user paying an annual fee for the right to use the product.

End-user-written software

This is normally only an option for a very small project where the end-user is perhaps a computer specialist in their own right. A computer-literate enthusiast in a Recruitment Department, for example, may use a database package such as Access to write an application to input and analyse information about prospective or new recruits to help plan future advertising campaigns.

The advantages of the end-user writing the software is that the requirements are precisely known so no problems of communication arise, and the software is likely to be developed quite quickly in response to a specific need. The disadvantages are that the end-user is very unlikely to provide any technical or user documentation so that when he or she leaves, the software will probably quickly fall into disuse.

This option is only useful for minor projects with a limited life-span.

> ➢ **Discussion: Fifteen or so years ago it was quite common for, say, an enthusiastic doctor at a GP's surgery to buy a PC and develop his own software for an application such as printing out repeat prescriptions. Does this still happen? If not, why not?**

Writing software in-house

Many large organisations have their own department of computer specialists for maintaining existing software and developing new software. It is estimated that as much as 75% of computer specialists' time may be spent on maintenance – keeping existing programs running and making changes to them as required. Any opportunity to participate in a new project is likely to be received enthusiastically. This approach also has the advantage that any confidential information or ideas are kept within the organisation and will not be given to competitors by outside consultants.

However, developing a major new system may require extra staff with specialised skills and such people may be difficult to recruit, especially if they are only needed for a relatively short time. The company may decide it is preferable to bring in outside consultants who have the necessary experience and expertise.

External consultants

For a major project, going to an external software house may be the only solution. The job may be 'put out to tender', with several companies submitting proposals and being invited to give presentations of their proposals before one is chosen. The more complex the project, the greater the pitfalls, and so great care is needed in the choice of consultant. Cost is always a consideration but a consultant who can point to several successful systems already installed may be worth the extra money. The relationship that a consultant builds with the client may be one of the most important factors in implementing a new system successfully.

> ➢ **Discussion: What criteria would you use in deciding between several external consultants who had submitted proposals for delivering a new system?**

Buying a package

If a package is available to do the job, this may be a very safe and relatively inexpensive way to acquire the new software. A package has the following advantages over specially written software:

- It is cheaper than custom-written software – the development costs of the package may be millions of pounds, but the customer may be able to buy it for a few hundred pounds, since sales are made to thousands of other customers;

- It is immediately available and already thoroughly tested so is unlikely to have major bugs in it;

- Documentation is usually available in the form of reference manuals, user guides and tutorials;

- Training courses may be available from third-party trainers;

- Technical support is usually available from the manufacturers via a Web site or telephone line (at a price);

- Other users of the package can be consulted as to its suitability before purchase;

- Upgrades are usually available every year or two.

Disadvantages of a package solution include:

- The package may not do exactly what you want it to do;

- It may not run on the firm's existing hardware;

- It may not interface with other software already in use in the organisation.

Leasing software

Some packages are leased rather than purchased. This means that the user will automatically receive regular upgrades, and the initial expense is less. In the long run, of course, this option may be more expensive.

Modifying existing packages

Sometimes a package is bought and modified. This is in general a very dangerous option as it means that the manufacturer will no longer provide any technical support, and the modifications are likely to cause errors in other parts of the software, which therefore require more modifications, and so on.

Software testing

All software has to undergo a rigorous testing process before it can be released. When a new system is developed, the testing process may typically consist of five stages:

1. **Unit testing**. Each individual component (such as a subroutine or code for a particular function) of the new system is tested.

2. **Module testing**. A module is defined in this context as a collection of dependent components or subroutines.

3. **Subsystem testing**. This phase involves testing collections of modules which have been integrated into subsystems. (For example, the Purchase Order function may be one of the subsystems of an Accounting system.) Subsystems are often independently designed and programmed and problems can arise owing to interface mismatches. Therefore, these interfaces need to be thoroughly tested.

4. **System testing**. The subsystems are integrated to make up the entire system. The testing may reveal errors resulting from the interaction between different subsystems. This stage of testing is also concerned with ensuring that the system meets all the requirements of the original specification.

5. **Acceptance testing**. This is the final stage in the testing process before the system is accepted for operational use. It involves testing the system with data supplied by the system purchaser rather than with simulated data developed specially for testing purposes.

Testing is an iterative process, with each stage in the test process being repeated when modifications have to be made owing to errors coming to light at a subsequent stage.

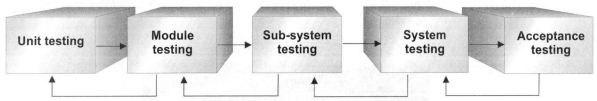

Figure 62.1: Stages in testing new software

Alpha testing

Acceptance testing is sometimes known as **alpha testing**. For specially commissioned software, this testing continues until agreement is reached between the developer and the system purchaser that the system works correctly and fulfils all the system requirements.

Alpha testing is essential because it often reveals both errors and omissions in the system requirements definition. The user may discover that the system does not in fact have the required functionality because the requirements were not specified carefully enough, or because the developer has overlooked or misunderstood something in the specification.

Beta testing

When a new package is being developed for release as a software package, beta testing is often used. This involves giving the package to a number of potential users who agree to use the system and report any problems to the developers. Microsoft, for example, deliver beta versions of their products to hundreds of sites for testing. This exposes the product to real use and detects problems and errors that may not have been anticipated by the developers. The product can then be modified and sent out for further beta testing until the developer is confident enough in the product to put it on the market.

Software maintenance

It is impossible to produce software which does not need to be maintained. Over the lifetime of any software system or package, maintenance will be required for a number of reasons:

- Errors may be discovered in the software;
- The original requirements are modified to reflect changing needs;
- Hardware developments may give scope for advances in software;
- New legislation may be introduced which impacts upon software systems (e.g. the introduction of a new tax).

Maintenance falls into three categories:

- **Perfective maintenance**. The system can be made better in some way without changing its functionality. For example it could be made to run faster or produce reports in a clearer format.
- **Adaptive maintenance**. Changing needs in a company may mean systems need to be adapted – for example, a single-user system may be adapted to a multi-user system. A new operating system or new hardware may also necessitate adaptive maintenance.
- **Corrective maintenance**. This involves the correction of previously undetected errors. Systems may appear to work correctly for some time before errors are discovered. Many commercial software programs such as Windows, Word or Access have bugs in them and maintenance releases are regularly brought out.

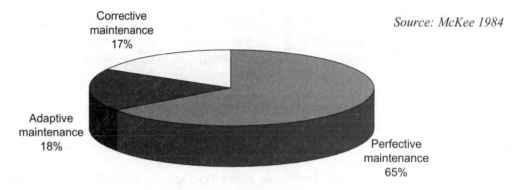

Source: McKee 1984

Figure 62.2: Maintenance effort distribution

> ➤ **What are some of the possible consequences of the millennium bug to different types of organisation?**

Maintenance releases

The maintenance process is generally triggered by requests for changes from system users or by management. The costs and impacts of these changes is assessed and if the decision is made to go ahead with the proposed changes, a new release of the system is planned. The release will very likely involve elements of adaptive, corrective and perfective maintenance. The changes are implemented and tested and then a new version of the software is released.

Minor changes in software packages are often released with version numbers like Version 3.0, 3.1, etc. Major new releases may be given numbers like version 4.0, 5.0 etc., or a completely new name.

Maintenance is often perceived by software developers as a rather inferior type of activity, requiring less skill than developing new software, and is therefore allocated to less experienced staff. This is probably one reason why such a high proportion of software costs are attributed to maintenance.

A study by Lehman and Belady carried out in 1985 resulted in a set of 'laws' of software maintenance.

---

1. **The law of continuing change**

   A program that is used in a real-world environment necessarily must change or become progressively less useful in that environment.

2. **The law of increasing complexity**

   As an evolving program changes, its structure tends to become more complex. Extra resources must be devoted to preserving and simplifying the structure.

3. **The law of large program evolution**

   Program evolution is a self-regulating process. System attributes such as size, time between releases and the number of reported errors are approximately invariant for each system release.

4. **The law of organisational stability**

   Over a program's lifetime, its rate of development is approximately constant and independent of the resources devoted to system development.

5. **The law of conservation of familiarity**

   Over the lifetime of a system, the incremental change in each release is approximately constant.

The third law above suggests that large systems have a dynamic of their own. Maintenance teams cannot simply make any changes they want to, because of structural and organisational factors. As changes are made to a system, new errors are introduced which then necessitate more changes. Major changes tend to be inhibited because these changes would be expensive and may result in a less reliable system. The number of changes which may be implemented at any one time is limited.

Maintenance is very expensive, being by far the greatest cost incurred in the overall systems life cycle. It is therefore cost-effective to put time and effort into developing systems which are as easy as possible to maintain.

Exercises

1. Before releasing a new package the software company carries out alpha and beta testing.
   (a) What are these two types of testing and why are they both needed? (6)
   (b) Explain why, once the package has been released, there may be a need for maintenance releases and how these might be dealt with. (6)

   NEAB IT05 Qu 8 Sample Paper

2. An examination board is considering developing a system which is to be used for maintaining and processing module test results of candidates.
   - Describe the different ways in which the examination board may be able to provide a software solution.
   - Discuss the issues the examination board should consider before choosing any particular solution. (20)

   NEAB IT05 Qu 9 1997

IT05 – Sample Questions and Answers

1. A manager has upgraded his desktop computer to take advantage of his company network environment.

   State **two** changes that you would expect him to see as a result of such an upgrade. (2)

   NEAB IT05 Qu 1 1999

Notes:

A bit of a trick question this, since you will get absolutely no marks for saying 'his applications will run faster' or ' he will be able to run the latest version of Microsoft Office'. The point is, he may not have changed his actual hardware, he's just had a network card installed, the sneaky so-and-so. Let this be a lesson to you. READ THE QUESTION CAREFULLY.

Suggested answer:

He will have an additional dialogue to deal with log-on, possibly including an ID and password.

He will be able to access files either on the server or on the other computers in the network, if it is a peer-to-peer network.

(Could also say, he will be able to use resources such as printers on the network.)

2. 'I don't care which version of a word-processing package the rest of the company uses. As a senior company manager I intend to upgrade my department to the latest version.' Give **four** potential problems this attitude may cause for other IT users in the company. (4)

   NEAB IT05 Qu 2 1998

Notes:

You have probably encountered problems with transferring documents written in one version of a software package between home and school, and that will give you one answer. For the other answers you need to imagine the problems it would cause within a large organisation. You could assume that there are some fairly major differences between the versions, if that makes the question easier to answer.

Suggested answer:

Documents created on the new version of the software will probably not be downwardly compatible so users in other departments will not be able to load and edit them.

Upgrading 'piecemeal' may cause difficulties with keeping track of site licences – the company may have a site licence to run a particular version of the software.

The computers in the department may not all be able to run the latest version of the software which probably will require more RAM, faster processor, more hard disk space etc. This may mean new hardware has to be purchased and could put an additional strain on the department budget. Current hardware may be leased and it would be expensive to terminate the lease early.

There is always movement between departments in a company and it is irritating and demotivating for, say, secretarial staff to find different versions of software when they move departments. Additional training may be required.

3. A hospital information system holds program files, which are rarely changed, and large database files, which are changing constantly. At present the backup strategy uses a tape storage device, and has the following characteristics:

    Each evening the information system is taken off-line and a full backup is made of the entire system. Three sets of tapes are in use and are referred to as sets A, B and C.

    > Set A is used one evening,
    >
    > Set B is used the next evening,
    >
    > Set C is used the following evening.

    This sequence is then repeated, starting the next evening, with Set A again.

    An advisor has suggested a change is required to improve this strategy. Give, with reasons, **four** changes that could be made. (8)

    NEAB IT05 Qu 5 1999

Notes:

Read Chapter 53 on Security and Backup Policies. You could suggest incremental backups, RAID systems, having more frequent or less frequent backups. Where are the backups stored? Remember, you must justify each point you make to get the second mark.

Suggested answer:

It is not necessary to backup the entire system every day. The hospital could use incremental backups so that on Monday, the whole system is backed up, on Tuesday, only the files created or changed on Tuesday are backed up, on Wednesday, only the files created or changed on Wednesday are backed up, etc. *(Now give a reason.)* This will reduce the amount of time spent on making backups.

The backup tapes should be securely stored off-site to give further protection against physical disaster.

The strategy should include regular restoration of files from the backup tapes to ensure that the backup system is working correctly and that in the event of a disaster the restoration process goes smoothly.

The hospital could use a RAID system (Redundant Array of Inexpensive Drives) so that all transactions are written to two separate drives, and if one drive goes down, the data is stored safely on the other drive. No further data will be written until both are up and running again.

(Could also say, need a backup log to keep records of which tape is the current one, and to keep a record of any problems with backups. Could use data compression techniques to reduce the backup time and amount of space required on storage media.)

---

4. You are the IT manager of a college. Your principal wishes to implement a computerised student identification card system. One way of providing the software for this system is to use a generic applications package, and to customise it to meet the project specification.

    (a) Describe **two** ways of providing the software other than using a 'generic applications package'. (4)

    (b) The college has a clearly set out IT strategy, however this project has not been included. Identify and describe **four** issues that should be considered when making a final choice from the above three methods. (8)

    NEAB IT05 Qu 5 1998

Notes:

A 'generic applications package' is something like a spreadsheet or database package which you can use to build your own application, in the same way as you are presumably doing for at least one of your projects. Look at Chapter 62 on Software Acquisition for other ways of acquiring software.

Suggested answer:

(a) The software could be written in-house using a programming language such as Visual Basic. This would require a team of experienced programmers employed by the college.

Alternatively, a specific purpose applications package could be purchased. The package would have to be carefully evaluated to ensure that it met the requirements of the proposed system.

(b) Four issues:

Development time: It would be a lengthy process to develop an application from scratch using a team of analysts/programmers. It would also be necessary to already have, or to employ, analysts/programmers with the necessary skills.

Reliability of the system: Special purpose packages have usually been tried and tested and are therefore on the whole robust and do not crash unexpectedly, as they have been tested in many similar environments.

Availability of user training: There is often an authorised training program and/or training manuals for a special purpose system, which there would not be for the other two options.

System documentation: Packages usually come with documentation already complete, whereas this would have to be written for a system developed in-house and is often a rather neglected part of a project.

(Could also mention upgradeability, software support issues, compatibility with existing hardware/software.)

---

5. A company makes use of a computerised flat file information storage and retrieval system. The company is experiencing problems due to the use of this flat file system.

(a) Describe **three** benefits that the company would gain by using a relational database as opposed to a flat file system. *(6)*

(b) The company currently has three files in use; customer, stock and orders. During conversion to a relational database system these files would need to be normalised. Explain clearly what you understand by the term normalisation. *(2)*

(c) Examples from the three files are shown below. Normalise these files explaining any assumptions or additions you make to the files. *(5)*

CUSTOMER FILE

Surname	Forename	Street	Town	City	Post Code
Smith	James	11 The Avenue	Bemersley	Ruston	RS12 5VF
Penfold	Jayne	67 Bathpool Road	Outclough	Wignall	WG5 6TY

ORDERS FILE

Surname	Forename	Post Code	Order Date	Item Ordered	Quantity Bought	Price	Total Cost	Paid
Smith	James	RS12 5VF	6/5/98	Magic Duster	2	£10.99	£21.98	Yes
Penfold	Jayne	WG5 6TY	1/6/98	Banana Rack	1	£12.50	£12.50	No
Smith	James	RS12 5VF	12/5/98	Winsor Doormat	1	£29.95	£29.95	Yes
Smith	James	RS12 5VF	12/5/98	Easee Food Grater	1	£11.99	£11.99	Yes
Penfold	Jayne	WG5 6TY	1/6/98	Winsor Doormat	1	£29.95	£29.95	No

STOCK FILE

Item Name	Price	Quantity in Stock
Winsor Doormat	£29.95	11
Magic Duster	£10.99	34
Electric Potato Peeler	£39.00	0
Easee Food Grater	£11.99	9
Banana Rack	£12.50	1

NEAB IT02 Qu 10 1998

Notes:

This is a very technical question and unless you have studied and understood database theory you have no hope. The good news is that if you have, this is an easy 13 marks. Remember that a flat file system is a system of separate unrelated files. A normalised database should not have the same information held on different files, except for the common fields that relate the two tables.

To answer part (c) you could start by first drawing an entity-relationship diagram so that you can see clearly how the three entities CUSTOMER, ORDER and STOCK are related. Your diagram should look something like this:

i.e. One customer may have many orders, but an order can only belong to one customer.

An order may be for many stock items, and a stock item may appear on many different orders.

Now the problem here is that you cannot have a many-to-many relationship in a normalised database (read all about it in Chapter 56.) You need to introduce a fourth table, which could be called ORDER_LINE (representing one line in an order consisting of several items ordered). The crow's feet turn round and you end up with:

An order has many order lines.

An order-line is for one item of stock only, but a stock item may appear on several different order lines (in different orders).

Now you can create new tables from the original ones. Looking at the existing tables, none of them has a unique identifier which can act as the primary key, so you need to insert a primary key field in each table, e.g. CustID, OrderID, StockID. The new ORDER-LINE table needs 2 fields to make up the primary key – Order Number and either Line Number or Item Ordered.

The tables as they stand are already in First Normal Form because they contain no 'repeating fields', i.e. none of them have 2 fields for the same variable like Item Ordered.

The second step in normalisation is to make sure that each field in each table is dependent only on the primary key. This will get rid of the redundancy in the tables, so that for example Customer Name and Postcode is only held on the Customer file and not on the Orders file.

Once you've done all that, you'll probably have got the right answer. You could consider removing the Total Cost field from the Order table since this is a calculated field and it is not necessary to store it since it can be calculated when required.

Suggested answer:

(a) Advantages of relational database over a flat file system:

Data independence – the structure of the database does not affect programs which access it so for example an extra field could be added to the CUSTOMER table without needing to change programs not directly affected by the new field.

Control over redundancy (less data duplication. i.e. the same data is not stored several times on different files, so for example the video name and customer name are not stored on the LOAN table, as they can be looked up from the relevant table.

Consistency of data – because data is not duplicated there is no possibility of holding inconsistent data on different files, for example if a customer changes address.

(b) Normalisation is the process of organising data in related tables in such a way as to remove unnecessary redundancy (duplication of data), ensuring that there is consistency throughout the database. It also ensures that the database is flexible enough to enter as many or as few items (e.g. customer orders) as needed and to easily query the database.

(c) The normalised tables will look like this:

CUSTOMER FILE

CustID*	Surname	Forename	Street	Town	City	Post Code
123	Smith	James	11 The Avenue	Bemersley	Ruston	RS12 5VF
124	Penfold	Jayne	67 Bathpool Road	Outclough	Wignall	WG5 6TY

ORDERS FILE

OrderID*	Order Date	CustID	Paid
001	6/5/98	123	Yes
002	1/6/98	124	No
003	12/5/98	123	Yes

ORDER-LINE FILE

OrderID*	Item Ordered*	Quantity Bought
001	MD1	2
002	BR1	1
002	WD1	1
003	WD1	1
003	EFG1	1

STOCK FILE

StockID*	Item Name	Price	Quantity in Stock
WD1	Winsor Doormat	£29.95	11
MD1	Magic Duster	£10.99	34
EPP1	Electric Potato Peeler	£39.00	0
EFG1	Easee Food Grater	£11.99	9
BR1	Banana Rack	£12.50	1

* = Primary key

Total Cost field has been removed from the Order table since this is a calculated field and it is not necessary to store it since it can be calculated when required. Primary keys have been added.

6. A computer has a computer network system.

    (a) Activity on the network system is monitored and an accounting log is automatically produced.

        (i) State **four** items of information that this log might include. (4)

        (ii) Give **four** reasons why such a log is useful. (4)

    (b) An IT consultant has suggested that the company changes from a peer-to-peer network to a server based network. Give **six** features of these network environments which contrast the two different approaches. (6)

    NEAB IT05 Qu 6 1999

Notes:

There are several reasons why a systems administrator might want to monitor activity on a network. Why do you think he/she might want to know who is using a network, for how long and what they are doing or looking at?

Suggested answer:

(a) (i) Four items:

Amount of time logged on for each user, and times of day logged on;

Workstation from which each user logged on each time;

Number of times network crashed and details of any error messages;

Density of network traffic at each hour of day/night.

(Could also say, details of files stored/updated/deleted, details of applications used/count of users per application, details of failed login attempts.)

(ii) The log is useful because it provides systems administrators with information about network load so that they can deal with performance problems, or make informed decisions about whether to upgrade the network. It also helps to identify any abuse of the system or hackers trying to log on, e.g. if someone has 500 attempts to find the correct password. It helps to identify the busiest times of day so that rescheduling of some activities could possibly be done.

(b) In a server based network:

There is no one machine controlling the network;

Shared software and data are stored on the server, on a peer-to-peer software is stored on individual machines;

Peer-to-peer is more suitable for linking a small number of computers where each user performs basically different tasks but sometimes needs to use data held on other computers in the network;

Software upgrades are easier to manage on a server based network since only one copy of the software is stored;

Security issues are harder to control on a peer-to-peer network;

The speed of access will vary with the number of users logged on in a server based network;

Backup is centrally managed on a server based network.

---

7. A supermarket chain has recently implemented a new stock control system in each of its branches. This has affected those staff who have not used computer systems before. Many of the staff have described the system as being 'user-friendly'. However, when the package was implemented in one particular store, it was not well received by its staff.

    (a) Give **four** features of software packages, that would merit the description *'user-friendly'*. (4)

    (c) Both physical and psychological factors can influence how people interact with computer systems. Both may have contributed to the poor reception of this system in that store.

(i)   Describe **two** such physical factors.

(ii) Describe **two** such psychological factors.

(8)

NEAB IT05 Qu 7 1999

Notes:

This should be easy enough. I've no advice to give!

Suggested answer:

(a) User friendly: Intuitive to use; context-sensitive help available; commands, menus etc. in familiar places on screen, with a similar menu structure to other packages. Wizards or short cuts available to perform common tasks. Effective use of sound/colour to assist users.

(b) (i)   Physical factors: could be placed in a noisy environment so that sound effects associated with tasks cannot be heard; could be badly positioned so that the screen is not easily read with glare or reflection; the choice of colour scheme could be poor.

(ii) Psychological factors: the system could have been introduced with no training or preparation and people could be biased against it; the users in this particular store may be older people who are afraid of computers or who have been using the old system for the past 30 years and don't want to waste all that expertise.

---

8.   A software company is preparing to release a new application program. Describe the two types of testing carried out before the final release of the software. Explain why both are needed.   (6)

NEAB IT05 Qu 5 1997

Notes:

The expected answer to this question is exactly what is in the specification (what used to be known as the syllabus) – alpha and beta testing. To do well in this exam you are strongly advised to become very familiar with the specification, which you will find in the back of this book. Use it as a basis for your revision.

Suggested answer:

Alpha testing (also known as acceptance testing). This is the final stage in the testing process before the system is accepted for operational use. It involves testing the system with data provided by the software house. It will continue until there is agreement among the design/development team that the system fulfils all the requirements of the specification.

Beta testing. This involves giving the package to a number of potential users who agree to use the system and report any problems to the developers. Microsoft, for example, delivers beta versions of their products to hundreds of sites for testing. This exposes the product to real use and detects problems and errors that may not have been anticipated by the developers. The product can then be modified and sent out for further beta testing until the developer is confident enough in the product to put it on the market.

Both types of testing are needed because in-house testing will reveal errors or omissions both in the systems requirement definition and in the system developed. These must be fixed before the application is given to outside users to test. The beta testing is useful because it exposes the software to a large number of users who may use it in unexpected ways, and it will be tried on machines with different specifications using real data. This is likely to result in errors or omissions coming to light, or to highlight improvements that need to be made before the software can be put on general release.

9. "The rise of de facto standards due to commercial sales success can only benefit organisations and individuals". Discuss this statement.

   Particular attention should be given to:

   - operating systems;
   - portability of data between applications;
   - portability of data between different computer systems.

   Illustrate your answer with specific examples. (16)

   Quality of language will be assessed in this answer.

   NEAB IT02 Qu 11 1999

Notes:

Look at the advice given for question 9 at the end of IT01 on writing essays. You need to make four hard-hitting points and discuss them for each part of the question. A further 4 marks are available for a general discussion of issues if you have not managed to reach 12 yet, but don't just keep wittering on and on in case in the end you say something worth a mark. The final 4 marks will be for quality of language and coherence of answer and you'll lose marks here if you don't stick to the point.

Suggested answer:

Windows has become a de facto standard for PC operating systems around the world. This has the benefit that whatever PC you buy, Windows will almost certainly be pre-installed and will be familiar to someone who has previously used a PC. It should also mean that because of the gigantic volume of sales it is extremely cheap but this is not in fact the case. Some critics would also say that Microsoft has done the world a disservice by stifling the creative efforts of developers who from time to time come up with much better operating systems, but cannot break the virtual monopoly enjoyed by Microsoft by virtue of its world dominance.

The strict control exerted by Microsoft over its operating system has, however, meant that only one version of, say, Windows 98 or Windows 2000 exists. This is in contrast to Unix, say, which has been develop and 'improved' by many companies, leading to hardware and software compatibility problems.

The virtual monopoly enjoyed by Microsoft with its Windows operating system may be challenged by a newer operating system called Linux, which is available free on the Internet. Some of the best programmers in the world have worked on it, and it may yet establish itself as a de facto standard. It is less 'buggy' than Windows and more efficient in terms of memory space. Many of Microsoft's competitors – IBM, Corel and Borland, are beginning to offer Linux versions of their software. This will be of great benefit to everyone because it is free – Windows 2000 costs around £260.

The portability of data between applications means that, for example, graphics created in Corel Draw or a pie chart created in Excel can be imported into Word. Objects can also be linked into another application such as a Word document, in such a way that when the spreadsheet or graphic is edited, the latest version will appear automatically in the Word document.

The ASCII standard is an example of a de facto standard for representing characters. It is used on all personal computers and enables the transfer of text data between applications and between different computer systems. On the Internet, the adoption of the TCP/IP protocol as a de facto standard has meant that it is possible to download information from computers all over the world. This has led to a huge increase in the number of people accessing the World Wide Web and is clearly an enormous benefit to all. Communications protocols such as the OSI standard protocol means that data can be transferred between different computer systems on a local or wide area network. The protocol lays down exactly what format the data has to be in and how it is to be transmitted.

Programs written in the language Java will run on any hardware platform – a great benefit to Web page designers and users as it is widely used in interactive Web page design.

Appendix A

AQA Specification Summary

Information and Communications Technology

Scheme of Assessment – Advanced Level (AS+A2)

The Scheme of Assessment has a modular structure. The A Level award comprises three compulsory assessment units from the AS Scheme of Assessment and three compulsory assessment units from the A2 scheme of assessment.

AS Assessment Units

Unit 1	**Written Paper**	**1 ¾ hours**

15% of the total A Level marks

Unit 2	**Written Paper**	**1 ¾ hours**

15% of the total A Level marks

Unit 3	**Coursework**	

20% of the total A Level marks   *60 marks*

A2 Assessment Units

Unit 4	**Written Paper**	**2 hours**

15% of the total A Level marks

Short answer, structured questions and an essay assessing Module 4.

Unit 5	**Written Paper**	**2 hours**

15% of the total A Level marks

Short answer, structured questions and an essay assessing Module 5.

Unit 6	**Coursework**	

20% of the total A Level marks   *90 marks*

AS Module 1 – Information: Nature, Role and Context

	Topic	Amplification	See Chapter
1.1	**Knowledge, information and data**	Understand the distinction between knowledge, information and data. Information has context and its meaning is determined by the context. Understand the nature of data: recorded facts, events or transactions. Understand the different ways in which data can arise; (direct capture or as a by-product of another operation). Describe the effect of the quality of the data source on the information produced. Understand the need to encode information as data. Understand the problems associated with the coding of value judgements.	8
1.2	**Value and importance of information**	Understand that information is a commodity and as such can have a monetary value, the level of which depends on its accuracy, its potential use and its particular intended use. Describe the overheads involved in ensuring that information is up-to-date.	9
1.3	**Control of information**	Describe the legal rights and obligations on holders of personal data to permit access. Understand that the sale of entitlement to access to data may mean paying for a more convenient form of access, the right of which already exists. Understand that files on individuals and on organisations that are non-disclosable have commercial value.	11
1.4	**Capabilities and limitations of information and communication technology**	Understand that ICT systems offer fast repetitive processing, vast storage capability, the facility to search and combine data in many different ways which would otherwise be impossible. This can provide quality information.	9
		Understand that the response speed of technology within ICT systems facilitates the use of feedback, e.g. maintenance of optimum stock levels, electronic fund/money management systems.	9 9
		Understand that there are limitations in the use of ICT systems and in the information they produce. Factors could include hardware, software and communications limitations in addition to inappropriate data models and data control mechanisms.	
1.5	**The social impact of information and communication technology**	Explain the benefits and drawbacks of the use of information and communication technology in manufacturing, industry, commerce, medicine, the home and education and teleworking.	1, 2, 3, 4, 5, 7

	Topic	Amplification	See Chapter
1.6	**Role of communication systems**	Explain the use of global communications between single or multiple sources and recipients, including public networks e.g. INTERNET. Describe the hardware, software and services required to access the Internet	6
		Describe the facilities offered and the relative merits of: telephone, fax, e-mail, teleconferencing, viewdata, teletext, remote databases and other relevant communication systems.	6
		Explain the use of the Internet for a range of activities including communication, information searching and information publication.	6
		Candidates should be aware of the recent developments in the area of communication systems.	6
1.7	**Information and the professional**	Recall the personal qualities and general characteristics necessary for a person working effectively within the ICT industry and as part of an ICT team.	1
1.8	**Information systems malpractice & crime**	Explain the consequences of malpractice and crime on information systems.	10
		Describe the possible weak points within information technology systems. Describe the measures that can be taken to protect information technology systems against internal and external threats. Describe the particular issues surrounding access to, and use of the Internet; censorship, security, ethics.	11
1.9	**The legal framework**	This section applies to current British legislation and its relationship to the Council of Europe Convention directives.	11
	Software and data misuse	Describe the anti-hacking provisions of the Computer Misuse Act. Describe the principles of software copyright and licensing agreements.	10
	Data protection legislation	Recall the nature, purpose and provisions of the current data protection legislation of the Public Register. Recall the type of data covered and various exemptions from the legislation. Recall the definitions of processing and consent to process. Explain how the requirements of the legislation impact on data collection and use. Describe the obligations of data users under the legislation. Recall the rights of individuals under the legislation.	12
		Recall the role of the Registrar in encouraging good practice, acting as Ombudsman and enforcing legislation.	
1.10	**Health and Safety**	Describe the provisions of the current health and safety legislation in relation to the use of information systems. Recognise that health and safety guidelines cover the design and introduction of new software.	13

AS Module 2 – Information: Management and Manipulation

	Topic	Amplification	See Chapter
2.1	**Data capture**	Describe methods of data capture and identify appropriate contexts for their use. Understand the concept of data encoding.	15
2.2	**Verification and validation**	Understand the distinction between accuracy of information and validity of data.	16
		Explain possible sources and types of error in data capture, transcription, transmission and processing. Describe methods of preventing and reducing such methods.	
		Describe appropriate validation techniques for various types of data process, from data capture to report generation.	
2.3	**Organisation of data for effective retrieval**	Describe the nature and purpose of a database and how they work.	17
		Understand that data needs to be organised in a database to allow for effective updating and retrieval. Understand how data can be retrieved to produce meaningful information.	19
		Recall the relevant advantages of databases over flat file information storage and retrieval systems.	18
		Select and justify appropriate file and database structures for particular applications.	
2.4	**Software; nature, capabilities and limitations**	Describe the need for interfacing with peripherals storage devices, input and output devices and display devices; describe the need for printer and other peripheral drivers.	28
	Nature and types of software	Describe the distinction between systems software and applications software; the purposes of operating systems.	21
		Describe the nature of package software, generic and specific, and of bespoke software. Describe the general characteristics of generic packages and the integration of objects and facilities for processing data protocols and standards.	22, 23
			22
		Describe the functionality offered by software which provides access to the Internet.	
	Capabilities of software	Describe the desirable features of packages that would be appropriate to particular users and activities such as: links to other packages; search facilities; macro capabilities; application generators; editing capabilities; ability to change or extend data and record structures; short access times; data portability and upgrade paths	23
	Upgradability	Explain the technical and human implications of package change/upgrade.	23

	Topic	Amplification	See Chapter
	Reliability	Explain the difficulties of thoroughly testing complex software.	23
2.5	**Manipulation and/or processing**	Describe the different modes of operation; batch, interactive, transaction, real-time and identify appropriate contexts for their use.	24
		Describe the characteristics of processing data in the form of text, pictures, numbers and sound.	25
2.6	**Dissemination/ distribution**	Describe the need for suitable output formats and orderings to communicate the results of data interrogation and undertake report generation.	19, 22
2.7	**Hardware; nature, capabilities and limitations**	Describe the broad characteristics, capabilities and limitations of current input devices, storage devices, communications devices, processing devices and output devices and identify appropriate contexts for their use.	14, 15, 26, 28
2.8	**Security of data**	Understand the importance of and the mechanisms for maintaining data security. Describe the distinction between security and privacy.	27
		Understand simple processes that protect the integrity of data against malicious or accidental alteration; standard clerical procedures, passwords, levels of permitted access, write protect mechanisms, backup procedures, restoration and recovery procedures.	
	Backup systems	Understand the need for regular and systematic backup and procedures for recovery.	27
2.9	**Network environments**	Describe the characteristics and relative advantages of network and stand-alone environments.	29
		Describe the difference between a Local area and a Wide area network. Describe the elements of network environments.	
2.10	**Human/ Computer interface**	Understand the need to facilitate an effective dialogue between humans and machines.	30
		Explain the need to design systems which are appropriate to users at all levels and in different environments; the impact of clarity of structure and layout.	
		Describe how the user-interface can be designed for effective communication with the user.	
		Describe the advantages of common user interfaces between different generic application packages.	
		Describe the advantages and limitations of a natural language interface.	

A2 Module 4 – Information Systems within Organisations

	Topic	Amplification	See Chapter
4.1	**Organisational structure**	Understand the basic concepts of organisational structure.	36
4.2	**Information systems and organisations**	Understand the difference between an information system and a data processing system. Understand the role and relevance of an information system in aiding decision making.	36
	Definition of a Management Information System	Recall that an MIS is a system to convert data from internal and external sources into information. This is communicated in an appropriate form to managers at different levels to enable them to make effective decisions for planning, directing and controlling the activities for which they are responsible.	37
	The development and life cycle of an information system	Recognise the existence of formal methods, the need for clear time scales, deliverables and approval to proceed.	38
	Success or failure of a Management Information System	Understand the factors influencing the success or failure of an information system: inadequate analysis, lack of management involvement in design, emphasis on computer system, concentration on low-level data processing, lack of management knowledge of ICT systems and their capabilities, inappropriate/excessive management demands, lack of teamwork, lack of professional standards.	39
4.3	**Corporate information systems strategy**	Describe the factors influencing an information system within an organisation: management organisation and functions, planning and decision making methods, legal and audit requirement, general organisation structure, responsibility for the information system within an organisation, information flow, hardware and software, standard, behavioural factors e.g. personalities, motivation, ability to adapt to change.	40
	Information flow	Describe the methods and mechanisms of information flow within an organisation both formal and informal and the constraints imposed upon this by organisational structures.	42
	Personnel	Understand the levels of task/personnel within an organisation: strategic, implementation, operational and relate the needs of these three levels to the information system.	36

	Topic	Amplification	See Chapter
4.4	**Information and Data**		
	Information	Understand management information needs; the concept of relevance and methods of interpretation.	42
		Understand that information has many characteristics and can be classified in many ways. Examples include:	
		Source - internal, external, primary, secondary; Nature - quantitative, qualitative, formal, informal; Level - strategic, tactical, operational; Time - historical, current, future; Frequency - real-time, hourly, daily, monthly; Use - planning, control, decision; Form - written, visual, aural, sensory; Type - disaggregated, aggregated sampled;	
		Discuss the value of information in aiding the decision making process.	
		Understand the difference between internal and external information requirements.	
		Describe the characteristics of good information and delivery: relevant, accurate, complete, user confidence, to right person, at right time, in right detail, via correct channel of communication, understandable.	
		Describe the advantages and characteristics of good information within an applications context.	
	Effective Presentation	Understand the effect that the method and style of presentation has upon the message – design in relation to the intended audience.	42
	Data	Understand that data may require translation or transcription prior to entry into the system. This can affect the accuracy of the data.	43
		Discuss the impact of quantity and quality of data on the method of data capture and the control and audit mechanisms required to manage the data capture.	
4.5	**The management of change**	Understand that the introduction or development of an information system will result in change; this must be managed. Factors could include re-skilling, attitude, organisational structure, employment pattern and conditions, internal procedures.	44
4.6	**Legal aspects**	Understand the need for a corporate information technology security policy and its role within an organisation. Factors could include prevention of misuse, detection, investigation, procedures, staff responsibilities, disciplinary procedures.	45
		Describe the content of a corporate information technology security policy.	46
		Describe methods of improving awareness of security policy within an organisation, cross referencing to training and standards.	47

	Topic	Amplification	See Chapter
	Audit requirements	Understand that many information technology applications are subject to audit. Understand the impact of audit on data and information control. Describe the need for audit and the role of audit management/software tools software. Understand the function of audit trails and describe applications of their use; e.g. ordering systems, student tracking, police vehicle enquiries.	45
	Disaster recovery management	Describe the various potential threats to information systems. Factors could include; physical security, document security, personnel security, hardware security, communications security, software security. Understand the concept of risk analysis. Understand the commercial need to ensure that an information system is protected from threat. Describe a range of contingency plans to recover from disasters and relate these to identified threats. Describe the criteria used to select a contingency plan appropriate to the scale of an organisation and installation.	46
	Legislation	Understand that the implementation of legislation will impact on the procedures within an organisation. Describe the methods of enforcing and controlling data protection legislation within an organisation. Describe the methods of enforcing and controlling software misuse legislation within an organisation. Describe the methods of enforcing and controlling health and safety legislation within an organisation. Discuss the implications of the various types of legislation.	47
4.7	**User Support**	Describe the ways in which software houses provide user support; relate these to cost and package credibility. Describe the range of user support options available when using industry standard packages. These could include: existing user base, support articles, utilities, specialist bulletin boards, communications systems eg Internet, e-mail. Select and justify an appropriate user support system for a particular context. Explain the need for different levels of documentation related to user and task.	48

	Topic	Amplification	See Chapter
	Training	Explain the need for different levels of training related to user and task.	49
		Understand the need for continual skill updating and refreshing.	
		Describe the methods by which users can gain expertise in software use and discuss their relative merits.	
		Understand the need to develop training strategies to respond to growing user awareness.	
4.8	**Project management and effective ICT teams**	Understand why projects are often sub-divided into tasks and allocated to teams.	50
		Describe the characteristics of a good team; leadership, appropriate allocation of tasks, adherence to standards, monitoring, costing, controlling.	
4.9	**Information and the professional**	Discuss the social, moral and ethical issues associated with the introduction and use of information and communication technology systems as they affect a professional working within the industry.	51
		Understand that 'codes of practice' exist separate from any legal requirements with which professional organisations are expected to comply.	
		Understand the need for a code of practice for ICT users in an organisation.	
	Employee Code of Conduct	Understand what is meant by an employee code of conduct; responsibilities, authorisation, security, penalties for misuse.	51
		Describe the contents of such a code of practice.	

A2 Module 5 – Information: Policy, Strategy and Systems

	Topic	Amplification	See Chapter
5.1	**Policy and strategy issues**	Understand the need for an information management policy. Understand the strategic implications of software, hardware and configuration choices for an organisation. Appreciate the range of needs of different users.	52
	Methods of enhancing existing capabilities –	Discuss the reasons why organisations may wish to upgrade hardware/software provision - factors could include hardware/software development, organisation ethos, task driven change, software change. Understand that hardware and software exists which allows packages to run on different platforms.	52
	Future proofing	Understand the advantages and disadvantages of the approach.	
	Backup strategies	Describe the different options available for backup systems and understand the implications and limitations of their use. Understand the strategies for backup scheduling and storage of backups.	53
5.2	**Software**		
	Evaluation of software	Describe the mechanisms/procedures for software evaluation. Establish client/user needs, establish software capabilities and match.	54

	Evaluation criteria	Understand the need for establishing evaluation criteria; these include
		
		Agreed problem specification
		Functionality
		Performance – use of benchmarks
		Usability and human-machine interfaces
		Compatibility with existing software base
		Transferability of data
		Robustness
		User support
		Resource requirements including hardware, software and human
		Upgradability
		Portability
		Financial issues –
		   development cost
		   development opportunities
			54

	Topic	Amplification	See Chapter

	Evaluation report	Understand the function of an evaluation report and know that the content will include:
		  methodology used
		  actual evaluation
		  recommendations
		  justification.
			54

5.3	**Database management concepts**	Explain the purpose of a database management system (DBMS). Explain the role of the database administrator. Explain what is meant by data consistency, data integrity, data redundancy and data independence. Explain the concept of entity relationships and data normalisation. Explain the concept of a client/server database. Recall the relevant advantages of a client/server database over a non-client/server database.	55,57 57 56
5.4	**Communication and information systems**	Describe the use of networked systems for various applications. Describe the network infrastructure required to support the World Wide Web.	58
	Applications of communication and information systems	Select and justify an appropriate networked system for a particular application.	58
	Distributed systems	Understand that distribution can apply to both data and control. Describe the uses of distributed databases and understand the advantages and limitations of such distribution.	58
5.5	**Networks** **Network security, audit and accounting**	Understand the particular security, audit and accounting problems associated with networks, and recall the steps which can be taken to preserve security. Describe the measures taken to protect network traffic against illegal access. Understand the reasons for using audit software in providing a network service. Understand the reasons for using accounting software in providing a network service.	59

	Topic	Amplification	See Chapter
	Network environments	Understand how a network environment affects the user interface provided: security, control of software, control of files - access rights.	59
5.6	**Human/ Computer Interaction**	Describe the psychological factors that affect human/computer interaction; user friendly, give help to novices, provide short cuts for experts, make use of human long term memory to maximise efficiency.	61
5.7	**Human/ Computer Interface**	Recall different approaches to the problem of communication with ICT systems and discuss the resource implications of sophisticated HCI. Discuss the implications for customising software to develop a specialist HCI.	61
5.8	**Software development**	Understand that there are different ways of providing software solutions to specialist applications: - user written, internal development team/department - external software house to specification. Describe the possible criteria for selection of software solutions to specialist applications and their place within the corporate strategy.	62
5.9	**Software reliability**	Describe methods of ensuring that software is reliable - α testing, β testing, agreements between software houses and purchaser for testing. Understand the need for maintenance release(s). Understand the reasons why fully tested software may fail to operate successfully when implemented as part of an information technology system.	62
5..10	**Portability of data**		
	Protocols and standards	Explain the need for portability of information; ease of transferring numerical, graphical and textual data between applications. Describe the need for standards for interchange of text, numeric data and graphics, for hardware and software, and for common operating systems.	60
		Understand the protocols and addressing mechanisms used to support the World Wide Web.	60
	Communication standards	Understand why protocols are required and know of the existence, benefits and limitations of standards.	60
	Emergence of standards	Recognise the existence of de facto standards based on historic precedent and sales success in comparison to formal standards.	60

Appendix B

Book List

Book List

The following books have been invaluable in the preparation of this text and are a useful source of information for staff and students. All prices are approximate, as obviously they tend to increase over time.

General texts

Alter, Steven **Information Systems A Management Perspective (2nd Edition)** (1996) Benjamin Cummings ISBN 0-8053-2430-5 £25

Good American hardback book, full of useful information, case studies and beautiful colour illustrations. An excellent book for the library.

Heathcote P.M. **Tackling Computer Projects in Access with Visual Basic (3rd Edition)** (2000) Payne-Gallway Publishers ISBN 1 903112 22 2 £9.95

Useful advice for project work, with sample projects.

Hussain KM and Hussain, Donna **Information Technology Management** (1997) Butterworth & Heinemann ISBN 0-7506-2656-9 £35

Awfully expensive but it is a very good resource for second year work. A good book to have in the library.

Laudon, Kenneth et al. **Information Technology and Society** (1994) International Thomson Publishing. ISBN 0-534-19512-1 £21.95

An excellent American textbook which deserves to be on the library shelf of every school and college offering A Level I.T. Too long and detailed to be used as a student text but a wonderful reference book. Weighing in at 3lbs, too heavy for the average student's schoolbag.

Laudon K. and Laudon J. **Management Information Systems (5th edition)** (1998) Prentice Hall
ISBN 0-13-906462-1 £25

An even weightier tome (literally), about 800 pages but covers most of the syllabus. A good reference source although it is aimed at undergraduates and would be rather daunting for the average A Level student. Good value for money.

Parsons J and Oja D **Computer Concepts (3rd edition)** (1998) Course Technology ISBN 0 7600 5500 9 £20.95

Another useful American text, beautifully illustrated. A good reference book covering a large part of the syllabus in a rather roundabout way.

Stern, Nancy and Stern, Robert **Computing in the Information Age** (1996) John Wiley and Sons Inc. ISBN 0-471-11061-2 £20.00

An excellent American text, beautifully illustrated. A good reference book covering a large part of the syllabus in a rather roundabout way. Includes a CD ROM.

Zwass, Vladimir **Management Information Systems** (1992) Wm C Brown ISBN 0 697 01538 6 £18.25

Good general text, good value for a hardback book.

Books for specific topics

Barrett, Neil **Digital Crime** (1997) Kogan Page Limited ISBN 0-7494-2097-9 £12

Written by an ex-hacker with a rather poor grasp of English grammar, but who is nevertheless extremely knowledgeable on all aspects of computer crime and the law. An interesting read.

Bawa, Joanna **The Computer User's Health Handbook** (1994) Souvenir Press ISBN 0-285-63207-8 £10.99

Well-written, informative reference book covering all aspects of Health and Safety for computer users. A good chapter on user interfaces.

Bruton, Noel **How to manage the I.T. Helpdesk** (1997) Butterworth Heinemann ISBN 07506 3811 7 £19.99

All about helpdesks.

Cavoukian, Ann **Who Knows** (1997) McGraw Hill ISBN 0-07-063320-7 £18

A good book on privacy issues in the computer age.

Collins, Tony **Crash – Ten Easy Ways to Avoid a Computer Disaster** (1997) Simon & Schuster ISBN 0-684-81688-1   £20

Very entertaining case studies of computer disasters, including many over-ambitious projects which didn't come up to scratch. Good material for 'factors influencing the success or failure of an information system'.

Evans, Alastair **Data Protection Policies and Practice** (1987) Institute of Personnel Management ISBN 0 85292 385 6 £10

A very thorough treatment of the Data Protection Act and all its implications, with guidelines for security policies as implemented in various organisations such as B.P. and Kodak.

Gates, Bill **The Road Ahead** (1996) Penguin Books ISBN 0-14-024351-8 £ 7.99

A wonderful account of how to establish a de facto standard by one who knows. Also a generally entertaining account of the current state of technology and (self-fulfilling?) predictions for the future.

Kallman E.A. and Grillo J.P. **Ethical Decision-making and Information Technology** (1993) McGraw-Hill ISBN 0-07-033884-1 £14.95

A fascinating book on ethics in computing, with 18 case studies illustrating all manner of ethical dilemmas, excellent for class use. A good book to order for the library.

Sommerville, Ian **Software Engineering (4th Edition)** (1992) Adison-Wesley ISBN 0 201 56529 3 £23.95

Good reference book for all aspects of software engineering such as systems development, maintenance and testing. Designed for undergraduates.

Whitehorn, Mark and Marklyn, Bill **Inside Relational Databases** (1998) Springer ISBN 3 540 76092 X £19.50

Excellent book on database theory with examples in Access. Highly recommended.

Other resources

BSA Guide to Software Management

The Business Software Alliance is an organisation dedicated to stamping out the illegal use of unlicensed software. They produce a FREE folder, CD and presentation floppy disk. Good for a couple of lessons at least! Their address is

BSA Europe, First Floor, Leconfield House, Curzon Street, London W1Y 8AS. Tel: 0171 491 1974

User support/Help desk software

A good resource for this topic is Network Associates, Minton Place, Victoria Street, Windsor, Berks SL4 1EG. Tel 01753 827500. They produce McAfee HelpDesk software and have a good (free) sample CD and information sheets.

Index

Successful ICT Projects in Word (2nd edition)

by P.M.Heathcote
February 2000   208pp   ISBN 1 903112 25 7

This text, updated for the 2001 syllabus and Office 2000, covers the essential features of Word from basic editing and formatting right through to advanced features such as templates, macros, customised toolbars and menus. It is suitable for students on a number of courses such as 'A' Level or GNVQ ICT, HNC and HND in Business Information Technology and Access to HE.

It gives ideas for suitable projects and explains how to complete each phase from Analysis and Design through to Implementation, Testing and Evaluation. AQA Project Guidelines and a mark scheme are included in an Appendix.

Successful I.T. Projects in Excel

by P.M. Heathcote
January 1999   208pp   ISBN 0 9532490 5 0

Excel is a powerful and versatile spreadsheet program which is eminently suitable for project work at every level from GNVQ (e.g. Advanced GNVQ I.T. Units 3 and 13) to degree work. This book is also invaluable for staff development, and caters for users of Excel 97, 7 and 5.

A sample project demonstrates how to lay out a complete project report, and the AQA project mark scheme is also included. The template for the sample project as well as a sample chapter entitled 'Project Ideas' are available on the web site www.payne-gallway.co.uk

Successful I.T. Projects in Access

by P.M. Heathcote
May 1999   224pp   ISBN 0 9532490 6 9

This book will help students to complete a project in MS Access, using version 7 or 97. It covers database design, creating tables, forms and subforms, queries, importing and exporting data to other packages, analysing and processing data, reports, macros and some Visual Basic for Applications. It includes advice on choice of projects and a sample project.

It is suitable for students on a wide range of courses such as 'A' Level or GNVQ ICT, HNC and HND in Business Information Technology and Access to H.E.

Successful ICT Projects in FrontPage

by Matthew Todd
May 2000   208pp   ISBN 1 903112 28 1

This book is designed to help students on an 'A' Level, GNVQ or similar course to design and implement a Web site using MS FrontPage 98 or 2000. It assumes no previous knowledge of FrontPage and takes the reader from the basics such as entering, editing and formatting text and images on a Web page through to advanced features such as writing scripts, gathering data from forms, and making use of active components. A wide range of examples is used to illustrate the different facilities of FrontPage, and a sample project shows students how to tackle and document each stage of project work.